PRAISE FOR *MILL TOWN*

"The book of a lifetime; a deep-drilling, quick-moving, heartbreaking story of one working-class family in one working town, which is also the much bigger American story of how harm settles on and in some of those who love the country most." —Robert Macfarlane, author of *Underland*

"Arsenault combines memoir with investigative journalism in this tale of the toxic paper mill at the center of her Maine hometown, an area now nicknamed Cancer Valley." —*People*

"Part beautiful memoir and regional history, part investigative journalism, part environmental diatribe countered by a poetic ode to place. In short, it's a fraught love letter to that fragile American entity, the small, rural, working-class town." —Stephanie Hunt, *The Post and Courier*

"*Mill Town* poses hard questions that challenge the tacit acceptance of ecological destruction as the price of economic health." —*Los Angeles Times*

"What Arsenault presents, with mesmerizing lyricism and endearing honesty, is the story of a dying town wedded to a paper mill that once anchored the local economy while also bringing pollution and cancer. *Mill Town* puts forth larger questions of the human relationship to the environment, of the violence done to the land that eventually translates into the devastation of the people that live on it." —Rafia Zakaria, *The Baffler*

"A valuable addition to the literature of New England's industrial legacy, something many residents have either forgotten or choose to ignore, to the region's detriment." —Alex Hanson, *Los Angeles Review of Books*

"Reportage, memoir, and the refusal to seek easy answers clasp hands to bring us a searing, compassionate story of people rooted in and committed to a place that keeps breaking their bodies and hearts. . . . With love and sorrow, wed by eloquent prose that moves with keen pacing, Arsenault traces the story of her family and the many families who have been battered along with their despoiled environment. This book is an essential answer to the urgent question: At what cost comes progress?"
  —Garnette Cadogan, *Literary Hub*

"A rich, rewarding read that defies easy categorization. Despite the gravity of its subject, *Mill Town* is, at its heart, a love letter to the people and places of Arsenault's childhood and a plea for a cleaner, brighter future."
—Jessica Lahey, *Air Mail*

"In this masterful debut, the author creates a crisp, eloquent hybrid of atmospheric memoir and searing exposé. . . . Bittersweet memories and a long-buried atrocity combine for a heartfelt, unflinching, striking narrative combination."
—*Kirkus Reviews* (starred review)

"[A] powerful, investigative memoir . . . This moving and insightful memoir reminds readers that returning home—'the heart of human identity'—is capable of causing great joy and profound disappointment."
—*Publishers Weekly* (starred review)

"Arsenault's compelling debut asks readers to consider how relationships between humans and nature impact our bodies and environment. . . . [A] powerful memoir."
—*Library Journal*

"An imposing work of narrative nonfiction."
—Harvey Freedenberg, *Shelf Awareness*

"Clear-eyed and self-deprecating, Arsenault is a welcome guide through the history of Mexico and Rumford, capturing the voices of their inhabitants, the stories they tell, and the confidences they keep. She is tenacious in her search for answers, tender in her interactions with her mother and their neighbors. A riveting blend of reportage and memoir reveals the secrets of a paper mill town."
—Michael Berry, *Maine Sunday Telegram*

"For stretches, it is pure memoir—and first-rate memoir at that. . . . In other places, the book is a compelling and taut work of industrial investigation [and] Arsenault is meticulous in her research. *Mill Town* is haunting and heartbreaking, charming and funny . . . and utterly exceptional."
—Alan Adams, *The Maine Edge*

MILL
TOWN

RECKONING WITH WHAT REMAINS

Kerri Arsenault

ST. MARTIN'S GRIFFIN
NEW YORK

Published in the United States by St. Martin's Griffin, an imprint of St. Martin's Publishing Group

www.stmartins.com

Portions of this book appeared in slightly different and condensed form in *Freeman's* and *Literary Hub*. All interior photos taken by the author.

Art on title page: lines © shaunl/Getty Images; river © Abstract Aerial Art/Getty Images

Certain identifying details have been changed.

This book was printed on paper bleached without chlorine gas, chlorine dioxide, or any other chlorine-based bleaching agent.

The Library of Congress has cataloged the hardcover edition as follows:

Names: Arsenault, Kerri, author.
Title: Mill town : reckoning with what remains / Kerri Arsenault.
Description: First edition. | New York : St. Martin's Press, [2020] | Includes bibliographical references.
Identifiers: LCCN 2020019303 | ISBN 9781250155931 (hardcover) | ISBN 9781250155955 (ebook)
Subjects: LCSH: Arsenault, Kerri—Family. | Working class—Maine—Mexico (Town)—Biography. | Mexico (Me. : Town)—Biography. | Mexico (Me. : Town)—Social life and customs. | Rumford Mill. | Rumford (Me.)—Biography. | Paper industry—Environmental aspects—Maine—Oxford County. | Paper industry—Health aspects—Maine—Oxford County. | Pollution—Androscoggin River Region (N.H. and Me.)—Anecdotes. | Androscoggin River Region (N.H. and Me.)—Environmental conditions.
Classification: LCC F29.M49 A77 2020 | DDC 974.1/75 [B]—dc23
LC record available at https://lccn.loc.gov/2020019303

ISBN 978-1-250-79968-5 (trade paperback)

First St. Martin's Griffin Edition: 2021

10 9 8 7 6 5 4 3 2 1

For John Freeman

Find out just what a people will submit to, and you have found out the exact amount of injustice and wrong which will be imposed upon them; and these will continue till they are resisted with either words or blows, or with both. The limits of tyrants are prescribed by the endurance of those whom they oppress.

—Frederick Douglass, in a speech concerning West India Emancipation, delivered at Canandaigua, New York, August 3, 1857

CONTENTS

MILL TOWN

PREAMBLE

MEXICO, MAINE IS a small paper mill town that lies in a valley, or "River Valley" as we now call the area, because I suppose you can't have one without the other. The hills are low and worn and carved by the waters surrounding them, and trees line the rivers, which confine the town. Coursing through the valley's midsection, the Androscoggin River.

Just across the S-hook in the river, in the neighboring town of Rumford, the mill's smokestacks poke holes in the white plumes they create. *That's money coming out of those smokestacks,* our fathers used to say about the rotten-smelling upriver drafts that surfaced when the weather shifted. That smell loitered amid the softball games we played beneath those stacks and lingered on our fathers' shirtsleeves when they came home from work, allowing us to forgive the rank odor for what it provided.

Where stack meets sky, the wide, slow-moving Androscoggin pivots and bleeds south and east, under bridges and over rapids, pushing through dams, slinking around islands and along inlets, skidding through other mill towns of Jay, Lewiston, Topsham, Brunswick and picking up flotsam and jetsam or passengers in canoes. In the calmer sections, its velvety waters press on with the slow caress of lava and despair. Vapid pools form when the water has nowhere else to go, sheltering the river's secrets in dark lagoons, where they congregate in the muck and fester like complicity. Sometimes the river pauses or eddies when it meets an obstacle and diverts into other routes, into unpredictable detours following the edges of its design. Yet it proceeds nonetheless.

Rivers are living bodies that need oxygen, breed life, turn sick, can be wrecked by neglect like human bodies, which we often think of as separate, not belonging to the landscape that bore them out; they tell a story, these bodies. They are the story.

In deep grottos of the past, the great polar ice cap melted into glaciers, and its calving mass crawled north, carving long, deep ruts that became the lakes and rivers of Maine. Our geologic past foretold everything about our future. But in this future, lives are un-lived, secrets never revealed, and stories remain unwritten about how much we all lose. In this future, I learn of asphalt lakes, people bulleted with disease, burning tires scarring the sky, the forsaken buried in unmarked graves, the evisceration and erasure of home. In this future, we pardon legislators who convince us nature will sort itself out. In this future, we will have forgotten everything that came before, and our only legacy for those who will supersede us is the promise of ruin. It started early, this ruining of bodies and the yawning of leaders who didn't care about a landscape so altered by us it's reciprocating the abuse.

When I walk along the Androscoggin and over its bridges, I try to see the river as it was or could have been. Even in its current spoiled state, it's still a thing of great agency, the transactions of its waters an awesome sight, wearing down granite and earth with the repeated force of its movement. Down at the rocky outcrops when my father was a boy, a park with a bandstand and grassy plateaus wrapped the town with music and tranquility. There, you can imagine the thunderous negotiation of the river's turbulent waters as they passed, defeating the submissive notes of flutes and clarinets. Before my father, my grandfather walked in the same park where shrubs and flowers and little stones drew a path amid the shade of chestnuts that were about to die. Before him, Abenaki crouched along the Androscoggin's edge to catch salmon lofting on its tide. Salmon had long flung their way upstream from the

Atlantic to spawn, swimming past floodplains and alewives that gathered in the river's current. Gristmills and pollution and dams and the lawmakers discouraged their run-ups but the hopeful salmon pressed on until they disappeared except for the few each year who still hurl themselves up and over that first dam wondering if by tenacity they will prevail. Their fate, it remains unknown.

WHAT GOES AROUND, COMES AROUND

FROM THE PORCH steps of the house where I grew up, you'll see the end of the road. There, the pavement dips down to reveal the town's only traffic light, a gas station, and the roof of the Family Dollar store. Behind the store lies the Androscoggin and just beyond the river, the paper mill's largest smokestack emerges like a giant concrete finger. From anywhere in town, you can orient yourself to this stack, or by the ever-present *ca-chink ca-chink ca-chink* of the mill's conveyor belts, and find your way home even from a pitch-black walk in the woods. When mill shutdowns occur for holidays or layoffs, the smokeless stacks resemble the diseased birch trees dying throughout New England.

To the right of the porch you'll see a street of clapboard homes, silent but for the occasional snarl of a jake brake on a logging truck or a motorcycle shifting gears. A mile or two out of town, the road narrows, and small creeks knit through pastures shadowed by hills, a working farm or two, a long straight road, cut hay, muddy cow paths, rotting leaves, or black ice, depending on the time of year. The seasons, they calendared our lives.

Farther up the road you'll eventually bump into the North Maine Woods. If you look at a map, you'll get an idea of the yawning jurisdiction of the area, which lies (generally) within the twisted pavement of

Route 2, Interstate 95, and the Canadian border, their lines lassoing the wilderness within. The Woods are a deluge of spruce, fir, hemlock, and beech, a steady brown and green canopy fractured by silvery brooks or iron gray lakes. The damp mossy understory and thick brush, claustrophobic with tangled twigs and scant cabins, hide the chewed-up dirt logging roads that colonize the backcountry. I didn't pay much attention to those darker, deeper woods because there were already so many trees right in our backyard.

My mother stayed home while my father worked: her making pot roast, him making smokestack money. As kids, we explored the world through textbooks and made classroom dioramas of what we thought a Mayan village or a Midwestern dairy farm looked like. The rest of the world seemed to be New Hampshire or Canada. Families didn't go on overseas vacations and rarely traveled interstate. Our lives were focused inward . . . Red Sox games, union strikes, and grousing about the weather.

Monumental philosophical ideas were surfacing across America—feminism, environmentalism—however, there were no movements in Mexico but for people walking across the mill's footbridge to work. We were more likely to dry bras on a clothesline than burn them. We lived in a Shrinky Dink world where everything was there, just smaller. We were lucky in this, felt safe with our doors unlocked at night, and ameliorated most of our sins within the latched doors of St. Theresa's confessional. At nighttime football games, we watched our fire-twirling majorettes toss their batons skyward in a spinning, blazing fan. They caught them dead center every time. Those kerosene-soaked batons in the dusk of autumn, they smelled of permanence.

From October to April, oil-burning furnaces heaved in our basements while outside, the violence of chainsaws making firewood meant things were getting done. Winter insulted us with frequent storms that hurled wet pillows of snow into our faces or horizontal pellets of icy rain onto our footpaths. In a weekly dirge, we'd crack the ice on the walkway or throw one fat shovelful of snow after the other into white pyramids while our breath funneled out in smoky vapors. Passers-by on their way to work, unrecognizable in the bulk of their warmth, would wave a shallow hello as we huffed through our chores. As people and winter lumbered along, sidewalks became glacial, leaving everyone to walk in the middle of the road. We all complained, yet nobody ever thought to leave. Weather was just something we endured.

One year blended into the next with only slight differences in star athletes or town leaders and sometimes one turned into the other. Family businesses occupied Mexico's Main Street, anchored by the Chicken Coop—"Good Eatin' That's Our Greetin'!" their tagline declared in flat red paint. The Bowl-O-Drome, Lazarou's car dealership, WRUM, RadioShack, Dick's Restaurant, the Dairy Queen, the Far East Restaurant (the "Chinah Dinah"), a carwash, and Maddy's Pizza murmured with people doing their thing. Businesses opened and closed with the seasons and the sun. Before my time, Boivin's Store, Stanley the grocer, T.M. Stevens Dry Goods, a theater, a livery, a dowel mill. Once there was even a hotel. At the rim of town, the mill footbridge, where three generations of my family and exponential relatives crossed, as did most millworkers who spread cretons on their toast before clocking in. We were stamped out like Christmas cookies, as good French Catholics were.

Everything else we needed was in Rumford, the larger of the two connected towns and the commercial center of our community. At times there were deep rivalries and frictions between Rumford and Mexico, but we were always tethered by blood, two bridges, a dependency on the mill, and by around 2009, schools and a single grocery store.

Overall, what we needed we had. Everyone knew everyone and we liked it that way—for what other way was there? *It was quite the place,* my mother always says. *There was never any reason to leave.* In our nuclear family of seven, we always had enough food, plenty of hand-me-downs, some spanking, and an unspoken love for each other, because frankly, nobody really spoke much about love at all.

In the drowsy dusk of summertime when the sun dipped under the foothills and the humidity of the day invaded kitchens and bedrooms, people flocked to their porches. There, they chatted while night knit itself into a tight blanket. As the sun sank, one by one, mimicking fireflies, house lights flicked on and porch lights flicked off and people streamed inside for the evening. The sounds of clinking dishes, faint music, vehicles purring, and light-as-vapor laughter scented the air. Night fell like a bruise.

During those school-less summer days, I often sat on the dusty curb in front of our house and counted the out-of-state license plates as they sped by on their way to somewhere else. When I could finally drive, I'd cruise around with other teenagers, pivoting our used Monte Carlo in the Tourist Information Booth parking lot before another revolution through town. My parents thought the Information Booth was where all the "druggies" hung out, but really it was a harmless venue in a small town with nothing else to do but drive around in circles.

My parents shaped their own well-worn paths. While my father walked back and forth across the mill footbridge to and from work, my mother lugged laundry up and down the cellar stairs, day after day, one skinny arm cradling the laundry basket, her free hand gripping a Vantage, a cigarette brand whose packet featured a bull's-eye graphic design. With a screech and a whack, the screen door would slam shut after she elbowed it open. She would dump clean laundry on the kitchen table, snap each article of clothing three times, fold them sharply into tight wedges of fabric, and stack them like the reams of white paper my father brought home from the mill. When the screen door wore out, my mother replaced it with a new one that already came equipped with a squeaky spring. She left it defective, announcing herself into infinity with only my father to hear. His hearing, long dulled by the hum of paper machines, was the perfect match to her perpetual clamor. My mother, she'd let her Vantage expire before finishing it and send me to fetch her a new pack from the corner store. *I'll time you,* she'd say. *Now GO!* And off I went. She didn't need to tell me twice.

Things stayed in this balance, with minor adjustments every now and then, until America's working-class towns started to ebb alongside the industries that nourished them. The future? We knew nothing of it. Our horizon trembled like a fragile convex meniscus, brimming away from the landscape that held it. All of what was before us was not as bright as what had passed.

· · ·

I LEFT MAINE in 1985 after graduating from high school to attend Beloit College in Wisconsin, where an oily, vomit-like smell—the "cheese breeze"—gusted from the nearby Frito Lay Cheetos factory. Even in the funky scrum of Wisconsin air, I believed I had left my past behind. All the old ways and places fell out of view. Little did I know there were armies of us across America who felt this way: hopeful young adults from small towns who were trying to find our way, another way. What none of us foresaw, however, as we marched down those roads not taken by our parents, is that leaving home can be as complicated as living there and as inescapable as our own DNA.

After college, I lived in dozens of places and rotated through dozens of low-wage jobs: short-order cook, cocktail waitress, ski coach, dishwasher, nanny, graphic designer, shipping manager, chairlift operator, gardener, copywriter, high school gym teacher, real estate assistant, to name a few. In 2001, I married a US Coast Guard officer, but in 2009 a permanent job and home still remain out of reach. His duty stations, while not always perfect, are always determined by a perfect stranger (his military detailer), so the only constant in our mobile life is that we are constantly mobile. With him, I slingshotted around the world and back only to return home each time with a dimmer sense of "home," though my parents still live in the same house and my four siblings have settled in the Northeast. I keep returning to Maine, of course, but my visits are always focused affairs: holidays, weddings, family birthdays or anniversaries, and funerals like my grandfather's, which brings me home now, in April 2009.

. . .

SPRING HAS ARRIVED in Maine with driveways full of snowplow debris; salt stains, shredded earth, and derelict mittens lie in the wake of its embracing path. Dirty buttresses of snow linger like pocked monoliths, meting out the season's arrival. The swollen Androscoggin pushes flotsam downriver in the commotion of spring's thaw, and soon, hatches will burst along its surface until summer opens like an oven.

My mother comes out to the porch where I'm standing. The house sighs with winter's leftover lethargy. "Want to go for a walk?" she asks, her face pinched with the sharpness of her father's death.

We head up Highland Terrace and stop to peek in the windows of an abandoned house, one I always liked, with its wraparound porch, turreted roof, and buttercup-yellow paint. "The owner is sick but refuses to sell," my mother says as we walk across its battered porch. So this once elegant home sits there, shedding its brightness, yellow flecking the half-frozen ground. Spray-painted in the road near the driveway: "Fuck you, bitch." The fug of the mill swallows us.

We reach the top of the hill, and from there, my old high school. To the east, snowmobile trails; abutting them, the mill's landfills. To the west, the football field slices the horizon. Beyond, lazy fingers of smoke lick the sky.

Inside the school, my mother stops in the office to chat with the principal she knows well. The lobby's smells—warm mashed potatoes, Band-Aids, and damp socks—remind me of Greg Chiasson, my high school on-again, off-again, lumberjackish boyfriend. Greg lived near the town incinerator, whose sweep of ash always whispered across his front lawn. I loved Greg like I would a sorry stuffed animal, one who had lost an eye or whose fur was rubbed raw. Kelly, a girl who wore her black, perfectly feathered hair like a weapon, was in love with him too. When he and I fought—usually over her—I'd listen to sad songs on my cassette player over and over until he called for my forgivingness in a pattern of pain and redemption.

I only saw Greg once after graduating from high school. He visited my parents when I was home from college one Christmas break. He and my mother chatted while I leaned against the kitchen countertop. "Peckerhead," my father said when he saw Greg. He called all the boys I dated Peckerhead, but only if he liked them. If he didn't, my father would sit at our kitchen table like a boulder while the boy fidgeted by the kitchen door in blank-faced silence.

My mother and I leave the school and follow the dirt path behind the football field past Meroby Elementary, where I got in a fistfight with Lisa (nee Blodgett) Russell. Lisa and I took turns swinging horizontally at each other's head until a teacher intruded on the brawl. When I looked in the mirror that night, I was sure I looked different, the way you think you do when you lose your virginity. It was my first and last bare-knuckled fight, except for a few unconvincing swipes at good old Kelly one night after a dance. She volleyed back with sharp red fingernails.

Down Granite Street, an untied dog follows us, growling.

"Just ignore him," my mother says.

The dog sniffs my heels, his tail down. He sits down in the road. I walk faster, looking over my shoulder until we are out of his sight and he is out of ours.

We skirt the Green Church, the library, the town hall, the fire station, and through the mostly empty and oversized parking lot at the Family Dollar where someone is inside a parked car eating their lunch. Nearby, Lazarou's car lot is filled only with puddles, and where the bowling alley used to be, a sunless cavity notched into the side of a hill. Behind it, St. Theresa's, our shuttered Catholic church where I received my first Communion, the sacrament of Confirmation, and made my first confession to Father Cyr. *I'm sorry I lied to my parents,* I said to him, though that itself was a lie.

On the corner at the traffic light is a newish gardening store, newish to me anyway. Lawn decorations, perennials, stuffed animals, and miniature tchotchkes for terrariums strain the well-stocked metal shelves. As in many small towns, most of the mom-and-pop shops have closed over the years. In their place, discount stores like Walmart or local iterations like Marden's Surplus & Salvage, Wardwell's Used Furniture, the What Not Shop thrift store, and other such secondhand outlets and pawn shops appeared, as if everyone here deserves only leftovers.

I'm inspecting a snow globe when I hear my mother shout, "Kerri, guess who's here? Do you know who this is?" Inevitably, she plays this remembering game, often in the grocery store, where she will stand next to someone, grab them by the arm, and ask if I remember so-and-so, and I will stand there, frozen in the frozen foods, staring at my mother and so-and-so, everyone's eyes like dinner plates, waiting for my answer. *Sure, yes, I remember you!* I had said yesterday to Mr. Martineau who lived across the street from my grandfather. After Mr. Martineau left my mother told me he has Alzheimer's. *He doesn't remember you,* she whispered.

"Kerri, come see who's here!" she shouts. I walk toward her, my steps jiggling the shelves of dollhouse-sized terrarium décor as if I'm Gulliver. My mother raises her arms upward like a magician: "DO YOU KNOW WHO THIS IS?" she asks.

"Hi," the woman next to her says. "Long time no see." I don't recognize her beneath dry yellow bangs that slump over round eyeglasses hiding her pink powdered cheeks. On her bulky sweatshirt, something plaid.

"Yeah, what is it, about twenty years?" I say, looking for my mother who has wandered off.

"Where do you live now?" she asks, leaning on the counter, arms crossed like a fortress.

"Oakland," I say quietly, feeling bad, not knowing why.

"Wait, Oakland, Maine?" she asks.

"California," I say. "Near San Francisco."

"Oh," she says. "I went there once. Didn't like it. The people are not very nice. I never found anything good to eat."

I look around for my mother, the exit.

"It seems quiet around town," I offer. "Much less going on than when we were kids."

"Not really," she says.

"Really?" I say, wondering if she means there is something going on or there isn't. "I went by the Recreation Park yesterday. It's just so . . . so different," I say.

I glance at her around the periphery of her glasses, our conversation. She stares at me over the top of her rims, as patient as a road, looks at me without blinking: my leather jacket, my Prada eyeglasses, my expensive jeans.

"Nope," she says. "You're the one that's different."

My mother reappears and as we leave the store she says the mill plans to shut down Number 10 paper machine, and others are on a transitional schedule, meaning they too may slither to a slow, hissing halt. In the past few decades, with technology displacing people and digital media overtaking print, the production of coated magazine paper—our mill's primary product—has become as precarious as the livelihoods of the men and women who make it.

"Nobody will want to live here anymore," my mother says, panning her hand from one side of the street to the other. Homes sag with ruined lawns.

Around the block, we pass Kimball School, where I and generations of my family attended K–4. On Friday afternoons the entire school gathered in my Aunt Linda's homeroom, where she taught fourth grade, to sing endless rounds of Chuck Berry's "My Ding-a-Ling," a tune that filled innocent kids with vague titillation with its refrain:

My DING-A-LING!
My DING-A-LING!
I caught you playing with your own ding-a-ling!

The teachers would throw open the folding partitions between classrooms as Aunt Linda banged out the melody on her upright piano. By the end of the song we were shouting: MY DING-A-LING!! MY

DING-A-LING!! The tremendous glee of teachers singing alongside us felt embarrassing, as we were old enough to know something, but not old enough to know anything specific. We felt complicit somehow, blushing as we looked at our teachers and shouted louder and louder, drowning out my aunt knocking on the piano pedals. We were told the song was about some kind of bell, and I always imagined it as a giant cowbell, like the ones we rang during ski races at Black Mountain.

Doctor Edward ("Doc") Martin gutted Kimball School years ago and transformed it into a medical office, erasing the linseed oil and warm crayon smells I once loved. After he died, the building closed permanently. Weeds now root in the tar playground and broken glass breaches the milkweed surrounding the maple tree where we sought shade during recess. A rusty chain-link fence girdles the property.

Down the street, my grandfather's house is buttoned up, his car truant. Remnants of crabgrass and soggy leaves flatten his once thriving garden. Mr. Martineau, whom my mother and I saw at the grocery store yesterday, emerges from the house across the street. He waves. We wave back.

My mother and I walk home in silence. Halfway there, I run my hand along the cool green iron railing that parallels the sidewalk and snag my sweater on it. Rusted, dismembered bits of iron are scattered about. On my way home from school, I'd dive under that railing and roll down the banking, climb back up the hill, and repeat the action until grass stained my clothes. Afterward, I'd run home, as if my head was made of that same iron rail and my house was magnetic north.

I see the porch of our house from several blocks away, and it looks as it's always looked only smaller, as things often appear when you are older.

My mother and I stomp our feet on the porch to dislodge road grime from our boots. "I can't imagine what will happen if the mill closes," my mother says as she opens the door. "So many people are out of work already," she clarifies. "It will be a ghost town." I take off my coat while my mother digs out the local newspaper, her forefinger thumping a news article about the mill. "We have to sell the house," she says. But she has been saying this for years.

• • •

THE NEXT DAY, I go for a run through Strathglass Park, a collection of two-family homes designed by noted architect Cass Gilbert and funded by the mill's founder, Hugh J. Chisholm, to accommodate his employees around 1902. Brick-by-brick (around five million), Chisholm assembled the buildings, for what he hoped would be a long-lasting industry, with long-lasting materials: slate roofs, granite foundations, handmade balustrades and headers, concrete steps, plaster walls. He even provided ranges, hot water tanks, laundry facilities, electricity, and wallpapered the living rooms.

In an 1894 letter to his engineer for the power company, Chisholm wrote: "One of the ambitions of my life is to see Rumford Falls develop into one of the model towns of New England and a place that every resident living within its border will be justly proud of . . . a place where working men of moderate means are to have placed in their easy reach the comforts that only wealth can furnish."

His was a progressive and unusual claim. Chisholm wanted to eliminate the tenement housing he felt cheapened such mill towns as Lawrence and Lowell, Massachusetts, and ushered in slum violence. But there's no real evidence such rampant violence existed. By 1904, Chisholm's realty company constructed one hundred and eighty-six dwellings and two boardinghouses, all available at low rental rates.

As I run through Strathglass Park, broken snowmobiles and other lifeless remnants litter front lawns while listing, half-baked additions or porches scab once pristine houses. Sheets shroud leaded glass windows and garbage lies in heaps alongside scattered woodpiles. Dog-shit-covered snow accompanies abandoned bright plastic toys, and wind chimes tinkle above the din of a yowling mutt. The road is a glacier. I mince along the icy path ahead.

Wandering around in this forlorn landscape, I think Mexico *is* a ghost town, a home all but vanished but for its dull eggy odor. It complies with my memory of it—the glancing dreams of betterment, how spring mud forecasts hope, the continuity of trees and paper—yet

it also does not, a blend of nostalgia and something else as unrecognizable as the back of my own head. *It's not where we grew up,* a childhood friend said to me recently. So what is it? It's home, that much is true, and home is the heart of human identity, a blurry backdrop like that fake plastic tree I leaned on while posing for my high school yearbook photograph.

LIVING THERE, LEAVING THERE

After the Gulf of Mexico's *Deepwater Horizon* oil spill in April 2010, my husband receives transfer orders to Curaçao, a former Dutch slave-trading colony in the Netherland Antilles, to work as part of an oil spill prevention team in the wider Caribbean. By June, we leave the soft eucalyptus air of California for a steamy island with dentate plants, dial-up Internet, and laissez-faire racism. We rent an apartment in the main city of Willemstad with a 280-degree view of the Caribbean Sea. We manage to fit in, find our way around supermarkets, friends, beaches. We evade dengue fever, jellyfish, tourists, expats, children. We start wearing flip-flops and drink coconut-infused cocktails at dusk while watching the horizon for the green flash. I learn to play tennis. We snorkel off the reef in front of our apartment. Paradise, or so I am informed, is composed of such elements. But paradise is hot. Hotter-than-the-center-of-the-sun hot. In Maine, family and friends huddle in their homes away from winter's silvered edge. They have no sympathy for me.

But there's something off, something un-paradisiacal, I think one night—as I look toward town and over the tiled rooftops of the candy-colored buildings, an oil refinery's smokestacks snort off gases in fiery spasms in competition with the equatorial sunset. Downwind, the school and Wishi, one of the poorest neighborhoods. Upwind, me. The school, I learn later, often dismisses students early because kids get nauseous from the junk those stacks cough up—at a clip of 335,000 barrels of oil processed a day. But the kids have nowhere to go because their homes lie in the path of pollution that trade winds carry into their open-windowed, un-air-conditioned homes. The sea-level neighborhood is also adjacent to "Asphalt Lake," a large swath of nearby Schottegat Bay so named for its black, sticky-textured water, a legacy of one hundred years of the refinery's waste disposal practices. The harbor smells of tar and dead fish and rotten fruit, and black residue in the water smears anchored boats. Residents of Wishi will later complain of a green substance that glazes their lampposts, mailboxes, and fences, which turns out to be harmful levels of vanadium pentoxide, nickel, and sulfur, all leaking from the refinery. I wonder, as I look at flames tossing up to the sky, what such brutish landscapes must do to a mind, a body, a spirit over years, decades, across generations. Cumulatively. To this day.

Back in Oakland, California, my husband's job illuminated how disadvantaged people in Oakland's port faced threats the more fortunate did not. I knew also of minority communities, some even of Acadian descent like myself, living near plastics and petrochemical companies in Louisiana and on the fence line between employment and disease. I compile a list: residents living near mountaintop mines in Virginia; close to ash pits in Kingston, Tennessee; in proximity to natural gas fracking sites; aside oil spills in Angola; near oil-production facilities and industrial projects in the Niger Delta; or next to now Chevron's "rain forest Chernobyl"; or in Chernobyl itself. Palestinian farmers on the edges of Israeli settlements. Love Canal, New York; Times Beach, Missouri; Flint, Michigan, all infernos of another kind. As the wind frisks the oily sea, the flat line of the horizon severs the ocean's surface until there's nothing left to see.

By sunrise, Wishi and the threads of those tragic narratives get buried beneath stacks of other headlines and the ordinary affairs of the day, like the car on fire in the empty parking lot across the street and, later, plunderers stealing parts from its blackened carcass.

My mother emails me at a regular clip, noting earthquakes and hurricanes in far-flung lands, sending a zucchini bread recipe, discussing Christmas plans. I read biographies of consequential men, watch HGTV, and mope around town under the ruthless Caribbean skies. I shelter at my husband's office to use his high-speed Internet and start working again on my family tree, a project I began back in 2001.

I had discovered my grandfather William's obituary folded up in a book, and it provided particulars I'd never known: that he was born in Pinsdale, Prince Edward Island (PEI); the names of his parents (Thomas and Obeline); where he worked in the paper mill (the bleach room); that he became a naturalized US citizen and died of metastatic stomach cancer not long after he retired in 1969, when I was two.

With time on my hands, I try to break through ancestral brick walls, such as finding Obeline, whose parents were still MIA. I also want to learn more about the history of our town and my grandfather's work in the mill. *You should talk to Terry Martin,* an old friend from Mexico responds innocently enough to my online queries. *She knows all about French Canadian and Acadian history, so probably your family, too.*

I had known Terry and her husband, Doc Martin, as a kid, but only slightly. She was a pretty and aloofish mother, a nurse who smiled without showing her teeth, the way someone does when they know something you don't. Doc Martin was the designated town physician and a heavy-eyebrowed man who spoke with the deep gruff voice of a superhero villain. I saw most parents that way, as children do: one-dimensional adults like in Charlie Brown cartoons, vague outlines with exaggerated attributes, intruders who interrupted the more important contours of childhood like filling your pockets with rocks or poking things with sticks.

The Martins lived in a Federal-period farmhouse on the outskirts of town. It contained seven fireplaces, antique oil murals by New England artist Rufus Porter, a Louis XV writing desk, an inlaid Hepplewhite candle stand, a Chinese Chippendale table, a sixteenth-century Mexican chest, and shelves of poetry. While my parents' house was comfortable and pleasing enough, the Martins' elegant fittings introduced a yearning I had yet to understand.

I send Terry an email. "Someone said you could help me with our town's history and my family tree," I write.

She replies with the cryptic and unsettling response that my inquiry is not at the core of the story, that there's a much larger issue afield, full of "state-wide lying and deceit," that the answers to my questions are complicated and protracted. "Play your cards close," she advises.

My curiosity always overthrows warnings or practicalities so I make a date with her to get on the phone. I had spent a few months as a journalist traversing the occupied Palestinian territories and met nervous Israeli soldiers who blatted out gunshot with the cavalier stance of spitting on the ground and hung out with Palestinians who had nothing left to lose. Surely, I can handle whatever Terry has in store for me.

"The town you left is not the same town," she says at the start of our Skype call a week later, her voice cracking over the poor connection.

"What's that have to do with my genealogy?" I ask.

Terry laughs. "Your father and grandfather all worked in the mill, right?"

"Yes," I say. "And my mother, both grandfathers and grandmothers, and my great-grandfathers."

"My family did too. They sold their farm, took the train to Maine, left their villages to move to a new country, and worked in the mill. Then they got sick."

She continues as I think of my father's prostate cancer operation in 2008.

"My husband, he tried to speak up about what was happening," Terry says. "When he stumbled on what he thought was causing all the cancer in town, they did everything to destroy us."

Destroy us. State-wide lying and deceit. Play your cards close. Her words sound a little dramatic, maybe paranoid. I had come to her for genealogy, and here she was diverting the entire thread. Yet Terry poked at the edges of a cumulative and persistent nagging that had been growing in me, a slow dawning something back home just wasn't right, made more pronounced the longer and farther I lived away from Maine and fortified by my mother's emails that included a never-ending loop of obituaries containing the phrase "Died after a battle with cancer." Friend, family, young, old, healthy—the big C seemed indiscriminate. *What the hell is going on there?* I'd ask her. *Everyone dies of cancer here,* my mother would say. But the battle with cancer is a fight nobody ever wins; it's just a small skirmish in a long and complicated war.

It's difficult to understand a place when you are so far removed from it, as I had been for years. But it's just as hard to see when you are too close, as when I was young and living at home. While distance provided perspective, I needed to go back, to see what I couldn't see from here. So I buy a plane ticket and fly to Maine to see what I had missed. Apparently, I had missed a lot. *What you don't know won't hurt you,* my mother always said offhandedly. She was dead wrong.

WHAT GOES UP
MUST COME DOWN

FOREST AND PRECIPITOUS curves hem in the forty-two-mile road from Mexico to Rangeley where Terry lives. On the outskirts of town, FOR SALE! signs disfigure houseless parcels of land, and purply cones of flowering lupines grace roadside ditches.

Rangeley has a year-round population of about 1,100 with one foot planted in the wilderness and the other in tourism. It's a landscape where you can get a hot dog for lunch while still being surrounded by what Henry David Thoreau considered "wild" in his book *The Maine Woods*. Near town center, Rangeley Lake abuts a solemn Main Street. Motorboats hunker around the edge of its inky water. In a couple of weeks, the town will drone with an armada of children, slamming screen doors, the nonchalance of flip-flops, *fwapping* waterskis, the hum of cicadas. A breeze carries clouds across an indecisive sun.

I meet Terry at the Church of the Good Shepherd, where she directs the choir. Singing tapers off then chatter echoes in the high-ceilinged room. When Terry sees me, she walks down the aisle and gives me a hug. Her chunky turquoise necklace pinches my neck. I haven't seen her for about twenty years, but as it is with people from small towns, decades compress into minutes. Her face is smooth and pink, her hair a soft yellowy nest.

"It's so good to see you!" she says and I can tell she means it. The slipstream of her floral perfume strays onto my sweater. She turns and announces to the choir, "Kerri's from the Rumford and Mexico area."

As I follow her to the altar, one of her singers, an elderly man, says to me, "I used to be Ed Muskie's driver, you know. He was a nice guy," the man continues. "Very important to cleaning up the river."

• • •

WITH CHOIR PRACTICE over, I tail Terry in her black Jeep Cherokee to her four-acre property just outside of town. It sits on a knoll where she would be able to see Rangeley Lake if all the trees in her yard weren't blotting it out. Her house is a one-floor affair socked in by pines and wind and filled with things that migrated there from her small antique shop at the end of the driveway.

She shows me the guest room where I'll stay for the night. Terry's antique-dealing days are mostly concluded except for an occasional treat like the sable coat she purchased at the Brimfield Antique Show that hangs in the guest room closet. She pulls the coat down, tosses it on, says, "It was already dead, right?" The coat swallows her.

We grew up in the same town, and she knew my parents and they knew her. I knew her kids, who went to school in Rumford. We endured the same winters, enjoyed the same continuity of community and family, and understood that our past is inseparable from our present-day lives. We came from the same stratum. It's not long before we're trying to figure out if we share any Acadian ancestors. Acadian generally means we had familial roots in the French colony of Acadia, which was originally centered near the Bay of Fundy, spreading later into the present-day Atlantic provinces of Canada and parts of northern Maine.

"You should talk to Dot Bernard from Rumford," Terry says. "She knows the family tree of everyone in town. I'll introduce you."

As for Terry's immediate family, her father worked as an embalmer at Meader & Son, a funeral home in Rumford. Later, he worked as a milkman during the day and as a projectionist at the movie theater at night. Gangly and sloped-shouldered as if apologizing for his height, he'd make an appearance at the dinner table every night but even then seemed to be elsewhere, the blank square in a game of Scrabble. After her parents' divorce, Terry's mother convinced her to enter novitiate at a Catholic boarding school in Salem, Massachusetts. *A place of witches and nuns,* Terry thought. *Which am I?*

The nuns immersed the young postulants in the Catholic doctrine that insisted on poverty, chastity, obedience, silence. The nuns also fought to purge individuality by making their wards share everything, even brownies sent from home, which they would be forced to divvy up with the sweet-toothed nuns. For two years, Terry walked in a straight line and kept her mouth shut in her heavy black wool uniform, itchy with unforgiveness.

One weekend while the nuns marched around the convent doing chores, the girls snuck up to the attic. In this hideaway, time lay bare against the slanted sunlight under the old timbered roof. As the sisters dusted and prayed below the floorboards, the girls peeked out a tiny window into the grass below. Terry's periscopic view through that small perch gave her another perspective, one that had been pretzeled by her parents' divorce and perhaps god and the nuns themselves. There went a cute boy, mowing the lawn.

It was right then—April of her second year—Terry resolved to leave. But not without discouragement. Every night by Terry's bedside, Mother Superior coaxed, alleged, argued, insisted: *Out there one could make mistakes. God wants you for a reason,* she cooed. *To leave would be against God's will. True freedom exists inside.*

· · ·

I unpack the groceries, pour two glasses of red wine, and start chopping onions for the dinner I promised to make. Terry watches like a shadow. She tells me a story, one of many she relays over the next several years. Sometimes her stories feel rehearsed as if she's worried about saying too much, as if I might be a spy. I tell her I'm trying to learn about my family, not necessarily hers. She remains unsure, as do I, what to reveal, and our mutual skepticism is exacerbated by my uncertainty about what I seek. We pirouette around this show-and-tell and I find myself pressing her to disclose things, but she hides them in pockets of subterfuge where they seem canted and dark, a lean-to of pain.

The bedrock of her story goes something like this: One day in the early 1980s, a small package landed on Doc Martin's desk. The package contained a study conducted by the American College of Surgeons that examined over 1.5 million cancer cases in 700 hospitals in the United States. Prostate and colon cancer were almost double the national per capita average for our hospital. Cancers of the uterus, cervix, pancreas, and rectum were also significantly higher than the rest of the nation. Doc Martin brought the report to the board of directors at Rumford's hospital.

"They said the report was bullshit," Terry says. "After they saw it, the report disappeared."

Subsequently, the Maine Department of Health conducted a Chronic and Sentinel Disease Surveillance from 1984 to 1986, which showed a high incidence of lung disease, aplastic anemia, and cancer in our community. The state epidemiologist said those findings were preliminary and inconclusive.

In 1985, when I graduated from high school, the Maine Department of Environmental Protection (DEP) was alerted by the US Environmental Protection Agency (EPA) that dioxin—a toxic by-product of the chlorine paper-bleaching process and mill sludge waste incineration—was found in fish downstream from seven Maine paper mills, including ours. Of the seventy-four sites tested by the EPA, the Androscoggin contained one of the highest concentrations of dioxin in whole fish. But the DEP downplayed the findings in the media, saying the dioxin amounts were "not very severe at all."

Dioxin had long been known to be harmful. It was used in the herbicide/defoliant Agent Orange in Vietnam (1961–1971), allegedly causing three million Vietnamese and thousands of US soldiers to become ill; Agent Orange had unknowingly been used in motor oil to keep dust down on the streets in Times Beach, Missouri (1972–1976), rendering the town uninhabitable by 1983; dioxin was determined to cause cancer in rats (1977); dioxin savaged the town of Love Canal, New York (1978); dioxin poisoned Seveso, Italy in a chemical accident

(1979); and by 1985, the EPA determined there was sufficient evidence to declare dioxin a probable human carcinogen.

Do no harm, Doc Martin's Hippocratic oath insisted, and he followed it to the letter. He triangulated the fish test results, the hospital study, and the well-known information about dioxin and began to suspect dioxin was to blame for the elevated cancer diagnoses in our towns.

Subsequently, and for years, he tried to drum up concern at local meetings, wrote news editorials, spoke to his patients and friends, appealed to state and federal legislators, and pressed the hospital, mill management, and town selectmen to consider, pay attention to, or evaluate dioxin's harm.

Terry shows me a letter he wrote to then governor (now Maine senator) Angus King: "The paper companies own the town they are in, lock, stock and barrel. They will do and say anything to have their way and for years have controlled the DEP of our state." Doc Martin also noted that two of his patients in six months were diagnosed with Ewing's sarcoma, a rare bone cancer occurring at the rate of about thirty-five cases in the United States per year. "Our representatives in Augusta scoff at such cases. . . . They say we don't have any higher incidence than anywhere else in the state. Hogwash! It isn't true."

The blowback to Doc Martin's mission was fierce, according to Terry. "First, he was discredited by his peers. The hospital reported him to the IRS, the State Board of Medicine, the State Medicaid program, the Medicare program. That caused audits with all of these agencies. He was even unwelcome at our bank. Finally, he was denied access to the Rumford hospital. He had no time to fight environmental issues because he was busy fighting personal ones."

• • •

Doc Martin grew up in Mexico, Maine, too, and intended to do something special with his life, for that's what everyone expected him to do, especially his mother, who would barge onto the football field if anyone hit her son too hard during his high school games. At age sixteen he earned his pilot's license, and on a lark flew a Piper Cub under two bridges in Rumford. His dream of becoming a Navy pilot materialized the moment he rocketed over the Androscoggin's turbid waters.

He attended Colby College on a football scholarship, but his education was interrupted by a stint in the US Navy in 1945 in Pearl Harbor. There he made an impression, not through his piloting skills, but by winning a boxing match against Carl "BoBo" Olson, who eventually became the world middleweight champion in the 1950s. During those waning days of war, Doc Martin's fading pilot dreams were only sustained by his proximity to the Navy's legendary plane, the Vought Corsair F4U. Otherwise known as "the Whistling Death" for the shrill sound it emitted during high-speed dives and for the thousands of Japanese blotted out by its six wing-mounted machine guns, the Corsair landed and took off with a teasing frequency from nearby Ford Field. Doc Martin's fearlessness was superseded only by his arrogance; on a quiet day in Pearl Harbor he walked onto Ford Field and without permission hopped into the nearest Corsair and took off. He would fly a fighter, war or no war.

Whoever is in that Corsair, return it to the airfield immediately, someone bleated on the radio. *I repeat, under the threat of a court-martial, I order you to return to the airfield immediately!* Despite the threats, Doc Martin flew until he ran out of gas. He figured he'd be punished anyway, full tank or empty. Two Navy planes finally escorted the gull-winged killing machine to the ground, where officers handcuffed Doc Martin and locked him up in the brig. After the war, he graduated from Colby, attended medical school at the University of Vermont, and came home to start his family practice in the only place he really loved—Rumford. *My son, the doctor,* his mother would bray to anyone listening.

Terry met Doc Martin at the Rumford Community Hospital, where she was working as a nurse and he as a family doctor. *Have dinner with me tonight,* he asked, he stated. So she did. Four months later: *Let's get married,* he asked, he stated. So they did.

As the sausage simmers in the pan, Terry sketches out more coverups that went beyond the borders of our town. Her outline, though blurry around the edges, shapes my life for the next eight years . . . because it is my story, too.

"I want to show you something," she says as she stuffs logs in the woodstove and a tape in the VCR. "Rangeley has its problems, but at least the air is clean," she says as she laughs and presses play.

We watch a 1991 episode of the TV news series *Chronicle,* titled "Cancer Valley." The Boston NBC affiliate, WCVB, who produced the program was inspired by a 1991 Associated Press headline and the story behind it: "PAPER MILL CHEMICALS FORM PALL OF CONTROVERSY OVER 'CANCER VALLEY': SEVERAL CASES OF A RARE LYMPHOMA IN MAINE TOWN RAISE CONCERNS. BUT NOT EVERYONE BLAMES EXPOSURE TO THE PULP PROCESS." The article revealed four people in Rumford and Mexico were diagnosed in rapid succession with non-Hodgkin's lymphoma, a form of blood cancer associated with exposure to toxics produced in the papermaking process.

Resident Dan St. Cyr and his fifteen-year-old daughter Danielle, who suffered from leukemia, made appearances in the documentary. I remember Danielle, who was three years old when she was first diagnosed. Our community held fund-raisers to help pay for her treatment, and her picture was always in the paper. Hers was an unwelcome celebrity. She looked old but as vulnerable as a new bird with no feathers. At the Dana-Farber Cancer Institute in Boston where Danielle was being treated, twelve of the twenty-eight patients on the children's ward lived within a twenty-mile radius of Rumford, according to Dan. He said to *Chronicle:* "People in the area accept cancer almost the way you'd accept getting a cold. It's just a part of life." The numbers were so skewed that Dana-Farber called Doc Martin and asked, "What the hell's going on in Rumford? We're getting all these kids with cancer coming in from your town."

In "Cancer Valley," as Doc Martin performed a bedside call on his boyhood friend Art Zinck, whose cancer had metastasized to his colon, Zinck told Doc Martin God spared him for one reason: to tell people that when he worked in the mill he released water from the Androscoggin (classified then as an industrial river, meaning it was not suitable for human consumption) into the town's drinking water supply under direction of mill management. At first, mill management denied the practice, but later amended their position and said the State of Maine allowed them to augment the water supply when their reservoir got too low. This was done five or six times a year.

"I'm sure the water district filtered the water," I offer.

"The real problem," Terry says as I slug my wine, "is that nobody ever told the community about this practice. They took away our right to know."

The *Chronicle* segment never aired in Maine, according to Terry. "It was too controversial," she says.

From what I find out, that's probably true: "It's doubtful it played many places in Maine, as it would be necessary for the viewer to have WCVB, the Boston-affiliated channel," *Chronicle* wrote in response to my inquiry.

At his private medical practice, Terry says, Doc Martin's patients talked. They sensed he was on their side, knew he was looking in corners where others hadn't looked, felt certain the mill's practices were questionable, believed pollution caused their illnesses. One millworker told Doc Martin about the time his boss ordered him to bury mercury-tainted waste in the riverbank across from the Dairy Queen in Mexico. Others recounted mill chemical accidents or spills, like the one believed to have sent dozens of high school students scurrying with nosebleeds to the school nurse. One patient told him how from 1982 to 1985 they were ordered to put xylene (a toxicant) and methyl ethyl ketone (a hazardous solvent) in fifty-five-gallon drums, seal them with screw caps, and place them in dumpsters supplied by a local trash disposal service who hauled them to Farrington Mountain (the mill's landfill), violating environmental regulations on handling hazardous materials. *Don't say anything,* mill supervisors insisted. And Doc Martin's patients didn't— except in those conversations sealed by the good doctor's oath. *Plus,* they said to him, *if nobody believes a doctor, why would anyone believe us?*

I refill my wineglass and turn off the stove. Terry sets the table then pops in another tape—"Return to Cancer Valley"—*Chronicle*'s ten-year follow-up to their 1991 documentary. By then, Art Zinck and Danielle St. Cyr had died; Janice St. Cyr, Danielle's mother, had been

diagnosed with brain cancer; and Doc Martin had been diagnosed with prostate cancer.

The bodies begin piling up. Terry and I break to eat.

"You know . . . Ed wrote a novel about Rumford. About a lone physician fighting the bureaucracy of small-town medical politics," Terry says as we sit down. "The protagonist is named 'Lucky' Johnson and he worked at the Rural Community Hospital in a mill town called Liberty, Maine. Of course Lucky was Ed."

"I'd love to read it," I say.

"Maybe not yet," Terry says.

. . .

"WE TELL OURSELVES stories to live," Joan Didion once wrote. Maybe that's what Doc Martin had been trying to do to prevent himself from going mad. Like him, like Didion, I had been viewing what had been happening in Maine from a safe remove. Practically everyone always called our community "Cancer Valley" in a jokey way, yet nobody ever took the nickname seriously, even myself, even to this day. *It smells like farts!* kids from other high schools would say about our town because of the mill's sulfur emissions. And so it did. You'd think a town with a nickname like that would have troubled me a long time ago, but I suppose normal is just what you get used to. I had been a bad witness to whatever had been going on, and like most of us who had lived there or still do, I didn't bother to connect the dots if indeed there were any to connect.

In 1990, the year before "Cancer Valley" aired, I was living at home. I had just graduated from college, sent out dozens of resumes to newspapers and magazines, and received only one offer: a fellowship from *Mother Jones,* much to my surprise. Their letter indicated I'd receive a small stipend (I think) or none at all. In either case, I read it then threw it away without mentioning it to anyone. The stipend wasn't even enough to pay a modest rent, never mind the enormous student loan debt crouching in my mail. The chance of working in publishing, I thought, was completely out of my reach. Alternatively, a full-time job offer in Maine awaited my response: teaching high school gym class, a job my mother helped arrange. There was also an opening for a junior high soccer coach that same fall. What choice did I have?

After the teaching and soccer-coaching gigs ended, I coached skiing by day and waited tables by night until a ski injury forced me to suspend both. Soon, the hole in the floor of my 1970 Saab grew bigger until snow drifted through the floorboards. Eventually the Saab became marooned at the ski area then buried by the nocturnal work of those who plowed the parking lots every night. When enough snow melted, I urged the Saab out of its slumber and drove it back to the pink trailer I was renting. One day, I took a right-hand turn and the car just kept going right. I paid someone to tow it away and never saw it again. My parents, in sympathy, gave me their weathered K-car, which I eventually sold for a few hundred dollars to a line cook so I could buy pots and pans and pay off my Discover credit card bill, which I had maxed out to subsidize my student loans and make constant repairs on the delinquent, feckless Saab. My financial debt was only superseded by my ignorance. I was a sliver away from what was happening in my town yet it was background noise to my more selfish aims of trying to make my way. Was this true for everyone else? Or was I just telling myself a story, too?

. . .

"It took courage for you to leave Mexico," Terry says as we gulp down the last chit of wine, her eyes rimmed with tears.

"Not really," I say, thinking I almost *didn't* leave. My first Christmas home from college, I got engaged (but quickly broke it off). Plus, I never saw myself as courageous, at least not in any way Terry meant. I am scared of the dark, of lightning, of trees, Bigfoot, large jumpy dogs, bears, bugs, hugs, tests, perfume, of not having enough food, of succeeding, of failing, of drowning, of striking out by watching a pitch glide by. Like my father, I feel uncomfortable when the spotlight focuses on me. Me leaving happened in some small unknown aperture of providential design. Yes, there are plenty of people more courageous than me. "It takes courage to *not* leave," I say. Terry mumbles something and looks out the window.

Most of us take the easy way out, I think. We take the least stressful path, move away, avert our eyes, live upwind or upstream. And why wouldn't we? Nobody chooses to live a fraught life. Terry? She looked fear and love right in the eye and stayed. She stayed and reared three kids who went to public school and are now saving the world one life at a time: one is a children's brain surgeon, one is an environmental and social justice activist, and one will soon become a single dad whose love for his child could fuel a mission to Mars. Terry, she was the courageous one.

Finally, we watch a short video of Doc Martin being interviewed in 2001 as he lay in hospice at his house. Doc Martin had nothing but time. In a few days, he would die.

"Do you think things will change at the paper mill?" the filmmaker asks.

"No," Doc Martin replies, his eyes concave, dull as chalk.

"He was my hero," Terry says, looking at the screen. "But he was also my enemy at times. I know he was frustrated, angry. He wanted results and couldn't get them. If the mill could take water from the Androscoggin and fill the town reservoir with it, what else are they capable of doing?" she says in a mix of thoughts, her words like a blender on high with the cover off. "Nobody likes a dead hero, someone once told me." Terry laughs uncomfortably as she clicks off the VCR.

Doc Martin may not have been a hero dead or alive, but his data, as Terry recites, indicates success: he practiced medicine for approximately 40 years; delivered over 2,500 babies; was married for 32 years; fathered 9 children (3 with Terry); collected 100s, maybe 1,000s of antiques; wrote a 420-page novel on the Abenaki Indian Nation; survived prostate cancer for 14 years; and founded the local Acadian Heritage Society.

We end the night and I slough off to my bedroom and lie there staring at the pine-tree motif wallpaper. Terry shifts into the living room to play the piano. I fall asleep to images of cancer-deflated bodies and crescendos of Bach.

• • •

THE NEXT MORNING in a small windowless room in the basement, thirty years of Doc Martin's personal journals—bound, dated, meticulous—annotate a wall of shelves. I flip a few pages. An entry from 1989: "Around the first of February they made a diagnosis of cancer of the prostate on me. . . . I was shocked to say the least but fortunate to have it be in an early stage which was a 10-year survival rate of 70%. Of course 30% don't make it . . . I hope I am not in that category."

It told a lot, this entry, the way he designated his disease to percentages, to data, the way he registered a downgraded shock ("at least") in a reserved way as if he were preparing the journals to be read by the public and for the public good, the way he halfheartedly foresaw hope like he didn't believe it himself, coming at the end of the sentence, his own life sentence it turned out. While he died only a few years earlier than you'd expect the average man to die, he wasn't an average man or a data point or someone to recklessly overlook. He was an egomaniacal jerk at times, a father, a doctor, a husband, and someone whose life was perhaps abridged by the very environmental pollution he sought to understand.

Terry brings a few journals upstairs, lets me leaf through them as we drink coffee in the shadowy cool of her kitchen. They are filled with news clippings, opinions on art, family history, patient notes "disguised as poetry," Terry says, looking over my shoulder as I hesitate on one page.

"I often despised him," she says to my surprise and I close the book.

"Why?" I ask.

"He abused me. Emotionally and mentally," she says and her hand goes up to her mouth. "He was largely a difficult man to live with," she finishes without looking me in the eye and pours herself another cup of coffee.

I hadn't known. Didn't know what to say.

"There are a lot of personal things in there, about me, about my family," she says nervously, pointing to the journals. Porcelain rooster plates and green-checked wallpaper throw cheer against Terry's worried face. "I often consider burning them."

"Can I borrow some before you do?" I ask carefully, half-jokingly, trying to put her at ease. She puts a hand on the journal I'm holding.

"No," she says, her face clamping shut. The antiques dealer she's hired to vacate her shop knocks on the back door and she turns to answer it.

. . .

I leave Rangeley and head back to Mexico. As my car lists through the rutty frost heaves, I watch for moose, a creature as tall and dark as the trees from which they emerge. Their brown hide absorbs light, rendering the beast near-invisible. Moose can't see well so tend to wander into byways filled with fast-moving cars. Friends who survived hitting a moose say they never saw the animal until blood and fur had coated their windshields, their nerves bankrupted by the slow, unceremonious crunch of glass and metal when they smash into the creature's unsuspecting legs.

Just outside the unincorporated area of Township E, a moose and her calf stumble out of the woods into the road. I stop. The cow stands on the double yellow line, her beard dripping with water and moss. I toot the horn. The cow pivots her head in a slow, uninterested stare. A few moments later, she and her calf clop off into the tree line, oblivious to my intrusion, as nearsighted as I was to what had been happening in my hometown.

It was here in Township E in 1988, as porch sitters played cards or drank beer, for it was an unusually warm fall night, they saw one or two unmarked yellow dump trucks drive by toward the outskirts of town. The trucks returned to town empty. Folks didn't attribute much significance to the commotion, as logging trucks were always barreling down that same route. A few days later, the porch sitters noticed more trucks, then more, until thirty trucks snarled up the road. A man who lived near that sleepier fringe of town where the convoy had been pivoting put on his boots and hiked into the woods after the trucks decamped. Now he had never been to Egypt, but Egypt was the only thing that came to mind when he peeked through the trees and saw colossal pyramids in those woods near the upper reaches of the Swift River and our town's drinking water supply.

Those piles, come to find out, were made of mill sludge (from the nearby paper mill in Jay, Maine)—toxic material scraped from the bottom of chlorinated settling tanks—like pathogens, heavy metals, and persistent toxics such as polychlorinated biphenyls (PCBs) and dioxin. Naturally, residents were upset and called for a public hearing.

The mill insisted the sludge would not cause the watershed harm. That the law was very clear, that permits had been issued and site inspections had already been done. The sludge, they said, was a "winter stockpile," which sounds cozy, like a stack of wood, a cache of sweaters, a squirrel's hoard of food tucked away in a tiny forest pantry.

Resource Conservation Services (RCS), the "organic recycling company" contracted to haul the sludge, concluded, based on a risk assessment study it commissioned from Envirologic Data, that even though the 5,000 cubic yards of sludge contained toxics, even while the parameters of those risks weren't exactly defined, the mill's "sludge recycling program" wouldn't result in an unacceptable level of lifetime excess cancer risk to residents.

State representative Ida Luther wrote a letter to Maine senator

George Mitchell about the term "stockpile": "As in the book *1984,* the prostitution of language allows everything. An industrial dump becomes a winter stockpile and that makes it all right."

When "organic recycling companies" who do "risk assessments" tell us something is acceptable or unacceptable, we generally go along. We pay them to furnish us with facts. Plus, who of us has the time or knowledge to chase such things around? Lifetime risks, however, it seems, are as individual as the whorl of a fingertip, and based on many factors like how much you smoke or how fast you run. While studies or governments often determine risks for everyone, based on some chart I don't yet know, it should probably be up to the person facing the risk to determine its level of acceptability.

I wonder if we have become inured to this kind of discourse, a gaslighting of sorts in which the definitions of words are as slippery as the sludge itself. If we aren't sure what things mean, our circuits get scrambled and we lose the thread, then we lose control. And if we lose control, someone else takes over, and where are we then? Whether it's "winter stockpile" or "organic recycling company" or "acceptable risk" or "inconclusive studies," it all starts to feel inconclusive itself.

This contortion of language illuminates the gap between truth and perception until the two concepts converge and we no longer know what's what. As I drive back into Mexico, my understanding of all I had just learned feels as amorphous as the wet, steamy pile of sludge in Township E that apparently had no liner underneath to curb its movement.

. . .

Doc Martin's journals are an anvil of responsibility, and Terry, an executor of something un-executable, her inheritance a stack of evidence no court of law will ever see. For the next eight years, the journals live in suspended animation, residing somewhere in the same vicinity as Terry does: between entrapment and escape, truth and secret, shame and pride. Catholics do this. Humans do this. We accommodate what wounds us, pick at our open sores, let the scars heal to angry red bumps.

For years, Terry and I go back and forth about the contents of the journals. "I'd rather not have you read that," she says, moments after handing a journal to me. "It's too personal." Then a few months later, "I can't tell you how relieved I am to talk about this." Then, "I'll have to discuss it with my kids." Some days she will praise Doc Martin for his genius, for the good he did in town; some days she wrestles with her compliance to a man who bullied her into living in limbo even though he's been dead for nearly twenty years, forcing her into survival mode where her only weapon was silence, a silence she can't seem to crowbar open. An asshole to some, a hero to others, his personality mirrored the dualities of the medical profession and the mill itself: with the good came the bad.

Terry's acts of retreat and progress in unmasking him, in reckoning with what he left behind, mirror in some small way what I feel every time someone asks, *Where are you from?* Like Terry, I simultaneously defend and disparage where I grew up, not because I'm nostalgic for the way things were; because I'm nostalgic for the way I *thought* they were.

"Domestic abuse is a difficult thing to be honest about," Terry writes to me in an email. "Fear is the great motivator as it encourages one to hide. I spent the better part of my life trying to cover up the fact that

Ed was an abuser. He verbally abused me for our entire life together. And now it is expected of me to continue to hide the secret that I hid for all of those years into eternity? Why is it that everyone wants to protect the abuser?"

HOT AIR

The "Cancer Valley" episodes asked questions my family, our towns, and I hadn't asked: was the mill responsible for the proliferation of cancer and if so, how did we stay silent knowing it was true?

The mill was indignant about the accusations leveled by the films. The mill's communications manager, Jeff Nevins, wrote a letter to *Chronicle*'s Chris Stirling: "'Cancer Valley' was one of the most disturbing pieces of 'journalism' we have ever seen . . . based on unsubstantiated allegations." He went on: "It's this kind of journalistic abuse that must make the large majority of responsible, unbiased, and fair-minded journalists cringe with professional embarrassment."

Andy Drysdale, a Boise spokesperson, responded to Nevins's memo by calling "Cancer Valley" a "piece of trash." Scribbled at the bottom of the typewritten note: "We are yet to see any hard evidence or supported studies for the content! Who would want to move to Rumford and Mexico?"

Resident reactions were mixed about the possible effects of the film. Business owners worried it was bad publicity that could anesthetize their revenue. Some worried a controversy would sully town pride. Millworkers didn't want to lose their jobs. Other folks just didn't want to die. Those who were already sick got mad. The mill kept reiterating there were no facts to back up such destructive claims and didn't seem concerned the film's claims might be true.

A hummock of paranoia built up around town, reinforced by an action the mill subsequently took: the year after the first "Cancer Valley" episode was released, the mill filed a request with the DEP to increase its boiler emissions, which meant toxics would increase too. By significant amounts.

About two hundred alarmed residents turned up for a public hearing about the emissions increase. A de facto panel of town leaders, mill management, and environmental experts quashed citizen discontent by informing them the predicted elevated emissions were within legal limits, that the mill was basically within its rights to toxify the town. Cries of complaint rumbled through the room. Doc Martin asked if more research could be done before pressing on. The panel basically folded their hands, said *no,* then they were done.

"There's an old saying around Mexico and Rumford by a misinformed few," Doc Martin later wrote in a letter to the DEP, "that the stench in the air is the smell of money. What should be added is the smell of death and suffering."

The permit went through, but the frustration of the citizens didn't die down. In 1994, the EPA funded and helped form a study group, the Northern Oxford County Coalition (NOCC). Outside facilitators tasked the twenty-five local stakeholders with determining whether people were getting more cancer in Rumford and Mexico than elsewhere and if so, was that somehow precipitated by pollutants from the mill? They formed subcommittees and set to work analyzing studies on water, air, and human disease.

Hostility, accusations, skepticism, fear, insults, and unfamiliarity with consensus-building tactics crippled the process right from the start and beleaguered the efforts of the facilitator, so he left and was replaced by Consensus Building Institute (CBI) and an epidemiologist from Rutgers to help detangle and defang the mess.

Tempers simmered down but stakeholders stayed frustrated by the incomplete cancer data they were forced to use, which didn't include data on dioxin, one of their main concerns. And their worries weren't out of the blue. Dioxin scandals had been trending across the US:

1981–83: Ann Gorsuch (the mother of Supreme Court Justice Neil Gorsuch), the EPA administrator, is accused of trying to ease regulations on dioxin and avoid cleanup of hazardous waste sites that contain dioxin and other toxics.

1985: Dioxin found in fish downstream from our mill, provoking concerns about how dioxin enters the food chain. The EPA determines that dioxin is a probable human carcinogen.

1986: Activist Carol Van Strum's and Paul Merrell's report, "No Margin of Safety," on the risks of dioxin and how the paper industry contributes to those risks, is released.

1987: Dioxin residue found in paper products like milk cartons, tissues, coffee filters, tampons, paper plates.

1987-88: Van Strum documents how the EPA colluded with the American Paper Institute (the paper lobby) to downplay dioxin's dangers.

1987: Maine's state toxicologist Robert Frakes quits because he says his dioxin warnings were manipulated by the paper industry.

Also, in 1988, six Boise Cascade paper mills (including ours) had discharged 1.5 million pounds of chloroform and chromium into the air. How did mill management react? In their newsletter, the "Wrap Sheet," they crafted a notice: "We know of no scientifically credible data that would suggest that the employees of our mill or the residents of our community suffer from an abnormally high cancer rate—from chloroform or from any other substance associated with our facility. Therefore, we know of no reason for anyone to be alarmed at the report associated with this highly questionable data."

Yet our mill's union requested the National Institute for Occupational Safety and Health (NIOSH) test its workers to see how much toxics were in their blood as compared to the local population. NIOSH found the toxics in employees' and residents' blood were basically the same, that millworkers were not exposed more than anyone else, therefore there was no need to worry. But to me, residents *and* employees getting doses of the toxics didn't vindicate anything. It established cause for concern that everyone was susceptible to the pollution's reach.

NOCC went forward anyway and did what they could with what they had. After two years of work, they concluded cancer rates in Rumford were significantly elevated when compared to the rest of Maine. For men: respiratory cancers, prostate cancer, and non-Hodgkin's lymphoma, the latter 100 percent higher than expected. For women: colon, endocrine, and thyroid cancer, the latter more than 200 percent higher than expected. Yet when lifestyle behaviors, genetic predispositions, environmental and occupational exposures, age, gender, race, and other risks were factored in, NOCC found it difficult to come up with anything definitive and determined their study inconclusive, as most studies of the sort are. Their recommendation? Further analysis. But money and energy flatlined and everyone quit.

CBI, their facilitator, in a postmortem report said they felt residents saw them as "a bastion of academic pretension and liberal activism" so it was hard to get anything done, which suggests some of the study's failures were the fault of residents, not of the facilitators who lived outside the confines of this town. From residents' point of view I could see how CBI's whole top-down approach could have felt paternalistic, even condescending. Maybe CBI held themselves above and apart from those they claimed to help, and in doing so, weren't able to see residents eye to eye. And this imbalance teased out a defensiveness that was already lodged in our town gestalt. I had lived it myself as a kid, where we eschewed those smarter or more worldly than us because they made us feel small, whether or not that was their intent. I remember harboring resentments toward white-collar professionals who were full of blue-chip solutions and not blue-collar common sense. We held on to these grievances like life jackets, as so many times we'd been reduced to caricatures or not treated as humans with intelligence. Our anger held us afloat.

It's also not uncommon for aid-driven organizations to swan in with a precalculated blueprint only to find out the blueprint's made for an imaginary scene, that they are dealing with individuals who have been suffering many things the organization has not. Perhaps CBI's assessment of the stakeholders emerged from this general resistance to outside help by interlopers, none of whom stuck around to see things through or felt what we felt.

There were truths to both sides of the whole NOCC exercise; people were getting cancer yet there was no proof the mill caused it. This almost Orwellian Doublethinking, in which two beliefs are both accepted and irreconcilable, doomed the NOCC exercise from the start, for they canceled each other out.

. . .

AFTER NOCC DISBANDED, Terry didn't give up. She started an activist group called the Toxic Waste Women with four other women: Anne Morin, a neuroscientist; Jenny Orr, a psychologist and biochemist; Ingrid Eriksson, an orthopedic surgeon; and Shirley Damm, a baker.

In the winter of 2004, just outside of Rumford at Anne's B&B, the Toxic Waste Women met in a room imbricated with board games, a big-screen TV lodged in one corner, and cast-off furniture crouched all around. They watched as Denny Larson punched a hole in an industrial plastic bucket with his Makita cordless drill. "The bucket is the human body, the bag is the lung, and the pump is the diaphragm that brings in the air," he said as he brandished each part in front of his T-shirt that read, "PASS THE BUCKET."

Denny's MacGyver-esque device was actually a sophisticated but inexpensive version of an EPA canister to capture air in fence line communities or "Sacrifice Zones," a term the US government used during the Cold War to describe areas of radioactive contamination that was later repurposed by journalist Steve Lerner in his book of the same name. The term refers to low-income or otherwise disadvantaged communities disproportionately exposed to some of the most poisonous toxics because of where they live and who they are.

Denny trained what he called "Bucket Brigades" to help citizens engage or feel less helpless about the air pollution skirting around their town when governmental or environmental agencies wouldn't, couldn't, or seemed to give them suspect data. "It's on the same idea as a neighborhood crime watch only this is for environmental crimes," Denny said to the room.

Once you drew air into his EPA-approved buckets (he worked hard to get his methods approved so the EPA would consider his results credible), they would be sealed and mailed to a laboratory in California, where the contents were tested to determine what, if any, toxics were contained within.

"I used to send out a manual for this stuff but people would screw it up," Denny said. The women sat up straight. Anne's face tightened as if she was about to say something, because she usually was. "It must be airtight," Denny clarified. "You don't want anyone questioning your results." The strain of the moment softened.

Typically, Denny explained, there were no air monitoring devices in industrial zones, and if there were, they were often installed ten to twenty miles away from the source of industrial pollutants or sometimes even upwind. Bucket Brigades fortified community arguments that industry crossed the line, figuratively and literally, with their pollutants. "They will try to intimidate you," Denny warned. "But document it or it never happened."

The women leaned in as Denny spoke.

"It's very clear that there's significant air pollution here that's not being monitored. And if it's not being monitored, nothing can be done about it."

"What about the TRI?" Terry asked.

The EPA had established Toxic Release Inventory (TRI) monitoring in 1986, a federal program that collects data on specific toxic chemicals released into the environment by industry. However, what these industries report is determined, collected, and submitted by the companies themselves, as Denny alluded. Also, TRI releases are calculated, not actually measured—again, by the companies themselves. Companies also have accidental toxic releases, which are not recorded at all. Many of the toxics (around 93 percent) included in the database lack proper safety assessments. Illegal discharges are not reported.

Denny said when he was working in Port Arthur, Texas, a refinery reported a million pounds of TRI, but when added to the "upsets," or accidental releases, it was closer to six million pounds of TRI. The year before Denny came to Rumford, our mill released, according to the mill, 706,236 pounds of toxics directly into the environment.

"TRI is interesting," Denny said. "But it's not data. Turns out TRI is the best guess made by mill engineers. But you don't breathe estimates."

The day after Denny's demonstration, he and the Toxic Waste Women drove to Mexico in their three-car caravan and parked in the crescent-shaped lot across from the Far East Restaurant on the banks of the Androscoggin and popped open the trunk of Denny's car.

"God, it smells!" he said, looking across the river at the mill, then reminded them the buckets only test for gases, not particulates. "Smell," Denny said, "correlates to danger. No one makes an odorless chemical in isolation."

The temperature outside rose from twelve below earlier in the morning to six degrees, yet it was an unscrupulously bluebird day. As they got out of their cars, gusts of wind flattened a door against someone's leg, and flags hurtled in the wind's fuss. And the odor, along with the wind, kept shifting. The squalls along the river motivated the group to move their operation up to Granite Street, a higher road where less wind sought to ruin their intent. Air was hard to catch when it blew around.

"I can't stand the smell. It gives me a headache," Terry said, getting out of the car. "This must be a good location."

The plastic tube from pump to bucket had hardened because of the cold, making it tricky to insert into the bucket opening. "I can't feel my fingers," Anne said. Jenny warmed the stiff tube with her breath.

"Someday I'll have a big bus painted with the words *Terry's Toxic Tours*," Terry said as she rubbed her hands together and laughed.

They managed to get a sample, despite the wind, the cold, and their inexperience. Denny took a photograph of the women holding their buckets: "Look, Anne and Jenny and a bag of air!" he said as he laughed.

With each bucket at $75 each and the tests around $500, the Toxic Waste Women quickly used up their money from a small grant they received, then started paying out of pocket. They obtained some samples over the course of a few months; however, the tests were inconclusive. With no local or political will to back them, the Bucket Brigade dissolved alongside their good intentions.

. . .

JOHN PATRICK, THE state representative for Rumford and a mill employee, told a story during the House's first regular session in 2001 about how he was gassed at the mill, which meant chlorine in a gaseous state was accidentally sprayed in his face. When the chlorine reacted with the water in his lungs, it produced acid, so he would have felt like he was drowning.

John said, "Like a loyal employee with my eyes burning, my sinuses burning, my lungs burning, dizzy, lightheaded and vomiting, I went down to [mill] first aid. They gave me some Milk of Magnesia and told me to take it easy for a while and sent me back on the job."

His condition worsened and he went to see Doc Martin, who said the mill probably hadn't noted on his record he was gassed. Later, when John developed chronic bronchitis and pneumonia, he asked to see his mill health chart and "just like [Doc Martin] said, word for word, 'employee has flu-like symptoms.' They weren't there to help me out. They were there to protect themselves."

• • •

HUMANS GENERALLY PREFER unambiguous situations. We like to know what's around the corner, in our lungs, in our water, or in the wind. We like to know what evidence we can depend on so our choices about where we live, how we act or don't act, are based on fact not fear, an emotion sometimes as irrational as flowers that have no scent.

When you are told one thing, then another, or nothing at all by various parties who are party to questionable deeds—like John Patrick found—it accentuates the overall feeling of suspicion, which is as debilitating as worrying about the viability of your already tenuous job or health. For millworkers especially, this adds a terrible irony to the mood, coiling around their allegiances like a caduceus. So when environmental regulators, scientists, or mill doctors say local cancers are within the normal range—that risks can be controlled, that industry is not to blame, and we are not to worry about things we can't see like the pollution that leaks through our towns—people deploy coping mechanisms to stem their alarm: hypervigilance, blame, and nonempirical belief systems, or develop traumatic neuroses like PTSD. The uncertainty, combined with actual illness, can eventually cause us to distrust medicine, scientists, doctors, facilitators, lawyers, government officials, neighbors, everyone, and everyone else even if they seem to have our best interests at heart. And it is the overall ambiguity—when the arbitrary overshadows the reasonable—that leaves people helpless, paranoid, confused, angry, incredulous, psychologically adrift, as I was starting to feel myself.

NOCC's uncertain conclusions also mirror the imprecise boundaries of cancer itself, a disease that can develop slowly, a physical disaster not bound by space or time. Cancer emerges if cells mutate by chance and multiply out of control when they no longer have instructions on what to do. So when cancer strikes, it can feel arbitrary, vindictive, adding to the sense we've lost all control. The cause of cancer and the path of dioxin are both hard to pin down, a whack-a-mole exercise where the truth seems provisional.

If nobody or nothing is causing us to die or get sick except in average percentages, there is always the possibility someone or something is *letting* us die by widespread inaction, or "death by indirection" as Rachel Carson described the invisible, stealthy threats that imperil our world. Because we are—people are getting cancer and dying at what feels like an alarming rate.

CONNECTING WITH DOT

DOT BERNARD'S HUSBAND pulls up on his riding mower and lifts his chin, inquiring without speaking, *Who are you?* He cuts the engine. It ticks away and he looks at the Florida plates of my rental car. The wet green smell of fresh-cut lawn strangles the air.

"I'm here to see Dot," I say. "I'm friends with Terry Martin."

"Well, just knock, if she's expecting you," he says, starts his mower, then lurches off over the clotted hillside.

Dot answers after one knock, as if she's been waiting for me by the door. She is tiny and smells of fabric softener. Diagnosed with cancer years ago, the doctors didn't give her much time. She made amends, cleaned out the house, readied herself for death. But death took its time. She's been housebound for eleven years. Shaking her hand is like touching a bird claw.

"My stomach bothers me. Can't keep weight on. Afraid I might fall," she says as she shuffles into the yawn of her office door.

Her slow decline granted her time to figure out her family tree, which sags in brittle manila folders inside the file cabinet next to her desk.

"Terry said you could help me fill in the gaps in my family tree," I say, I ask.

"What are you looking for?" she asks.

"My great-grandmother, Obeline," I say. "I can't find any record of her death or birth. And some guy named Captain Gallant that took care of my grandfather." Dot doesn't respond. "I don't recall learning anything about Acadian history as a kid, even though our phonebooks are filled with Acadian names," I say.

Dot sits down and pulls open a drawer. "People seem to be curious about the past much more than they are about the future," she says as she bends over her files and starts digging around.

Of course I was curious about the past. My social studies teachers taught us about Captain John Smith's outpost in Jamestown and the pilgrims who landed in Plymouth, Massachusetts, and I thought they were the only part of American history we needed to know. I never learned anything about Prince Edward Island except by way of *Anne of Green Gables*—a children's book set in PEI—and even that, only through extracurricular reading. Our town, our schools, our state, our country remaindered Acadian history out of the curriculum altogether.

Hours slip by. We talk about PEI, where to find genealogical records, where my ancestors likely had lived, and eventually we talk about cancer—hers and the millworkers' she oversaw in her role as secretary in the mill's personnel department. "Speaking French was suicide for those seeking management jobs," Dot says. "And of course, they only hired older men to work in the bleach room. Most men who worked there died a few years after retiring, around age sixty-seven. That's why they wouldn't hire the younger ones to work there. At first, I thought the mill hired the older guys due to their experience or because it was a special job working in the bleach room. The men were made to think that anyway."

I tell her my grandfather William worked in the bleach room and he died of cancer just after retiring. Dot nods.

"The mill didn't want to take care of young guys who got sick. And anyone who worked in the bleach room got sick. The mill didn't say this of course. I figured it out."

"Why didn't you say anything?" I ask.

"I didn't want to cause problems," she says, closing the file drawer.

I leave Dot's and drive to the airport and fly south. As my plane skitters down the tarmac in Curaçao, I'm still thinking about Dot's conclusions. Had William known the dangers of working in the bleach room? Did he care? Did he have the luxury of caring?

· · ·

WILLIAM'S FATHER, THOMAS, grew up in Howlan, Prince Edward Island, a small settlement of flat windswept fields consisting of one or two roads and a handful of homes. The youngest of seven children, Thomas was a self-employed fisherman and helped farm his family's hardscrabble land. His wife, Obeline, died young, and his land and PEI's economy gave up on him, too. With four children, he knew what he had to do.

Thomas went to Maine to seek work in the mill like so many of his friends before him. He entrusted William to a man known simply as Captain Gallant, so Thomas could be a little flexible in his job search. Families did that back then, at least in our circles. If a child was orphaned or needed shelter, someone provided a home, related or not, no questions asked. My father never knew Captain Gallant's first name. "He was just Captain Gallant," my father once said. "Nothing more, nothing less."

As soon as William was a little older, he moved to Maine and he too started walking across the footbridge to work in the mill with his father to convert wood to paper pulp using the Kraft process, so named for the German word for strength. Every day they scooped up wood chips and heaved them into a digester, a rocket-shaped vat around ninety feet high. The digester "cooked" the chips in a broth of white liquor (sodium hydroxide and sodium sulfide), steam pressure, and high temperature. The lignin, the glue that binds the wood fibers together, dissolved under the assault. The brown cellulose, which is the main component of paper, stayed behind. From there, they would remove any leftover lignin then proceed to bleach the pulp white. Elemental chlorine was used back then as a bleaching agent, until regulations forced mills to switch to Elemental Chlorine-Free (ECF) technology, which was the term used for chlorine dioxide. Our mill switched in 1997. While both elemental chlorine and ECF produce dioxin, the latter produces significantly less.

It was the 1920s and William was employed and single, enjoying the rumble of the postwar economy. He was an "honest and faithful" guy with blue eyes and a "swarthy" complexion, according to his National Guard records. I've only seen one photograph of him and in it he's wearing a bolo, his salt-and-pepper hair slicked back, his eyes deliquescent. He looked as if he was about to release a long-held breath or punch someone in the face. He lived a little fast, drank a little too much, as did many in that era because they didn't suspect the hardships yet to come.

As the mill prospered and expanded so did its immigrant population: while able-bodied Acadians fled south to Maine, Italians, Poles, Lithuanians, Irish, and Scots in other parts of New England were steered north in a steady industrial headwind by Rumford's good wages and dependable jobs. They arranged themselves in town by nationalities, languages, churches, neighborhoods, traditions; Acadians made *tourtière* (meat pie) in their apartments on Waldo Street and went to the Le Paresseux Club (the Snowshoe Club) where they dressed in red wool knickers, wool shirts, and sashes, and raced around on snowshoes. Italians opened the Sons of Italy club in Smithville, an area where I played summer softball on a field we called the Spaghetti Bowl because of its proximity to the population living nearby.

The town fathers weren't pleased with the influx. In a 1907 editorial to the *Rumford Falls Times,* Waldo Pettengill, the first president of the mill, wrote, "The entrance into our political, social, and industrial life of such vast masses of peasantry, degraded below our utmost conceptions, is a matter which no intelligent patriot can look upon without the gravest apprehension. They are beaten men from beaten races, representatives of the worst failure in the struggle for existence. . . . Next to the liquor problem, this question of the emigration is the most serious that the American people have to contend with."

Fifty thousand Maine KKK members at the time mirrored what Pettengill insinuated and advanced an anti–French Catholic agenda. The KKK considered French Catholics subservient, a dark-skinned race that stole jobs, defiled American culture, and spoke in pagan tongues (Latin masses, French). These sentiments sprang partly from the belief that loyalty to the pope precluded loyalty to America, and if your views questioned American anything, then you needed to go. Their zealous leader, F. Eugene Farnsworth, a former hypnotist and barber from Missouri, insisted the KKK's message and acts were focused on fraternal rights, political leverage, and "Americanism," a belief that Americans of Anglo-Saxon origin were superior to immigrants, which really just disguised racism with national unity.

Though mill management despised "Herring Chokers," as they called Acadians in a derogatory way, they loved us as laborers. The tenets of Catholicism—discipline, loyalty, duty, family—worked in management's favor and made us ripe for exploitation and servile employees. And we willingly complied. Our dark history—being driven from the Acadian homeland in 1755—also steeled us for the sometimes unpleasant and often treacherous work at the mills. The wages were that good. An 1881 Report of Labor Statistics from Massachusetts stated:

> With some exceptions the Canadian French are the Chinese of the Eastern States. They care nothing for our institutions, civil, political,

or educational. They do not come to make a home among us, to dwell with us as citizens, and so become a part of us. . . . They are a horde of industrial invaders, not a stream of stable settlers. . . . These people have one good trait. They are indefatigable workers, and docile. All they ask is to be set to work, and they care little who rules them or how they are ruled. To earn all they can by no matter how many hours of toil, to live in the most beggarly way. [T]o work them to the uttermost is about the only good use they can be put to.

As more Acadians moved to Rumford and Mexico, the more they were resented by Protestants like Pettengill, with someone saying Acadians were making the towns a "veritable Gomorrah." Besides the violence perpetuated by the KKK, the name-calling, and the scorn of town leaders, Acadians were also targets of legislation of their tongue.

For my ancestors, language had always been an avenue of control. In 1539, France's Ordinance of Villers-Cotterêts ruled that Parisian French would serve as the official language of the land, which was different from the language my French ancestors spoke. Not long after the decree, those ancestors carried their unclipped, loose vernacular to Acadia and eventually to Maine. There, my great-grandparents kept the accent alive until 1919, when Maine legislators designated English as the legal language of instruction and forbade French to be spoken at schools. Then, as in France of 1539, a people lost their mother tongue to the ideations of the state and social pressures of the time.

● ● ●

My GRANDMOTHER, HORTENSE Dumas, born in 1912 the illegitimate child of Mary Duguay and Martin Dumas, lived in various apartments in Rumford with her mother, who took in boarders or lived as a boarder herself, both women abused by those who sheltered them. At age seventeen Hortense began work at Rumford's Continental Paper Bag Company, a subsidiary of the mill, one of many women who operated the 190 bag machines and made twelve to thirteen million bags a day.

Hortense met and married William in 1931 when he was twenty-five and she was eighteen. As the Great Depression expanded, the US economy contracted, and the mill's paper production slumped. William was in and out of work and he and Hortense sank into the economy's spongy morass. The forecast for the couple's marriage fared no better. My father was born at the edges of this unstable terrain in 1933.

Hortense began an affair with a railroad man from Massachusetts named Frank Jordan when my father was five. Frank's original name was Supernault, one he changed to cover for some crime of his past, though Supernault always sounded like the fake one to me. Frank came and went to Rumford with the rhythm of the train schedule, until one day Hortense left with him, leaving my father and his older brother with William, who lived in the mill's bachelor quarters where there was no room for two young boys.

Unable (or unwilling, as my mother suggests) to provide a home for his sons, William ferried them to the Healy Asylum, a Franco-American facility run by the Grey Nuns, forty-five miles south in Lewiston. The nuns' mission at Healy was partly to alleviate the suffering in Lewiston and maintain the ethnic identity of the city's large Franco-American population. The nuns believed whoever lost their French language, lost the faith. *Elles sont venues, elles ont servi:* "they came, they served" was their motto.

On his first night at Healy, the nuns forced my father to bathe last in the tepid, root beer–colored water after dozens of boys before him. They explained (in French, which my father did not understand) how new boys needed to earn fresh bathwater, and for the duration of their impoundment, my father and his brother would be separated within the brick walls that held them.

I'm sure it was worse than my father conceded when I once asked him about that time. Who would want to remember eating food with mold and mealworms as others have acknowledged since? Who would want to remember wetting the bed and having your face shoved in pissy sheets; being forced to kneel on a blanket of dried peas; having your bottom beaten purply red; watching as kids with Down syndrome got shaken like dog toys; or hearing yourself called by a number not your name?

Months later, William settled into an apartment he could afford, and retrieved the boys from Healy. Sometimes they lived with him, sometimes with relatives and neighbors, my father and his brother scattered like birdseed.

My father's early memories clung to him like the odor of his clothes that went unwashed for weeks when he was a kid. "I hadn't thought much of it then but looking back, my childhood was a horror," my father once said. "I don't remember ever taking a bath except at Healy. I must have stunk."

• • •

THE WORKING-CLASS, AS Dot suggested, we tolerated our fate silently, and silence became part of our topographical makeup, looping through our lives like the long, quiet walks my parents and I took around town. These silences show up in my family tree too, in the absence of genealogical evidence I can't seem to find and in diseases revealing themselves when it's already too late. Silence also seemed to be an Acadian thing, how we lost our tongue, kept our complaints to ourselves, took it all on the chin. I began to see how it connected to what Dot said; we buried things pretty deep. I was just trying to fish it out from the dark waters of our past.

As Mainers, as New Englanders, as working-class Americans, as Acadians, we were also programmed not to whine, so a kind of fatalism slipped unconsciously into our routines. Eventually that fatalism transformed over generations into something else . . . a handing over of control to the powers that be. In doing so, we curtailed our independence, our identity, maybe even our lives. It wasn't a deliberate act. It was just a slow-moving turnstile of resignation to accept what was on offer, whether we wanted it or not, just like the rotten-egg smell hovering over our isolated town.

I talk to a friend about my exchange with Dot and he says my family faced a Hobson's choice. (A diehard Boston Red Sox fan, he originally thought it referred to Butch Hobson, the famed Red Sox third basemen who had to choose whether to play the 1978 season with bone chips in his elbow or not.) Thomas Hobson, the actual inspiration for the phrase, was said to have owned a large stable of rentable horses in seventeenth-century Cambridge. His customers tended to favor the fastest horse, so soon the poor animal wore out with overuse. Hobson declared a new policy stating customers could only rent the horse closest to the door (which he kept rotating) or go without. With the shadow of unemployment looming like the mill's smokestack does over our town, millworkers face a similar choice—between something or nothing—which isn't really a choice at all. It's an inevitability.

In order to try to better understand this thinking, I read a few studies that examine the phenomenon of organizational silence in the US workplace. In one, participants were asked if they would speak up if they knew something was wrong at work. Eighty-five percent responded "no," mostly because they feared being viewed negatively even if they weren't being negative. It didn't matter if they worked in coal mines or corporations or operating rooms, even if a patient's life was at risk; so it appears that such silence was a costly dysfunction in many ways. Author Margaret Heffernan received permission to repeat the studies in Europe and in every country she polled, she got the same results: around 85 percent of workers prefer to remain silent rather than speak out.

Other researchers couldn't understand, however, why such silences were repeated . . . how one illogical act upon another becomes a powerful norm. Silence, it seems, is an accumulating force, like the accretion of trauma in the domestic abuse Terry bore. This negative feedback loop contains no exit strategy and mirrors how toxics, if left unattended, will grow exponentially until they're impossible to control. I used to think our lives orbited around love, for love was why we bothered to get up in the morning. But after talking to Dot, and considering my town, my family, my own stifled voice, life seems to revolve around the silences we're afraid to violate. And as the studies show, this isn't just a problem in Mexico, Maine. It's a human problem.

• • •

TERRY AND DOT handed me a baton in a race with no track. While my husband is off in Brazil for work and the crushing heat of Curaçao

keeps me inside, I start a timeline, plotting dates in my family tree alongside Doc Martin's claims, studies, dioxin details, and environmental regulations passed. Soon, however, the information is more than I can govern in a simple path. So I make four timelines racing in parallel tracks. But they run aground out of the gate. I try making notecards. I consider using a scatter plot. I stick push-pinned memos to my office walls. I three-hole-punch my way into a mismanaged mess. I start a genogram—a chart similar but more expansive than a family tree—that shows three-dimensional relationships, connections, and patterns across generations and throughout the community, and indicates ties with the mill are not just economic; they are emotional, genetic, psychological, social, cultural, physical. The information forks into five dimensions and I follow each route to its apparent dead end. I throw it all away and make another timeline on a long piece of brown paper, one of death and of cancer in family, in friends. Its horizontal line reaches almost to infinity.

I pack up Dot's books to return to her, but before I mail them, I read her obituary in the *Rumford Falls Times*. I call Terry.

"Keep the books," she says. "Dot won't need them and you do." Then Terry tells me more information, data I can't figure out where to place.

After Doc Martin died she began compiling a "house history" by walking door-to-door on Mexico's Middle and Kimball Avenues, where she polled residents about disease in their family homes, asking them when they bought their house, who the previous owner was, who lived there, and who in their house—past or present—had cancer.

"I had no money for a real scientific study," Terry says. "But basic physics says all those chemicals that go up in the air . . . they have to come down somewhere."

She found cancer cases divided and multiplied like cancer cells themselves at every house and through generations of families. In one home, both parents and one child died of cancer. One man who worked in the mill had prostate cancer, three of his five children had been diagnosed with cancer, his wife suffered from fibromyalgia and lung disease, while another of his children died from cardiac arrest. One family, wiped out completely. The diseases included the familiar and the unpronounceable: brain tumors, prostate cancer, lung cancer, colon cancer, leukemia, stroke, pituitary cancer, liver cancer, cervical cancer, breast cancer, precancerous polyps, PCOF ovarian syndrome, kidney disease, pancreatic cancer, lentiginous melanoma, rhabdomyosarcoma, liposarcoma, asbestosis. Some people even gave Terry copies of medical records, death certificates, pathology reports, because they were so desperate to understand what was making them and their families sick. I grew up in that neighborhood, as did my grandparents, my uncle and aunt, and all their friends and neighbors. I knew them all. I had never known of their suffering. How to chart that?

HAPPY DAYS

THE PAST HAS always been an animating force in Rumford and Mexico. We lionized it, revered it, practically took it out to fancy dinners and gave it awards. Why wouldn't we? We believed with no reason not to that our previous successes would usher in an equally triumphant future. But this belief got mixed up with longing and nostalgia, and we looked more backward than forward. Because of our regressive sentiments, we never seemed to relieve ourselves from the past, a presence so acute it sabotages our town's future like a tetherball match, where the ball's own retrograde velocity ends the game.

I join a Facebook group where we reminisce and celebrate the *remember when*s of leaving our doors unlocked at night and speeding home to the mill's nine o'clock whistle after playing hide-and-seek. The administrator of the group won't allow any posts except for the happy memories of the *good old days,* even if they are about adversities our towns once faced, leaving us to commiserate without being explicit that the former iteration of our community was replaced by some menace we are oddly not allowed to express. His rules of procedure underline the general belief that our past was always better than the present. But that's a concept fogged by distance from the past's oppressive systems and ways. Our collective fantasy also doesn't consider the struggles we experienced, like how the landscape we loved was shifted beneath our feet by toxic and invisible deceit. Pretending everything's fine, and nothing bad ever happened in our town, seems like a prescription for a skewed point of view. This silencing of anything but sepia-toned reveries absolves that page administrator of complicity in the very things he hopes to ignore by preferring one version of history over the other, even if that history is not complete. He allows our past to remain great even though it wasn't always so. What about people like my grandfather who may have been poisoned by the industry that sustained him? Or rivers that yielded fish we couldn't eat or rivers we couldn't swim in or leaders who led us astray? Was that past so great?

What's the use of digging up the past? I am often asked, ask myself. How far did I need to go to make sense of how the past relates to what's happening today? Apparently, I didn't have to go that far. I only had to look in our backyard. And in our backyard grew steep-sloped woods, where as children we'd race through the thicket on fast-moving sleds, tree branches clawing our faces. We didn't bother removing the twigs from our snowy path until we needed them for our snowmen's arms. Buttons we liberated from my mother's sewing tin became their eyes, and we used a half-rotten carrot for a nose. As winter wore out, the sun and wind would flatten him into a grimy wad, leaving the entrails of his decoration in the half-frozen lawn. As spring turned to summer we played hoops on the hot-topped patch my father installed at the edge of our woods, *so you don't become cheerleaders,* he said to me and my two sisters. The basketball court foiled the cheerleading, but, to my father's disappointment, attracted cute high school boys who practiced layups every afternoon.

Swarms of neighborhood kids fed our backyard and we gathered there on weekends and after school: the McDonalds (two girls), and not far away, the Goodoffs (four girls, one boy), the Zanonis (five boys, two girls), the Woods (one boy, one girl), the Arbors (four girls, three boys), the Martins (six girls), the Chessies (thirteen kids), the Blodgetts (fourteen kids), and my Arsenault cousins (five boys). The Gotto, Witas, Petrie, Dugas, Freeman, Bedard, Watson kids, and assorted only children like Bobbilyn Mercier rounded out the crowd. Our backyard was big enough to field two full soccer teams with subs. It often did.

What may be great about our past *was* our backyards, even if sand-wiched by bachelors who had no patience for balls bouncing mis-takenly in their property. On the soft grass, the cold snow, or on the hot-topped courts and streets, we sorted things out amongst ourselves like quarrels and fair teams. Backyards taught us about losing, playing together, crushed dreams, how to ride bikes with no hands, or build forts with nothing but branches we ripped from trees. We wandered a little beyond the boundaries of the land that enclosed us but our back-yards made their mark.

The house anchoring my family was a four-bedroom clapboard New Englander with a roomy two-story barn attached via a long cold shed. Until my parents installed a shower in the sole bathroom around 1990, we washed our hair in the kitchen sink at breakfast, the scent of cinnamon toast and Gee, Your Hair Smells Terrific mingling with my parents' morning cigarettes. At some point, they renovated our kitchen and quit smoking, but the stingy heat that pursed through the vents in the floor, the creaky stairs, the mercury glass–colored walls, they stayed as they were. When things staled, my mother glued wallpaper to the plaster or carpeted the floor or shifted the doilies to soften the angles of the oak furniture that adorned the rooms.

Our household population consisted, at various junctures, of my parents (Maddy and Tom) and in order of birth: Kelly, Amy, me, Tom, and Joel, and throughout the years, a militia of cats and kittens, a couple of miserable dogs (that I wanted but neglected), and a lone rab-bit named Peter. As the middle child, I got less attention and liked it that way. My two older sisters laid out a path for me to follow and my brothers provided reinforcements later on; I benefited from the space in between.

A smaller house was connected to ours through a door in my bed-room, linking me to the daughters of our long-term renters. We would whisper through the keyhole to each other until my parents Sheet-rocked our secret portal for reasons unknown. After the blockade, we formulated a complicated knocking code to communicate with one another, which we could have eliminated by simply meeting up in our shared backyard.

Only one other house preceded this one, and it was just across the street. When I was eight years old we paraded furniture and toys to the current one, then owned by Amelia and Frank Knaus, who decamped from the former Yugoslavia for America at gunpoint when Tito's soldiers knocked on their door asking for their son. When the Knauses sold the house to my parents, Mrs. Knaus left her wicker furniture and perennials and Mr. Knaus left his asparagus, his barn-sized wood ladder, and the red plastic holy water font on the frame of the dining room door.

One by one as we left home, my siblings and I stored our belongings in the barn and promised to remove them once we settled. The longer those boxes lay there on the floorboards, the less meaningful they became, like Mr. Knaus's asparagus that had gone to seed.

• • •

IN THE MIDDLE of my husband's job transfer from Sweden to California in 2007, I returned home to help my parents organize their house and barn, which had maddeningly accumulated stuff as if through osmosis: tools, old skis and sleds, a baby crib, the golf balls my father rescued from the rough, things the tenants stored or abandoned, and bits my mother inherited from her mother nine years before. I dusted off half-refinished furniture, tossed jars of nails and crates of moldy magazines, some things broken or worrisome, others loved but useless. Some of my own belongings, stored elsewhere in the US while I was living overseas, arrived and added to the snarled mass.

For a month I cleaned, pitched, cataloged. I held a yard sale. My father and I drove stuff to the dump, to the secondhand store. I held another yard sale. Even though it was her stated goal to get rid of things, my mother constantly thwarted my efforts. *I just don't want to talk about it,* she'd say, teary-eyed, as she stuffed a broken teacup back into her cedar chest. My mother unpacked and repacked the salt-and-pepper shaker collection, a bride doll in a faded silk dress, and my great-grandmother's mandolin, undecided if she should save these things or give them to me. We went through the books, kept on a shelf in the shed, and I grabbed a first edition of John Irving's first book, *Setting*

Free the Bears, but most others were brittle paperbacks we chucked in gleeful recognition—finally here was something we could do without.

I used to work as a project manager for a company that created custom gifts for museum shops nationwide. My boss there previously worked as the president of Goebel, the maker of those collectible porcelain German Hummel figurines. Despite recessions, wars, inflation, he claimed business in the porcelain statuette world remained unshakable. Americans are the biggest collectors in the world, he noted, and tied fiercely and inextricably to "things" (air quotes his), even if the "things" they save represent nothing except nostalgia. They were placeholders, reminders of a happier past, until the day comes when we can't remember anything but the item itself.

My aunt had collected Hummels even though she bore no connection to the German tableaux, so my old boss's theory made sense. In the carpeted living room away from daily living, the guileless, expensive characters atop her upright piano were tempting to someone like me who was attracted to such evocative and off-limits things. If I got too close to them, a snarled *hands off!* from my watchful aunt. Every time I see those Hummels now, usually at garage sales or antique shops, they are still hermetically sealed off, a glass between them and me to keep their value pristine. My mother owned not Hummels but a set of antique piano babies, bisque figurines (also German) found in many Victorian middle-class homes, often used to hold a tablecloth or piano shawl in place, a piano we did not have, which my aunt did. I always helped my mother keep those cherubic gesticulating babies dust- and fingerprint-free because I loved them as much, if not more, than she.

While my mother may have balked at discarding certain objects, she always ran a tight ship, vacuuming twice a day whether it was needed or not, ensuring I finished everything on my plate whether I was hungry or not, and insisting that I needed to go to college—something she did not have the luxury of doing. She parented us as most mothers did in the 1970s: within an inch of our lives, dressing me and my sisters in pleated Polly Flinders outfits and my brothers in spotless shirts even if we were just climbing on jungle gyms. If she spanked us, we'd mumble *I'll call the child abuse hotline* and she'd pretend to dial the phone. If we threatened to run away, she packed our gym bag. I did things because she *said so*. "If I didn't have you kids . . . ," she said to me once, her thought trailing off like a small stone pinging down a rockslide.

While I was home that month in 2007, I found in the upstairs hall closet her rhinestone tiara, the crown she was awarded as Queen of the Rumford Winter Carnival in 1962 when she worked in the mill's personnel department. At the time she wore her jet-black hair in a pixie cut and her polyester minidresses showed off her good legs and small frame but it was no beauty contest. To win the crown, she sold the most tickets to the Winter Carnival gala at the Rumford Armory featuring the "Deansmen," an all-male a cappella group from Bates College. We were never allowed to touch the jeweled coronet, but its sparkly, silvery hardware was irresistible to my raccoonish love of shiny objects, so I'd sneak it out of its yellowy tissue paper and wonder why such a thing lay hidden beneath old blankets.

After a five-year hiatus, the Queen competition was reinstated and renamed the Rumford-Mexico Winter Carnival, and my mother—who in those five years had married, had my sisters Kelly and Amy, divorced, and remarried—crowned the next Queen using a different crown. The local newspaper published a photo of my mother and the new Queen, and in it, Kelly and Amy accompany her, wearing velvet dresses with white Peter Pan collars as stiff as Communion wafers.

As I lifted the now slightly damaged keepsake out of its nest, I thought of the crown I received when I was sixteen for being elected homecoming queen, though my crown was made of the finest mill paper instead of faceted glass. That crown connected my mother and me, enthroned together in a contest she undoubtedly won: she worked hard for hers and I did nothing except choose the right king—my long-suffering Greg. I tossed my crown away long ago, as it was far more transient than what my mother had been entrusted to preserve, so who was I to tell her what to throw away?

One day my father unearthed a few pages of a journal he kept hidden under a plastic tablecloth in the shed: "I Think I Should Start at the Beginning," handwritten in his loopy scrawl. I had encouraged him to write and I think those pages were all he wrote. I've not seen the journal since and can't recall what it said. He was always a word-smith, acing his crossword puzzles before I could eat a bowl of Froot Loops, and loved to use archaic words in light conversation know-ing those listening would usually be too embarrassed to ask what he meant. My mother was also a good writer but her words were usually spoken out loud or kept to herself. There was no journal to tie her down.

Her forsaken crown reminded me of her first husband as he too was part of a broken but resuscitated past. She married her high school sweetheart, a handsome and capable boy, but after five years of mar-riage he started looking around. Eventually, he left her with two babies and his tuition bill from the University of Maine. My mother was a buoyant, forgiving woman and bore life as it was, not as it was sup-posed to be. Absorbing the gravity of the situation so her daughters wouldn't have to, she fell in love with and married my father, making a sensible home out of ruins. The ex appeared decades later and my sisters got to know him *like an uncle,* they'd say, and he began infiltrat-ing their lives with new wives and step-siblings who called them *sister.* One Christmas, when the ex worked as a Florida real estate flipper, he mailed my sisters an enormous box of things we figured he must have bought at a secondhand store: tacky, tangled costume jewelry, previ-ously worn clothes that didn't fit or suit them—abandoned odds and ends, the shine on them long gone. After my sisters opened the box, they adorned themselves with the trinkets of his dubious generosity and we laughed. A few years later, he sent my oldest sister, who was in the process of adopting a baby from China, a life-sized, lifelike Asian doll that for years she was afraid to throw away.

The ex eventually apologized for everything and my mother accepted. She has always been far more gracious than me. The ex's reputation as a selfish man made me think his expression of regret was solely for him-self. His smooth-operating procedure was always a liability according to others who know him, a slick, puppy-eyed man whose *sorry*s could never replace what my father shored up. Did anyone not remember his thoughtlessness when I did? Or did I remember it all wrong?

Sometimes our recollections can be suspect because memory accumulates actual events and muddles them with how we want them to unfold. *You used to lock us out of the house in the winter,* my siblings and I would tease my mother. *You bundled us into snowsuits, sent us out to play, and locked the door behind us, only letting us inside for lunch.*

I never did that to you kids! she'd always huff. It was five against one and we'd corner her with our allied reminiscences. *It doesn't matter anyway,* she once said. *I wasn't there to entertain you.*

Those addenda she tacked on put us in our place, as was her job as a mother of five. This way of editing the past was probably a muting device she inherited from her mother, Bridget, who eliminated all photos of my mother's ex from family albums, rigorously decapitating one Polaroid after another, leaving nothing but photographs full of menacing holes where his head should have been. When I think of the ex, his peripheral presence is like the pain of a splinter in your fingertip you can't quite see, and I sometimes wish he remained the headless amputee he had become at my grandmother's exacting hand.

After my parents and I finished decluttering the barn that long summer of 2007 and it was time for me to go, I called my siblings and told them to come get their labeled and tarp-covered stuff.

· · ·

My parents put the house on the market sometime in 2008. Although they loved that old house it always needed something, like a child who never left home. A new roof on the barn, a paint job, a furnace, tree removal, septic repair, excising skunks living under the shed. The house sat for a while on the market. They received no reasonable offers, so they dropped the price. Then dropped it again. Below market value. Then again. Nothing made a difference. Not the wood floors or the airy rooms or the old-growth trees shading the porch. Not the grassy yard, the basketball court, the big barn, or the turn-of-the-century practicality of the house itself. While upriver properties earned around $150/square foot, in Mexico they idled around fifty dollars. The real estate market and my parents' lifetime investment had run out of breath.

When I asked their realtor if there was anything else they could do, she said, "Nobody wants a view of a paper mill."

. . .

In 2011, four years after I cleaned up the barn, my parents' house sits unsold with weeds coagulating in its backyard, yet they make an offer on a smaller house in Rumford and it's accepted. I ask my mother, what will they do? "If the bank takes our house, who cares?" she says.

I fly home from Curaçao in August to retrieve anything I left behind and to help my parents ready for their move. As I wander through the house—probably the last time I ever will—I snap photos of tabletop vignettes filled with the loot of childhood: the porcelain reproduction French King Louis XV lamps; the carnival glass candlestick; the Larkin desk; the mother-of-pearl opera glasses; a match holder; a plastic bag filled with plastic bags. I only brought my zoom lens so all the shots are close-ups, as if I am seeing the world from Alice's point of view after she drank the potion that made her shrink.

My mother plonks down a box on the kitchen table. A sour breeze from its contents feathers the air. I pick up a mill newsletter bearing a photograph of her planning the Winter Carnival Ball on account of her "firsthand knowledge" of the Queen's duties.

'Were you ever bothered by the pollution?" I ask, sniffing the newsletter, then pushing it toward my mother's nose.

"It was the smell of money," she says, shoving it aside. "Plus, we just had a lot of pride."

Pride.

I heard this word a lot when I was growing up. We were proud to be from Rumford or Mexico. We took pride in the mill, pride in the paper we made. We scrawled "PINTO PRIDE" on pep rally posters to honor our school mascot. Mill managers instilled pride in their workers. What did it mean, this pride?

I learned from an early age to be conspicuous was to be coarse. You didn't speak too loudly or too much. You blended in. This sameness, it turns out, was partially the source of our pride—we were all in it together, no matter what "it" was. We were a community and, like most communities, were proud of what we did, even if it was something we didn't necessarily like. It was part of the same unspoken social rules that also felt claustrophobic, so it was difficult to differentiate the two. It was a subtle force, like airplane cabin pressure—massive but invisible. In this togetherness our loyalties to each other and to our town were fierce, even if the intimation to conform was benevolent.

This absolute loyalty didn't stop at the edge of town; it extended to hopeless causes like the Boston Red Sox and the New England Patriots, who for decades disappointed us with their fruitless company. But we stuck with them because that's what we did despite their unwillingness to love us back. This mix of sameness and loyalty and pride and stubbornness made us tight. As we created this shelter for ourselves, it also meant outsiders remained outside. People "from away" weren't allowed into the sanctity of our tribe, and we certainly didn't want to be part of theirs. Solidarity was a matter of safety and comfort, but it was also a matter of hardheadedness that didn't always serve us well.

The mill, the main source of this pride and connectedness, provided us with what seemed like limitless opportunity, the tentacles of its fortune reaching into the county, the region, the State of Maine, America.

Our reliance on the mill and our pride was like our Catholicism: we were given something to believe in while ignoring our own suffering, all the while waiting for the big afterlife party in the sky. We depended on the mill, as did lumberjacks, whose lopping of the trees was seemingly anathema to the very thing relied upon to earn an income. Trees grew back, that much we knew, but our resurrection, it would have to wait.

It was often difficult to tell where the mill ended and where our personal lives began. In the 1920s, mill employees published *The League,* a compendium of work and community activities. In it, you'd learn, for instance, "Charlie Gordon was seriously ill Thursday A.M." or "Joe Provencher is in his second boyhood for he is wearing short pants again." The newsletter also reported mill first-aid-room statistics, town-wide events, movie times, attendance at mill fire drills, and changes in the sulfate mill, the bleach plant, and the finishing room. You'd see pictures of "Cutter" girls who worked in the mill's finishing room and dressed in "daring ankle-length dresses" whose "blue bonnets and sashes were made of fine Oxford paper" at the Labor Day parade. You'd see vintage photos of the workers adding bleach to vats of pulp, or working in the Kraft mill—gloveless, barefoot, smiling as if there was no end to the prosperity.

The newsletter's name changed to *The Oxford Log* in 1952 when the mill was in its prime. In it, you'd learn about Johnny Norris, who worked on the supercalendar machine (which gave paper a highly glazed finish), who found his New York City vacation "hot and confusing." Or about Hollis Swett of the "Island Division" who got caught in a lightning storm while fishing at Weld Pond. *The Oxford Log* published profiles of high school basketball stars who were sons of millworkers and of Nick DiConzo, a paper tester who prepared the ski jump for Black Mountain's Winter Carnival.

"The people in Mexico and Rumford were wonderful," my mother says as we page through the newsletters. "Everyone was so civic-minded and we focused on family."

Her longtime childhood friend, Brenda, walks into the kitchen and says hello.

My mother continues: "It was like *Happy Days*. You know the show? We lived like *Happy Days*."

Brenda signals her agreement.

I ask my mother if this was true for when I was a kid; did we live like *Happy Days*?

"Yes, but I don't know what happened after that. It's when our kids had kids that everything changed."

"You mean like me?" I ask. "It changed in my generation?"

"Yes," she says. "We had our parents' and grandparents' values. Your generation has different values."

Brenda says, "Your generation had too many choices."

• • •

AFTER MY PARENTS move into their new house, they lease the old one, unknowingly, to petty drug traffickers. My mother tries to evict them with phone calls but they respond with legal threats. Not one to be bullied, my mother enlists the help of an off-duty police officer to accompany her to the renters' lair. She's successful in her eviction, but before the drug dealers leave, they disfigure the interior in small but expensive ways: countertops scratched, an unusable pantry door, water damage in the basement, and scarred grass where they parked their vehicles on wet lawn.

The next renters are interested in buying the house but can't get a loan, so my parents finance it themselves, giving them two months rent free with the agreement they fix it up, paint it, and buy new appliances. But the arrangement simply doesn't work out.

Then, the house is rented to another couple who doesn't pay the sewer bill ($450) or the water bill ($100) and never service the furnace. The furnace firewall eventually cracks ($4,530) and ServPro cleans the house because of pet urine stains and odors ($1,200). When the renters leave, my parents hire a landscaper to care for the overgrown yard ($1,300) because the couple had ignored that, too. Since the insurance ($135) and accrued mortgage ($310) have to be paid each month on top of discrete expenses, my parents' savings are nearly gone. That Christmas my siblings and I buy them oil to fill their dwindling tank.

None of this makes sense. My parents, grandparents, and great-grandparents, like so many Americans, did everything right and in the right order, taking into account dental care and used skis. They gave us rules, didn't break any, crossed borders and learned new languages to get good jobs. They drew pensions when they retired, didn't use credit cards, owned their homes, bought modest cars, kept their cash liquid. They went to church, mended clothes, didn't waste time, ate enough (not too much), sent us to college on one income if that's what we wanted to do. They provided a backdrop and a backyard to happier days and were unselfish to a pathological degree. They were the working-class, the fulcrum on which America rested. Yet my parents couldn't sell their house and retire with what they promised themselves all along. They were like the damn tetherball: right back where they had started from without going anywhere at all.

Small towns like ours have always been preserves of earlier times, of better times, where the past provides respite like a childhood story we know by heart: in our architecture, our traditions, the way gossip or good news travels faster than the Latter-day Saints who knock on our doors. But I sense a new version of rural America setting up shop every

time I come home that's not happy at all. It's one in which I never see backyards filled with neighborhood kids settling their differences and then going home at dark. It's one where retirees can't retire because they still need to work because they can't sell their house because the landscape is all torn. What had gone wrong? Was this change related to the pollution I thought was making us all sick or some other affliction? Or is this new America because my generation had too many choices, as Brenda said, or because our parents did not?

WITH GREAT POWER

IN 1779, JONATHAN Keyes settled in Rumford. He was followed by thirty or so families—land grantees of British and Protestant descent—whose names can still be found on town maps and in local phonebooks today: Kimball, Howard, Abbott, Hemingway, Swett, Merrill, Walker, Farnum, Elliott, Putnam, Stone. The settlers sustained themselves on corn, potatoes, wheat, and wild blueberries proliferating on the south side of White Cap Mountain, built homes out of rough-cut logs, and sculpted coarse windows from greased paper.

The outpost boasted no reliable roads connecting it to civilization beyond. Birch, maple, pine, poplar, beech, and hemlock scaffolded a wilderness that, according to the Reverend Daniel Gould in his 1826 book *The History of Rumford,* provided "lurking places for Bears and foxes." Over in Mexico, the satellite settlement to Rumford, corn, potatoes, hops, and wheat garlanded the fields. The Swift River, a younger tributary that forked into the Androscoggin at its most precipitous bend, hosted three gristmills, which, compelled by the Swift's velocity, pulverized farmers' grains. A steam mill, a toothpick manufacturer, a cheese maker, and a carriage factory rounded out Mexico's commercial pursuits.

By 1800, Rumford grew to 262 people; ten years later, the population had tripled. Six years after Maine became a state in 1820, nearly 1,200 citizens lived in Rumford, whom Gould described as "industrious and enterprising, laborious and active, and of course healthy." The town supported three taverns, six stores, two through-roads, a handful of churches, a paint mine, a saw mill, one lawyer, two physicians, a post office, forty newspapers, tradesmen, craftsmen, and five paupers. Mexico's population was smaller in industry and population but expanded quietly in proportion to Rumford's. Why the influx to such an isolated valley? Partially for that very reason; at the time, Maine was one of the last frontiers in New England.

What came with that frontier were virgin stands of white pine, a lightweight and decay-resistant wood used by early settlers for fencing, houses, timber, shipbuilding. "Pine was the prince of the forest," Richard G. Wood wrote in his book *The History of Lumbering in Maine, 1820–1860*. Actually, it was fit for a king; Edward Randolph, the Surveyor of Pines and Timber appointed by King Charles II in 1685, emblazoned the tallest, straightest Eastern white pines in New England with a King's Broad Arrow, which reserved them exclusively for Royal Navy ship masts. Some trees were as tall as 152 feet, some six feet in diameter, and at least one was around eight hundred years old. "The Pine Tree Riot" in New Hampshire in 1772 saw lumberjacks defying the king by harvesting the earmarked trees anyway, one of the first signs of American rebellion against its colonial status. As the king made his mark on the landscape, the landscape started making its mark on the people who lived there.

The sleepy burgs of Rumford and Mexico weren't immune to the economic and political forces percolating across America. Our community bled out with the heave-ho of the Revolution (1775–1783); the Civil War that stole half of Rumford's workforce (1861–1865); the lure of the Gold Rush (1848–1855); and the building of the railways (1830ish–1890) that spirited off lads seeking more tillable land in the Midwest and the giant trees of newer frontiers. By midcentury, steam and steel unseated the wood shipbuilding industry, and the exodus continued. By 1870, around 116,000 Maine-born residents had fled. Soon only a few hundred people remained in the depleted agrarian towns of Rumford and Mexico. Wilderness eventually overtook deserted farms along the lowlands by the Androscoggin. Underneath, granite—unforgiving and abundant.

Enter Hugh J. Chisholm, the founder of our mill whose marble bust welcomes visitors in the first-floor foyer of Rumford's town hall. The town hall is listed in the National Register of Historic Places and its nomination states the structure "relfects [*sic*] the aspirations of a community which viewed the future with abounding confidence." This confidence came from Chisholm himself.

My lifelong view of and information about Chisholm were shaped by two books my parents owned, which I find on the shelves in Rumford's historical society on the second floor of the town hall: *A History of Rumford*, written by the mill's public relations man, John Leane, in 1972 and his booklet, *The Oxford Story: A History of the Oxford Paper Company*. Leane's texts include any number of flattering descriptions of Chisholm: "a visionary," and "driven," and an "indefatigable" man with a "sixth sense." Leane also conveys an unmistakable emphasis on the mill's integral part in the town's development. As a kid, I broke the spines of those publications with my constant scrutiny of their pages in an effort to find a link between my family's contributions and Chisholm's ambition. And today, I try again.

I flip through many other documents and they also express a similar posture toward Chisholm, describing him as a "genius," with "dazzling accomplishments" and as someone "always at the service of the good citizens of Rumford" or at least always there "in spirit," as the *Lewiston Evening Journal* wrote in 1905. Chisholm's son said in a speech at the Newcomen Society in North America that his father had the "ability to understand and encompass a complex subject with seemingly little observation and a minimum of basic data."

Colonel Fred Dow, son of General Neal Dow (Father of Prohibition) said in a biography of Chisholm: "Few men of his age and, at the time, of limited means, would have the foresight, the ability, and the courage to penetrate a wilderness and arrest a mighty river, as he did the Androscoggin in its unshackled useless flow to the sea and to compel it to render service and create wealth for man."

In other words, it's as difficult to find anything on my family as it is to find anything difficult about Chisholm, anything contrary to what

Leane proposed and others augmented. His persona, in everything I read, seems as flat and studied as the black-and-white portraits of him I also discover, as impenetrable as his marble bust in the foyer below.

Only two pages of Leane's *History of Rumford* are devoted to "The Curse of Pollution," as if our mill's environmental issues manifested from hell, not the other way around. Chisholm, he came to us by way of a different kind of divine intervention.

Chisholm's father, Alexander, "a gentle and lovable scholar" who "felt a deeper interest in . . . the profound lessons of the Greek philosophers, than in the fluctuations of the stock market," drowned in Toronto Bay near where he lived. The burden of supporting the family fell on Chisholm at age thirteen, so he stopped going to school and started collecting, packing, and selling produce in his neighborhood instead.

"Elders patted me on the head and called me a natural trader," Chisholm said in an interview with the *Los Angeles Times* in 1908. Chisholm did such a good job he was soon hired to sell candy and newspapers on the Grand Trunk Railway from Toronto, Canada to Detroit. "I got magazines, a month old for five cents apiece, and sold them at the regular prices, which in some instances, returned a profit of 600 percent," he told the *Times*. "I made money from the start."

By around age fourteen he and his brother Charles controlled distribution on five thousand miles of railroad, from Chicago, Illinois, to Portland, Maine, and as far east as Halifax, while employing over two hundred boys outfitted in brass-buttoned coats and trainmen's caps with patent leather visors.

The same pioneering spirit and railroads that stole Mainers away also shepherded tourists like Henry David Thoreau toward the state. Seduced by its "wildness," Thoreau lauded the majesty of Maine and wrote about it as one would a lover, presupposing man was part of nature and nature possibly God incarnate. Thoreau bounded through the forests of Maine, rhapsodizing even about the grim reality of a soaking rain. Maine Central Railroad amplified Thoreau's idyllic descriptions with their 1890 slogan "Vacationland," and that helped fill their half-empty railcars with tourists who wanted to experience the authenticity that Thoreau convinced them was being lost to industrial worlds but that Maine still possessed. And the Chisholm brothers sold souvenir guides and postcards to all of them.

In 1872, Chisholm divested his shares of the news distribution business to his brother and moved to Portland, Maine and started a lithographic printing company to publish the guides and postcards himself. He also invested in a wood pulp mill, an iron foundry, a power company, railroads, and a small paper manufacturer near my town. Thoreau's subtle but articulate plea for conservation was drowned out not just by the caravans of tourists he pied-pipered to Maine, but also by the felling of trees Chisholm required to make his paper products to sell to those tourists. It was a near-perfect closed loop system.

Between 1850 and 1890 about 350,000 tons of linen and cotton rags provided pulp for US paper manufacturers: about 85,000 tons were imported, the cleanest from Egyptian mummies. As paper manufacturers built faster, wider, and more efficient paper machines, papermaking productivity mushroomed, as did the need for pulp. Rags and mummies were not limitless, and the pulping of their fiber couldn't be mechanized on any large scale. Subsequently, scientists went to the woods to see what they could find. So did Chisholm.

Chisholm was primed to profit from a nation well fed on a diet of oil, railroad, banking, and industrial success stories. It was the golden age of the American Dream and scaled-up success, where men like Cornelius Vanderbilt, who worked on a ferry at age eleven, went on to monopolize steamship and railroad empires. From the rattling windows of the Grand Trunk, Chisholm had seen the undeveloped forests of Maine, the paper goods tourists consumed, and how the railway system, with its five thousand miles of tracks, provided an ice-free and convenient route that connected raw materials to civilization. So in 1882, when Chisholm first glimpsed the short, precipitous 176-foot drop of the Rumford Falls into a 300-acre pool and forest all around, he saw opportunity; where lumberjacks and shipbuilders saw mast poles and planks, he saw paper. He wrote in his journal about that moment: "The idea of developing and making productive this great mechanical power before me and of planting a city in the wilderness was what came to me then." Rumford contained the resources necessary for paper manufacturing: trees, water power, and a straight shot to the coast on rails such as he worked on as a child. Maine was his geographic destiny.

Under secrecy and with the help of Rumford resident Waldo Pettengill, a man who could "squeeze a penny 'til it was blue," Chisholm began to gather data on the average rainfall, the river drainage, and reservoir storage capacity. By August 1890 he had purchased (with Pettengill's aid) around 1,400 acres of land on both sides of the Androscoggin, obtained riparian and transportation rights along the river, and had begun to amass an eco-industrial trifecta of raw goods, power, and transportation. He established Dunton Lumber, Rumford Light and Water Company, and Rumford Falls Power Company, which published a brochure to attract prospective entrepreneurs. Chisholm constructed canals and dams and hydraulics to control the flow of the river, which would eventually power the paper mill he was building. He inserted water mains, electric grids, and sewer lines, built schools, controlled two banks, and started newspapers. He constructed railways and roads for moving goods and people in and out of the area. He drew up plans for the brick Strathglass Park homes, commercial buildings, bridges, and shopping centers, and hired immigrants from Lithuania, Italy, and Ireland to erect them. He built a boom company to catch the logs coming downriver, a sulfite pulp mill, and set up Rumford Falls Realty to rent the homes at Strathglass Park. He donated land to almost every church in the area and constructed a skating rink for the "healthful outdoor amusement for the workers in the mill" and paid to have it lighted at night. Allegedly, one Christmas he also furnished turkeys to his workers.

By 1898, Chisholm and his partner William Augustus Russell combined seventeen pulp and paper companies, including the Rumford mill, to establish International Paper, then and today the biggest paper company in the world. In 1902, our mill produced its first sheets of paper, and shortly after, the brick homes of Strathglass Park housed the millworkers whom he employed. Within the year, the US Postal Service commissioned Chisholm to manufacture all their postcards (at the rate of three million a day). In twelve years, Chisholm's Rumford mill became the largest book-paper maker in the world under one roof.

While most residents of Rumford and Mexico welcomed the boon, skeptics remained, especially those who felt tricked by Pettengill. One resident wrote a letter to the editor:

Is this town going to be owned, operated and run by one man, as his private property, and for the benefit of his pocket book, or are the citizens to have a say as to how its affairs are to be conducted . . . ? Was it for any philanthropic idea that he would built [sic] a Utopia here? Not at all. It was with the sole idea that there was money in it—for him! That by doing so, he would be richer, have more power to wield in the financial world; have a little city up here in the wilderness which would obey his commands as the City of New York, where he comes from, listens to the commands of its boss.

The success and expansion of "Magic Town," as a *Boston Globe* reporter called Rumford, looked to be unstoppable, and almost four thousand people streamed into town looking for work, including my Acadian great-grandfathers, Thomas Arsenault and Pierre Gaudin.

• • •

I TAKE A break from my research to walk around town hall. On the second floor, I skirt the perimeter of the bright, high-ceilinged public meeting room that smells of old varnish and fresh paint. Historical photographs decorate its walls. On the first floor, town offices and the courthouse. I sneak inside. The antique fixtures are only slightly modified to meet modern-day courtroom needs. Above, a recessed ceiling with trompe l'oeil designs. Behind the judge's bench, "The Birth of Law," a mural painted by Henry Cochrane portraying Moses in a red robe, his wild eyes rolled skyward, aimed at a flaring thunderbolt and up toward the panopticon of cupola and clock that rest on the town hall's roof, as if the biblical past was commandeering time and law itself. Moses clenches the Ten Commandments to his chest to supply society—as Chisholm did too—with guidelines we supposedly lacked.

At the end of the day I'm disappointed (but unsurprised) not to find anything about my family in the archival records of the town. What's in or what's out by deed or command are decisions made by those with knowledge or prestige: historians, experts, even modest archivists at small town halls. We depend on experts to collate and curate the past so the future will know what went on. It's a powerful profession, more powerful than we sometimes understand, because the facts they choose to memorialize or highlight can be corrupted by motives other than just their job. We are vulnerable, in a way, to their all-seeing eyes observing and recording history as it unfolds while most of us are just getting through our day. And when history's makers (Chisholm) are aligned with history's recorders (John Leane), the resulting output is a skewed artifact all its own.

While Chisholm may dominate the recorded history of Rumford, the specter of my ancestors looms over me as did New Hampshire's "Old Man of the Mountain," the naturally occurring granite relief that looked like a human profile when approached from the north. As a kid, in summer we'd take rides through Franconia Notch where the Old Man lived, to seek relief in the cool highway passes and gorges darkened by the shadows of mountains. I was always surprised when we'd roll around the bend and see him appear, like a figurehead on the bow of a ship cantilevered out over the edge of a great fog.

In 2003, after too many facelifts of steel rods and cement, years of exposure and weather caught up. His face fractured and tumbled into the wooded valley below. What remains today of the Old Man, besides his missing profile, are broken-off, downriver alluvial deposits. Below in the viewing plaza, however, if you position yourself just right, interactive sculptures create an illusion of the Old Man to allow future generations to see him as I once saw him, too. Looking at the sculpture is like looking at history itself, a grand illusion shored up by those who seek a specific point of view. Meanwhile, my family's past, here and there in those low floodplains of legacy, gold.

I walk home after the historical society closes and glance up to the building's clock. The time is all wrong.

BLIND SPOTS

In a sepia photograph my maternal great-grandfather Pierre Gaudin sits on a giant stump in front of a logging camp: arms crossed, a thicket of wavy hair, a long-handled ax buried in the woodpile next to him. Pierre worked as a logging camp cook (a "cookee") in northern Maine when he was young, where he fed lumberjacks who toiled in the woods ten hours a day severing tree trunks with toothy, two-man crosscut saws. The drafty cabins where Pierre worked were fueled by woodstoves that warmed their bodies and dried their socks. In more primitive camps, a hollowed-out log served as a sink or bench, and pine needles, a crunchy, fragrant mattress. Men slept in splintery hewn bunks stacked around the "stink pole" where they strung their half-washed clothes like steamy, sour ornaments. In wintertime, they'd harness downed trees to oxen and slide them across packed snow to ease the wood's weight. By spring, viscous mud slowed the movement of the harvests, but lakes and rivers swelled into liquid highways, which lumberjacks used to raft the flotilla of trees toward Maine's coastal ports to be sold and sent throughout New England and the world.

Every day Pierre rose at 3:00 A.M. and made Paul Bunyan–sized breakfasts for his hungry mob—biscuits, codfish, donuts, partridge, tea, potatoes, rice, molasses, coffee, macaroni, pickled beef, cookies, bacon, cakes, and "the great trinity" of beans, pork, and bread. Logging camps without good cooks shuttered, and inferior cooks were ousted by grumbling crowds of muscle-fisted men. A cookee's tasks boosted not only productivity but morale. As soon as the men bolted down their breakfast, Pierre assembled an equally massive sack lunch. After the lumberjacks left for the day's work, he began preparing their next meal to keep up with their 9,000-calorie-a-day intake. In an endless circle of cooking and cleaning, his job was as vital to the paper industry as the pines the lumberjacks felled.

Pierre had lived a rural life under vast stippled skies in the one-church burg of Tignish at the northern tip of Prince Edward Island. The country's main industries of fishing and farming offered meager opportunities for his generation; the bankrupt soil made farming unprofitable and fisheries were increasingly being exploited by American colonies to the south. Pierre's father and grandfather worked as shoemakers, and when Pierre was a child, he thought he would be one, too. Canada's tanking economy and impoverished land pushed young men while the lure and proximity of lucrative factory jobs in America pulled them. From about 1840 until 1930, almost a million French-speaking Canadians immigrated to the United States, with the largest percentage going to New England to work in its paper and textile mills.

Pierre's work as a cookee was lucrative but provisional, and he saw no long-term merit to the work. And if everyone was leaving Canada, so were their shoes, so shoemaking held less promise than a seasonal and arduous job. Working in Rumford's new paper mill could provide everything he needed and things he probably never dreamed of enjoying: electricity, running water, vacation, a weekly paycheck. The mill's location, however, was remote, near nothing but dark-needled trees. To compensate for the isolation, the mill offered new employees ten cents an hour, where in other parts of New England they were offered only five to seven cents an hour for the same work. Both rates surpassed what Pierre could earn as a cook for rowdy, hungry men. For that kind of money, he would put up with pretty much anything. There seemed to be only one choice to make. So at the age of twenty-one, Pierre booked a one-way ticket to Maine on the Grand Trunk Railway.

In Mexico, he met and married Isabelle LeBlanc, who was born in the small French-speaking village of Rogersville, New Brunswick, and had moved with her parents to Maine ten years prior. They were part of *l'emigration en chaine* (chain migration); one family member would depart, settle in the US, and send for other family members, and so on, until homes heaved with relatives and streets became *petit Canadas*, compact satellite versions of Canada and home.

Pierre started going by the name "Peter" and began working in the mill while Isabelle worked making paper bags until she had children. Meanwhile, Pierre fixed up their house, sanded its maple floors, installed an indoor toilet, and every morning still rose at 3:00 A.M. and made fresh bread for his family. After breakfast, for twelve hours a day in the mill's groundwood room, he would monitor logs rattling up a flume before they dropped onto the floor. There, he chopped the wood into four-foot lengths and soaked them in water in preparation for the debarker, a slatted rotating drum that slaked off their dampened skins. Pierre would feed the stripped logs to the woodchipper's gaping maw, an inexhaustible steel mouth where rotating blades would mince the once noble trees to the size of cornflakes, spitting them into the air in perfect arcs. Bark, rocks, and other debris fell into a pit where another person (my sister, one summer) shoveled them into another area for disposal. As the chips piled up in the millyard, they formed tall pyramids and moistened the air with the sharp resiny smell of fresh-cut wood.

Besides the five kids they already had by 1918, Pierre and Isabelle also "took in" an older child, Arthur, whose father returned to PEI after Arthur's mother died. No official adoption papers ever passed between the parties, even though the relinquishing father had lived just down the street. I never met Arthur because he got gassed in 1956 while working in the mill and died two years later after the chlorine gas exposure, at age forty-seven. In his employee records, just like in John Patrick's, the mill doctor wrote Arthur "had a cold." My mother says of his death: "He didn't have a cold. He was never right after that. He was practically green."

Intelligent, kind, and much loved by the community and his employer, Pierre was offered a mill manager job—but in Minnesota. Pierre saw a streamlined future, one with a quiet office in the Midwest instead of the pulverizing appetite of the debarker. Isabelle refused to budge. *I won't leave my mother,* she said. Pierre's choices boiled down to one. Like so many immigrants before and after him, he adapted: green or not.

I remember Isabelle's sweet and doughy smell, her thick accent I hardly understood. Twice the size of Pierre, her dark, pinned-back hair lay flat against her serious face, her neck a stump. She was both scary and safe, like ballast in a ship, and I only knew her until I was three. She told me a story once that went something like this: A girl lived in a rambling old house (to me, a castle like the one in *Cinderella*). The girl was allowed to explore any room except one she was explicitly told not to infiltrate. Of course, like all curious girls, she went in anyway; the not-knowing was more powerful than whatever was forbidden. When she opened the door of the embargoed room, something terrible happened, but it was beyond my grasp of language or metaphor to recall exactly what. For years, I thought Isabelle had crafted the story to keep me from sneaking into her bedroom, a narrow space on the first floor next to the kitchen. Even when I tried to peek inside that room, my grandmother Bridget—with quick reflexes and a few swear words—would slam the door shut, her voice a jackhammer. "Goddamn you kids!" (It was always plural.) "Get. Out. Of. That. Room."

After Isabelle died, I was allowed to select from her lair a few things to keep. Piles of letters, magazines, medicine bottles, rootless jewelry, and half-knitted things settled beneath the blurry smell of powder, baby aspirin, and long-dead lilies. Textiles leaked out of her dresser. I chose a faux mother-of-pearl brooch with "ISABELLE" scripted in twisted metal and a few postcards I still keep on hand. Bridget exhumed the rest of the room's contents to the attic, a place I begged to see, too.

I promise not to touch anything, I'd press.

Bridget's face would condense into a roadblock. *NO!* she would always retort. Occasionally, she would announce, *I'm going to the attic,* and I'd long for the chance to accompany her, to see where all those upstairs trips led. She might as well have said she was going to Disneyland, though I would have preferred the attic even to that.

Sometimes she relinquished small treasures she poached from up there and secreted them into my tiny willing hands when I appeared at her house on Saturday afternoons on my bike: a graduation photo of her and her twin sister, a postcard from PEI, an old broken toy bank. Relegated to the first floor of my grandparents' house, I made peace with her restrictions and surrendered myself to snooping through the stale remnants within the kitchen drawers.

It wasn't until I was older that I figured out Isabelle's story was a version of "Bluebeard," the French folktale of the violent but magnificently rich man who lured women into his opulent home.

He would give each new wife a key to every room and tell them not to enter one particular room, and of course, like the girl in Isabelle's story, they always did, for which they were bludgeoned to death. The bodies were left there, turning the prohibited room into a bouquet of rotted corpses for all but the last wife, who managed to escape.

As a young girl, there were a lot of doors I never opened because I didn't have the nerve or the key, but the unknowing can leave a person unmapped and undone, like the lies John Patrick or Pierre's adopted son Arthur faced as they started to drown in their own throats.

• • •

MY GRANDMOTHER BRIDGET was a poker-playing, foul-mouthed woman who taught me to dive off a crumbling wharf. *Sink or swim,* she'd say as she sent me into a turbid, leech-filled pond with an unglamorous push. That push was one of generosity, not cruelty; in New England sometimes the two acts get conflated. Pushed off a wharf or out a back door to play, or motivated to behave by terrifying stories, the women in my family believed independence trumped overt affection.

Bridget's can-doism was intrinsic to "the Greatest Generation," *her* generation, who survived economic and actual annihilation in the Depression and the war. As a patron saint in matters of survival, she saved everything: teeny pieces of wire, broken dry cleaner hangers, coffee cans, and sample glass vials of perfume from the drugstore. *These things may come in handy,* she'd say as she washed and pinned plastic Wonder Bread bags to the clothesline, the red, blue, and yellow polka dot design flaking off in the wind.

As a young woman Bridget lived at home with Pierre and Isabelle while working in the mill, marshaling and sorting fresh white sheets of paper, julienning her fingertips as the Depression raged around her. In 1936, a flood decimated Rumford and Mexico. The heavy snow that year, an abrupt spring thaw, then rain on top of rain vandalized bridges, flushed sediment and wastes downstream, and whooshed five thousand cords of lumber down the Androscoggin into Merrymeeting Bay. The freshet, on the way through town, bore a bobbing crop of orange pumpkins aloft on its flood tide that were thieved from a farmer's wrecked barn. The flood also ushered Gerald Epps into Bridget's jurisdiction.

In order to relieve unemployment, the federal Works Progress Administration (WPA) dispatched unskilled and otherwise jobless men from Missouri to decommission a branch of the Maine Central Railway that had been damaged and abandoned after the flood. The workers burned railcars, scrapped locomotives, and tore tracks from their beds until all that was left were the men executing the demolition. One of them was Gerald, a handsome, thick-haired southerner from Harrisonville, Missouri, who declined a football scholarship at "Mizzou" to take a job with the WPA. Gerald liked his Lucky Strikes and Canadian whiskey and often walked with a slight limp from his days on the gridiron. He wore clothes, many noticed, as top of the line as the cars he drove, even if his income underperformed his aspirations.

After a short courtship, Bridget and Gerald married in 1939, his accommodating Southern-ness tempering her fierce practicality. Their brief union produced two children: my mother and her sister. When

Bridget found out Gerald was sleeping around with other women, they divorced and Gerald moved back south to marry a blond bombshell who clerked at a drugstore. It was Bridget's second husband, Ernie, not Gerald, whom I called grandfather; did it matter if we didn't share the same blood?

Ernie Pariseau grew up in Central Falls, Rhode Island, where he and his father worked in a textile mill winding threads on bobbins. They were among the thousands of Canadian immigrants whose ancestors moved there during the Civil War to provide labor for the textile shortage. Ernie's father and sister died young, his father at age thirty-four from a mill accident and his sister in his own arms when she was five. By 1942 his mother had died, too. No longer the breadwinner for his family, for he had no family left, he joined the Army.

When I was six he gave me some francs he brought home from Marseilles, the multicolored bills inscribed with his handwritten memoranda in miniature small caps, the kind of memorializing he was prone to do. His writing appeared on almost anything blank—his pocketknife, a jar of nails, my pink Huffy bike, the boat he constructed from a *Popular Mechanics* magazine, and noses of B-17 bombers. He also painted curvy Vargas-type women on those planes to accompany American pilots on flight missions during the war; a small pleasure, I imagine, in the act of killing or dying.

Ernie's battalion hit Utah Beach in August 1944 and began its sweep to Berlin two months after the Normandy landings. Anne Frank had been arrested, but Germans were surrendering all around, and within a year, Goering would be imprisoned and Paris would be liberated. I like to think Goering's pilots saw Ernie's airbrushed and idealized women skimming the sky while American bombs rained over Bremen. Perhaps the pilots were confused by the scantily clad pinups or maybe even titillated before they pinwheeled to the earth in a fiery tantrum.

I was born twenty-two years after World War II ended, but the lingua franca of that war—Sacrifice, Courage, Victory, Honor—was transmitted from Ernie to my mother and then to me. Over the years, the narratives were reworked, retold, and sometimes augmented like a shiny glaze on a terra-cotta pot. They underscored the selflessness of

American soldiers and colored the way I thought about war; it was a quixotic necessity, shored up by patriotism, perhaps even a little romantic.

Ernie took photographs during his trek through Europe, marking each set of negatives with *Paris, the Elbe River, Switzerland, Nice, Baesweiler, the Riviera.* One pale blue envelope addressed to *Outdoor Life* contained a negative but no evidence of it being sent. In it, Ernie stands next to a P-47 Thunderbolt nicknamed "Little Evie," adorned with a menacing toucan holding a skull, I assume painted by him. Behind him, more parked Thunderbolts, muted by a flat field of grass beneath their wheels and open sky above. His photographs also show soldiers goofing around in the fields of Germany and, in one, they stood on the wings of a downed Nazi Stuka dive-bomber, seeking diversions amid the devastation that lay around them. An emblem of terror, the Stuka would dive at its target, drop a bomb, then jerk skyward so quickly the excessive G-forces on the aircraft could cause its pilot to experience temporary unconsciousness or blindness. Stukas were in and out, lethal in accuracy and in flight, and emitted a metallic, terrible whining sound. When out of action, they flew in wedges, like geese heading south for the winter.

I supplemented blank spots in my war knowledge by flipping through the Time-Life series *This Fabulous Century.* It was in those books I first learned about life and death beyond Mexico, Maine: in Robert Capa's photographs on the fields of Córdoba and in the irreparable scars left behind by the Enola Gay's soft mushroom of death. In seventh grade, I also read *The Diary of Anne Frank,* though I was more scared of being locked behind a wall without a toilet than of the Nazis who hemmed in poor Anne.

After the war, Ernie attended Rhode Island School of Design for a year on the GI Bill, a benefit that expanded and enriched America's middle class by paying tuition for returning soldiers seeking higher education. The perk especially helped underserved populations, which then like now supplied the majority of our troops. On summer break, Ernie heard the Rumford paper mill was looking for workers for their massive ten-year expansion. Tugged by the promise of good wages,

Ernie moved to Mexico in 1947 to make a little money before fall semester. He dropped out of college and never returned to Rhode Island after meeting Bridget, who, like her mother, had no intention of leaving Maine or her family.

Ernie kept his job in the mill as a paper machine tender for over forty years until he retired and grew corn in his garden while his two stepdaughters twirled batons and married local boys. Ernie, Bridget, Isabelle, Pierre, my mother, her sister, and adopted Arthur were tight because they had to be in that three-bedroom house, and they ate all the homemade bread Pierre could stuff into their mouths before he left for work each morning.

. . .

"I LOVE YOU all very much, but if I had it all to do again, none of you would be here," Bridget once said to my sister Kelly as a Virginia Slim seesawed on her lip.

She urged Kelly, home from college that summer, to become an airline stewardess, as Bridget always loved the idea of faraway lands even though she'd rooted herself to just one. A few tour-bus trips to Boston for veterans' events and visits to Missouri to see her twin sister, otherwise she never went very far. It always made me a little sad, this confession to want another life than what you had. My grandmother's life was prescribed not by her but by the weight of some predetermined rendezvous, as was Ernie's, whose art career was cut short by other goals. My parents and grandparents believed we'd go to places they couldn't, and while we accrued more mileage than they ever did, I'm not sure my generation could ever repeat the wholesale sacrifices they made, sacrifices made at such great cost. Their lives *were* transactions in a larger sense. They helped turn trees into paper and paper fed the pollution, and when the pollution flowed back into their bodies and the bodies of water that fed the growth of trees, the process would start all over again.

Bridget was diagnosed with colon cancer in 1997 when I lived in Portland, Maine, and she stayed with me when she needed treatments at the hospital across the street. *They got the cancer!* she told me one day when I came home from work, but really, the treatment got her. After months of chemotherapy, she was bedridden and living in a nursing home, in and out of the hospital and in and out of consciousness. The last time I saw her alive, neither of us knew the other.

My mother called me one day to come home as soon as I could. When I pulled up to my grandparents' house, everyone was already sitting on the porch as if they just got out of church and were having a snack. *She's already gone,* they said about Bridget, her body carted away before I arrived. If it wasn't for the traffic or the time I took to pick out my shoes, I thought, I could have seen her off. It felt selfish to drive back to Portland the next day while her corpse was being vaporized at the funeral parlor. Her death certificate said she died of radiation colitis, a condition that gutted her insides until she was a carcass of her former self; however, the doctor had told us the cancer was nowhere to be found.

I had taken her and my grandfather's proximity for granted, figuring they would always be there when I was not. They, like most of my ancestors had up until recently, floated in my periphery like a blind spot that evaded my direct view.

WATER UNDER THE BRIDGE

In the mid-1800s, as small pioneering hamlets up and down the Androscoggin grew into viable municipalities, the populace began furnishing the river with a miasmic and untreated deluge of raw sewage. Log jams, caused by the fury of the river's spring thaws, dispensed resinous brown sap and bark in the calamity of the push. With all those logs came sawmills, and with sawmills, sawdust slurrying the water and killing off Atlantic salmon, the last of which were seen suffocating downriver in 1816. By the start of the twentieth century, when my great-grandparents arrived in Maine, factories dominated the banks of the Androscoggin and generated tons of waste, adding to the evolving river cocktail. Upstream and downstream, manufacturers tossed in their dyes, fibers, and toxic substances. Into the sky went their pollution and particles. Hydroelectric dams impounded natural flow. Plumes from effluent pipes greased the river's waters.

Industry, along with everyone else, believed in the adage *the solu-tion to pollution is dilution,* so for a little while, rivers and skies were able to recuperate without aid. Mother Nature, however, could do nothing to remedy what caused the legendary twenty-foot walls of urine-colored toxic foam emerging from the canals forty miles down-stream or cure the asphyxiating fallout from the twenty-one dams that tempered the water and powered the factories. Years and years of flotsam and effluent choked what fish remained. Aeration dimmed. Water temperature rose. And in 1941 when manufacturing's con-comitant pollution reached a stinky zenith, the smell emanating from the river was so appalling people fled town or shuttered themselves in. Coins in men's pockets and silver sets tarnished overnight. Stores closed. House and car paint peeled like burnt skin. Residents vom-ited. Laundry hung on clotheslines blackened with ash. Citizens de-manded action.

As a gesture of progress, the Maine legislature created the Sanitary Water Board. Poorly funded from the start, the board wielded no real power except to hire an engineering firm to perform an impact study on the river. The report showed 96 percent of the pollution derived from industrial wastes, with 92 percent from pulp and paper mills; more specifically, it originated from sulfite liquor, a by-product of the wood-pulping process of the time. "Few streams in the United States of comparable size showed evidence of such extreme pollution," the report announced. While the population of Rumford hovered around ten thousand, the industrial discharge equaled what more than two million people would expect to produce.

The report recommended mills wait to discharge the sulfite liquor and other wastes when water flow and temperature could dilute them better. When International Paper of Jay, Maine, the Brown Company in New Hampshire, and the Oxford Paper Company in Rumford, Maine—who were responsible for the mess—ignored these recommen-dations, Maine attorney general Frank Cowan, in an unusual environ-mental action for 1942, filed a lawsuit against them. The case resulted in an order by the Maine Supreme Court demanding the mills reduce their discharges at once. Editors at the *Lewiston Daily Sun* wrote in

response: "Only the foolhardy would desire clean water at the expense of slashed payrolls, lost industry and a ghost town."

In response to the order, in 1947 the three mills built a waste holding pond—the lagoon—downriver in Jay, Maine, to contain the four hundred tons of sulfite liquor that was tossed into the river every week, but the pond's clay lining leaked. Upstream, the Brown Company built an additional holding pond. It also leaked. Three years passed with no further action until the three paper companies agreed to an abatement plan and Dr. Walter A. Lawrance, then head of the chemistry department at Bates College, was brought on as rivermaster to help manage the noxious mess. From 1947 to 1978, Lawrance tried.

Herb Knight, one of Lawrance's students at Bates, sampled river water at various locations to understand the pollution load generated by the mill. Knight remembers "an ugly brown sticky substance" formed on the surface of the twenty-two-million-gallon lagoon. "When the temperature dropped, [the mill] would dribble the stuff in the river rather than just dump it all at once." The river already contained things called "cellulosic fines," he says, another by-product of the pulping process. The sulfite liquor combined with these cellulosic fines to produce a "grayish, foul material we called shit cakes," Knight says with an embarrassed laugh. "There must have been about one hundred acres of it floating in the river."

Lawrance and his assistants kept meticulous reports of water samples to monitor the dissolved oxygen content in the water. They recorded extensive information about the weather, wind velocity and direction, humidity levels, river color, water surface conditions, and air temperature. In his descriptions of river odor intensity and type, he categorized them as "earthy," "musty," "rotten eggs" or "pig-pen," which he clarified as: "The name is quite descriptive of the odor, which is very similar to the somewhat sweetish but unpleasant odor usually present in pig-pens. . . . Pig-pen appears to vary in different locations . . . in the Lewiston area [downstream from Rumford and Mexico] . . . it possesses a more 'cadaverous' flavor."

Lawrance added sodium nitrate to the river—about seven thousand tons of it between 1948 and 1960—to kill bacteria, raise the dissolved oxygen level, and blunt the stench. He also tried, in 1969, to re-create the river's natural aeration by installing "bubblers" in Gulf Island Pond, the water area, but it was only a temporary, mechanical fix. Some people lauded Lawrance's efforts. Some, however, remained suspicious; they thought "perfuming" the water with the sodium nitrate didn't solve the underlying problem, and scientists feared the unnatural nutrient load only added more pollution. Both were right. The river was being paralyzed by both action and inaction. And the bubblers *were* a makeshift solution, unsustainable for a river of its size. Lawrance too was stuck in a no-man's-land between economic and environmental prosperity and his own dubious authority to do anything about it except with the inefficient technology he had at hand.

Decades later, the smell became less offensive and less frequent, and the flat, floating, encyclopedia-sized pieces of shit cakes dwindled. "The pollution was exaggerated," Knight says. "The media didn't balance between reality and conjecture. Now there's a boat launch where sludge used to float. It was a great leap forward."

. . .

My mother was born in 1942, one year after the public outcry against the Androscoggin, one year before Lawrance started working as rivermaster. In 1952, the mill put out an ad seeking an entry-level pipefitter; my father applied and got the job. Except for a tour in the Army (Colorado and Indiana) during the Korean War, he remained a pipefitter for the next forty-four years. My parents were sandwiched between a stinky past and a hopeful future. And theirs was a future nurtured by glossy magazines like *Better Homes and Gardens, Good Housekeeping, Harper's Bazaar, House Beautiful, Reader's Digest, Saturday Evening Post, Seventeen, Town and Country*, and *Vogue* our mill made. We also made paper for publishers like Doubleday, the Encyclopedia Britannica, Macmillan (my publisher), and Condé Nast, as well as envelopes, industry trade magazines, product labels, and catalogs for Sears, Roebuck & Co.

To make that kind of paper required virgin wood, bleach, clay, resin, casein or starch, and other chemicals to coat the paper to give it that sheen. It took a lot of other resources as well. The mill owned 750,000 acres of land that held approximately 3.6 million cords of wood. Every day, the mill produced 530 tons of pulpwood using 13 paper machines that pressed out 17 miles of paper; it took 33 million gallons of water to sustain this rate of production. The mill also maintained a deep bench of two people per position.

In 1958, the National Geographic Society entered into a fifteen-year contract with the mill to make paper for *National Geographic* magazine. The windfall, while providing steady work for the town, also brought with it a windfall of pollution that exacerbated the toxic load Lawrance was already managing. The mill had been making coated paper since 1913, but for *National Geographic* they had to install a state-of-the-art machine to produce the bright white paper with a smooth finish and good opacity for the photographic images the magazine built its reputation on. From the end of World War II to 1966, the mill invested over $130 million into new machinery. By the time I was born in 1967, our mill was producing some of the best specialty papers in the country and maintaining one of the largest payrolls in the state. Our economy flourished. As the mill kept modernizing and expanding, each year the mill's newsletter, like the town's future, got brighter. And each year the river and the skies above seemed dimmer and dimmer no matter what Lawrance did.

. . .

By 1970, when I was three, the Androscoggin's dissolved oxygen level was exactly zero. *Newsweek* named it one of the ten filthiest rivers in the United States. Everything in the river died. And when I graduated from high school in 1985, the EPA revealed its creatures contained some of the highest dioxin levels in the country. *Don't eat the fish,* we were always told, but we couldn't have anyway because we never saw any to catch. There also were no swimmers or boaters in the river William B. Lapham once praised in his 1890 book *History of Rumford,* noting the Androscoggin as "beautiful" and the scenery "picturesque and often grand."

If you squint, the Androscoggin still fits Lapham's description. But if you open your eyes, you'll see what was invisible to me my whole life: the mill's pollutants hovering low over the naturally formed glacial bowl of our valley or in the toxic stew congregating in the riverbed. What I did notice when I was young was the rainbow-colored foam eddying on the river's edge, which was as enchanting as the gray "mill snow" that floated softly up from the smokestacks and down upon any surface in town. What did we all do? We plugged our noses and placed our drinking glasses upside down in the cupboard so ash wouldn't get in our milk. The pollution was as trapped as we were.

I still gag every time I drink a glass of water, a reflex that emerged when I lived within a football field's reach of the mill and the Androscoggin. At the time, I sweetened our mephitic drinking water with Tang or Zarex or drank no water at all. But as an adult, the memory of our water's brackish and sweetish chemical smell/taste, combined with the sour air above it, precipitates what feels like smothering when I put glass to lips.

Dioxin, cadmium, benzene, lead, naphthalene, nitrous oxide, sulfur dioxide, arsenic, furans, trichlorobenzene, chloroform, asbestos, mercury, phthalates: these are some of the by-products of modern-day papermaking. Non-Hodgkin's lymphoma, lung cancer, prostate cancer, aplastic anemia, colon cancer, liver cancer, esophageal cancer, asbestosis, Ewing's sarcoma, emphysema, cancer of the brain, cancer of the heart: these, I find out, are some of the illnesses appearing in our towns. Occasionally in curious clusters, sometimes in generations of families, often in high percentages. And in every news article I read, every scientific study I try to dissect, when people tried to link the mill's pollution with these illnesses, logic was met with justification, personal experience with excuse, stories with statistics, disease with blame.

There's a lag between exposure and diagnosis, experts declared. *People could be exposed from other sources,* scientists explained. *There were uncertainties,* decried environmental agencies. *Continued follow-up is needed,* said the mill. Meanwhile, people quit jobs or school to care for sick family members; lose health insurance because they lose their jobs; and put canisters on pizza shop countertops to pay for medical bills.

. . .

ON FEBRUARY 26, 2012, I read a headline in Maine's *Kennebec Journal:* "SOME LABEL TOXIN [*sic*] SPIKE AS POSITIVE; PULP AND PAPER INDUSTRY SAYS INCREASE IS A GOOD SIGN, STATE OFFICIALS NOT ALARMED." The article states that 9.6 million pounds of chemicals from paper mills were released by eighty-four Maine mills between 2009 and 2010, an increase of 1.14 million pounds over the previous year. Our mill is the number one producer, releasing over one million pounds. Dr. Molly Schwenn, director of the Maine Cancer Registry, tenders an explanation in the article. She says contributing to Maine's high cancer rates are "lower levels of education, high rates of poverty, unemployment, and lack of health insurance."

While it's difficult to see how pollution could be a good sign of anything, as the headline suggests, it's more difficult to critique the importance of a manufacturing surge from my current privileged and remote spot. I know firsthand that money in the pockets of my father, my grandfather, my great-grandfather meant new maple floors, indoor plumbing, cars, college for me, or money in the bank for a future rainy day. For others, a manufacturing surge may mean something as simple as three meals a day or a stove that works or a winter jacket that's warm.

It's Maine's constant conundrum, an American story, a human predicament, and the very thing Ed Muskie struggled with as he tried to protect our country's water and air—what are we willing to tolerate and whose lives are we willing to sacrifice for life itself?

It seems the less you have—in education, money, health insurance, or work, as the article cites—the more you are prepared to endure. And that signifies what's out of balance in a world gone askew, in a world where the definition of "need" has transformed to "greed." Even if suddenly the current surge goes away, its absence will never compensate for the toxics generations of us absorbed, so the long-term benefit to the increase in pollution is for those who manage factories from far away.

If our "state officials" are not "alarmed"—i.e., looking out for the people or the environment they've been elected or hired to protect as that headline suggests—what would shock them instead? In a few hours on Google, I found statistics someone, anyone should have been alarmed about. Does a lack of education or poverty contribute to cancer, as Dr. Schwenn implied, or was it the other way around?

1989: Our mill discharges 1.2 million pounds of toxic chemicals into the environment.

1989: Our mill is fined $1.5 million by OSHA for 531 safety violations and fined $98,150 by the state of Maine for illegally polluting or exceeding discharges to the Androscoggin.

1990: The National Institute for Occupational Safety and Health conducts a study at the mill and determines that "malignant neoplasms" (cancers) increase by three percent for every year worked at the mill.

1991: According to Maine's chronic disease surveillance study for the period of 1984 to 1986, of the sixty-four people diagnosed with aplastic anemia in our county, twenty-one were Rumford residents, which was three times the rate of anywhere else.

1991: Five millworkers are diagnosed with non-Hodgkin's lymphoma.

1988–2002: Our mill releases over 25 million pounds of toxics.

2005: Maine's death rate from cancer surpasses the national average.

2008: Our mill is among the top Maine industries releasing toxics into the environment.

2010: Toxic environmental exposures associated with childhood illnesses cost Maine about $380 million.

2011: Rumford releases over two million pounds of toxics, ranking number three in the state.

2012: Cancer is the leading cause of death in Maine and the Rumford paper mill is the top producer of toxic chemical releases.

2014: Cancer remains the leading cause of death in Maine.

FAMILY AND OTHER
ACTS OF OMISSION

IN OUR ETERNAL migrations as humans, when we pass over rivers and oceans and bordered lands, we leave our histories behind, so a human yearning to know what came before us is as fixed as the nose on our face. I long dreamed of a road trip through France where my ancestors once lived, to see what they saw, even if the land had (undoubtedly) changed, and to trace the lineaments and geology that led them away. It seems important to have a conversation with their landscape, to know where my people came from even if those links to France have long expired. So in March 2012, when my husband is summoned to attend a conference in London, I conjure a broad itinerary based on places listed in my family tree and book my flight. With the conference over, we take the train to Paris, rent a car, drive through the flat, tree-lined back roads of the Loire watershed and the riverine areas that flow toward the coastal port of La Rochelle, and stop in those towns that appeared in my family tree.

Our first night we stay in Blois, a town two hours south of Paris, once occupied by the Germans who bombed the town to smithereens during World War II. The Royal Château de Blois, however, was saved by French residents who destroyed homes to create a firebreak as German fires gnawed at the château's gates. Before dinner, my husband and

I head to a bar under the shadow of the château, where I talk with a few men. *Arsenault?* they say. *That is an old name. There are no Arsenaults here anymore.* Later, when we're alone with our wine, my husband says he was startled by how similar their expressions and gestures were to mine and how much they looked like me. In the descending darkness that soon outlines our path, I want to believe I'm connected to them, but it may be too easy to mistake beliefs for facts, to see what I want to see.

The next day, we visit the nearby Château de Chambord, a sixteenth-century castle built by King François I as a hunting lodge in the Sologne marshlands. It's a spectacular site with 440 rooms and 365 fireplaces, one for each day of the year. Stag antlers line trophy galleries and coffered ceilings drape the stone-floored rooms. At its center, a double-helix staircase that consists of two sets of stairs wrapping around the same newel post but containing separate entrances and exits. As my husband and I ascend on independent paths, we catch glimpses of each other through small apertures in the design. We meet up later at a designated spot, a balcony where we stare into the sharp March air. Gardens slumber, and a road slices a thin line through the landscape.

On the suggestion of both Terry and Dot, three days later we roll into La Chaussée, a commune not much bigger than a Home Depot. It's remarkable only in its un-remarkableness, fairly empty midday as I stand in the middle of the road scanning the dusty town. Looking around at the flat farmlands, I could be standing in the potato fields of PEI or Maine. I've been looking forward to seeing La Maison D'Acadie, a museum devoted to the history and migration of Acadians to North America. But nobody answers my knock at the door.

Nearby, an eleventh-century stone church sits gray and cool in the center of town with not a human in sight, its steps worn and polished by centuries of use. According to Terry, it was from this church her ancestors (and mine) said their prayers, boarded a boat, and floated downriver to La Rochelle, where they eventually sailed for the Maritime Provinces of Canada. I'd like to believe in this myth because of its convenience to where I stand, but Acadian history and identity are more complex, as I'm learning on this trip. Many Acadian records were destroyed or never existed at all, so it's hard to piece together a cohesive narrative or complete my family tree. What evidence remains is largely circumstantial, like so many Acadian lives became. The closest evidence historians find are similarities between people from certain regions in France and the oldest Acadian families who shared, among other things, surnames, a common vernacular, a glut of dike builders, and an aversion to war.

. . .

BEFORE ACADIA, BEFORE Maine, and before salmon struggling upstream, Jehan Terriot, my tenth great-grandfather, was born in 1601 near La Chaussée, as his surname shows up on the parochial registers of the time. When French seigneurs (feudal lords) and land developers began expeditions to settle their interests in Acadia, they needed men like Jehan—*défricheurs d'eau* (the clearers of water)—to tame the tides that forsook the seigneurs' agricultural aims. Jehan left behind the disease, food shortages, and feudalism, and French seigneurs got settlers who could urge back the ocean with their hands, a skill they had deployed (but in significantly different terrain) in France since around 1024.

Once Jehan crossed the thrashing Atlantic and came ashore, he would have encountered virgin forests and land flush with game, coal, and cod, a fish so plentiful boats would be slowed by their fleshy mass. He would have been greeted by the Mi'kmaq, a seminomadic, Algonquin-speaking people who crossed the Bering Strait from Asia to North America thirteen thousand years ago. French fishermen and fur traders had been trading with the Mi'kmaq since the early 1500s, so they perceived little threat from the French colonists. The Mi'kmaq taught them skills to navigate harsh winters and became their closest allies, inland guides, and, in some cases, spouses. Without the Mi'kmaq alliance, it's doubtful the Acadians would have survived those first lean years.

In the Bay of Fundy, a body of water surrounded by present-day Nova Scotia, New Brunswick, and Maine, the tide surges and retreats fifty feet twice a day, yielding 160 billion tons of seawater—more water than every river in the world combined—leaving rich organic matter in its wake. To turn those mudflats and marshes into fertile agrarian sites, men like Jehan built *aboiteaux*, U-shaped wood sluices fashioned from hollowed logs that allowed fresh water to exit the land at low tide and prevented the salt water from returning at high tide through swinging wood doors and a small one-way valve called a clapper. The space in between the salt and fresh water is where the magic happened, where it went from useless to useful, transforming the land and eventually a people.

Excavations show early Acadian homes often followed a one-room design for sleeping, eating, and working. Historian John Mack Faragher writes about their lifestyle, "as in the household, so in the *hameaux*," meaning the shared space of the home mirrored the shared space of the hamlet (hameaux). The hameaux and the aboiteaux—community-created systems and community-maintained projects—fostered a collective ethos and slightly more balanced ownership of the land. As the Acadians cultivated these relationships with each other and with the Mi'kmaq, they farmed their way into relative peace and prosperity and helped construct a distinct culture and identity from France.

Acadians populated their homes with large families of ten to twenty children (with low mortality rates) and ate a healthy, protein-rich diet of shad, salmon, bass, cod, beef, sheep, hogs, rabbit, teal, and moose, supplemented by brassicas, wheat, chives, peas, beets, root vegetables, leafy greens, apples, pears, and cherries from their orchards and shared gardens. Disease, pests, weather, jealousies, and tragedies also accompanied their lives, and I'm sure arduous days careened into short, blank nights, only to be relieved by another day's work of pushing back the forests by root and stone and stemming the salty seas. But overall, it seemed pretty good up there under those fretful, powerful skies, living off your potential and your land.

Some say the name Acadia derived from "akadie," a suffix from the Mi'kmaq language meaning "place of abundance." Giovanni da Verraz-zano, an Italian explorer, was said to have christened the region after the pastoral poem "Arcadia" by Jacopo Sannazaro, which describes the idealized landscape in the central Peloponnese, a territory lauded since

Virgil. There were other claims too, but whatever the truth, it was this very fecundity that French and British powers desired and fought over. Acadians were also ambushed and pillaged by jealous New Englanders who desired the Acadians' fertile meadows.

Continental arguments spilled over into their corresponding colonies with regularity, and political boundaries shifted almost as often as the tides. Acadia ping-ponged between French and British jurisdiction, changing hands nine or ten times beginning in 1604 until the Treaty of Utrecht in 1713 wherein Acadians became British subjects and became mostly isolated from their French counterparts of the larger New France. This was a defining moment in Acadian identity in which they were defined not just by a geographical marker or the aboiteaux. Almost three generations had been living in isolation from France, and their developing cultural identity of independence, optimism, cohesion, forgiveness, humor, faith, pride, work ethic, familial tenacity, and perseverance still persists to this day in their descendants' DNA.

Acadians didn't want to fight the British, their French countrymen, or the Mi'kmaq, yet they still wanted to reap the benefits of the colonial enterprise that kept them afloat. So Acadians clung to their neutrality in war and peace and the British generally left them alone as long as they didn't take up arms against them. But over time, paranoia fogged the minds of British leaders. *Acadians,* they thought, *may be dangerous to the king's goals and primed to revolt.* At the beginning of the French and Indian War of 1754, the British gave the Acadians their final ultimatum: leave or swear allegiance to the Crown. Most refused to take sides.

In 1755, tensions between France and England climaxed, and the fear and suspicions the British nursed toward Acadians led to irrevocable acts: overnight, the British and their New England allies removed at least half of Acadians from their homes in *Le Grand Dérangement* (literal translation: the big bother or big disturbance).

The quietness of that translation ignores the violence of the act and its racist intent. It was Britain's solution to a long and vexing problem: the French, and alongside them, the Mi'kmaq. Some scholars consider

Le Grand Dérangement a genocide, and some see it as the predecessor to American Manifest Destiny. Other Acadian critics, researchers, and lay genealogists prefer to use the term *La Déportation,* but that nullifies the savagery because it only addresses the expulsion and not the hatred behind it. Some delineate the actual removal with the decades of wanderings that happened later (the diaspora), which makes sense. But diaspora, deportation, dispersion, removal, exile, expulsion, big bother—the terms *generally* refer to this: in September when apples started to ripen, grain peaked, and the sun waned, at the command of British colonel John Winslow under Governor Lawrence, proclamations were posted in Acadian villages requesting men and boys over the age of ten to gather to hear the king's new resolution. Acadians were too busy in the season's tasks to realize this was a ploy to herd them into controllable groups.

At a proposed time and place, Acadians mustered and were told, "Your Lands and Tenements, Cattle of all kinds, and Livestock of all sorts are forfeited to the Crown with all other [of] your Effects, saving your Money and household Goods. And that you yourselves are to be removed from this Province." Effective immediately. Those Acadians who refused to move were urged on by soldiers with bayonets.

My ancestors took what they could carry in the arms that had worked so hard to tame the tides. Then, single file and bewildered, they marched toward the vessels awaiting them in the harbor. Men were sent first. During that grim parade, women and children lamented, begging soldiers to let them accompany their husbands, fathers, brothers, sons. The women sang a dirge:

> Let us bear the cross
> Without choice, without regret, without complaint;
> Let us bear the cross,
> However bitter and hard.

Within hours, families ruptured and were ripped from their land. A separate ship arrived for elders, another for women and children. The king's men burned villages to houseless lumps. Dikes were breached and broken by the hands of New England foot soldiers who were in service to the British Crown.

Captured Acadians were sent to the American colonies as the British wanted to disperse them and prevent them from returning to French control. They were not well received and endured hardships in their rejection: disease, unsanitary conditions, starvation, death. Later, during the second major phase of the expulsion in 1758 after the capture of Fort Louisbourg (a pivotal moment of the Seven Years' War that ended French colonialism in the Maritime Provinces), the British rounded up Acadian refugees who had earlier avoided capture by fleeing to PEI and Cape Breton. These Acadians were either imprisoned in Halifax or dispatched to England. Some ships sank, with major loss of life. Other refugees were sent to France and became wards of the king.

Acadians were never deported to Louisiana, the Caribbean, South America, or the Falklands. They migrated to these areas after the war trying to find a place to settle. A small group went to Haiti and then Louisiana around 1765 and became the nucleus of the "Cajun" identity, a word from the corrupted "Acadian." However, most who went to Louisiana did so after 1785 when the King of Spain (who now owned Louisiana) sponsored hundreds living in France (basically on welfare) to populate the colony with Roman Catholics. This was the only major resettlement of Acadians as an entity in their own right. Of course, many others returned to the Maritime Provinces and some stayed in America, but no cohesive group coalesced. By the time the manhunts were over around 1763 with the Treaty of Paris, the Acadian population was halved, and New Englanders wrested what land and homes weren't disemboweled by the Brits.

Some families—including the Arsenaults—survived the diaspora by escaping and hiding in the forests until all the ships got under way. They must have felt unmoored in that precarious island hide-and-seek, tiptoeing through the red dirt, shushing their babies, hoping winter didn't come early.

Colonel Winslow, like Doc Martin, kept a journal during this time, recording his correspondence and observations as if writing for reputation and posterity. Winslow's notes, therefore, present a sanitized and one-sided narrative and minimize the Acadian reaction to the horror. He calls their removal a "scene of sorrow" of "Unplesant [*sic*] Business," and notes nothing more than how they were "greatly struck." Historians have tried to conjure what Acadians must have suffered, how it felt to be decimated, silenced, scattered, erased. But the only physical reminders of their presence in Acadia are ancient willow trees planted by its first settlers, ruined sluices, and the mouths of empty cellars.

• • •

HENRY WADSWORTH LONGFELLOW's 1847 poem "Evangeline: A Tale of Acadie" tells the story of Gabriel Lajeunesse and the poem's heroine, Evangeline Bellefontaine, a star-crossed couple separated by the expulsion on their wedding day and reunited, many years later, whereupon Gabriel dies in Evangeline's arms. The romantic poem begins: "This is the forest primeval. The murmuring pines and the hemlocks; Bearded with moss, and in garments green, indistinct in the twilight."

Longfellow, who wrote from his upper-class New England milieu, never stepped foot in Acadia or he wouldn't have considered it a forest primeval; much of the land had been cleared by European settlers for over two hundred years by the time he put pen to paper. The Mi'kmaq were not expelled as the Acadians were, but when they lost their main ally (the Acadians) in the deportation, they signed treaties that basically relinquished control of their lands and ended up as most tribes did, shoved into the corners of their own nation.

The poem was, as Longfellow admitted, about constancy and virtue, which was unsympathetic to the Acadian trauma, which Faragher insists derived from racist policies not the fealty of women. The poem also papered over New England's complicity in carrying out the brutish collaboration in the Acadian removal and New England's long history of persecuting the French for their Catholicism. Worse yet, subsequent historians were influenced by Longfellow's sentimental tone.

After their removal, Acadians were fractured into small groups and dispersed across the globe. They never did reassemble as a people on a land. And like most victims of trauma, Acadians of the time stayed largely silent in their exile, for who would want to relive the murder or diaspora of your people? For me, "Evangeline" appropriated, swallowed up, blunted the truth of Le Grand Dérangement and became a totem of suffering, revered and believed as truth by many people, including Acadians, to this day. It functioned, absent one of our own, as a creation myth, to give weight and expression to Acadian history by an outsider who had no understanding of the racism and devastation Acadians endured.

But am I also an outsider myself? Years of dialogue have been devoted to discussing what it means to be Acadian. Even in my Acadian social media groups some people believe you can't be Acadian unless you live in what was once Acadia. Others believe DNA or culture determines your Acadian viability. Some scholars and politicians consider speaking French an important Acadian identity marker but that's problematic too, since our language was ripped from our mouths in so many ways.

In Wikipedia, Acadia is described in past tense, as it no longer enjoys a dot on a map. Maps are so fixed in our consciousness it's hard to dismantle the concept of belonging and identity behind their arbitrary lines. So what happens when we move, as my French and Acadian ancestors did or as I've done so many times myself? Who are we then if we move between nation or nationality, disenfranchised or unmoored, defined by our landscape without the agency to define it ourselves?

Pélagie-la-Charrette (Pélagie: The Return to Acadie) by Antonine Maillet better conveys the diaspora at the center of Acadian identity than Longfellow did. Maillet's tale follows a widow, Pélagie LeBlanc, who leads a band of exiled Acadians via oxcart from Georgia to the Maritime Provinces. The journey forces the characters—who speak in the ancient Acadian dialect—to reassess what home means. Is theirs a physical journey to an actual place or to another kind of landscape, one of a shared sense of culture, exile, or DNA? Or is it a more elusive trek, just the map of their *experience* in trying to find such a thing?

"I have avenged my ancestors," Maillet said upon accepting the Prix

Goncourt she won in 1979 for writing *Pélagie*. Since the surnames of her characters—Cormier, LeBlanc, Landry, Poirier, Leger—appear in my family tree, it seems Maillet avenged my ancestors, too.

. . .

IN THE DUSK of our France trip, my husband and I head to Angoulême, a commune built on a limestone plateau where my eighth great-grandfather, Francois Dumas, was born. There, I see the Charente River again in a new light from the promontory, as the orangey kickback of the sun flares against the Roman Catholic cathedral. The sky darkens and we roulette down the steep ramparts of the town. At the river's edge, we see the Angoulême Paper Museum, built from the ruins of the former Le Nil factory, a paper manufacturer that operated alongside the pristine waters of the river. It seems as close to my French ancestors as I'll ever be.

Another road on another day—we drive across a bridge over the Charente near Rochefort. Below, the watery landscape of snaking estuaries alters the map with the tug of the tides. Excavators and workers with helmets and bright orange vests maintain the dikes now. I see no remnants of my ancestors' original dike-building work, yet their finger-prints are all over the place, as abraded as I'm sure they were.

In Rochefort, I walk around town, through the arsenal and Corderie Royale, a seventeenth-century cordage factory turned maritime museum, its expansive bookshop flush with history of the region where for centuries Arsenaults supposedly lived. But the books I want are written in French, a language I never nailed down and one my ancestors lost years ago. The stories in those books are as untouchable as La Maison D'Acadie's displays, behind a locked door just out of view. Outside, I take the path alongside the Charente's marshes, once navigable until mills and locks were erected to control the water's path. Brittle yellowy reeds bend toward the silty waters in the sweep of a soft wind. There's really no homestead for me to see.

In our hotel room that night, I look online at photographs of La Maison D'Acadie. Mannequins and dioramas of medieval France colonize the eyeless ethnographic displays in a simulacrum of identity, ribboned off from descendants like me in so many ways. In that remove, I find it hard to get purchase on what these people (*my* people) were all about. I feel as connected to them as I feel toward the paperclip that falls to the floor as I shuffle my itinerary around. They could have been any models in any country from any period where electricity wasn't yet used, which may in some way illuminate the periphrastic machinations of identity itself; it's constructed, not bestowed, I suppose, with the materials we have on hand, and how others see us, not just how we see ourselves.

We visit other French towns with faraway, fairy-tale, recherché names: Chinon, Loudon, Chartres, Cheveny, Chatellerault, Saintes, the names of them ancient and deep like the soil under my feet. Scarred gravestones, ruins, bastides, fortresses, dovecotes, abbeys, rivers, daffodils, and cats sunning themselves in medieval windows—I think I'll remember it all but I don't. As I search through graveyards and forgotten hamlets I take photographs, but later can't recall where or why I took them: an old iron hinge, a carousel, a masted ship, blurred fields through a car window. They become the memory, these photographs, a rudder to navigate the trip and tribute I had so carefully planned.

But photographs can be deceitful, like the ones my grandmother so expertly ruined in the throes of divorce, beheading her ex-son-in-law in every shot. Even in their mutilation, however, in the absenteeism carried out by my grandmother's sewing scissors or in the unidentifiable shots I take in France, images tell another story, witness to the cargo our minds can't carry, a pulse impossible to capture.

Like the water that came from the sea and returned after converting in the aboiteaux, my ancestors were forever altered by their migrations and movements—as was I after visiting the lowlands of France. I realize I'm still connected, as we all are, to the earth's own biography that coughed us up so many thousands of years ago, and that the complicated layers of identity, like Acadia itself, linger in a space not within a cartographer's artistry and agenda.

Recent epigenetic studies suggest emotional or physical traumas can be passed down in our DNA. In the prenatal environment of malnourished mothers of the Dutch famine of the 1940s, certain genes were silenced in the unborn children and remained silent, causing latent and negative effects on their health and their family's health for generations. Another controversial study suggests DNA plays a part in social stratifications. Neither study is conclusive, but the idea that our past is connected to our future isn't magical thinking. I see the scars from those traumas inflicted by Colonel Winslow's hand in my family tree, underdogs who survived while formidable efforts were made to snuff them out; Acadians persist like the willows that bore witness to the horrors of 1755, a tree that can sprout from a finger-sized cutting jabbed into the ground.

MARGINS OF SAFETY

IN 2012, MY husband's military orders send us to Washington, DC. I pack snorkeling gear, sell off our air conditioners, close our bank account, shove leftover rum into boxes, rent a townhouse (sight unseen) near Capitol Hill, and book plane tickets. As our household goods sail north, we move into an empty house, my husband goes to work, and I drive to Maine to visit my parents. I haven't seen them for over a year.

On the way, I stop in Freeport at L.L. Bean's flagship store. After two years in Curaçao, Bean's feels bloated and overpolished, and I feel battered by the sheer amount of things available to buy. I get lost, as everything has been moved since the last time I was here. Cascades of down-filled jackets abut a trout pond where kids seem to be terrorizing the fish. Walls of shoes are arranged in profile, missing their partners. Upstairs and downstairs I travel, like I'm in an M. C. Escher painting of log home design. Racks of sleeping bags hang like carcasses, and in the hunting section I see actual deer, stuffed, preserved, looking as if they are hunting me. The trickle of a fountain (or is it the pond?) disguises the beeping of cash registers and the shutters of cell phone users taking selfies one after another.

Bean's sells nearly everything you need and many things you don't, 24 hours a day, 365 days a year. Clothes, guns, skis, bikes, tents, couches, fishing licenses, ukuleles, knot-tying courses . . . you can even buy a holiday, like an eight-hour canoe tour down the Androscoggin, complete with a lobster roll lunch: a "quintessential Maine day," according to a brochure. If you don't eat lobster but enjoy the lobster aesthetic, Bean's offers lobsteralia: beach towels, hooked throw pillows, key chain fobs, lollipops, or a brass door knocker, all of it red, boiled, dead.

I can't remember the first time I ate lobster, but while waitressing from age fifteen to thirty, I served it to thousands of tourists, many of whom weren't sure how to approach a red corpse resting on their plate. I'd crack open the shells for them, revealing the tender white meat and tomalley—the soft green substance considered a delicacy—and slash my fingers in the process. The instruments of the meal always augured an annihilation: heavy metal crackers and forks to coerce the stubborn meat out of its casement; burying the flesh in a tub of hot butter; the plastic bib we wore featuring a red lobster as if to warn the critter before we boiled it, *death is nigh.* When I think of the tonnage of lobster shells I saw clack and congeal on diners' plates, I'm reminded of something Barry Lopez once wrote about arctic whaling, about how gulls and fulmars would feast on abandoned whale carcasses in a "carnage of wealth."

We hardly ever ate lobster in my family, if at all. Neither did my Uncle Whitey, who was a lobsterman ("bugs," he called them). I always found something menacing about them, the way your teeth bounce on the meat, the way the claws open and close like pliers, their rubbery antennae, eyes protruding like 3D pimples, teeth in their stomachs, clear blood, the way they molt, their captivity right up until the moment of their demise, the way they sound like they're screaming when boiled in water.

I look quickly for those coffee tables made from retired wood lobster traps I always found attractive. *The furniture is in another building,* I'm told by a courteous employee pointing the way.

My sister once dated a lobsterman and he told me the traps were like an underwater food truck, waiting for lobsters to crawl in and have a snack. You sink a trap—I think most are now made of metal— weighed down with something like bricks so it can race to the ocean floor. The lobsters enter the trap through a funnel-shaped net and drop into the "kitchen" to find herring or fish heads strung from a bait bag or string. Unable to pass back through the narrow conduit, they crawl up to another funnel-shaped net and drop into the "parlor." In the parlor they become trapped again, that second egress a sleight of hand that tricks the critter into thinking it's escaping. A backdoor exit allows the undersized juveniles to leave, but adults have no way out, like how I feel when I'm navigating Bean's.

After buying some DEET and wool socks and not finding any lobster trap coffee tables, I walk outside. The sun slaps my face and a sixteen-foot-tall all-weather Bean boot shadows the main exit door.

I escape Freeport and take the back road to Rumford that parallels the curves of the Androscoggin all the way to Lewiston, a city about twenty miles northwest. I pass farmhouses and a church, an old cemetery or two. Cars are negligible until you reach Lewiston's city limits, where I'm pestered by traffic and strip malls and the beat-up center of town.

Lewiston, where my mother would take us school shopping every fall, to Kmart, to the mall, to Levinsky's, a nearly one-hundred-year-old discount store where we'd stock up on dungarees and cords. Once a booming textile manufacturing town with early twentieth-century French Canadian emigres and its own stacks perforating the skies, Lewiston still boasts one of the largest French-speaking populations in the United States, even though the mills where they worked are now mostly adjourned, replaced by other economic developments and a flourishing Somali community.

At the city's perimeter, Bates College, a selective, private liberal arts school founded by Benjamin Bates, the founder of Bates Mill, a textile factory that once supplied garments to Union troops, and later, the middle class with cotton terry loop bedspreads. When I was in high school, getting a scholarship to Bates usually meant getting a job at the Bates Mill, not going to the school christened with his name. The Bates Mill shut down in 2001 and the EPA declared it a "brownfield" (a contaminated site) and the renowned Bates bedspreads are now made by another company and sold online.

I had begun contacting people from the Cancer Valley videos because I was disturbed by what I saw in those films. I will track down Richard Clapp, who grew up along the Androscoggin in Lewiston, one block from Bates College. Richard appeared in the Cancer Valley films in his role as an epidemiologist and director of the Massachusetts Cancer Registry. During the formation of the Maine Cancer Registry, he served as a consultant in Rumford alongside Doc Martin.

When we eventually speak, Richard will tell me more about dioxin, a by-product of the paper-bleaching process that belongs to a class of chemicals called persistent organic pollutants, which resist the normal processes of degradation in the environment and in our bodies; its half-life is seven to eleven years, but we never stop accumulating it so we take it to our graves. More than 90 percent of our exposure to dioxin is through our food supply, in the fatty parts of living things like fish, clams, meat, and in their products like butter, eggs, and cheese. Dioxin also accumulates in the breast milk of nursing mothers; nursing infants are exposed to dioxin levels *77 times* higher than the EPA recommends. Because dioxin is bioaccumulative, the further up the food chain it travels, the more concentrated and toxic it becomes. At the top of the food chain: the human body.

Dioxin I learn can also be found in scant amounts in bleached paper products like tampons, coffee filters, tissues, baby food, diapers, in fertilizer on baseball fields, in gardens, in human placenta, on farms, as fuel for our paper mill, in contaminated sludge like what was buried in Township E.

In 1994, researchers also discovered "unacceptably high" levels of dioxin in Maine's lobster supply, predominantly in the tomalley (which acts as the lobster's liver and pancreas), with minuscule amounts in the meat. Maine drafted lobster consumption limitations and recommended women and children not eat the tomalley because it may contain harmful levels of dioxin. "The message is not 'Don't eat lobster,'" the Department of Environmental Protection poorly clarified. "Go and buy it, enjoy it, but just eat the lobster meat." The State Marine Resources Commissioner concurred: "It's not as serious a situation as it undoubtedly will want to be played by some."

In 2009, the Maine Center for Disease Control & Prevention advises *everyone*, not just pregnant women and children, to refrain from eating lobster tomalley because it can "accumulate certain contaminants found in the environment" without naming dioxin as the source of those certain contaminants. The warning goes even further out of its way to be vague: "There is no known safety considerations when it comes to eating lobster meat," it disclaims.

I will ask Richard why the government allows any acceptable amounts in our food stream for such a dangerous toxicant. "These decisions are based on politics," he will say. "They have nothing to do with health or biology."

• • •

IF YOU WANT to measure the amount of dioxin in your water, you will need at least $3,000 of equipment and access to a lab, because dioxin is measured in parts per trillion. Even so, Richard will say dioxin is not water soluble. It is carried in the silt and sediment that creatures like lobsters and clams ingest. If you wanted to measure the amount of dioxin in something like lobster meat, that our government says is okay to eat, you'd never get a reading because the level of dioxin would be so low no tool could accurately measure it. So, I wonder, how do they know the meat contains even minuscule amounts? And if we can't measure dioxin in our water, why do they sell tests that say we can? Maybe there's something I'm getting wrong, but the logic is paralyzing at best. How does one go about measuring the impossibly minuscule? So we measure it in fish, whose fat contains measurable amounts. Why not test it in humans, or are we too scared to look? As Rachel Carson made clear regarding the pesticide DDT, gross neglect of the environment shouldn't be the only standard to judge disasters by; it's the little things that count.

As my knowledge of dioxin accumulates, I start to learn a new alphabet, one of limits and values and regulations that are supposed to keep us all in good health:

- TLV® (threshold limit value): the level a worker can be exposed to a substance day after day for their lifetime without adverse effects. These are set by the ACGIH® (the private, nonprofit American Conference of Governmental Industrial Hygienists) and are sometimes commonly referred to as tolerable daily intake (TDI) or acceptable daily intake (ADI). ACGIH® also establishes the BEI® (biological exposure indices), which pertain to physical agents in the workplace. The ACGIH® standards are widely accepted internationally but are not enforceable.

- PEL (permissible exposure limits): employee exposure to substances set by OSHA (Occupational Safety and Health Administration).
- REL (recommended exposure limit): employee exposure to substances set by NIOSH (National Institute for Occupational Safety and Health).
- MCLG (maximum contaminant level goal): non-enforceable goal of no known risk or expected risk to drinking water.
- MCL (maximum contaminant levels): enforceable standards for the highest level of contaminant allowed in drinking water.

• • •

I UNTETHER FROM the Androscoggin on the familiar, insufferable two-lane road choked by logging trucks and a slow-driving pickup hovering unperturbed near the solid yellow line on my way to Mexico. I wave, as I always do, to the seven-foot-tall painted plywood people someone lodged onto their front lawn. Down the road, I blow the horn at my grandparents' graves, then rumble over the bridge that spans the Androscoggin. At the traffic light in Mexico, I look up the road toward our old house but keep on driving by. When I finally pull in to the driveway of my parents' new house, my father is trimming the overgrown hedges while my mother hangs laundry on the clothesline.

"Do you need help?" I ask my father as I get out of the car.

"Nah, I can get it," he says as he severs the TV cable with an inattentive *clip*.

We talk briefly that night about my ancestral research in France made the month before, but my capers are divorced from the small deeds of yardwork and clean clothes billowing on a string. What we don't talk about—and never really do—are my concerns about the cancers infiltrating our town and about its future health. Disease and family are two separate paths, two explorations I continue to make, and I catch glimpses of one as I mark steps in the other, and that more serious conversation seems as far away on this warm day as a double helix staircase in the marshlands of France. My parents do what they do every day and I think they'll do the same things forever, as children are prone to think.

After my visit, as I travel back to DC, I picture them in my mind's eye; one moment, my dad is running down the first base line and my mom is winning beauty contests with her black hair, but in real time, they're driving slowly at night, spooked by fast cars and the darkness blinking back at them, or cutting TV cords in the hedge. They jump around in time and memory like balls of mercury resisting constraint. The only way parents stay put is if we stay put with them. And that's something I never do. When my parents and I chatted over breakfast before I left, I experienced a different kind of carnage of wealth than the one Lopez described, one of constancy, something my parents always provided.

MAKING YOUR MARK

By late summer 2012 our household goods finally arrive in DC. When I look at the loot dumped at our door, I find myself momentarily paralyzed by our breadth of acquisitions. Throughout our marriage things just arrive—either by design, act of God, or globalization's muse—and we don't have the guts or the heart to throw anything out, not even the nails my husband plucks from the road. He'll say, *I may need this someday,* but we usually don't. So many items end up in the scrum: books nobody wants (we can't throw away books!), the coin-embedded ashtray from Guatemala (we don't even smoke), the Georgian vodka (tastes like bunker fuel), an oil-stained rock from Valdez (for what?), the Hamas flag shoved into my hands in Jenin. I unpack the pencil cup the Bangladeshi navy gave my husband as a gift (we can't throw away gifts!) and the twenty-three assorted backpacks, gym bags, and suitcases we (ironically) shipped in a box. Some of our goods we acquired on purpose: a couch, skis, and the bookcases and tables to hold and display the stuff that's like plankton coming through on the incoming tide. Although we moved every three or four years, friends were always astounded by what we brought along. What were we supposed to do, just throw it away? Stuff: it finds us wherever we live. From one box I pull a stack of Ernie's calendars my mother had rescued from a load bound for the dump.

Every year Ernie received a freebie calendar from his oil or insurance company and filled in its squares daily, inscribing them in a font the size of a tick. He never used them to schedule things, as most people do, but instead recorded events at day's end, which seems counterintuitive to a calendar's purpose.

APRIL 16, 1988:

34° WET SNOW

44° SUN OUT 2PM

BRI[DGET] HOME FROM POKER 1:30 AM. WE WERE UP

AT 7 AM LEE TOOK SHOWER

HAD LITE BREAKFAST

LEFT FOR FUNERAL. ALSO

LIN[DA] PICKED UP MOM. I WENT

OUT SCOOPING WET SNOW

(& EXERCISED) BRI &

I WENT TO 4 PM MASS.

BRI GAVE ME HAIR CUT.

VACUUMED ALL OVER HOUSE

5:57am-7:26pm = 13:29 [sunrise-sunset]

FEBRUARY 27, 1990:

BRI PICKED ME UP AFTER WORK FROM HOSP. (I.C.U.) TESTS WERE FAVORABLE NO HEART ATTACK.

FEBRUARY 28, 1990:

BRI & I MOVED SOFAS AROUND TO MAKE WAY FOR THE NEW SLEEPER WE GOT AT SEARS.

In one year, Ernie brandished troughs of zucchinis, renovated a bathroom, and one cold day in January he "walked around kitchen 150 times" for exercise. Except for a brief observation regarding Christmas foodstuffs, "all sorts of goodies," the entries are blow-by-blow chronicles, with nary a hint of intimacy from the man who penned them.

He was endearing and told corny jokes on cue.

What do you call a cow with no legs? Ground beef, he'd say, not waiting for our answer.

What do you call a boomerang that doesn't come back? A stick.

Hey, could you pass the mustard, please? my brother Joel would ask Ernie while eating a hot dog, setting him up for the predicted punch line. *I get disgusted if I don't have my mustard!* Ernie would say as he grabbed the yellow squirt bottle.

While he loved a corny joke, the real riddle was his interior. I never tried to unpack what lay beneath his stoicism, and he never ceded entry. It wasn't that I was indifferent, but I was born into a culture of discretion, only one generation removed from postwar respect for and deference to things people didn't want to share; ours was also a culture absent of mental health professionals or family members who would ask us how we felt. Emotional or personal confessions were not part of our milieu. At some point we became stranded in this silent contract even if we wanted to decamp; because how do you bring up talking about not talking if you are tutored in the reverse?

I pore over his calendars, looking for the key to this one-man fortress. He noted important events like the Exxon *Valdez* disaster and my mother's birthday, which entry reads: "maddy jo's birth 47." Maddy Jo, my mother, nearly the same age I am now, with all those days in between then and now condensed into the size of a postage stamp with four words in red pen. Sunrise, sunset, the weather, and Red Sox scores preoccupied most of the squares. "Always next year w/red sox . . . lost 4 straight against oakland in playoffs." I find an entry: "❤ D-day june 6, 1944 44 years ago," with that tiny inked heart giving away his own.

Ernie pressed on, one day at a time, finding satisfaction in the ordinary task of canning seven quarts of pickles. Though mundane, it seemed those moments made up his life, fragments of a day fortified by the square that enclosed them. This was how he lived, how most of us live. Years boiled down to days and days to hours and hours to a list of things we get done.

. . .

I SAW BRIDGET and Ernie all the time when I was a kid, sometimes daily, as they lived just down the street. We hunted for Easter eggs at their house in spring; played tag football in their yard after turkey, orange salad, and green bean casserole on Thanksgiving Day; spent Christmas afternoons with them opening presents while snow piled up as high as the packages under the tree. When the white winter sky ruptured into night, the twinkle of holiday lights would lead us home. The rest of the winter we'd beg Ernie to pull us around in the sled attached to his Ski-Doo. He'd circle the edges of his yard until we were dizzy from gas fumes and the smoke trailing from his cigar, our lashes sowed with ice crystals.

Wash your hands! he'd bellow at us after we came inside from our ride. His compulsive cleanliness applied to everything, even eggs. *They come from a chicken's ass!* he'd say as he washed them anew; Ernie's TLV or PEL or ADI was low. Bridget would cushion his commands with Dentyne, Fresca, and the uncomplicated love grandparents often provide.

Ernie suffered from glaucoma for years before he died and it made his decline into old age feel prearranged. *DAD! DO YOU KNOW WHO THIS IS?* my mother would yell when someone walked into his room. Disembodied voices resonating in and out of earshot must have been bewildering as he groped for a glass of water, a piece of celery.

When we moved him into a veterans home, everything else withered, too, and his once sharp memory got mixed up with the absence of sight, as if the two were mutually dependent. The last time I saw him alive, the cool, thin, cucumber-colored skin of his hand touched mine: *WHO'S THAT? WHERE IS DREW? IS HE HERE?* Ernie hollered. My mother insisted I talk to him about things to trigger his memory—his neighbors, the camp he built—or sing songs he used to love. It felt chaotic, this final loud conversation, and the anecdotal detritus seemed to push him off the edge of dementia.

My mother, her sister, and a used furniture dealer unceremoniously emptied Ernie's house not long after he died in 2009. When I asked my mother if I could look through what remained, she refused. *I don't want you kids going through anything,* she said, like her own mother had often declared. My father and I went anyway, using a key he hid in our barn.

Up in the attic, I unspooled frail Christmas wrapping paper and flipped through illegible letters in French. Decayed silk fabric perished in my hands. All those plastic bread bags my grandmother so carefully washed and dried on her clothesline flaked away like dead skin. A trunk I opened expecting something, anything, was full of rotted nothings. As we rummaged through the rest of the house, I tried on my grandfather's hand-tooled leather belt, took a few old *Popular Mechanics* magazines, his family photographs, and the glass deer eyes he used for his taxidermy work, which were overlooked like so many things families leave in the wake of their sorrows.

When his milky eyes shut for good, leaving papery pockets where his vision used to be, the detailed marginalia my grandfather scribbled had concluded forever. Although his life was as straightforward as his calendar—a friend's funeral followed by a list of chores; a ♥ designated to a day that killed thousands—the family photos he left behind are more ambiguous. As I lift them out of the moldy cardboard box I rescued them from, I see no marks, no notations, no names on their reverse. For a guy who labeled everything, his ancestors remained blank, their identities lost alongside his life. Maybe the larger mystery about my grandfather is not what he left behind, but what he did not.

Photographs have always been a subjective version of the truth, as were Ernie's calendars, I suppose. A moment frozen in time, a choice about what the creator would like to remember, a record of something seen, worth seeing, worth recording, worth showing to someone else. Flipping through the photos, I see Ernie's are mostly formal cabinet cards of what appear to be relatives, their lives stalled for a shallow mise-en-scène like my high school photo with the blurred tree. Wedding pictures with old-fashioned brides, everyone wearing their Sunday best, including the portrait of a nun. Men in World War I uniforms train their inanimate eyes somewhere off to the distance. Maybe to their early graves. Or maybe they're looking at their own largesse of "stuff" somewhere in the room. One man keeps reappearing in different photos but never makes it past a certain age. A few informal photos show people sitting on a porch or at the beach, everyone lined up as if waiting for the bus. Their postures relaxed, their clothes askew. Someone even took a picture of a canoe. Another, maybe Ernie's half-sister, who died in 2010 and was cremated with no funeral, no wake, and no notification to her family.

In the background of the portraits, flocked wallpaper, Persian carpets, mahogany furniture, the bit of lace on a baby's dress. A doll, a piano, a girl reading, a string of pearls. There's a sense of stability and yearning in their confident stances, in the set piece of who they wanted to be or were for that day. Textile families, French Canadian immigrants, Rhode Island laborers like them were generally excluded from oil portraitures that dignify gilded frames in museums and less modest homes. An image, however, can outlast and perhaps out-tell something beyond what is represented, as the art critic John Berger wrote. While these strangers are frustratingly unknowable, the more I look at them, the more I recognize who they are; they show the social transformation of the working-class made whole by a young girl holding a book.

APRON STRINGS

My parents visit me in DC in November 2012, and we attend a military singalong, a Senate session, tour the White House, and walk around museums and monuments to fill in the blanks. Although they are both curious, my parents are incompatible travel mates: my mother moves fast, seeks new experiences, while my father explores more deliberately, examining a rock he picks up from the landscape that bore it out. They came from different environments, she and he, so it makes sense they participate in the world in different ways; my mother's is an ongoing moment and my father's is more a considered past.

After a full day walking around the National Mall, my father crawls up the thirteen cement stairs leading to our townhouse door. "My hip's bothering me a little," he says, grabbing the scabby grass on the side of the steps. I try to help but he shoos me away, gets up, dusts off his knees. I don't think any more about it and neither does he.

We spend another afternoon at the National World War II Memorial, which honors the sixteen million troops who served for the United States. Bas-reliefs, waterfalls, fountains, domed pavilions, elm trees, plaques, bronze wreaths festoon their battles and names. At its heart fifty-six granite columns symbolizing the states and territories surround an oval-shaped pool. The extensive scope of the memorial reminds me of a film I once saw at the Imperial War Museum in London. In it, soldiers at the Battle of the Somme hurtle toward their death in an endless frangible stampede, their acts both sharpened and dulled by volume and repetition. What it all meant became incomprehensible. Memorials, memories, they transform with each passing generation until they become a derivative of the actual events they commemorate, as it felt here in DC.

Maine feels so far away at this moment, even though my parents are right here. In the brindle of the autumn air, I want to break up with Maine if such a thing could be done, forget about everyone in my town who is so ill, about all the recurring things gone wrong. Maine's problems seem insignificant compared to the four hundred thousand lives lost because of the war, a war that defined my grandparents, my parents, and me in the thin wind of this November day.

On Thanksgiving Day I wear an apron my mother gave me last time I was home. She had kept it in a Ziploc bag in the basement, wanted to "save it," she had said, until my aunt harangued her to give it to me. My mother handed it over with a strict warning to take care of it.

"I can't believe you're wearing that apron," my mother stays as I stir the sputtering gravy. "You are going to ruin it!"

After we eat, my father announces he's going for a walk.

"Take my cell phone," my mother insists, shoving it in his coat pocket.

"I don't know how to use the goddamn thing," he says, which is true.

I tell him to stick to parallel streets, to walk to the Library of Congress and return, and I point the way. "Straight up and back," I say. "Stay away from streets named after states, they run diagonal to everything else." He nods and takes off.

My sister and her family arrived the day before and in the melee of the holiday afternoon, we forget about my father. A few hours later, it's my husband who finally asks where he is.

"If he's lost, he'll call," my mother says with the confidence of someone who knows how to operate a cellular phone.

I call him—no answer. I try a few more times. Still no answer. My husband and I set out on our bikes, making wide loops around Capitol Hill.

While we're gone, my mother reaches him, asks him where he is, tells him not to move, but he doesn't see any signs. Toward H Street, I see him standing on a corner, his hands in his pockets, looking around.

"Hey Dad!" I yell and give him a little jump. "Are you okay?"

"I figured I'd find you sooner or later," he says. I don't say that it was I who found *him*.

His absence, even for a couple of hours, unsettles us. My mother blames it on his lack of direction but I think he was just too busy looking around. It's easy to lose yourself like that, in the quiet post-holiday streets below the southern sun's autumn haze. Or was it related to his bum hip?

I find out, two years later, he called someone while waiting alone on Capitol Hill—Andrea, a family friend whose number appeared at the top of my mother's contact list.

He asked how she was, what she was doing, that sort of thing, as if they had bumped into each other at the corner store. At the end of the call he said, *I love you, Andrea. You know that, right?* and Andrea said *I love you* back, and he hung up the phone.

Andrea thought it was strange, so unlike my father both to phone and to say he loved her when he'd never done either before. But it was just like him: he didn't want to bother anyone after walking in circles for hours (with a sore hip) and admit being lost.

. . .

MY HUSBAND RETIRES from the Coast Guard in the spring of 2013 and we are faced—after six moves in twelve years, and now with no military detailer telling us what to do—with the dilemma of choice. Where do we want to live? I moved over thirty times in forty-six years to various towns, countries, states. I lived in a pink trailer, lousy apartments, dark basements, and a farmhouse with hungry sled dogs. Twice I couch surfed and once I lived in the former king of Sweden's apartment, built in 1914 for the Baltic Exhibition in Malmö. My husband and I bought and sold several homes and I even got my real estate license so I could do it for others.

I love moving, unlike most people . . . especially those first months of a new home, its walls blank with possibility. I was shortsighted when it came to empathizing with my mother's anxieties over relocating, even though she delighted in new experiences. To leave a place she spent most of her life must have been stressful on top of everything else she and my father were trying to do—age in place, see their kids grow old, watch their friends get picked off by cancer one by one. So when she held tight to those aprons I wasn't supposed to wear, I should have known the aprons were not aprons, they were disruptions to a long-held routine, strings difficult to sever.

I don't want to move back to New England after living so many places *not there*. The clannishness feels suffocating, the traditions stale. But we fall in love with an old house in Connecticut with chestnut floors in a town of two thousand souls where stone walls cross over forests and fields, so what can we do? As I pack to move yet again, I encounter the objects and things I keep moving from house to house. Some have shed their original function (like glass deer eyes) and have become something else, but like the aprons, my grandfather's calendars, Mr. Knaus's holy font, the damaged Carnival Queen crown, the photos I curate, the stories I've been told or tell myself, they are part of, not separate from, the landscapes in which I move or live.

VACATIONLAND

I CAN'T MAKE it home for my father's eightieth birthday cele-
bration in March 2013, so I create a slide show for his party at
my mother's request. I don't have many photos of him caught doing ordinary things, as our family never really used a camera with
any regularity. It was especially difficult to capture my father as he
never wanted to be the focus of a lens. Yet he is always there even if
in the corners of the frame: wearing a mustache and a shiny seventies
suit. Playing third base. Opening Christmas gifts under the tree. And a
freeze frame of a video where I'm four and he's hauling me down Black
Mountain in his arms. You think you'll remember your family as they
were but you can't, because memory is like a dream you forget to write
down and everyone ages too fast.

As I scour my thirty thousand photos, I find my father in a few
shots of places my husband and I had taken him: Walking across the
Golden Gate Bridge. Standing inside a redwood tree. On a train in
Sweden, on a boat to Alcatraz, eating a Danish in Denmark, walking
me down the aisle in 2001.

The photos prove he was a good sport, contrary to popular (my
mother's) belief. He gets anxious traveling, she always says, which
sometimes he did. He would say he only felt nervous with her
because she'd often get lost, which sometimes she did but only be-

cause she was uninhibited in exploring in a physical way, which he was not. If that is my mother's greatest fault, then his would be the opposite: staying too still. But on balance, their relationship was in balance and *neither* of them had a good sense of direction, at least in a literal sense. They came as a pair on vacations; I got him alone only once.

In 2002 my father and I drove to PEI to find Pinsdale, where his father was supposedly born. While we spooled out an agenda early on, we were also willing to follow a more meandering path. I was inspired by the online research I'd been doing where people would find records of their ancestral past and connect them with their present-day lives, as if scripted by god her or himself. Never had I experienced such an acute event. Instead, when I asked my online Acadian genealogy sleuths *Where is Pinsdale?*, nobody knew.

On the mostly flat, carless, three-turn, eight-hour trip from Maine to PEI, my father and I stopped once for a snack and talked a little about the information we hoped to find: Captain Gallant (his father's guardian), Obeline (his grandmother), Pinsdale (which we couldn't find on any map). My father was always a curious person, but in a smaller way than I, restrained by limited opportunities but not by his imagination, which too often I failed to try and excavate.

Make sure you go to Green Gables, friends urged before we took off, referring to the PEI farm that inspired L. M. Montgomery's classic children's book, *Anne of Green Gables.* The book, published in 1908, juggernauted its way into literary legend and has by now been translated into thirty-six languages and sold over fifty million copies. Around 125,000 tourists a year visit the idyllic property, where you can play eighteen holes of golf or buy red yarn braids to transform into Anne, the freckle-faced, adopted imp from the fictional town of Avonlea. PEI's history seems inextricable from or perhaps even dependent on *Anne,* and the industry built around the tale augments this indivisibility: a theme park, festivals, musicals, radio shows, plays, curriculums, academic conferences, museums, TV miniseries. The government of PEI even licenses *Anne*-related goods, events, and services, and the Green Gables estate is a Canadian National Historic

Park. And Anne herself? As far as I knew she was of British descent. It was not the PEI of my family lore, and I suspected *Anne* was not for me.

When we crossed the Northumberland Strait into PEI, my father said, "I regret not asking my father more questions about his past," and we left it at that. My mother wasn't along to break the silences, so the vacancy sat between us and became part of the trip like so many things we had never addressed. While we were marooned by habit and conditioning not to poke at anything too far below the surface of our comfort zones, our silence at times was as important as what was said. People can be uneasy with gaps in conversations and will fill them up with useless talk. "Omit needless words," I read in *The Elements of Style* a million years ago, and it's an edict I've lived by and plan to etch on my gravestone one day. The essence of the phrase is contained within the phrase itself, its three words saying all they need to say. That's how it was with my father and me at times, when words were just extra syllables in our mouths.

We spent most of our time examining church registers, graveyards, and museums in the villages of Tignish, Casumpec, Mont-Carmel, Rustico, Miscouche, Bloomfield, Palmer Road, and Howlan, where our Acadian family lived and some cousins still do. We talked to curators, priests, residents, and sometimes just people walking by. We couldn't find any record of Obeline no matter where we looked.

We met up with Joyce Desroches, whom I originally encountered online, as she had offered to help us once we arrived. Farms and pastures sheltered her house from the soft coastal winds. She greeted us in her driveway as we pulled in.

"Welcome to PEI!" she said, giving us hugs.

As she made a pot of coffee, I pulled out the notes on my family tree. Kitchens were where my family's business always took place and I could tell it was the same for her. In PEI, Joyce told us later, kitchens were also meant for trays of food, dancing, and fiddlers, like her daughter Anastasia, playing throughout the night.

"What can I help you find?" Joyce asked.

It was my first time in PEI and my father's too, but we felt instantly at home. I don't know if it was the strong black coffee or the small talk or the smell of grass simmering on the land.

"Pinsdale," my father said. "It's where my father was born."

Joyce looked at my chart.

"There is no such place as Pinsdale," she said. "The name of the town is Piusville." As with so many things, human oversight corrupted the facts and a typo in the archival record became an unfindable truth.

Finding out about Pinsdale/Piusville itself wasn't such a big deal, but if something so basic as the place we are born can't be found or is missing in the records history holds, it made me wonder about other bits left in or out of evidential accounts of the past. A transcription error stood uncorrected and untested, a question that remained unasked and unanswered like the ones my father lamented as we serpented over the Northumberland Strait. Genealogy is like that: what we find is not always what we seek and what we seek we don't always find. And those questions, sometimes they hover on our lips until it's too late to ask them.

On one of our final days, we approached a cemetery in the fading light of day. The majority of headstones engraved with ARSENAULT and GALLANT tilted toward the sea and the setting sun, their crosses lit by the orange sky.

"It looks like an Ansel Adams photo," my father said, to my surprise. I quickly snapped a photo of the scene.

We looked for Captain Gallant amid those graves, but Gallant was (and still is) a common Acadian surname as was the title, Captain, used by fishermen who owned and operated their own vessels. Figuring out the Captain's first name would be just as hard; the 1703 *Rituel du Diocèse de Québec* stipulated naming conventions for Catholic first names must include a male or female saint or religious figure. Joseph, which was popular for obvious reasons, appears in my immediate family tree no fewer than 202 times. In the end, our search for Captain Gallant was in vain so I left him alone in the aggregate of other absences, long buried in time.

We drove around the island to the places we knew my father's family was from, but there were no historical sites to view, no family to visit, and like my trip to France, there was no homestead to see except for Green Gables, a fictional home irrelevant to Acadians, as far as I could discern.

At the Miscouche Acadian museum, I bought an Acadian flag, created in 1884 long after Acadia had gone mute. The blue band, I was told, represents the Acadian patron saint, the Virgin Mary, who like her acolytes was forced to live in the margins, impotent against those who governed her. The star on the blue field stands for the mariners at sea, and the yellow of the star represents the pope, so presumably the Acadians' Catholic faith. For some, the Acadian flag stood for the Acadian spirit that lay in the rotted dikes along the shores of its bays, a staged identity to soothe a longing for an ancestral home, a longing I guess I also had because there I was buying a flag to connect myself to something more tangible than family names scribbled on a page.

. . .

UPON MY RETURN home I watched the 1985 *Anne of Green Gables* miniseries and later, the first season of the Netflix adaptation, *Anne with an E.* In the latter, I was surprised—but shouldn't have been—to see the only Acadian character in the form of the stoic farmhand, Jerry Baynard, whom Anne constantly berates.

In Montgomery's book, Anne was adopted to work as a farmhand because Acadians like Jerry were considered unreliable, as the author writes in the first chapter: "There's never anybody to be had but those stupid, half-grown little French boys, who as soon as you get them broke into your ways are off to the lobster canneries or down to the States." The Acadians of Avonlea, Montgomery is saying, are not only stupid and unreliable, but ungrateful servants too, for they leave as soon as they are trained.

Many of Montgomery's works, in fact, contain these kinds of othering undertones that never sat comfortably with me, nor did her fetishization of the PEI landscape that Anne is "of." It is that specific preposition "of" that troubles me most, as it mirrors how the book ignores the geographical trauma that Mi'kmaq and Acadians experienced, though they were "of" the landscape before Montgomery's Protestant ancestors kicked them out. In the book, Mi'kmaq and Acadians also exist only in peripheral (sometimes derogatory) ways. This erasure feels like a bigger gap than the silences my father and I bore, a gap filled with the bloated, commercial trappings and artifice of Avonlea.

Netflix had the chance to correct at least one oversight: keeping Jerry's surname of Buote (an old Acadian name), which was in the book, but instead they curtailed it to the more Anglicized Baynard, just as some people in Mexico did to make themselves more palatable and employable to our mill.

While I admired Anne herself—a plucky underdog who said what she meant and meant what she said, and who seemed to break barriers for girls of her time—I couldn't muster an appreciation of the story she inhabited because she is almost the only thing anyone remembers about PEI. Then again, if we stop reading *Anne*, will anyone be curious about PEI's history at all? I guess it depends on what silences we are willing to forgive and what we are not. In another way Montgomery got it right. Anne's story was aligned with the Acadian story: she had been kicked to the street and desperately wanted a place to call home.

· · ·

I HAD LEANED on photography to help me remember the trip to PEI, but when I tried to upload the photos to my computer after our return, all had disappeared but two: one of a red dirt beach near Tignish, and the other, a blurry image of my father climbing up a lighthouse stairway. While the photos were lost, I was able to reconstitute small conversations that occurred, places we went, and some silences we shared, yet it was a place and a time where so many things had already felt erased.

When I told my father the photographs were irretrievable, he pulled out an Ansel Adams book he had received as a Christmas gift. "See," he said, pointing to the photograph "Moonrise, Hernandez, New Mexico, 1941." The cemetery in PEI and the Ansel Adams photos looked remarkably the same.

A little over a month after Adams snapped "Moonrise," the Japanese attacked Pearl Harbor and the US entered the war. Shortly after our PEI trip in 2001, terrorists struck the World Trade Center in New York. Both photos—from PEI and New Mexico—their smattering of crosses in the fore, heralded the swiftness of light and life like the brilliance of a hawk negotiating the wind and were as ephemeral and sacred as that one vacation my father and I took alone.

• • •

"VACATIONLAND," OUR UNOFFICIAL state motto, appears on T-shirts, coffee mugs, brochures, and on Maine's car license plates since 1936, but Maine and my family vacations never held up to the glamour of that word. Most summers were spent at Garland Pond with Bridget and Ernie or in Kennebunk with Hortense and Frank, where they moved when my father was a boy.

Hortense was a chain-smoking, sardonic woman with a face like a dormant volcano who kept her emotions as tightly bound as her arms, which were always crossed over her chest, and she only allowed small giggles through her thin hand, which rose to cover her mouth when she laughed. When Frank entered the room, his egg-shaped bald head flirted with the ceiling, his voice booming and fearsome. He was affectionate in his toothless smile, the way an octopus was, embracing his grandchildren with a manic, repulsive grip.

In Kennebunk—a place known for its quaint seaside and affluent residents—Hortense and Frank lived closer to the town dump than to the beach. Their house choked with the smell of cigarettes and age, a sour, untidy odor I evaded by sleeping in the mobile trailer they parked in the driveway. For hours we'd sift through other people's trash for treasures with Frank or play on the broad front lawn with their dog, Bijoux, a crabby, spoiled Chihuahua. As for the beach, we would sometimes go and build sandcastles, but the riches I sought were buried elsewhere. I would rather paw through the dump and find a slightly damaged treasure than face a marauding jellyfish sloshing in the lazy waves or meet up with Frank in an unkempt upstairs hallway.

We used up the rest of our summer vacations on a plot of land stubbed by blueberry bushes and poison ivy just outside of town, where Ernie and Bridget built a camp: a two-story, open space structure. Spare furniture, puzzles, mismatched dishes, and a couple of animals my grandfather resuscitated with his taxidermy skills furnished the two rooms downstairs. Cots and old dressers equipped the upstairs' open, doorless loft. Camp was also a mind-set where the only running water was in the front yard, which also happened to be a pond, a pond in which I hated to swim.

Almost every weekend we dragged charcoal, drinking water, coolers, and enough DEET to bring down a jungle up to camp. After we claimed our beds, I'd pad along the carpet of dry pine needles in the woods and pretend to be in the wilderness; little did I know I already was. We caught hornpout with red hot dog chunks and plinked the sour scabby blueberries into washed aluminum tomato cans so my grandmother could make pancakes for us the next morning. At night we cooked dinner on an open hearth made from an enamel sink my grandparents ripped from their house during their kitchen renovation. Bridget would start the fire with tinder harvested from the woods, but we would always throw in other things just to see how they burned: hair elastics, tinsel, plastic coffee can covers, fish scales. With no electricity or running water, the only sound at night came from teetering gas lanterns and mottled voices of other families across the pond playing cribbage or rummy. In bed, I lay there and listened to everyone breathing while mosquitos buzzed about, sorties against DEET-less skin.

Ernie built a mint green and white, fifteen-foot, tugboat-looking craft out of plywood and fir (the "yacht"), which my husband believes came from the plans outlined in *Popular Mechanics.* Its construction cost him part of a finger, which he used as a prop for his never-ending magic tricks: *Now you see it, now you don't!* he'd tease, even though the digit was never really there. He would take us for rides on the yacht two at a time: *OK, Kelly, Jill!* he would holler, leaving the rest of us to wait our turn on the tilting wharf. He'd untie the lines then putter around the pond. Upon his return, he'd tie the boat to the wharf's cleats and swap Kelly and Jill out for the next two kids, always ensuring an older one was paired with someone younger. This activity would consume the better part of a day, to the enchantment of our parents.

Later on, when the yacht deteriorated beyond redemption in Ernie and Bridget's backyard, sometimes we'd joke about it and I'd wish I hadn't; the man built a boat that floated with plans from a grocery store magazine. Plus those protracted rides with orange lifejackets choking our necks were as sacred as the thin feathers of a blue-winged teal.

As teenagers, sometimes my sister and I went to Old Orchard Beach, two hours south, where we'd buy fries on the pier or browse T-shirt and taffy shops. On the beach, I'd smother myself with iodine and baby oil and lie on the hot sand, getting the tan that proved I had been somewhere.

In Mexico, we had lived on the edge of anxiety and illness rather than on the edge of the forest primeval even though trees outnumbered everything else, so "Vacationland" always felt like someplace to escape from and not to, somewhere you went, not where you lived . . . like the time I visited New York City in junior high school with the Bolduc family. I saw the city in all its gauzy grime: the smell of dried piss and sausage smoke; glamorous women in colored pumps clacking along

Fifth Avenue; loopy hippies leering at our country mouse clan. And as I leaned over the white wood barrier near Yankee Stadium's locker room, Bucky "Fucking" Dent (my father's name for him) touched my arm as he left practice. Though it seems corny now, visiting the Empire State Building was the best part of my trip, as I wrote in a paper for my high school English class the following year. From the observation deck, on that sharp sleek monument, I saw further than I had seen before. The wind up there, it took my breath away.

CUMULATIVE AND PERSISTENT

When my father retired from the mill after forty-three years, he received a toolbox (which he used), a Bulova watch (which he never wore), and asbestosis of the lungs. The toolbox decamped to our dusty barn and I found the watch years later in the garage, in perfect shape, on a shelf by the cat litter. As reports surfaced about the dangers of the asbestos he handled at work, manufacturers compensated him (and others like him) for the scarred lung tissue asbestos caused; sometimes he received three dollars, sometimes a few hundred. Eventually, the monies petered out, as did his lungs.

My father was tough, sometimes to a fault, and I never heard him complain, not even on the night he died. He told me once about how when he was a kid he walked around all day with a sharp pebble in his shoe, so that when he took it out, the relief was even greater than if it were never there at all.

In late summer of 2013, he collapses on the ninth hole of the golf course, face up, in the middle of his daily game. After months of tests, he is diagnosed with esophageal cancer and a few months later, lung cancer. My father asks us not to discuss his prognosis, because he doesn't want to know. We comply in mute alliance. Weeks of chemotherapy and radiation, a blood clot in his lung, a catheter, a feeding tube, an oxygen tank, the gloom of hospice, he shrinks to half his size.

"No taste," he says, tussling with a piece of pasta like it's barbed wire. He loses more weight and loses interest, too. My mother encourages him to start physical therapy, eat a Popsicle. He stares out the living room window while we whisper behind his back.

I go home almost every week that fall, the limbo-like season when New England maples defrock and the sun is a brief low slit casting glinty rays through unkempt branches of half-bare trees. Summer's nonchalance is long gone but winter's yet to turn its steely aim upon the soil, the houses, or the mice that build nests in walls, seeking the relative warmth of unpeopled spaces.

My mother doesn't want to be alone or leave my father by himself, afraid he'll die while she's out buying cheese. My sisters make a schedule for one of us to always be with her and I try to comply but sometimes it's hard to make the trip. When I can, I stay in Maine for weeks at a time but my sisters shoulder the bulk of the load. When I'm not there, I keep checking my phone for health updates they provide. Fall somehow skids into spring. I send home cookbooks for cancer, buy him subscriptions to my favorite magazines to keep his mind off his meds. I am repulsed by the ingredients listed on the cans of Ensure the doctor recommends he drink. It doesn't seem life-sustaining to me: corn maltodextrin, sugar, canola oil, and soy protein isolate. But there's only so much I can do from afar, and his decline feels like a lone, distant crow squawking in the wind.

There's a more horrible blip in this horrible routine and my father is sent to a hospice facility because there is no room at the hospital to adjust his oxygen so he can breathe. But hospice is a bad place to recover because hospice is a place one goes to die. Hospice workers ask my father when he doesn't or can't eat: *Do you want to talk about the end?* instead of feeding him a turkey sandwich or giving him a glass of ice. *He doesn't have to eat if he doesn't want to,* they say right in front of him. Their statements are in the same spirit, with the same resignation deployed when doctors inject morphine in his veins instead of trying to figure out what happened to his lungs. *He's had a good life,* hospice workers say under the angry waiting room lights. *Has he?* I ask and watch their mouths cave.

He rallies a little when we bring him home.

Back and forth I drive, five or six hours each way, from Connecticut to Maine. One trip blends into the other until I can't tell what month or even what year it is: April 5, Maine is buried in snow. April 20, there's not a white flake in sight.

Slowly, my father begins to eat. All he wants is pistachios, so I buy bags of them. *Those are too expensive for me,* he says, gobbling them up. We talk about baseball and books. He reads *The Art of Fielding* and we forget to talk about it. We watch movies. We sit around. He always loathed just sitting around, as do I. Once an outstanding athlete (golf, softball, bowling, skiing), he was known for being able to do a "tip-roll" at the eighth tower of Black Mountain's main trail when someone would shout "alley-oop" from the T-Bar. He'd plant his two poles downhill and spin on them and the tips of his skis in a pirouette then continue down the hill as if nothing had happened. Now he struggles to lift a knee. He starts physical therapy. I watch his slow march to nowhere: up, down, up, down, up down, updown, updown, Up. Down. Up . . . Down. . . . . . .Up. Down. By spring, he rolls his wheelchair into the driveway to bask in the yawning sun.

Late summer, 2014. I kiss my father hello and after a few minutes, he turns to the TV. My mother shouts something from the kitchen over the clamorous rattle of the TV show *Pawn Stars.* I slump in the overstuffed chair.

Over the next couple of days, I learn the new routine of their lives: my mother empties my father's catheter, changes his cannula, washes dishes, makes coffee, turns the heat up, turns the heat down, helps him to bed, tucks him in. One day the "oxygen man" who delivers fresh canisters, a nurse, their handyman, and a parade of strangers and friends amass then disperse, like a dandelion gone to seed in a quick wind. In the room where I used to sleep, big liquid oxygen tanks, with their constant threat of blowing us up to smithereens at the accidental drop of a match.

In the morning, my mother walks my father to the kitchen, her arms wrapped around his waist. I hear them murmuring in the hallway.

"Ain't much of a life," he says.

"What's the matter?" my mother says, slightly alarmed.

"I feel like shit," he says. "Just couldn't sleep."

My mother procures a voice-activated phone, a walker, the best hearing aids, a hospital bed, bathtub rails, hospice aides, ice cream, Netflix. The days drift. Dinner comes early. The late afternoon winter light hesitates, then crashes, darkening the curtained room. We fold ourselves into the furniture and flip channels.

"Do you or does anyone you know suffer from lung cancer? Give us a call at . . ." the lawyer on the TV beckons.

"Maybe I'll call," my mother suggests.

"What the hell are you talking about?" my father says.

"Your lung cancer. Maybe I'll call them about your lung cancer," she says.

"I don't have lung cancer," he says.

My mother tracks his oxygen levels, like volunteers have done on the Androscoggin, judging impairment by percentages, keeping the lower numbers at bay by turning up the O_2. The river's oxygen percentages lie somewhere between impaired and threatened, as do my father's. My father's body too seems to be a recycling unit for the toxicants that stream through his blood. But he, unlike the river, would never breathe again without a machine to help him, like the bubblers Rivermaster Lawrance had long ago installed.

"When I get better," he says as he hunches over, "I'll visit your new house." His oxygen tank hisses away in the other room, its plastic line leashing him to his chair. As he keeps trying to live he keeps dying at the same exponential rate as the town . . . an unbuilding of a body that had previously built a mountain.

. . .

WHEN I CROSS into Maine from New Hampshire across the Piscataqua River, one of the first things I see is what I always see: the state-funded welcome sign, "MAINE. THE WAY LIFE SHOULD BE." *Was there ever such a Maine as this?* I wonder as I speed up the Maine Turnpike. The promise of that phrase just never added up.

E. B. White wrote dispatches for the *New Yorker* from his saltwater farm in Brooklin, Maine. When he drove to Maine from New York, he, too, crossed the Piscataqua River. "I had the sensation of having received a gift from a true love," he writes in his essay "Home-Coming," following the same route. "Familiarity is the thing—the sense of belonging," he wrote. "It grants exemption from all evil, all shabbiness."

I'm tethered to Maine by this same sense of belonging, but also by a sometimes paralyzing ambivalence I wrestle to understand—an inexplicable love for Maine and what it represents, even if some of those things are false. I don't think it was ever really a paradise, except maybe for the Abenaki who fished the Androscoggin until their lives and the salmon they ate were choked out by dams or disease. Maine's story somehow became so appended over the years that the story became the story itself. It was like that game you played as a kid where you sat in a circle and one person would whisper a phrase in their neighbor's ear, and that child would whisper it to the next one, and so on. At the end of the circle, the last child would repeat the phrase aloud. Inevitably the murmured telling and retelling distorted the words so the original phrase was no longer recognizable.

In Maine, we clear-cut our forests while tourists exalt them. Pollution bankrupts the fresh air we advertise. We let dioxins invade our environment, which end up in lobsters tourists eat. We celebrate Thoreau's voice but drown it out with the growl of chain saws. What gives our town life could also be what's killing it. As the folksy Maine saying goes, "You can't get they-ahh from hee-yahh." In other words, the way life should be, the idealized state of Thoreau and tourists, may have never actually existed except in the landscape of our minds.

One night on the Metro-North train from New York City to Connecticut, my seatmate and I strike up a conversation.

"Where are you from?" he asks.

"Maine," I say.

"Fresh air! Woods!" he says. "God's country!"

God's country? Behind the glimmer of the hand-forged "Rolla Roaster Hot Dog Fork" from L.L. Bean and the lobster logo-ed gifts on the Maine Tourism Bureau website, there is a state perishing under the weight of its own advertisement and where "God" is noticeably absent.

· · ·

THE DAY AFTER Christmas 2014, I watch my father die. He keeps trying to speak, but only a thin awful wail emerges as he thrashes his body against steel bedrails and wrestles with sheets. I see in the outline of his body a lifetime of 7–3 shifts at the mill. I see in him, too, a lifetime of working for an industry that, in the end, led to his end. What he is trying to say, I'll never know, but I do know I no longer have to keep secrets from him or for him.

By dawn, my mother has stripped his bed and cleaned out his room to a certain degree. My five-year-old nephew wakes up, asks what happened, is confused by his grandfather's absence. My brother tries to explain to him the idea of heaven, death, and what it all means. I can see in my nephew's eyes it doesn't make sense. It doesn't make sense to any of us.

You look like your father! people always told me and still do. Our eyes, in particular, are/were the same blue-gray. We both have one that sags a little, as if we're falling asleep, at least in that one eye. In that sameness, I saw what he saw, or at least I imagined I did, especially on our walks around town where his repeated stories became so distilled. He'd narrate as we walked: *This is an historic spot,* he said one time, pointing to the road as we passed the grassy lot that used to be his high school. *This is where my friend Roger Gallant dropped a jar of mercury.* I imagined the balls of silver pinging along the road in tantric lines. We scuffed our boots across the thin snow to uncover a plaque of people who donated money for the plaque. He pointed to the name Roger Gallant, class of 1951. *That's him*, my father said. *That's the guy that dropped the mercury.*

CHIPPING AWAY

You'd think things would have changed. And they did. My father, after his retirement in 1995, for the first time in his life, canoed and fly-fished the Androscoggin. The fish, supplemented by a stocking program, started to reappear, which meant eagles—who ate the fish—could re-turn to the river, too. My father's blurry snapshots of the threatened raptors circling above the river proved the food chain was sorting itself out. The revived river activities (eagles and humans and fish) meant toxic releases to the water and air had decreased, which they had, be-cause federal and state regulations curbed the more grotesque offenses to the land: the Clean Air and Water Acts helped unclot our water and skies; Superfund regulations compelled corporations to clean up their messes; open trash incineration was no longer acceptable; and the EPA required paper mills to stop using elemental chlorine to bleach their products and started tracking certain toxic chemicals the industry re-leased to the environment.

In his postretirement days, my father also walked a lot around town. In those walks he rediscovered places like a trail down by the river where there was now brush but before the brush and the trail, just the river itself—a river his memories, his life's work, his blood—orbit around. I accompanied him many times on those walks and he always had a story to tell, most of which I can't remember because they seemed insignificant at the time. Later, when he got sick, I wanted to record his stories my-self, but then he'd suspect he was dying and we weren't supposed to let on we knew he was, even though he knew we knew. Our silence about his impending death circled around our conversations and around the twiggy paths we pretended were new. On them, we somehow found our footing.

. . .

My husband and I trace a familiar walking route one afternoon: down to the Mexico corner, Route 2, past Maddy's Pizza and the truss footbridge, take a right over the River Street bridge before finishing our circle through Rumford with a dip down to the suspension bridge, then back up Route 2 by Hannaford grocery store, a right on Hancock Street before heading home.

As we walk past the mill, we see a black oily ribbon the size of a stick of gum on the side of the road. I take a photo of it, pick it up, sniff it. It smells like rubber.

"It looks like a shredded tire," my husband says, angling it in his hand. I stick it in my pocket.

We keep walking and as we do, we see more pieces freckling the road. Then another then another then another as we follow the Hansel and Gretel trail of the glistening bits.

We look over the side of the railroad bridge. Mounds of the same material lie in open-topped railroad cars parked below, one after the other. Mixed in with the pieces, splintered chunks of wood that look covered in creosote.

"The cars are headed toward the mill," my husband says, pointing. "I wonder if they are going to the power plant."

It's cold. We're hungry. As we turn to walk back to my parents' house, I slip on a patch of black ice and break my camera lens. I forget about the cars of rubber and wood.

We return to Connecticut, and while doing laundry, the rubber bit *ka-chonks* out of my jacket pocket and onto the floor.

I get online. After a few hours of Googling things like "paper mill—rubber—power plant," I find out the rubber, as my husband guessed, is a piece of shredded tire, used in paper mill boilers as fuel (tire-derived fuel, or TDF). I also find Mike Blumenthal, former president of the US Rubber Manufacturers Association (RMA), who lobbied policymakers to enact legislation favorable to, well, rubber tire manufacturers. I email him and he responds right away. We schedule a phone call for later in the week.

• • •

SCRAP TIRES HAVE long been a nuisance. They are nonbiodegradable. When stockpiled, their shallow cavities collect fetid water and harbor mosquitos and rodents that carry disease and provide combustible materials a place to congregate. If they start on fire, the resulting toxic sludge creates serious groundwater problems because tires are no longer just made of rubber—their chlorine content is higher than some coals. And when chlorine combusts, you get dioxin. Moreover, the presence of tires piled in the respite of a forest's edge mars the natural landscape, and disposing of them is generally expensive or takes up valuable landfill space. A small percentage of tires are used for highway barriers, asphalt paving aggregate, underwater reefs, or are exported somewhere else.

In the early 1990s, the US government began looking for alternatives to fossil fuels. It made sense, economically and environmentally, for them to consider tires, a burdensome resource that was cheap, plentiful, and burned hotter than wood or coal.

"1975 was the first time tires were used as fuel," Blumenthal says over the phone. "It was at a cement kiln in Germany, right in the middle of the oil embargo when prices were going through the roof! You know how the Germans like to burn things. So they came up with the idea and said, *Ach du liebe!*"

"Our mill started burning TDF in 1994," I say as I look at my timeline on my desk. I realize the mill started using tires and mill sludge for fuel right after they received a permit from the DEP to increase their stack emissions.

Blumenthal is retired now and generous with his time and knowledge. He's a convincing and animated proselytizer, sermonizing me with his industrial marketing degree and preaching the benefits of burning tires for fuel, which included saving his RMA clientele a lot of cash and remedying the stockpiles in places like Colorado, where they feuded with the Rocky Mountain skyline. His key legacy was a policy the EPA ultimately upheld: the categorization of used tires as a fuel rather than a solid waste. Once tires were considered a fuel, the rules for getting rid of them changed, and those regulations rested in the hands of the state with that federal definition guiding the way. Forty-eight states adopted, in one form or another, laws and regulations on scrap tire management, including Maine.

When I try to ascertain Maine's TDF regulations, DEP administrators bury me in language difficult to comprehend without an engineering degree. The terms and charts I study feel complex by design, where even careful readers like myself are stalled by technical, abstruse language and cut off from what the public (me) needs to know. When organizations break down their information to more simple forms—FAQ sheets, memos, and bullet point lists—the facts become blurred, seem incomplete, un-nuanced, and thus a little skewed. When I look to online science or sociology journals—because their papers are usually peer-reviewed—I find more often than not I have to pay a relatively high fee to see what they say. I email friends with university accounts, but that can only go on so long. Plus I already know what all these documents and laws will say: that paper mills follow all the rules. And they generally do. It's the rules I need to decipher, not to catch the mill doing anything wrong. But decrypting those rules or figuring out who benefits from the rules is like catching pollution in plastic buckets. I even lob a plea on social media asking who can tell me about TDF and nobody responds. Are they still calling it TDF or is it called something else? I dig around there for a while in definition land and find several terms that could be substitutes for TDF, but I'm unsure if they mean what I think. Moreover, half the EPA.gov links are bad and I end up on error pages with nowhere left to go.

Scott Reed, the environmental manager at our mill, had explained their TDF process to me in an earlier email. Their two "very efficient" boilers that burn TDF (since 1994) also burn coal, gas, and biomass (since 1990), an umbrella term for any organic matter used as fuel, including bark, clean construction, demolition wood, and chipped railroad ties. The mill also incinerates a host of mixed wastes classified as fuels: creosote-treated wood, delayed petroleum coke, lime kiln rejects, oil, dewatered pulp and paper sludge, and mill waste (since 1993). Here is also what he said:

> As stated in the permit, these units meet federal New Source Performance Standards (NSPS) from 40 CFR Part 60 Subpart Db. They are also meeting emissions limits from State/Federal Best Available Control Technology (BACT) assessments for Particulate Matter (PM), Opacity SO2, NOx, VOC, CO. The Boilers will also be required to demonstrate compliance with federal Maximum Available Control Technology for boilers (Boiler MACT) by the effective date of that regulation. Compliance is demonstrated by both periodic testing and continuous emissions monitoring. The mill has been burning TDF since 1994 and was required to obtain an air permit modification prior to the use of TDF as a fuel. The overall facility air permit undergoes a renewal process every 5 years. Typically, a facility must apply for a permit modification prior to the use of a new fuel, at which time the regulatory agency can request additional information as needed for the approval process. Federal rules have also been developed under 40 CFR Part 241 that outline requirements for different types of traditional and alternate fuels.

I read the permit he cited and one paragraph of its thirteen pages said:

Emissions Limits
At the specific compliance date established per 40 CFR §63.7495 Rumford Paper Company shall comply with the applicable emissions limits for specific pollutants in 40 CFR Part 63, Subpart DDDDD, Table 2. For those pollutants which are limited both by this license and by Subpart DDDDD, the facility shall comply with the more stringent limit. [40 CFR §63.7505(a)]. The emission limits shall apply at all times the affected unit is operating, except during periods of startup and shutdown as defined in Subpart DDDDD, during which the source must comply only with the applicable limits of 40 CFR

Part 63, Subpart DDDDD, Table 3. [40 CFR Part 63, Subpart DDDDD, §63.7500(f)].

I continue to follow the vernacular breadcrumbs the best I can and look up all these acronyms to see what they mean:

BACT = "Best Available Control Technology means an emission limitation (including opacity limits) based on the maximum degree of reduction which is achievable for each pollutant taking into account energy, environmental, and economic impacts and other costs."

MACT = "Maximum Available Control Technology" applies if the boiler is an "area source" boiler, meaning: "Area sources are commercial (laundries, apartments, hotels), institutional (schools, churches, medical centers, municipal buildings) or industrial (manufacturing, refining, processing, mining) facilities that emit or have the potential to emit less than 10 tons per year of a single hazardous air pollutant, or less than 25 tons per year of combined hazardous air pollutants."

40 CFR Part 60 Subpart Db: These are the standards of performance for industrial/commercial institution steam generating units. They list emission standards for: sulfur dioxide, particulate matter, nitrogen oxide and the record keeping standards, parts (a) through (y).

40 CFR §63.7495 = This states "When do I have to comply with this subpart?" and enumerates all those reasons in (a) through (i).

40 CFR §63.7505(a) = These are the general requirements for complying with emissions limits in tables 1 or 2 or 11-13.

40 CFR, Part 63, Subpart DDDDD Table 2 = This table lists emissions limits for boilers like our mill operates (I think), which is a heat input capacity of 10 million BTUs per hour or greater. What's monitored is: hydrochloric acid, mercury, filterable particulate matter or total suspended material, carbon dioxide.

40 CFR, Part 63, Subpart DDDDD Table 3 = are the workplace practice standards, like tune-ups and energy assessments, visual inspections, inventories of systems, and other such internal reviews.

40 CFR §63.7505(a), Table 11-13 = these are "alternative emission limits" for new or reconstructed boilers that began after 12/23/2011 and before 4/1/2013, so they are different from Table 2.

In other words, it's goddamn complicated when burning so many different materials together, and it's hard to determine an exact pollution load, or for a layperson to even know what it means. Different fuels burn at different temperatures and not even all coal burns the same—it depends on where it's mined. Stack tests and trial burns could be considered a poor indicator of daily operations; normally tests appear to be performed at constant and optimum conditions; i.e., not real life. Daily emissions could vary wildly and we'd never know. Moreover, Bryce Sproul, from the DEP, says stack tests are only performed when new fuel sources are added, if there are suspected hazardous air pollutants, or if the state specifies anything else, therefore *regular* doesn't seem like something I can ascertain. In addition, Sproul says tires are considered just another fuel and not regulated specifically. It's also unclear as to who verifies the veracity of these tests, if they are verified by anyone but the mill itself.

I email the DEP and am told that "stack emissions may undergo testing for a variety of reasons": in effect, I am sent to look up more rules.

Mary S. Booth, Ph.D., studied eighty-eight biomass energy plants. She found that even the cleanest biomass plants emitted more nitrogen oxide, volatile organic compounds, particulate matter, and carbon monoxide per megawatt hour than coal plants and exceed emissions of natural gas plants by more than 800 percent for all major pollutants. In burning the contaminated fuels (i.e., waste-derived fuels) like construction debris or tires that our mill also burns, she found facilities can emit toxics like dioxin, furans, chlorine, heavy metals, benzene, lead, styrene, mercury, arsenic, and phthalates. I never come across discussions or regulations regarding butadiene, a toxic released when tires are burned. I do find it's one of the most potent liver carcinogens ever observed. Is the mill monitoring those, I wonder?

TDF is not considered biomass but Booth takes TDF into consideration, too, because it's tossed in with everything else. Booth says lax state regulations and permitting, and loopholes in the Clean Air Act, make it easier for industry to pollute. From what I understand from her paper, our mill could be legally polluting more than it did in the 1970s, when the Androscoggin was one of the dirtiest rivers in the United States.

When I confront Blumenthal with the information I've gathered, he responds with a question of his own: "If you get the so-called environmentalists in the room and ask 'em, *what is your number one problem with tires as a fuel?* And they'll say, *oh they create black smoke, they create odor, they are noxious and it will increase dioxin and blah blah blah.* Prove it. Where is your documentation? I have a report from the EPA that says dioxin formation is not a function of fuel combustion. I have emission reports showing that the emissions are below state and federal standards. Show me a peer-reviewed, valid scientific report substantiating any of your claims. No one in the world can disprove [mine]."

I ask him for these reports but he doesn't respond. I've no doubt some report exists, but I also have a report from the EPA that says it does consider TDF fuels a low-level source of dioxin and other toxics. And I also know Blumenthal's seen that report; he's thanked in the acknowledgments for "his assistance collecting source test data and for his valuable referrals and insightful thoughts on the utilization of scrap tires for productive purposes."

I follow up with Scott Reed, specifically about TDF dioxin emissions, and he says they're no better or worse than those of other fuels, which means TDF could pollute as badly as the worst and that's the most specific answer I get.

Like my father, on my walks through Mexico and Rumford, I always saw things anew, no matter how many times I walked the same routes or how many steps I took to connect the dots. Little did I know the new things I would find were new sources of pollution more furtive, more invisible, more locally bound than the toxic ash that looked like snow. It's an unbalanced burden we shoulder in Maine, to live in such a place where the parameters or boundaries of pollution are open to debate or too confusing to parse.

RITUALS

Wake.

When I started this reckoning back in 2009, I never thought I'd be as close to the subject as I am now. My father's death, some will think, is the center of this tale, but it's not. It happened along the way.

I drive home to Connecticut to gather some clean clothes for my father's wake and return to Maine with the gauzy headache of no sleep.

At Meader & Son, the funeral home, my family stands lined up like a broken wedding party with my mother at the fore, greeting everyone and returning embraces filled with other people's tears or their synthetic perfume. The same slide show I made for his eightieth birthday has been repurposed for this day. I see his face on repeat every time I greet someone at the door.

People kneel before my father's makeshift shrine: the photo I took of him at Black Mountain wearing his Chisholm Ski Club jacket; a glass-encased US flag folded into a triangle, as tight as my mother could fold; and an urn filled with his remains beneath a cross. Lilies choke the air while friends and family kneel in front of the gloom.

We gather at my mother's house after the wake and eat. It's all we can do. I think I made some kind of dessert that deflated on my drive from Connecticut. Meatballs float in a crockpot of unidentifiable sauce. I feel like a shrunken head.

That night, I look at my father's death certificate, his final salute, to see if all the details are correct. I'll look again four years later and see they are not.

My father's burial will wait until spring, when the funeral director returns from Florida and the ground yields its rigid mat.

I fall asleep under fitful, snow-spitting skies.

Funeral.

It's an insufferable winter day in January where we scuttle on skim-ice while the gray sky bullies us with its constant threat. We teeter into the church in small careful steps.

At the altar, I look up from the podium and over the crowd before I begin my eulogy. To the left, a raft of red jackets worn by the Chisholm Ski Club members who arrive together and, in unison, sit down with the whisper of their GORE-TEX skimming the pews. To the right, my family. I get through most of my speech until the last sentence. I look to my sister and give her my notes. "I can't finish," I say, croaking out the words as if my vocal cords are made of a plastic straw.

"Gee, thanks a lot," she says, half into the microphone and half not, and takes the page from my hands. Tight laughter ruptures from the nave.

My sister muscles through my words, then says a few of her own, which I don't register because those red jackets in the periphery keep catching my eye and my five-year-old nephew keeps looking around, asking my brother questions about God. "Amazing Grace" fills the church, then "My Way," the Sinatra version. My father loved those songs. He also loved "Raspberry Beret" by Prince for reasons unknown, and he played it on repeat for months when it first came out. I wonder why we didn't choose that song instead?

After the service, and downstairs at the church: *Sorry for your loss, sorry for your loss, sorry for your loss* on repeat, a serrated knife against the grain of our grief. People paste on sympathetic faces and our family coughs up our bleary-eyed thanks, for what else is there to do? *At least he lived a long life,* some people offered. That phrase, "At least . . . ," valuing quantity over quality, a demeaning traveling partner on funeral circuits with the meaningless "thoughts and prayers," erodes any humor I have to spare.

The day gathers in a cloud of hugs and casseroles. A few bursts of jittery humor detonate with the joy of a backfiring engine. I wear a black dress all day.

Again that night we sit in my mother's kitchen and eat and drink and talk about my father and the murder of my brother's close friend that occurred simultaneously with my father's death. We try to drum up funny stories about them both. Everyone's edgy, like a piece of glass has slit the sky.

The next day comes and goes, and more come and go after that. Grief sits on our shoulders like a nervous cat until it's spring once again.

Burial.

In June 2015, we hold a small graveside service for my father. A soldier plays taps. Another soldier kneels in front of my mother, says, "On behalf of the president of the United States, the United States Army, and a grateful nation, please accept this flag as a symbol of our appreciation for your loved one's honorable and faithful service." My mother's face macerates. There's not a cloud in the sky.

It feels cheesy but we all touch the urn, say goodbye, and bury him underground.

After the service we gather on my mother's front lawn under a tent. Neighbors drop off potato salad. Finger sandwiches dry out from the dry air. Clouds congregate late in the day. I drink too much wine.

My father and I used to visit cemeteries together. We'd survey gravestones, their shapes, inscriptions, carvings, flowers planted (or not), and note the unmarked graves of unbaptized babies stippling the perimeters. Forgotten or disused graveyards were always a solemn favorite and we felt beholden to their *in absentia* visitors. Old headstones featured eldritch engravings like skulls, willows, urns, women weeping, wild-eyed winged cherubs, broken columns, all signaling marital status, religious beliefs, social class, or a life cut short. Newer headstones sometimes bore photographs of the deceased, adding an emotional and unsettling tint to the scene. Their faces always looked like a foregone conclusion, as if they could have never been anything but dead. Below the soil they were. But up above on those bluebird days my father and

I shared in the quiet public finality of it all, the unseen were seen. The invisible, visible.

Mourning.

In spring 2015, I start going to estate sales again, long absent from my repertoire of weekend pursuits. It seems a way to moor myself to the companionship of death, to buy and safekeep things left behind by elderly people who quietly slip away despite full refrigerators or well-trodden paths to their mailboxes.

Near my house in Connecticut, an estate sale opens at 8:00 A.M. I take a number and wait my turn at the door. Across the street acres of stone walls scissor an adjacent field, signifying herds, territory, flocks, ownership, history. Some stones have fallen into despondent piles, indicating the slow tumble of time.

Someone calls my number. I go inside. Rooms are stuffed with cracked oil paintings, out-of-print books, artifacts, canisters and cookie jars, chandeliers (several), a grand piano, dried flowers. Drawers are open, doors ajar, everything's visible, even things that are usually not: sheets, socks, cookie pans, sewing notions, glue. It's as if someone turned the house inside out like a trouser pocket you're about to launder, showing the ugly interior of the fabric's linty seams. An anthology of home. Debris of emptied closets fills the sunroom in an exposé of intimates: nylons, an unopened package of cotton briefs, and a silk slip the fragile pink of a cat's inner ear. I hear a man say, *I like to look inside people's homes, see how they lived.*

Despite the foraging crowd, there is a stillness that comes from the chairs lined up along the wall, bedspreads fanned out like shrouds, and mirrors that no longer reflect anything but a price tag. In a bedroom, the silk of the headboard is tattered from the southern exposure like a membrane between life and death itself. Lamps are on, the bed is neatly made, and at a glance it looks as if the person's still alive but for the room full of buyers ruining the illusion. A woman's shoes sit on a low shelf. They are practical: low heeled, sturdy, well made, and once fashionable. Dirt is lodged in the soles of one pair that still holds the form, somewhat, of their previous wearer.

I return in the afternoon to pick up my purchases. The hum of the morning's possibilities has descended like the slow leak of a helium balloon. Dusk lies in wait. I squint at the field and see a faint imprint, a line in the grass where dairy cows wore a path with their hooves. At day's end, for years, they'd advance toward the barn tamping down the earth.

Inside, buyers have abandoned their rejects by the front door. Donut crumbs and half empty coffee mugs sit on the counter. The house is bereft with the sigh of pending twilight and broken dishes and a measured emptiness, which will continue night after night, day after day, until another person occupies the house. All those artifacts sold today will take on other meanings and folds, with a pause in between new owner and old. Clothes once pressed by their deceased owner will be ironed by a stranger; the family silver will simply become knives and forks; the broken mirror will become someone's trompe l'oeil.

Cars leave, lights go out, and the shag carpet is left trampled, flattened, a dirt path made by the footsteps of many. I leave with two fur coats and a lamp.

INTERLUDE

MILES DOWNSTREAM, THE Androscoggin joins and mingles with six other rivers at Merrymeeting Bay. But before the ocean pulls the river away, so many things have gathered in its draft: a tire, a plastic bag, chicken bones, car parts, a lone shoe, chromium, rotted wood, arsenic, a disagreeable tangle of wire, a shopping cart from a grocery store that no longer exists, polycyclic aromatic hydrocarbons, mercury, dioxin, even a corpse. This broadcasting of debris marks human territory, an affidavit to our lives, illuminating our shifting needs and greeds of the future, of the past. What inconsiderate creatures are we. This matter that rolls through time and space and landscape will eventually accrue. Does the accumulation add up to something else before it disperses at the aperture of the sea?

I remember when I was a kid, we'd toss a paper boat upon a stream and watch as it pitched about until it finally sank. When we repeated the act, the boat would always take a different path. We couldn't control its line. It moved with the current, but not within the jurisdiction of a straightforward timeline, mimicking a family tree, a multiplying cancer cell, or how the working-class declined in an aggregated mess. Trying to guess where the boat would stop was as difficult to pin down as where toxics berthed downstream or in our bloodstream or in the stream of our conscience or consciousness. Did you know asbestos, once found in our lungs, is as resistant to our body's natural defenses as that paper boat was to my guiding hands?

That corpse found in Merrymeeting Bay was a man who slipped off a dock and for a month was lullabied in death by the tides before searchers found him, as the movement of the six rivers forced his body to cascade far too deep. Water has always been futile to restrain but we try anyway; in steep canyons where we insist we live; in floodplains made of floodplains; in diverting or stemming water's flow with manmade tools; or even trying to restrain a tide beholden to the moon, a tide that killed a man without regret. The professional divers who tried to find the corpse knew this lesson well, which is why they gave up; water will always find the easiest path, a path that leads to other paths unforeseen. So many corpses never found such a peaceful grave as the one who was rocked in death in that watery bay.

. . .

WHEN THE TIDE inhales the ocean, sediment slips back in the upriver return, bulking up the bay's interstitial marshes until they become uplands, where humans build houses or bridges or industries or other monuments to themselves. When the tide exhales, sediment leaks into the ocean, carrying with it all those things we have tossed carelessly away, like debris from our activities or copper pennies flipped into water for luck. I read somewhere the practice began centuries ago when people would sacrifice coins to gods to ensure the continuation of clean water, something more valuable, apparently, than the coins surrendered. When did profits overcome such concerns?

My father said exits are more important than entrances, despite all contrary and clichéd claims. Nobody remembers how you showed up; they remember who or what you became because it's the last impression that lasts. After my father was cremated, I wonder what remains of the needle-shaped asbestos fibers that sliced and scarred tiny sacs in his lungs until stiffening them beyond repair. I wonder if they lofted up a chimney in a small puff of smoke and landed in the raging rapids above the dam, a manmade artifice author John McPhee calls "the epicenter of Hell on earth."

WHAT REMAINS

MY FATHER ALWAYS stooped to pick up pennies he found on the side of the road. If he found one heads up, he considered it good luck and would tuck it in his hand. Tails up, he would leave the penny alone. To him, superstition was superior to religion; he thought he could control the output with steady input. If he stood in the batter's box a certain way, he'd deliver a base hit. If he worked hard, his past would disappear. If he rolled the Eisenhower silver dollar he carried in his front pocket, as he did for decades, some unforeseen jinx would never occur. In the end, Eisenhower's slim hairline and bald head wore down, leaving only a wish of an outline, adumbrated by my father's own hand.

He held his talismans close. The square nail he took from a fence in Colonial Williamsburg became a story he could tell. His P-38, a small metal multitool that used to be part of US Army rations kits, became a tactile vestige of his past. Stones he plucked from lands he'd never see again became references to who or where he'd like to be. He even gave me a charm of my own: when I was away at college, he picked a metal nameplate off a paper machine with "BELOIT" pressed into the design and sent it in the mail. *They make our paper machines in Beloit,* he wrote, to remind me of where I was from. I wish I knew what happened to that nameplate and its emotional residue once held close by my father's hand.

• • •

THE NEXT TIME I'm home, my mother gives me a small veneered box topped with a silver metal figure frozen in a bowling stance that looks a little like my father as a younger man. It was the prize he won in 1970 for earning the highest bowling average. Inside, his expired licenses and membership cards, a wooden nickel, a tiny gold heart-shaped earring he must have found on the side of the road, and his father's matching black onyx gold-plated bracelet, tie clip, and signet ring.

"Your grandfather William lived larger than he could," my mother says, looking at the jewelry with contempt, snapping her words like gum. "He drove a new car while his kids lived like homeless people."

I feel a little defensive, not knowing this is how my grandfather was seen, how my mother felt. William died when I was three, so his image was not varnished by his early escape. "Well, Dad's mother abandoned him. She took off with another man. What about her?"

"William was just as bad," she says.

While my mother's accusations are perhaps deserved, I feel sympathy for William, this buying of shiny, pretty things while the world crumbled around him—even if it was partly his fault.

This getting and giving of property after someone dies always feels a little cheap, even though here I am participating in the practice myself. I've seen families destroyed over inheritances large and small, slit into tantrums and demands and warring sides. As far back as I can see, my family never left any valuable possessions in their dying wake. It's not that we were poor. We always had enough. But that didn't mean we didn't want more.

As a kid, I used to read *Richie Rich* comic books, featuring a golden-haired "poor little rich boy" of the same name. Richie always wore a suit and a red tie and was so rich his middle name was a dollar sign and the dots over the letter "i" in his name were diamonds. Richie's father, like Hugh J. Chisholm, was an industrialist of enormous wealth and provided Richie with gold-bedazzled possessions galore. One comic book cover showed Richie "camping," where he roasted hot dogs from

an ornate gold bench while a butler readied his linens and gold chalice for the meal. Richie's cabin-sized tent featured a TV and, in case things got rough, a Bentley nearby to whisk him off to other climes. Richie was so rich, he once used sapphires for a snowman's eyes. He epitomized what wealth could convey: a carefree life with the best toys money could buy. So when I look through my father's stuff, I can't help but wish that wooden nickel had been made of gold . . . not for me but for him to spend as he desired.

. . .

THERE'S A FRAGILITY in the landscape after death, like the skeleton of a leaf, in the negative space of its design. We are especially tender after a death not deserved. But what death is? We all know it's coming yet we are perennially unprepared. When Prince Albert died an untimely death, Queen Victoria grieved almost pathologically for forty years, punishing herself as if she had made his death occur. I read she kept Prince Albert's rooms as when he was alive, even had hot water brought in every day as if he were about to shave. She insisted on mourning rituals that increasingly shuttered her away from public life and I believe wore black until her own demise. Was this grandiose mourning a way to preserve Albert or herself? I am curious about this etiquette of death the Queen invigorated all those years ago, even though I probably won't follow any of its rules—like wearing black—even if they're meant to signal pain. At the same time, I feel rude; my father was just buried and here we are carrying on, with my mother already moving out his clothes. In a year or two or three, what will our grief look like, what will his legacy be, how will I preserve what he meant to me?

The death of our town father, Hugh Chisholm, is intertwined with my father's even though they were almost a century apart. When Hugh died in his Fifth Avenue apartment in 1912, the mill and town offices shut down operations and flew the American flag at half-mast. Town leaders attended his funeral in Portland to honor the industrial-sized legacies he left to our town: probably a future Superfund site and a paper mill of two million square feet of floor space over seventy-five acres, where my father worked and which eventually, I believe, caused his death.

Chisholm also proactively erected a tomb where he was to be interred, at the time one of the most expensive private monuments built in America. He modeled it after the ancient Roman temple in Nîmes, France, called the *Maison Carrée,* constructed during the reign of Rome's first emperor, Augustus Caesar.

In his last will and testament, Chisholm left his son, Hugh Jr., tons of cash and all his worldly possessions, including the Fifth Avenue apartment (that employed four servants) and a farm in Port Chester, New York, where he had raised thoroughbred Ayrshire cattle on five hundred acres of land. John Russell Pope, who designed the National Archives and the Jefferson Memorial, crafted the Port Chester house with wood-paneled rooms, boxed ceilings, leaded glass windows, intricate plasters, and decorated it with chandeliers, velvet drapery, hand-woven rugs, mirrored vanities, gilt-framed ancestral portraits, a billiard room, and built-in bookcases encased in glass that were stocked with leather-bound literature. So Hugh Jr. inherited all those furnishings, too. "He was never extravagant in personal habits," the *L.A. Times* wrote about Hugh Sr., but his multiple homes, his servants, the tomb, and the pricey cigars he smoked, whose vapors harmonized with his own pillowy white hair, suggested he lived more extravagantly than we ever guessed.

Hugh Jr. also inherited the mill. He expanded and improved its operations by diversifying its assets and bulldozing his way through the First World War and the Depression. After forty-four years of magnificent success, Hugh Jr. retired to the Ayrshires and to the Port Chester demesne. Now and again, he'd take out his boat the *ARAS*, a 1,332-ton, steel-hull, teak-deck, fourteen-bed, twenty-seven-crew luxury yacht he commissioned for $2 million from Bath Iron Works in 1930. He sold the *ARAS* in 1941 to the US Navy to be used as a gunboat in World War II. After the war the Navy decommissioned the *ARAS* but it was too fine a ship to mothball, so Harry Truman commandeered the sleek vessel for his presidential yacht, which sheltered such luminaries as Lauren Bacall, Winston Churchill, Dean Acheson, Lord Ismay, Anthony Eden, Omar Bradley, and other white people in ties who conferenced in the evanescence of their deeds of war. When Dwight Eisenhower became president, he declared the *ARAS* too rich for his blood and the government gave it up for good. Before Hugh Jr. died in 1959 in his skyscraper office on Park Avenue from a heart attack, he began selling off the prizewinning cattle.

Hugh Jr.'s son, William, inherited the New York estate and mill operations as well. A mill publication called William's reign "The Coated Age" because of the state of the art paper machine, the North Star Coater, he installed for *National Geographic*'s paper needs. He also built a research and design facility and reinforced the power plant's capacity. The schools were full, employment was up, and the baby boom was well under way. In 1961, William sold the Port Chester house and its surrounding five hundred acres to prominent residents who wanted to fend off overdevelopment of and encroachment on their neighboring country estates.

In 1967, the year I was born, William consolidated mill assets with Ethyl Corporation, a storied chemical company based in Richmond, Virginia, then he retired. No more Chisholms remained in our town affairs. William died in 2001 at his home in Greenwich, Connecticut, the wealthiest town in the state. The only things left of both New York properties are billeted at the Brooklyn Museum: photographs of the Port Chester home and four limestone Atlante sculptures that graced the entry of the Fifth Avenue townhouse that got torn down to make way for other midtown pieds-à-terre. I wonder if my father ever met or knew William, as they worked together at the same time, but I found no records to indicate William immersed himself within the folds of our town's affairs.

Boise Cascade paper company bought the mill in 1976 from Ethyl Corporation. After Boise, Mead, which merged to become MeadWestvaco in 2002. Then Cerberus Capital Management purchased MeadWestvaco in a leveraged buyout to form NewPage in 2005. Catalyst, a Canadian paper manufacturer, bought the private equity–funded NewPage in 2015. In one hundred years, our mill, like most of American manufacturing, went from natural resources to chemicals; from local to global; from making things with our hands to a more automated culture and disinterested funders, leaving laborers who no longer had enough to do.

Those in our town who remember the prosperous years the Chisholm trio wrought still speak fondly of them to this day. Because of Hugh Chisholm Sr.'s hardscrabble upbringing, I didn't begrudge him for his riches, even if parvenu. On the contrary, I had always aspired to the same, to be so wealthy I could leave an important legacy behind.

• • •

ON THAT TRIP to Manhattan when I was a teen, our group made a pilgrimage to Trump Tower. Like the golden hue of Richie Rich's comic books, the flashy brass of the Tower's atrium signaled triumph of the fiscal kind. The Escher-like escalators created a visual illusion, where I didn't know if businessmen in pinstriped suits were floating up or down as they left contrails of Drakkar Noir in their mechanized paths. We watched for an hour or two, perhaps to see someone famous like Trump himself or just to absorb the shine. It wasn't long before I felt small and out of place in my yellow Bronx Zoo T-shirt featuring lions in a cage while ladies in heels *clickety-clacked* across the marble floors. Perhaps I wasn't cut out for the richness I admired or was just wearing the wrong clothes. When I returned home, my New York trip made me a little embarrassed to come from where I did, yet it also evoked the envy of my friends. So I kept the feeling of it close at hand.

It's easy to scoff at gold-lacquered dreams or to say you'd rather have love or health over yachts or prizewinning hobby farms. The sacks of gold Richie Rich and Trump inherited and that Chisholm earned bought a kind of freedom that could erase misfortunes with the plink of a few coins. For many of us who have never had such abundance, a lifestyle like theirs (or even just health care)—to be so rich you didn't have to work or struggle so hard—I think is part of the American Dream, the very same dream my parents, my grandparents, my great-grandparents ventured to achieve. We never really expected to have that much coin, but in the act of striving for it, we ended up okay.

A book publisher once said something to me I'll never forget. We had been discussing diversity in the publishing industry because their

employees, on average, came from white, upper-class backgrounds (like her). When I asked why, she said maybe those from blue-collar backgrounds would rather make money than not, because publishing careers, on the whole, came with low financial plateaus. It made sense for a second; why would I choose to struggle if I had the choice not to? *But what of our other dreams?* I quickly thought, *the part where we get to do what we love not what we must?*

. . .

TRUMP TOWER AROSE as an edifice to signify its owner's wealth, but it symbolized additional sins. The $100 million tower was built on the footprint of Bonwit Teller, an art deco luxury goods department store that had embraced an extravagance of its own: crafted from limestone, platinum, bronze, aluminum, nickel, and garlanded with ornate metalwork and original friezes, Bonwit Teller also sold expensive perfumes, furs, and ladies hats in pilastered and paneled rooms. Before its demolition by Trump, the Metropolitan Museum of Art offered to rescue the friezes and other architectural remnants. But Trump had other plans. He envisioned a tall, "expensive-looking" building that showed off "real art, not like the junk . . . at the Bonwit Teller," he told *New York* magazine. So under his direction, the friezes were jackhammered, the metalwork disappeared, and the building was ravaged then sighed to the ground. And some of the undocumented Polish workers who helped build Trump Tower under dangerous conditions went unpaid until they took Trump to court.

The legacies powerful men construct almost always emerge from the debris of other people's lives, and ignore the moral and social violations they commit along the way. These architects of artifacts know they have the power to build then destroy the world, then move through it easily while most of us just watch it moving by. Indeed, to compare brave new worlds of shiny glass and gold and hand-rubbed marble to the monuments the rest of us erect—like graves by the sea or headstones in the grass—exposes a rift as deep as regular buttons versus the blind privilege of sapphires used for a snowman's eyes.

But even great riches can dissipate over time. When I follow the Chisholm family tree up and down the line, I see his descendants may have had problems as bad, if not worse, than mine. Cancer, alcoholism to the point of despair, and former debutantes who went off grid to shore up their mental health. A man named Colin Chisholm, who looks *identical* to Hugh Sr. and claimed to be related, has been imprisoned for fraud. And by 2014, the *ARAS* sat rotting and rusting in an Italian shipyard waiting for a $55 million makeover. While I feel sorrow for the Chisholm family's misfortunes, I wonder if they ever considered ours.

At home, I look through the rest of my father's personal things my mother stuffed into my hands: commemorative metal pins from events he never attended and a small piece of coral from a beach far away. Who will I give his personal effects to when I die? There's nobody after me. I'm the end of my genealogical line.

My father mustered these things together like building blocks of reality to create and navigate and express and give evidence to his life. Some he accumulated unconsciously, like the toxics in his lungs. I'd like to think my father's asbestosis was a ticking bomb unable to be defused, that there was nothing we could do. But it wasn't. It took its damn time, as long as it took for him to wear down poor Eisenhower's head.

STRIKE ONE,
STRIKE TWO . . .

MY FATHER WENT on strike twice. The second strike, the most turbulent, was in 1986 when Boise Cascade, the owner of the mill, required employees to fill in where the mill needed them with no regard
to their main job descriptions. Their pay or benefits weren't taking a
hit; this was a philosophical strike. Most workers feared a dilution of
their specialties would be the beginning of their slow-motion downsiz-
ing, and subsequently, a termination of their identity. My mother put
it this way: "Originally, if you needed a lightbulb changed, you would
have to call an electrician. If your father needed a pipe soldered, he'd
get a welder to do it. This was a major change."

On the evening their contract expired, we heard horns. Horns for
hours. Horns into the night while union members walked off the job,
got into their cars, and drove laps around the mill's main gate blaring
horns to express their grievances. Within days, Dick's Restaurant, a
local diner halfway between our house and the mill, vibrated with the
broody rumble of the unemployed. My father, who often left home
by dawn for the 7–3 shift, started going to Dick's instead, where he'd
pull up a folding metal chair with the guys and drink coffee that
tasted like it was brewed from twigs that dropped from the beds of
logging trucks.

I was home from college that summer and suddenly jobless, as I had counted on working in the mill. I wasn't alone. All of us kids on summer break had our eyes on mill jobs, on the wages you couldn't get anywhere else, yet we were told by our parents we would be disowned for setting foot inside. So I delivered newspapers instead, the same papers my father yelled at before heading to Dick's. Sometimes I followed him there, listened to everyone rehash strike headlines, plot out the day's picketing schedule, complain about the muggy heat. Even though Dick's was packed, the mill's downscaled production hushed the normal clatter of its operations and, in the balm of the late summer air, the intermittent silence felt like the warm breath of a sigh. And we drank it up along with our bitter coffee. In those fraught early hours of the strike, it felt a little like vacation.

Ten days into the dispute, Boise hired scabs, setting off a civil unrest. It was scab versus non-scab; you sided with the union or else. Picketers howled at logging trucks and banged on hoods of scabs' cars as they slithered through the mill's main gates. People vandalized homes. Neighbors fought toe-to-toe. Cars got keyed. Heads were bashed. A roustabout even fired gunshots. Some of the more harrowing battles, however, arose outside the picket line and in our homes; old friends became new enemies and family reunions and holidays collapsed all over town. At night, men and women gathered at the unofficial strike headquarters, the Hotel Rumford, for beer and blackballing super scabs, a special designation for millworkers who went on strike and returned to work during the strike, but in someone else's job.

Although I experienced the strike firsthand, I probably never considered the implications while I lived it. I was just a kid, wearing a red-lettered STRIKE! T-shirt like I did my Steve Grogan jersey, summoning the toughness I understood as part of being loyal to something even if on the losing side. We convinced ourselves we were better for not winning; being right was what counted. I remember standing in line to receive our family allotment of "strike food": industrial-sized and industrial-made bread, pasta, powdered milk, and "cheese food" the size of a kindergartner's torso. The cheese wasn't even dignified with a brand name like Velveeta, it just said "CHEESE FOOD" in practical Helvetica.

The chief of police, who also served on the board of selectmen, gave the scabs permission to leave their cars at the Mexico town hall parking lot and shuttled them by the incensed strikers who surveilled mill gates. Union members who got wind of the chief's decision drove to Mexico and surrounded the scabs' cars with their own. Fifteen guards from Metropolitan Security Services, a strike control organization hired by Boise, soon arrived, vaulted out of a pickup truck, and attacked the strikers, thumping bodies and heads. Strangers in riot gear pushing around our fathers and grandfathers, our mothers and grandmothers; this, for us, was war.

At a Mexico town meeting after the incident, my father spoke out, maybe for the first time in his life. With his voice wobbling in that hot, volatile room, he said he had thought about going back to work until "the Boise goons in Mexico only unified us more."

The strike disoriented people like my father, blue-collar workers who grew up respecting another man's rights and another man's job. When scabs crossed the picket line, the mill crossed a different one that underlined our powerlessness and took away my father's voice,

the one he was just beginning to find in that town meeting. Boise's contempt for such loyalty infuriated millworkers who, before the strike, always felt a neighborly regard from their employer and were given a say in collective bargaining. Suddenly they were being told what to do. My father believed Boise didn't want to negotiate in good faith because a broken union and a flexible workforce would grant Boise the upper hand in any future contract discussions. Yet millworkers thought *they* had the upper hand: they knew how to run that mill better than any of the corporate supervisors who had flown in from around the country.

Boise reasoned that foreign competition necessitated millworker concessions for their products to be more competitive in a growing global market. The parties brought in a federal mediator. Maine governor Joseph Brennan stepped in to ease negotiations. Nothing helped. Both parties were confident the other would surrender. Neither would. Boise underestimated the quintessential stubbornness of third-generation millworkers whose belief in the American Dream wasn't about to be crushed in the uncallused hands of absentee mill owners. The millworkers underestimated the economic, cultural, and political pressures outside the boundaries of our towns.

When Reagan broke the air traffic controller strike by firing eleven thousand striking personnel in 1981, my father believed the act was an assault on all unions. That betrayal was still fresh in my father's mind in 1986. "He will destroy the working man," my father always said about Reagan; and he wasn't wrong. Harold Meyerson of the *Washington Post* wrote that Reagan's strike breaking was "an unambiguous signal that employers need feel little or no obligation to their workers, and employees got that message loud and clear." My father's hatred of Reagan consumed our family and we weren't allowed to utter his name unless we called him "that fucking asshole," as my father constantly did.

It would be small to blame the demise of unions and the working-class on one event or even one man. Reagan also appointed, and the Senate confirmed, Donald Dotson as head of the National Labor Relations Board. Feverishly anti-union and pro-employer, Dotson was put in charge of protecting the unions he so obviously loathed. With

Dotson and Reagan at the helm, men like General Electric's Jack Welch sprang like Athena from the corporate boardroom head. Nicknamed "Neutron Jack" for his ferocious management style, Welch fired tens of thousands of his labor force, ruthlessly shuttering plants in a declaration that shareholders' interests superseded those of his employees. GE turned a huge profit and big corporations, emboldened by such measures, took note. The Supreme Court's *Citizens United* decision in favor of corporate personhood later confirmed that spending money is the same as and essential to protected speech, which allowed politicians to bankroll their interests as deep as their pockets would go. While spending money doesn't guarantee political outcomes (people still need to vote), the Supreme Court arguably legitimized the idea that the more money you have and spend, the more say you have. Before the 1980s and '90s rolled up their mats, Neutron Jack and many CEOs like him wiped their feet on the social contract between people and the places they worked, contributing to the decline of unions and obliterating the voice of the working-class all across the land.

• • •

ONE DAY, IN the middle of the strike, my nine-year-old brother Joel rode his bike to our grandmother's house, something we'd do when seeking sibling respite or a ham sandwich. "Let's go for a ride," she said to Joel, and they hopped in her brown Chrysler LeBaron, a car she operated with one foot on the gas and one foot on the brake. Joel thought she was taking him for an ice cream. Instead she drove him down to the picket line. As she skittered past friends and neighbors, she leaned on the horn for a half mile while screaming obscenities out the window in the general direction of the mill, jerking the car with each "You goddamn bastards!" It was how we all felt really—whiplashed by the stop-and-go decisions of the corporations that employed us and powerless against the federal government's laws that weakened us, so all we could do was scream.

After months of terse negotiations, workers cast their vote 2:1 in favor of returning to work. Everyone was just worn out. The new contract stipulated Boise could still assign workers to jobs they weren't trained for and everyone got a raise of fifty cents an hour, but it couldn't compete with the inflation that was taking hold. The Federal Reserve had induced two recessions in two years by raising interest rates, which helped people with financial investments, but not those who needed to make investments in their kids.

After it was all said and done, it felt like nobody won. Seventy-six days had cost Boise Cascade $30 million and the loyalty of their workforce. Of the 1,200 union members, around forty were permanently replaced by scabs and about 850 returned to work to what felt like a labor-unfriendly boss and a labor-unfriendly country. And seventy-six days taught the strikers not to trust their employers . . . or their neighbors.

Two storms arrived the year after the strike and caused extreme flooding in the Androscoggin. People, penned in by the river's rage, couldn't get in or out of town. After the water receded and summer gave way to early fall, in 1987 the Ku Klux Klan came striding through town to capitalize on the anxieties and animosities left by the flood and the strike; they believed they'd recruit new members from people who may have felt shuttled by shifting economic winds. A Rumford man invited them to rally and burn a cross at his farm. But citizen protesters outnumbered the Klan and the Rumford man. My mother and about 150 people stood their ground, shouting "Go Away, KKK!" while some objectors dumped putrid chicken manure on the man's property, hoping the stench would drive the Klan away.

When the landowner emerged from his house wearing a KKK T-shirt and brandishing a gun to the furious crowd, the protesters shouted him down. The KKK moved on the next day and left the landowner with the simmering embers of the cross and the loathing of most everyone in town. My mother mailed me a news clipping of the event, her angry face moiréed by the newsprint as if her rage had caused the ink to blur. The bad mood festered in Rumford and Mexico, alongside the mill's pollution, neither of which was washed away by costumed racists or seasonal bad weather.

The strike created a wound in our towns that never quite healed, and for a while, I thought that's why workers were called scabs.

Second- and third-generation millworkers eventually deserted the mill emotionally, though fiscally they couldn't. Despite the unfavorable contract the union was offered, men and women returned to work but remained pissed off about the whole ordeal until they retired, quit, or died. And even then, the sons and daughters of those strikers still bear lesions of the damage to this day, with broken families and friendships littering the town like the poisonous tailings of a long-closed mine.

In 2011, not long after Governor Paul LePage was elected, he removed a commissioned mural from the walls of Maine's Department of Labor that depicted Maine shoemakers, lumberjacks, shipbuilders, and unions on strike. A spokesperson for LePage stated the mural was "not in keeping with the department's pro-business goals" because of strike scenes and called the art one-sided, saying it didn't belong in government's halls. The artists filed a lawsuit against LePage for censorship, but it was dismissed, with the federal judge saying LePage's right to "government speech" ultimately superseding the artists' desire to convey historical truth.

On January 14, 2013, the labor mural was restored—but in the Maine State Museum, not the Department of Labor. Likely more people will see the artwork there, but its placement feels flawed, as if at the intersection of power and truth . . . and like America, the latter is being gutted by the interests of the former.

. . .

I REMEMBER WATCHING my father play softball that summer of 1986, fielding stinging balls hit down the third base line after he crept in to take away the bunt. He was quick, efficient. I never saw him make an error. When I was ten, he coached my summer softball team and insisted on the same kind of excellence. *You're throwing like a goddamn GIRL!* he'd yell at my throws from third to first if they weren't fast enough. But the worst infraction was striking out without swinging, by just watching the ball go by. It didn't matter where the ball lay in the batter's box. *You got two strikes on you!* he'd yell from the dugout. *Don't just watch the ball—SWING!* And I always did.

When my mother first went back to work (after having children and after the first strike in 1981) she made shoes at G.H. Bass. In the morning a horn blew, calling everyone to their position. "I laced those goddamn rawhide moccasin bows. You know the ones? My hands were so sore I had to soak them every night. It was like a goddamn sweat-shop," she said to me once. She worked until the horn blew again for lunch. "You stood there working with no break, all day until that horn blew, telling you what to do." Then the horn blew to indicate the end of lunch, then later, the end of the day. She never went back to being a stay-at-home mom. We needed the extra income, my mother reasoned, if five successive tuition bills were on deck. She didn't want her kids to be controlled by the bleat of wailing horns or Ronald Reagan's whims.

Before the strike, my father was the dutiful dad, attending all my athletic events—instead of me attending his—or showing up for sup-per at 4:00 P.M. after his work shift. And my mother, she used to be home making me grilled cheese sandwiches instead of picketing corpo-rations or men with pointy hats. After the strike, I saw them anew. My father was a regular guy who lingered over coffee at Dick's, shot the shit with friends midweek and midday, and on the third strike, he always swung for the fence. Meanwhile, my mother shredded her fingers.

• • •

I NEVER WORKED in the mill and never even saw the inside of it until the spring of 2016, when I ask Janet Chiasson, their human resources director, for a tour. *The mill long ago stopped offering tours*, she says, but she agrees to take me around.

Janet was the pitcher for my high school state championship soft-ball team and always competent in a way I never could be: steady and serious in school, where she deployed the same lethal focus as on the pitching mound. Hardly any girls could hit her when she was in the groove. Her balls rocketed out of her hand as fast as a sneeze. Janet's mother was a permanent and vociferous fixture in the stands at all our games while her father watched at more of a right angle. Both worked in the mill: her father as a machinist and her mother (later) in the roll wrap department. "My mother's cancer was a fluke," Janet says when

I ask about her mother's health. Her father died in 2004 (I'm not sure how) after forty-one years in the mill.

I drive to Maine for my tour and arrive at my mother's house mid-morning. As soon as I put my bags away and pour a glass of water, my mother sits on the couch and puts a harmonica to her mouth. "I have to show you what I learned," she says through its comb and starts playing "You Are My Sunshine" in a slower tempo than the song demands. She was always musical, but in a more admiring than demonstrative way.

I have seen over the past year my mother's grief fulcrum into an enthusiasm for undertaking new activities, things she had neither the time nor the inclination to do before. She started fly-fishing then sold off some antiques to buy a tent, a ukulele, gear from L.L. Bean. She even went camping. Several times. In high-heeled flip-flops. Her new proclivities for outdoorsy adventures surprised me. Her kingdom was usually inside.

She shakes her head and spits out the harmonica. "Shit! I can't remember! Here I go." She plays a few bars, then: "I spent three weeks teaching myself that friggin' song. Wait a minute!" I laugh at her intermittent swearing. She plays through the entire song.

She sets the harmonica down and says, "I had forgotten so many things over the years. The fun of learning something new. Being alone again."

"You went from living in your mother's house to living in your husband's house," I say. "You've never been alone."

She is quiet for a beat. "Hunh, I never realized that," she says, as she brings the harmonica to her lips.

* * *

THE NEXT MORNING, I arrive at the mill's lower gate where I watch a safety video and am issued earplugs and a hard hat. Janet meets me and escorts me into a huge windowless room, where the violent racket of Number 15—a paper machine the size of a city block—greets me.

A few weeks before, I had Googled "paper mill accidents" and watched videos of men being sucked into the rollers, their bodies pinched flat. I read about legs crushed, fingers lost, blasts, explosions, amputations, falling cranes, fires, gas leaks, or mishaps with "causes unknown." Such accidents are rare but feel accessible today, like when you look over the edge of a tall building with the irrational urge to jump.

Janet tears a piece of coated paper off a fresh roll and hands it to me. I sniff it, but my senses are vandalized by the roiling noise, the claustrophobic heat of the machines, the stuttering fluorescent lights. You could lose track of time, decades, your thoughts in here. I think of my great-grandfather, my grandfather, my father, how they must have been crushed by the input, the output, the hours they couldn't hear. I can't imagine working here a single day.

As Janet shepherds me around, I talk briefly to workers behind control panels or guys skirting the floor. I can't keep track of the details Janet relays, as I'm not allowed to take photos or touch anything. Mechanical things don't come easily to me when they are auditorily explained. I need to understand how things work in a much more physical way.

Janet introduces me to three men in the machine shop while she takes a call. The work area is tidy, but a century's worth of steam and grease and human sweat cake the tooling machines. Nobody says a word until someone's cell phone rings and one of the guys picks it up. Another machinist, who is in Florida on vacation, is calling everyone to say hi. They put him on video and the guys all laugh.

"Janet brought someone here. Wants to know what we do," one of the men says, snickering.

"The six guys working down here in the machine shop are putting out as much work as the twenty-eight guys that used to work down here," the caller says in serious tones.

"That's quite a drop," I say.

"We keep up," another guy in the room says. "There are *a lot less* machines running, so *a lot less* equipment, *a lot less* to work on. But *a lot less* emergencies."

I leave them alone with their phone call and walk around the shop. Machinist emergencies, I think, are probably *a lot less* alarming than the ones running on repeat in my head.

Machinists like Janet's father and pipe fitters like mine kept the whole operation afloat. When a machine broke down, machinists would make a new part. When a pipe needed fixing, my father got his wrench. That's how American industry used to be run; when machines failed, they were treated like a ship broken down at sea: fixed on the spot by trained and specifically skilled men. Indeed, all industry was more self-sufficient in earlier days, which meant it required more people to rely upon instead of a call center somewhere else. Since 1990, Maine has lost 13,000 out of 17,700 jobs in the papermaking industry (about 73 percent), with about 2,000 of those lost since 2013—so not only a lot less machines, equipment, emergencies, but also *a lot fewer* jobs.

When I leave the mill and its underlit rooms, I feel jet-lagged out in the fractaled spring sun, like Rip Van Winkle, who fell asleep for twenty years then emerged to a slanted world. The mill left an indent on me like the one I imagine Rip's face acquired from resting against the bark of a tree during his protracted nap. I had finally seen the other side—my father's side—and even though only a fraction of his life in the mill was revealed, like Van Winkle, I had crossed a threshold of some kind, and the world changed as soon as my perspective did.

• • •

I SEE JANET in the grocery store the next day and thank her for the tour.

"Don't make us look like rednecks," she says, laughing, knowing I was writing about the mill. "Did you see *The Rivals*? Don't make us look like that."

I had seen *The Rivals,* a Smithsonian documentary that explored the lead-up to the 2007 Class A state football championship between our high school team, the Mountain Valley Falcons, and the Cape Elizabeth Capers. In twenty-five years, Mountain Valley's football teams won over two hundred games and made it to the regional championship seventeen times, the class division championship eight times, and won the state championship four times. Attendance at those games was huge for Maine—around 2,000 to 2,500 people in a community where the population was 10,000, give or take, depending on the year.

The competition wasn't just on the gridiron; it was a cultural face-off between the haves and the have-nots, white collar vs. blue collar, so there was even more at stake. Cape (for short) outfinanced us on and off the field, and the documentary emphasized the ridiculous but sober tragedy of zip codes and tax bases to show there was no level playing field figuratively or literally: one was on artificial turf and one was on pocked crabgrass. But *The Rivals* wasn't really about opposing sides. It was about one thing being above or better than the other, the imbalance laid bare. Because even if Mountain Valley won, which they did many times, those kids' lives, as they said themselves in the film, were all downhill from there.

As I put my groceries on the belt to check out, a woman I grew up with works the register.

"Where do you live now?" she asks.

"In Connecticut," I say.

"Oh?" she says unhelpfully.

"In a farmhouse," I elaborate.

"Martha Stewart lives in a farmhouse in Connecticut," she reminds me.

"Mine is not like hers," I say.

"Connecticut's really expensive," she says.

. . .

As I DRIVE back to Connecticut, I consider all I had just done and seen and heard: the mill tour, my mother's new adventures and musical feats, and small interactions with old friends.

Janet's comment—"don't make us look like rednecks"—spoke to a dilemma I fight to resolve: what others think of the working-class versus how I perceive what it means to me. In the past, in a different system that no longer exists, the working-class were seen as honorable, hardworking, loyal people who made machines that made the machines that made the world go around. That's the identity I've always worn. Somewhere along the way as manufacturing declined, so did the perceptions of who we are. Now there's a sense Janet sensed: people see the working-class as rednecks who like their guns and bad food, don't care about the planet, are racist or just plain dumb. While there are always those who may fit that node, the former definitions also still apply and neither perception is wholly true. In fact, the majority of humans don't ever live up to clichés and can't or shouldn't be reduced and reduced and reduced to a single serving at an all-you-can-eat buffet.

Identity is more nuanced, I think is what Janet was trying to say, as nuanced as what happened halfway through *The Rivals*; the Cape coach admits he would rather be *us* than *them*, that he was envious of our community's passion for football, a game that bound us together as did the mill and made us in-tune to one another's losses and wins in a collective and empathetic way. He wanted what *we* had, which came as a surprise to me. Because while proud of my heritage, for all the things I watched my parents and grandparents do and how I was taught to be (per the past definition), remaining part of the working-class was never really the goal.

Technically, I'm no longer part of the working-class based on my husband's job, my address, and higher education degrees. That classification is even more complicated because I now live in a beautiful enclave an hour and a half from New York City where famous people buy summer homes and drink dry martinis as if they are dying of thirst, as the grocery store clerk surmised. The population hovers around two thousand and home prices hover around $700K to $1 million, with a steep climb from there. While not everyone is fabulously rich, most are comfortable enough. Very few, if any, struggle to buy groceries or train tickets to somewhere else. It's hard to sync these two lives, the perception with the reality and my background with my foreground, and declare myself part of the working-class, especially when I don't even have a job. So why do I feel like it's still part of me, including that redneck vibe Janet exposed? It's the same confrontation Mountain Valley High School footballers faced in *The Rivals*: myself against my inverse. As the Acadian refugees I'm sure wondered, can you be from a place that doesn't always welcome you back?

Connecticut is where I live. But home is a separate taxonomy with its inescapable cloak of influences, of church suppers, icy ski slopes, a backyard game of tag, or the bright reckoning of the sun at day's end. It's a sloppy first kiss, Coon Lyons who brought us sugared donuts on Saturday mornings, those chokecherries that grew along the neighbor's hedge. And it's the mill that I finally got to see. There is nothing in Connecticut or DC or Sweden or Curaçao that fulfills such bearings as these. Home also is a culmination of landscapes real and remembered that wad up in your chest like a knot, a knot that unfurls itself when the phone rings in the middle of the night. These landscapes define us, so no matter where we are in the world we carry them, even though they're never quite the same when we return. But we also define our landscapes, often gouging them with the wreckage of our debris.

THE PINE TREE STATE

My trips to Maine from Connecticut take on a Doppler-like effect of a motorcycle approaching, rumbling through a fixed point, then disappearing down the road. I always loved that sound, a sound most people hate, but the optimistic snarl of a motorcycle's engine reaching the vanishing point to somewhere I would have rather been reminded me of childhood summer days yet again.

I had been going home more in the months preceding my father's death and now because he is gone. I want to see if my mother is doing okay, that she doesn't face too many nighttime voids. When she took care of my father in those final months and days she said it was the closest they had ever been emotionally, and she became as patient with him as she had been as a mother to me. They were part of the same team, he and she, and with that membrane sheared, the transition between dinner and bed seems best avoided by loud TV and visitors like me and Father Joel Cyr.

As he pulls into my mother's driveway, I realize I haven't seen him much since high school, except at my father's graveside service that he emceed in 2014. In the back of his SUV, fishing gear, a tent, waders, hiking boots. "Just in case," he explains when he gets out of the vehicle. For him, I will learn, there's no clear line between fishing and religion.

. . .

FATHER CYR WAS assigned to our parish in the 1970s and arrived in a bright yellow Volkswagen Sirocco and with an affinity for a very dry martini. The hours leading up to the weekend soirees my parents threw filled our house with the sting of onion as my father urged them through the meat grinder to make spaghetti sauce for the forthcoming crowd. As part of the party prequel, my father would also smuggle the console TV upstairs so my sisters and I would not interrupt their fêtes. I'd sometimes spy on the grownups through the stair banister anyway, watching cigarettes flourish and highballs flash as everyone laughed and listened to Johnny Cash or *Jesus Christ Superstar*.

I always thought my parents the most glamorous, of course. My mother decorated herself with lipstick and jewelry she rarely wore, like the necklace with brown, orange, and yellow maple leaves attached to a chain of brown Bakelite ovals that sounded like poker chips when I collected it in my hand. And my father, he looked like a young Robert Mitchum with the sad and shy dangerousness of a man who had nothing left to lose, his eyes as striking and hard as a December sky. The morning after their parties I'd scrub their dingy ashtrays and scarf the leftover deviled eggs while prying from them stories about the night before. Remnants of my mother's spicy Jean Nate bath splash garnished the air.

Sometime after I made my Confirmation, Father Cyr transferred to Fort Kent, Maine's northernmost town, which is populated by a large percentage of Acadian descendants who fled the deportation. People often choose to speak French, including Father Cyr, who grew up there, retired there, still lives there. We always used to call him on Christmas Day, passing the phone around the table because it was his birthday. *My initials are J.C.*, he'd howl and tease over the phone. *And my birthday is December twenty-fifth. What do you think that means?*

One summer when I was a teenager, we vacationed in Fort Kent with the Chessies: Irene, Maureen, and Joanne. Our mothers packed six kids, two tents, and a cooler full of baloney in our station wagon and sped north to Fort Kent. We pitched our tent on the Canada-Maine border on the Saint John River, near the Fort Kent blockhouse and downstream from Madawaska's paper mill. At night we rambled parentless along the riverbank, slapping mosquitos while my mother, Irene, and Father Cyr drank cheap red wine at the nearby rectory. On the long drive home on Interstate 95, I remember staring out the window, watching pine trees and the flat landscape whiz by, in a repeated pattern, as if I were watching a Fred Flintstone cartoon where Fred would run through his house for what seemed an eternity, and the same table, chair, and window looped in the background as he raced on.

. . .

MY MOTHER INSISTS the three of us drive down to the falls to watch the rising full moon and we arrive in time to see it glance the hilltops in a haloed flame and sequin the river below. It's quiet but for the water glissading across stone and our voices splintering up toward the heavens. Our faces are clammy and cold from the waterfall's mist.

"Were you ever bothered by the mill when you lived here?" I ask Father Cyr.

"Life is stronger than death," he says.

"That doesn't answer my question," I say.

"People are willing to suffer some of the crosses of death . . . like pollution," he says. "For life."

I look at my mother.

"I was a young mother. My focus was on family," she says.

"There's an element of hope, that it's going to get better," Father Cyr says. "There was always the certainty of a paycheck, too. Plus, there was also a kind of richness to working in Rumford," he says and laughs. "All mill towns in Maine are poor, and the people stole a lot from the mills. I remember I'd say to the guys working there, 'I need some paper' and they'd say, oh yeah, yeah, don't worry, Father, we will get you some paper!' In East Millinocket near where I lived, lumber, electric wire . . . the majority of their houses are from stolen products from the mill! The comedy of sin!"

"Was it worth it?" I ask. "Not the stolen things, but living here. Was it worth the price?"

"There were always better opportunities where it was dangerous," he says. "It's always been that way. You have to have war to have peace."

. . .

FATHER CYR DOESN'T get up early like most sportsmen, considers the day as it comes. So it's 10:00 A.M. by the time we drive to Grafton Notch, a valley carved by the last ice age, to scout fly-fishing spots. On the way, Father Cyr pulls over to consult his DeLorme Gazetteer and I consult Google maps on my iPhone, but it's hard to get lost when there's really only one road to take.

He drives down a short dirt road and parks. We get out of the car and stand at the edge of Bear River, a tributary of the Androscoggin. White sky shunts into our eyes. Water runs narrow and shallow and the distant woods feather to thinning trees alongside the water's edge. "Perfect for casting," I say. Father Cyr nods but doesn't smile. Mosquitos curtain my body.

"I used to enter the woods and come out happy," he says scanning the land. "Now I go into the woods and come out sad. If anyone went into those woods today, they'd think wow, wow, wow!" He looks up and circles his hands above his head. "Compared to sixty years ago, it's nothing. Logging and clear-cutting has decimated not only the trees but ruined the solace and silence that comes from being among them. It's something nobody will ever understand again."

"Aren't Maine's woods 90 percent forested?" I say.

"Yes, but they include in their statistics the little trees, the ones the size of your finger," he says.

He also says many of those little trees are planted by the hands of the same people who will cut them down. With their neat rows, hand-planted trees also savage the architecture of surprise and authenticity he goes to the forest to find, so just planting them is not a solution to the demise of what they provide. What he says makes me think of the two-hundred-year-old stencils on a friend's living room walls that were ruined by a renovation job when her painter covered them with fresh paint instead of careful restoring of their lines: the walls' original surface as unrecoverable as an unbroken forest of Mother Nature's design.

My mother's foot is sore, so rather than walk in the rugged back-country we see from the car, we choose the more genteel sightseeing opportunities. We pull off at the popular places like Moose Cave, a forty-five-foot-deep, two-hundred-foot-long gorge into which, according to the legend, a moose once stumbled and died. My mother stays in the car because of the lumpy slopes we know await. Father Cyr and I hike down the path to a slitted cave created by slabs of rock that have tumbled into the gorge. Grooves and striations across the bedrock suggest movements of glacial ice and ancient geology that didn't advance in haste. At the cave, we shout into the void and our voices echo back. Under my feet, lichen and reindeer moss, named for the creatures who ate its spongy mats when they roamed the landscape. I swat mosquitos all the way back to the car.

We stop next at Mother Walker Falls, and it's an easy stroll, so my mother comes along. The three of us press against the safety railings as water thunders over granite boulders, its volume augmented by the fierce snowmelt. Pools of spent water slap lazily in smooth depressions of rock. Mica glints along the river's crooked path. The fishy smell of pulverized granite and quartz arises from the riverbed.

"It's not just the silence we are losing by losing the trees," Father Cyr shouts, barely audible. "It's this, too!"

We stop too at Screw Auger Falls where as a child I used to wade in its pools and granite grottos. A carpet of pine needles and tree roots in the shady groves muffle our voices. We sit for a spell and watch the hiss of water making its way downstream.

• • •

THE NORTH MAINE WOODS, where our mill has long harvested trees and a bit farther north of where we sit, is the largest undeveloped forest in the Eastern United States and much of it is only accessible on foot, skidder, or hand-paddled boat. There are no motels or Starbucks, and you can drive for hours without seeing a building. You have to fill up your gas tank before setting off up there because there's not many places to buy fuel either.

The thicket of private and public lands in the Woods consists of about ten million acres where basically nobody lives. Sometimes private lands are in the middle of public parcels or vice-versa; picture land archipelagos with negligible governance, detached but related like the West Bank and Gaza. Ownership changes frequently, so it's hard to say who owns what at any given time, but in general, about 90 percent is privately owned. Of that acreage, historically, fat swaths were owned by a few timber or paper companies that preferred the acreage in which to grow their trees, but now the Woods are owned by many entities, including investors, conservation groups, real estate investment trusts, institutional pension funds, and by private citizens like Roxanne Quimby.

Quimby moved to Maine in the early seventies after graduating from the San Francisco Art Institute. She felt a kinship to the Woods and Henry David Thoreau, who inspired Quimby about the inherent goodness of living deliberately and of nature and self-reliance, so she built a small cabin in the Woods with no electricity or running water. In the mid-eighties, she met Burt Shavitz, a beekeeper, and together they started selling beeswax products at fairs and festivals and called it Burt's Bees, which became a profitable skin care business.

Quimby bought out Shavitz and continued Burt's Bees herself. As her profits grew, so did her land holdings in Maine, including the acquisition of over twenty-four thousand acres (Township 5 Range 8, adjacent to Baxter State Park) to add to the sixteen thousand acres she already owned, making her the second-largest private Maine wilderness landowner. At some point Quimby wanted to preserve and protect what she so cherished and she set out to make her land a national park.

When I first heard about Quimby's idea, sometime in 2003, I reacted not unlike some people from Maine did—*this is our state not hers.* We liked the Woods just how they were, thank you very much. We could hunt, fish, snowmobile, hike, paddle, log, ski, camp, and snowshoe with nobody telling us, in general, what to do, even the private landowners who allowed all those things. Some opponents to her efforts just wanted to live in solitude, telling her to just butt the hell out, and in the independent but self-sabotaging spirit of Mainers, words like *federal overreach* and *Ban Roxanne* spilled into conversations in diners and onto bumpers of pickup trucks across the state. At one point the town manager for Millinocket wrote a letter to the editor in the *Bangor Daily News* saying to Quimby, "Leave us and our way of life alone." Other opponents were concerned a national park would hurt industries and families that produced Maine's forest-related products: lumber, pulp, furniture, paper, and wood, which comprise the state's largest exported goods. And with five paper mills closing between 2008 and 2016, leaving approximately 2,500 folks unemployed, a national park could ruin livelihoods of people halfway ruined themselves.

In a *Forbes* interview, Quimby agitated objectors by accusing Maine of being a welfare state filled with "a large population of obese and elderly people whose major landowners are committed to a forest products industry model that hasn't worked in years." She said of the state's leaders: "They're tone-deaf when it comes to the environment." So it wasn't just the gift Quimby intended to bequeath to the nation that troubled some folks, but her persistence to do so in such a condescending tone.

Quimby's acolytes argued a national park would create other kinds of jobs, ones more sustainable than knocking down trees and making them into books or magazines. They wanted to keep the forests un-answerable to skidders and other commercial enterprise except per-haps the business of tourism, which was a pretty lucrative bet; in 2017 Maine's national parks will bring in around $285 million. Quimby argued she wasn't doing this because she wanted to "call all the shots" but so all Americans could have a say in the land's use.

Paul Corrigan, a former Baxter State Park ranger and Quimby ad-vocate who lived in nearby Millinocket, told me: "It felt meaningful knocking on doors to tell folks about [the park]; writing supportive op-eds; going to Washington to lobby Maine's congressional delega-tion; getting behind Roxanne's gift to the American people. I knew I was rescuing my hometown. If you toss a drowning man a life jacket, it won't matter if it says 'Property of US Government' on it."

I worked in the tourism industry in Maine, feeding visitors lobsters, selling them clothes, teaching them to ski. So I understood how adver-saries saw her: as another tourist backpacking in her ideas of what con-stitutes the essence of Maine and shoving it down our throats. We had lived with a tolerant disdain for tourists, feeling both used by and reli-ant on them, a conundrum we've yet to solve; it was like our codepen-dent relationship with the forest itself. Tourists came, enriched us, then left us with a tenuous economy at the mercy of Vacationland whims. Also, their infrequent visits to their (often) second homes made town centers as sleepy as the dead ache of frostbite. Quimby didn't appear different—in principle—from paper companies either, who came from "away" and spent their money and influence to use Maine's resources as they saw fit.

Quimby's controversial rhetoric underscored an argument the book *The Paper Plantation* makes: just because the forests had been managed one way (a tone-deaf way) for so long, didn't make it right. Ralph Nader's Center for Study of Responsive Law, which fostered his philosophy of consumer protectionism, published *The Paper Planta-tion* in 1973 and it surveyed the seven major paper companies that controlled Maine's paper industry and forests. The book proposed that paper companies contributed to the "relative poverty and stagnation" of the economy by encouraging a dependence on forest-related jobs while "fattening the pockets of the out-of-state owners and managers of the large paper companies." Because of this dependence, Nader's group concluded Maine was a colonial state with a "one-crop economy with a one-crop politics" with environmental and human costs. The state was also lenient toward paper companies in taxation and enforcing laws, and in return, state leaders gained industry allies and votes, which kept both parties in power. And so it went. Year after year, the same recursive power plays kept paper mill owners rich and their workers poor. Was it any different now?

Between 2003—when I first learned of Quimby's quest—and now, I understand the issues better, and I grew to see the virtue and value in Quimby's ideals and ideas. My small-mindedness leveled at tourists was a holdout from my past, a past responsible for ruining the landscape she was trying to protect. I applaud her for jamming a crowbar in the center of the state's ambivalence toward outside influence (leave us alone! but give us your money!) and prying it wide open. Otherwise, who knows what would happen to the woods/Woods as long as humans plod the earth. If her national park becomes a success, I also know what tourists can support; their money paid my college debt as I served them lobster and beer. Plus, I hadn't lived in Maine since 2001. Wasn't I a tourist now, too?

Though the national park didn't directly affect my town, its potential creation asked questions on familiar themes: Save the environment or save the forest-related jobs? Give the woods/Woods to the tourists who propose to guard them or to the locals who will use them for economic prosperity? Do we yield to government regulations or business pursuits? Loggers, coalitions, environmental groups, tourists, nature lovers, pinwheel-eyed liberals, hunters, hikers, and disenfranchised millworkers, Chisholm, Quimby, Thoreau . . . we all wanted the same thing; we wanted the woods/Woods for ourselves.

The unasked question always floating beneath the discourse of the national park proposal was this: Who can own the woods/Woods, or nature itself? Is it even possible to possess the solitude Father Cyr described when he walked amid a canopy of pines? Could Quimby or the federal government own the moose that wrecked our cars or old growth trees? I wondered/wonder then/now, and thought/think I knew/know the answer. It's whoever coughs up the most cash.

In 2016, President Obama designated Quimby's donated acreage as Katahdin Woods and Waters National Monument and everyone just kept plugging away. Nothing terrible up there has happened since. But change in attitude comes slow in Maine, as slow as the time it takes for a pine tree to grow to full height, which is around fifty to sixty years.

• • •

I NEVER LIKED being in the woods, in the knitted vastness of it all. It makes me nervous, all that hemmed-in space with insects needling my skin. Whenever I was forced to go camping, I would always long for the accoutrements Richie Rich took on his outdoor trips. When hiking, if I saw heavy equipment or a clearing in the woods, my unease vanished: *A sign of civilization!* or so I thought. A logging road can be beautiful to the fraidy-cats of the world like me who see Bigfoot in every rotted stump, black bears in every shadow, murderers every time a squirrel scurries through the crunchy leaves. I'm not sure most Mainers feel this way, but my relationship with the outdoors is pretty fraught. I was brought up by dirty water and under skies that rained ash. Natural landscapes, subsequently, always felt antagonistic instead of passive scenes to enjoy. The bears, black flies, and Bigfoot were really just a metaphor for other anxieties.

In 1999, my then boyfriend/now husband convinced me one Labor Day weekend to go to Birch Island on Holeb Pond, about four hours from Falmouth, Maine, where we were living. Holeb Pond, with lowlands and waterways and trees, endless trees, is ground zero for biting insects and scary things hiding behind trees. I went anyway, to appear as woodsy as he probably thought all Maine girls were.

We stayed at "Whiskey Jack," a camp built in the late 1800s for sportsmen, abandoned in the crash of 1929, and purchased by my boyfriend/husband's cousins in the 1980s. To access the camp, we drove an hour from Jackman, Maine—a place already on the fringe—on lumpy, tree-choked dirt roads that braid through part of twenty thousand acres of terrain near the Canadian border. We parked our car, offloaded our provisions into the canoe we hoisted down from the roof, and paddled a mile and a half to the shore of Birch Island. I had no way to leave, no Richie Rich Bentley to whisk me away.

After we cleaned up the camp and stocked the fridge, we cast a few lines down at the water's edge. The perch gobbled up everything we threw at them. After an hour, we poured two beers and sat on the porch and watched a pair of mergansers diving for food, our voices an intrusion to their delicate splashing. At dusk, a chorus of loons moaned low, then high, then low, their wolfish howls meeting up with the sinking sun. We fell asleep to their doleful mourns. Overnight, fog snuck in, smothering the pond.

Years later, loons will become a "species of moderate concern," meaning their populations are in decline because of what humans leave behind, such as lead poisoning from fishing tackle and mercury contamination from coal-fired plants. When the loons' unhatched eggs and livers are tested by the Loon Preservation Committee in New Hampshire, researchers will find other chemicals like flame retardants, dioxin, industrial cooling agents, DDT, and chlordane, the latter two both legacy pollutants banned long ago. Mergansers too experienced a cumulative decline of 24 percent from 1966 to 2014, with toxics thinning their eggshells and reducing their prey. These are just two creatures that detect and forecast environmental hazards humans likely will face, too. But the demise of species we poison, disturb, or decimate prophesies more than an imbalance in nature; it indicates a blight in the political, cultural, social, moral, and aesthetic choices we've made. And we repeatedly chose death over life.

. . .

On August 20, 2018, the CDC will release data collected from the Maine Cancer Registry that shows childhood cancer rates in Maine are much higher than the national average.

"These events are random," Dr. Nadine SantaCruz, a pediatric neurosurgery-oncologist, says on Maine's WMTW television.

"Most cancers among children involve no known genetic predispositions or environmental influence," says Dr. Stanley Chaleeff, a

pediatric hematologist and oncologist, about the results. And so it goes. Although both doctors hint at the possibility of environmental factors, neither makes the final call.

The same week of August 2018, I will read in the news about how a spate of dead seals wash up on the shores of Maine's coast. Researchers link their deaths to decades of chemical pollution released into their environment. Marine biologist Susan Shaw, in the *Portland Press Herald*, says young seals are immune-suppressed from birth. "When some pathogen comes along . . . they are very susceptible to becoming very sick and dying very quickly." By the end of August 2018, over four hundred seals have died. While Shaw was able to conclude toxics are killing seals, I wonder how many kids or parents will have to die before scientists start looking in such obvious places as in the junk we toss away.

Thoreau spoke up for wildness. Rachel Carson spoke up for bald eagles; Father Cyr spoke up for trees. But who will speak up for the trivial perch that snap at the ends of our hooks, or the mosquitos that crucify me? Will we wait until they are in danger to voice our disgust?

We also say in our homes and churches and halls of government we value human life, a species at the very top of the food chain, but even there, we insert a hierarchy that determines who among us are species of moderate concern: poor people live downwind and downstream more often than not; rich people can own the Woods more easily than others; one football team gets plastic turf while the other gets mud-soaked grass. Who then will speak up for those of us at the bottom rung, for my father and grandfather and my mother and grandmother, whose livers or uteruses or lungs or colons were never tested as carefully as the loons of New Hampshire or the fish in the Androscoggin or the lobsters in Merrymeeting Bay or the seals in Blue Hill, Maine?

"In Wildness is preservation of the world," Thoreau wrote, but as he aged, he too felt national parks had become overcrowded, too political. He too lived in a nice clapboard house in town with servants and a piano in his parlor. He too always felt "relief to get back to our smooth, but still varied landscape" of less wild places. He too saw the need for compromise when sometimes his texts indicated no such thing. This begs another question; if folks like Thoreau, Roxanne Quimby, John Leane, or Paul Bunyan are unreliable narrators for the Woods and the state, who then shall it be? Who gets to tell our story of logs and paper and land? Father Cyr? God? Hugh Chisholm? Or is it Stephen King, who seems to understand best the horrors of living in Maine? And whose voices will be stifled when we finally choose our spokesperson? The meek will inherit the earth, Father Cyr told me many years ago. He just never said what condition it would be in when we finally assumed ownership.

• • •

I SAY GOODBYE to my mother and Father Cyr, and on the way out of town I stop by my father's grave. There's no mausoleum, no oval-shaped pool, no kitted-out boat or aloof building made of gold. Under the crabgrass lie some of his cremated remains. Some are home on my mantel inside the bowling trophy, where they mingle with the things he found on the ground. For a while my mother tried to keep up his gravesite with fresh flowers but they always withered away too fast. I'm glad she didn't opt for a photo of him on the headstone, because in the aftermath of his death, two years on, I still can't look at pictures of him. In them I remember his emaciated body, sacrificed so I could have a new pair of shoes to start school every fall. And in his eyes, I see me.

HOPE SPRINGS ETERNAL

WHILE DRINKING MY morning coffee in June 2016, I read an article in the *Lewiston Sun Journal:* "NESTLÉ WATERS EYEING RUMFORD'S PRIMARY WATER SOURCE," meaning Nestlé Waters North America, a Swiss multinational food and beverage company and the largest food conglomerate in the world, is negotiating with Rumford's Water District to extract high volumes of water from the drinking water supply and bottle it under their flagship Poland Spring brand, a brand originating in Poland, Maine.

I learn the fate of Rumford's water rests with the Water District, a group composed of Superintendent Brian Gagnon and three unpaid appointed trustees—Harrison Burns, Jolene Lovejoy, and James Thibodeau, in order of birth, who all meet once a month at 3:00 P.M. midweek. While they are appointed by the town selectmen (who meet twice a month and create town policy), they are overseen and governed by the state, so Rumford residents and the selectmen have little say in what the Water District decides; their main objective, according to their basic bylaws and charter, is to manage the affairs of Rumford's water as they see fit.

The Water District's meetings and duties, normally, are not exciting, not even on the most exciting day. Their agendas list things like dump truck bids, new door signs, paving. But from 2015 to 2016, a few more unusual agenda items kept appearing: (1) aging infrastructure (2) Downtown Project (3) Water District Charter and (4) Poland Spring.

1. The aging infrastructure refers largely to the 123-year-old water main that's about forty-eight years past its prime. Its pipes were laid out by Hugh Chisholm, pipes now crumbling under sidewalks that are crumbling themselves. The calculated cost to the Water District is about $500,000, money the Water District doesn't really have.

2. The Downtown Project, slated to begin in 2017, refers to Rumford's downtown overhaul, which includes renovating sidewalks and roads and building new sewer lines. If the town already has everything exposed, it makes sense for the Water District to replace the old water mains.

3. The Water District Charter, which recently changed, authorizes new and expanded unilateral powers for the Water District, including the capability of contracting out the extraction of high volumes of water to corporations for interstate commerce without the approval of anyone except the Water District trustees.

4. Poland Spring refers to discussions of Nestlé's interest in Rumford's water supply and presentations to the Water District by Mark Dubois, natural resources manager and geologist for Nestlé. If a contract with Nestlé is signed, the income from Nestlé would easily pay for the new water mains the Water District can't afford. The Water District has already signed an agreement allowing Nestlé legal entry to the land, and Dubois has already taken initial samples from Rumford's aquifer to see if the data lines up, which means: can the aquifer maintain a pull on the water supply from both Nestlé and the town? The tests come back "favorable," meaning it's a good site for Nestlé to exploit.

Most of these agenda items are discussed at 3:00 P.M. midweek.

Bottled water companies like Nestlé often face opposition in communities like Rumford. Critics complain the company is predatory, targeting desperate communities like ours with promises of jobs and money, and in the end providing little to no income stream at all. While Nestlé says they want to work together with these places—to donate monies for the schools and be part of the town fabric—when it gets right down to it, Nestlé sees water as a commodity and they are there for one thing. A map of their territories would show a series of vulnerable or fiscally unstable towns. Many opponents to Nestlé see water as a right—as critical as air—not something to be sold or auctioned away. Some opponents just don't want trucks rumbling through their towns or chewing up their roads. Environmental activists see Nestlé's activities as nearsighted or motivated by greed because the amounts they extract from the ground are beyond what's ever been extracted before. Others have complained about Nestlé's child labor abuses and trafficking, and yet others complained of their environmental violations and greenwashing. Nestlé has been boycotted around the world for its marketing of baby milk formulas. They have also been sued for fraud.

When companies like Nestlé publicly approach water purveyors, their corporate teams have usually already done lots of footwork, taking advantage of the often weak and outdated local or state laws governing water rights. The only thing to stop them once they eye a site is a groundswell of citizens if citizens can organize fast. But it's hard to impede the steamroller of a wealthy corporation with a deep bench of legal teams who know the lay of the land, so to speak, more than we.

Terry Martin reads the same article I do and tells her daughter, Rebecca Martin, to call me.

"I'd like to assemble a public information session for Rumford," Rebecca says over the phone. "Will you help?"

"Yes," I say. "Whatever you need." After I hang up, I wonder if I had thought her request through carefully enough. I don't want to appear like a know-it-all, someone swanning in with outsider ideas, especially when I am woefully uninformed of the issues at stake. I'm also writing about this town. Should I even be getting involved? But my impulse says water is worth protecting. And if I can help in any way I should.

In 2014, just two years earlier, Rebecca read a similar article in her Kingston, New York, newspaper: Niagara Bottling (a Nestlé competitor) was considering extracting about 1.75 million gallons per day from her public water supply. Rebecca, already a community activist, moved

fast. She studied complex water laws and state water politics, dug into Niagara's portfolio and dealings, communicated her findings, and rallied fellow citizens to lend her a hand. Within five months, she drove Niagara right out of town.

Back and forth on email we go, and decide to feature a panel including me, Nickie Sekera, a well-spoken, highly informed Maine activist who has firsthand knowledge of Nestlé's activities; Nisha Swinton, from Food & Water Watch, a nonprofit that helps communities by providing resources about water issues; and Rebecca herself. To lure residents there, we plan to show *Tapped,* a documentary about the bottled water industry, and more specifically, how Nestlé's presence has affected citizens of Fryeburg, Maine, where Nickie Sekera lives. We get on social media, advertise, write a press release, call friends and family, invite town leaders, including the Water District. On June 27, 2016, the day of our educational forum, we buy donuts and coffee, set up about fifty folding chairs at the Rumford public library, and wait.

The town manager is a no-show, as are Water District trustees. One selectman shows up but leaves after the movie is done. My mom is there along with some of her friends. We take questions from a bothered crowd eager to learn more. Many are outraged at Nestlé's and the Water District's gall, stating they were surprised to learn about the potential arrangement in the news. A handful of people linger and ask if I'll help organize more meetings and I gladly volunteer. I pass out a paper and gather emails, then lick the donut powdered sugar from my fingertips. From here, things happen fast.

I exchange emails with the small group of concerned citizens I had met at the library and we plan to attend the next Water District meeting on July 6 at 3:00 P.M. midweek and agree to come prepared with rigorous questions about what happens next in the Nestlé discussions. We arrive en masse, fidget on our folding metal chairs. Someone from the Water District makes a joke about how nobody ever comes to these meetings, *hahaha*. I point out it's because of the time they are held, at 3:00 P.M. midweek. The Water District folks don't respond.

We ask polite questions one at a time while the trustees face us from a table five feet away:

"Can we change the time of the meeting?"

"How do I go about getting your financials? What is your revenue?"

"What is this really going to bring in besides a lot of trucks and a lot of people unhappy not knowing the security of their water for the future?"

"Are the taxpayers going to have a say? Could we form a citizen committee?"

Some people make statements that are really questions between the lines:

"I own a farm near the proposed site. I moved here because Rumford is affordable and I could live a good life, but if it's going to be interrupted by Nestlé, I don't want to be here anymore. Tons of young people want to move out of Rumford because of the way it's always been. But Rumford's dying. Will this save it or bring in more dying later on down the line?"

"I used to drink Nestlé's Fiji water like it was going out of style but once I learned that plastic containers under Nestlé and under Poland Spring are made from petroleum—that's oil, people, that's oil! You're drinking out of containers made from petroleum by-products."

The trustees respond through their lawyer, who sits amid them and moderates the meeting from the point of ridiculous subterfuge. He responds to every question we ask with "They'll answer your questions in due time," like a robot stuck in 2001 or 1984 or some such dystopia where everything goes wrong.

"When did you start negotiations with Nestlé? You must be able to answer that," I ask.

Harrison Burns doesn't like my question, gets a little gruff, and says something under his breath.

"They'll answer your questions in due time," says the lawyer who has nothing to say.

I ask more questions: "Why do you have legal counsel here? Who pays for your counsel? Has Nestlé contributed any money for it? Who has oversight of the Water District? Does the Water District operate using any bylaws? Why are your meetings at 3:00 P.M. midweek?" I get the same nonresponse.

People sit on the edge of their seats, others make statements from the floor, arms crossed, someone with a baseball hat pulled down over their brow grumbles at a trustee by first name. A newcomer to Rumford, a young man, speaks passionately about how Nestlé's operation and its caravan of trucks would ruin the peace and the land he sought when he moved here not long ago.

"Who's paying you to be here?" he asks the lawyer, frustrated by the silence in the front of the room. "You are stonewalling us, conspiring in the dark with Nestlé who takes beautiful water and puts it into cancer-causing plastic bottles, that will ruin the lives of people in our community and people all around the world. There will be consequences to your actions. Big ones."

Jolene Lovejoy slams the gavel hard, rising from her seat, her eyes steeled. But it's Harrison Burns who finally speaks up: "Just a minute now," he says, a little gruff. "Nobody's conspiring!"

The young man argues back: "You are obviously getting talking points from Nestlé and whoever else. They have a well-planned way, come to towns that are desperate and recommend this code of silence from people who control the water. You provide no answers. No accountability. No transparency. There are sacrifice zones all over the world like this, where once beautiful lands have been laid waste."

Jolene takes the floor. "We are not evil. We're not dummies," she smiles and says slowly in a condescending tone. "This isn't our first rodeo. That's the closest I've come to being pissed off. We're not stonewalling you. Some things require discussions," she says in a way that seems to indicate she doesn't want to discuss a thing.

The tension dissolves with the dispassionate attorney's: "They'll answer your questions in due time" and we carry on. The attorney tells us to submit our questions, on paper, as if Nestlé's money has made the Water District mute or unable to hear, and they promise to respond in kind by their next meeting in one month. A woman asks if citizens can be in on those discussions but the lawyer says the board won't meet privately to discuss anything as it's not allowed.

"If you are going to answer our questions at the next meeting," she starts, "but, as you say, you won't meet privately before then, how will you get your answers?" Conversation and laughs flare up all around.

"We will put our agenda up on the bulletin board," Brian says.

"But that doesn't answer my question," the woman says.

Jolene interrupts. "We are dragging this out."

Someone tries to get them to change the time to a more reasonable hour but the board says the time works for them, that they've always held their meetings at this time. A few minutes later, the meeting adjourns.

Jolene rises from her seat and approaches me fast, comes a little too close to my face. "Who are you?" she demands.

She may not know me but I know her, as does everybody in town, and she likes it that way. She served the town for many years as a scrappy, surefooted Republican: on the school board with my mother; as selectman for eight years; president of the town advocacy group Maine Municipal Association Executive Committee; director of Tri-County

Mental Health Services; on the board of Maine Citizens for Clean Elections; on the board of Black Mountain ski area; and honored as a "Community Hero" for fundraising for Safe Voices, an organization that offers shelter for victims of domestic abuse. She's trim and perky and her short white hair shows off her tan. Jolene lives down the street from my mother, suffers no fools. Which I kind of like.

"I'm Maddy's daughter," I say.

"That makes sense!" she says as she puts her hand on my shoulder. "I love your blouse, by the way." She's wearing a cute sweater herself, a cardigan that ties at the throat. Her straight white teeth look a little sharp.

• • •

IN 1844 HIRAM Ricker suffered from indigestion. So he started drinking spring water from his Poland, Maine estate. Suddenly, he felt better. He shared this same water with friends and neighbors and they all felt better, too. Hiram took all those good feelings and started selling and distributing his spring water in barrels throughout the state. Its reputation and reach went as far as the Chicago World's Fair in 1893, where it was declared the purest water of all. Doctors, with the testimony of that medal, prescribed it to their patients for their various ills. And Ricker, bolstered by all the good feedback, advertised his water as "Celebrated for its purity and wonderful medicinal properties throughout the world" and labeled it "the leading Medicinal and Table Water endorsed by the medical profession" that fixed a number of ills. "Cures Dyspepsia. Cures Liver Complaint of long standing. Cures Kidney Complaint. Cures Gravel. Drives out all Humors and Purifies the blood," one advertisement stated. Business became so lucrative, the Rickers expanded their homely wayside inn into a grand resort, the Poland Spring House, and offered Maine's fresh air and waters as therapeutic and curative amenities to the leisure class. At the resort, you could play tennis or walk on the one thousand acres of land with three lakes in which to swim. Afterward, you might read a book from the six-thousand-volume library under fifteen thousand square feet of covered verandas until evening, when orchestras played at elegant Saturday evening balls.

But there were no real special properties of that water beyond it being clean. There were little—if any—drinking water standards at the time, and so much of what came from the tap had a good chance of being impure or contaminated. It was the absence of dirty water that made everyone feel better, not the discovery of a fountain of youth. Eventually, clever marketing made the water seem like a magic elixir made of something as pure as people thought their souls to be.

The resort fed water sales and water fed the resort. The business grew so much the Rickers built a bottling plant in 1906. It was a win-win for everyone except for those outside Ricker's guarded gated land because the resort was only open to "the representative people of our country," meaning the elite and well-to-do. The Rickers feared, according to the Maine Historical Society, their grand hotel would be overrun by "pic-nickers and excursionists," which was code for the Franco-American millworkers, like my great-grandfathers, who lived nearby.

The same year the Rickers built the bottling plant, Congress passed the Pure Food and Drug Act, the first federal effort to monitor food and drug quality with a "truth in labeling" edict. Poland Spring happened to be on the cusp of old and new. On one hand, their water was pure but the claims about it containing medicinal properties (under the new regulations) would be pretty hard to prove. On the other hand, Ricker's reputation had already been cemented so even if doctors' medical claims were no longer slapped on Poland Spring labels, people believed them to be true.

Poland Spring may still be making snake oil salesman claims but now in three-piece suits in airy boardrooms all over the globe. On some Nestlé labels, the company claims 100 percent of their bottled water comes from natural springs and a class action lawsuit filed against them in 2017 argues they may be guilty of fraud for making such a claim. The lawsuit also states that for Nestlé to gather the eight billion gallons of water a year they sell from the eight natural springs in Maine, each spring would have to flow at a rate of 245 gallons a minute, or more forcefully than a two-inch-diameter fire hose at forty pounds per square inch. My husband compares that force to a P250 gas-powered pump—so named for its 250 gallons a minute flow rate—that the

Coast Guard deploys in emergencies to ships when they are taking on water and are about to sink. The water jets from those USCG pumps are like portable geysers, spitting water overboard as fast as they can. I can't imagine such a spring.

. . .

I EMAIL MARK Dubois—Nestlé natural resources manager and geologist—to tell him I have a few questions and he agrees to meet me for lunch. At a diner across the street from town hall at the appointed time, we introduce ourselves. He's a little jumpy, a little sweaty in the hand.

We sit at a table close to the door and notice we're the only ones here. Water is poured and small talk ensues. I order a salad and he orders the same. I'm tempted to order a beer. But it's still only noon.

When I pull out my voice recorder, he demurs.

"You can't record this," he says, a little red in the face.

"Why not?" I say. "You know I'm a writer and you agreed to meet."

"I will only talk if you turn the recorder off," he says, so I do.

He doesn't say much anyway, now that he's on alert. I state we are still on the record even though there's no tape.

"Who determines where Nestlé drills for water?" I ask. "Is that you?"

"Mother Nature decides," he says with a bit of a smirk.

"That's bullshit," I say, "and you know it is," and we both laugh. But he sticks with his story.

"Mother Nature provides the water. Nestlé just extracts it. The earth provides and we just use our geological expertise."

I stab my iceberg lettuce, look him square in the eye, and see nothing but fog. "Tell me about yourself," I ask, knowing the answers before he says anything.

He grew up in Maine and attended Maine schools, he says, trying out his local guy shtick on me. Because of his Maine pedigree, he acts as if we are friends, which would normally be common ground, but his demeanor comes off as a trained spokesperson rather than a geologist or someone drilling holes in the earth on Mother Nature's advice. I've seen him quoted in newspapers to a nauseating degree about Poland Spring's plans. He's even used in their Twitter ads.

"I'm from Maine too," I respond and look at him with hard eyes. "From here, actually. From Rumford and Mexico. But you already knew that, right?" I ask and pause. He looks confused. "You know my sister. She waters the plants in your office. She heard you or someone in your office say something about me," I say as I push my plate aside.

"What's that?" he asks as he drops his fork.

"She overheard you saying that you were used to 'dealing with' people like me. What kind of people do you think I am?" I ask. Mark has no response.

My kind of people, I think he thinks, are the uneducated people from the small towns of Maine whom Mark believes he can outmaneuver with his plaid shirts, his Maine heritage, and his geology degree.

We finish our lunch at a crossroads we apparently never cross and my subsequent efforts to contact Mark all fail. When Nestlé sets up a community liaison office in Rumford I knock at the door and nobody is there. I step back and look at the opening hours on their sign, which indicates there are none: "CALL FOR APPOINTMENT," it reads. I call a few times but nobody ever calls back. I see Mark at public meetings and information sessions but he won't even look me in the eye.

. . .

ALTHOUGH THE TOWN selectmen have nothing to do with the decision the Water District will ultimately make, our small group of concerned citizens would like to enumerate our concerns about Nestlé at the selectmen's July 21 meeting.

Over email, our group collects data and information about why they don't want Nestlé in town and I collate the notes and write up talking points. When July 21 comes around, the group asks if I will make the presentation. I suggest someone else from the group do the deed, but they defer to me. I have to get special permission to speak, since I don't live in town, but the selectmen all know my mother and say it's okay.

On July 21, 2016, our group files in. A smatter of talk here and there as everyone sits down. The selectmen sit at tables facing us in our wood chairs. My mother and I and the local reporter sit in the front row. Most of the group loiters near the back. Antique lights hang high above our heads, leaving cruel shadows across everyone's faces. We listen to other matters on the agenda before I speak: reports from firemen and budgets and things of no urgent concern. The sleepy eyes of some board members flutter under the stinging lights.

Jeff Sterling, the selectmen chair, introduces me and as I walk to the podium I think to myself, *what am I doing here?* Everything happened so fast but I guess that's the idea; when Nestlé moves, they move quickly. It's hard to keep up.

Before I speak, my mother, who hasn't been to town meetings in years, stands and addresses the selectmen. She calls them out by first name, using her sternest high school secretary voice: "You shouldn't be doing anything without getting the approval of this Nestlé issue from the people of this town." Finally, some of them open their eyes.

I introduce myself and begin, my voice an echo in the large, wood-floored room: "Everyone here probably agrees that Rumford could use an economic injection and everyone here also wants to do what is best for the town. But that is not Nestlé's aim. They attend to their bottom line. Rumford citizens and the environment are not part of that bottom line."

I cite Nestlé's habit of putting corporate rights over public rights. I present data showing an increase in heavy truck traffic may require constant road repair. Nestlé doesn't seem to care about the communities they exploit, that their products have been boycotted around the world, that drinking from plastic bottles can incur health costs. I talk about how bottled water plants wreak havoc on the health of people living near those plants and bring up other complaints about Nestlé over the years. I mention how Maine residents felt Nestlé's presence decreased the quality of life in towns like Fryeburg and Hollis. And, I ask, if they are pumping water from the town well, is it really spring water they are trying to sell?

Someone stands up and interrupts: "You can live twenty days without food but you can only live five days without water. Water is everything. Without water there's no life." A few selectmen roll their eyes.

"We believe Nestlé's request to tap into our water supply represents a change in the nature of our water use and the volume of extraction so profound it merits deliberation beyond the scientific data Nestlé intends to provide," I say as my final plea, look around the room, and step away.

The meeting ends as it began, with friendly small talk and the scraping of chairs. Everyone, Jolene and my mother included, goes out for a beer.

• • •

OUR GROUP STARTS calling itself Western Maine Water Alliance (WMWA). Someone makes a logo, I start a Facebook page, a website, someone else tries to procure a pro bono lawyer, and others enlist the help of like-minded nonprofit groups and meet with leaders of the town. While I'm in Connecticut Googling away, those in the group get their feet on the ground and ask for a moratorium on any decisions about Nestlé. They circulate petitions. Anti-Nestlé signs crop up around town. I post notices of our meetings on a Facebook page, the one where we only discuss the past. The administrator removes them all.

Nestlé holds an "information session" at town hall and I head home to attend. The room is set up like a trade show with different experts at separate stations so Nestlé objectors can't gather in one spot. We spread out and our voices all collide in the acoustically challenging room so our tape recorders don't catch all that's said. I ask geologists and hydrologists what makes Poland Spring water spring water if they are taking it from the town aquifer? Their responses are muddy, misleading, confusing. I record their statements, send them to the lawyers who eventually sue Nestlé for fraud.

As the WMWA grows larger, my role grows smaller. New members, once they get on the email threads, wonder who the hell I am and why someone from Connecticut should be involved. I wonder the same; who are these people taking over my group? The email threads get longer and people are added to the distribution list. More meetings are held where I can't attend. I suggest using Zoom or Skype but most of their meetings take place in an Internet-free Grange Hall. Someone takes notes but the practice soon filters away. It's hard to keep track of all that's going on; I lose sense of the narrative thread, of the ideas I once had about how to keep Nestlé away, like working *with* town leaders instead of antagonizing or blaming them.

Weeks go by. I sense a deeper unease about my role from a new member who ultimately considers himself the new skipper of the WMWA. He begins to leave me out of email discussions, then forwards me a select few—with his comments in ALL CAPS. Maybe I contributed to this ALL CAPS response, but I'm not sure how.

By October, I can't attend WMWA weekly meetings or have coffee at their homes because I'm so far away, have other commitments in Connecticut and New York. My work assignments, a new job coaching a ski team, perimenopause, and driving back and forth to Maine start wearing me out. The 2016 presidential election hovers in the background like an effigy I can't quite see but it drains me nonetheless.

I start receiving even fewer emails and hardly any calls, as they gear up for more local pursuits. The ALL CAPS emails continue and I start to work behind the scenes, emailing town leaders to understand what can be done. By fall, someone from the WMWA says it would be better if I weren't involved. *You no longer live here, you're not really from here anymore, you need to be in town to understand the group's needs* is the general tone. A few people go along. Others are agnostic. I try to convince them millions of people work together remotely, from different places and points of view. But they are not buying my online solution to their local needs. For them the injustices are more acute.

I am a little surprised and upset and get on the phone with one member, defending my right to be involved. Just three months ago they were *thanking* me. What had gone wrong? When I reiterate remote work is easily done, they say *no thanks we'd rather not* and ask for the passwords to the group's social media accounts. Was there a larger group resentment or distrust of me stewing for some time? Had I missed the signs? It was like an ugly breakup, but one where I later had to face the ex all the time.

One person, sympathetic to my fall from grace, peels off from the group, a group that's becoming more divisive and political in ways I'm not. Selectmen email me, asking where I am, but I no longer feel it's my place to say a word. I bow out before Christmas, confused, annoyed, mad as hell.

My response to their rejection mellows over time but every once in a while I think, who are they to decide where I'm from? Three generations of my family are buried in Rumford and Mexico and I was "from there" longer (technically) than most of the people in the WMWA. I'm under no illusion this gives me the right to boss anyone around or have more of a say, but my family as part of the historical makeup of this town *does* give me insight that perhaps others don't necessarily have. My connection to town also needn't deprive them of theirs. Nobody is more authentic, nobody more artificial; we just see what's unfolding from different points of view. I also just wanted to get shit done, to unleash a rejection of my own to compensate for all the injustices I had been seeing over time: that of Nestlé's overwhelming insistence on profiting from the water of communities across the world. What Nestlé was doing wasn't much different than what Ralph Nader's group ferreted out, but instead of paper, water was the resource to be extracted and sold.

I continue to read news of the WMWA's work and cheer them on in silence and from afar. Their petitions and moratoriums and protests and votes all fail to move the Water District to say *no*. The WMWA doesn't fail for lack of heart or smarts but perhaps because of the Water District's apathy and Nestlé's lure. Their failure felt like my failure, too, even in my perceived uselessness or inauthenticity to them.

In December, Nestlé and the Water District announce tentative contract terms: fifteen to twenty years of extracting twice the amount of water from the ground as currently used—up to 150 million gallons per year from Rumford's two town wells and in exchange the Water District would receive payments of $12,000 a month and up to $400,000 dollars a year, none of which will filter through to the town itself except through the coffers of the Water District's bank, an organization that only answers to the state. Nestlé suggests they'll invest $250,000 per year for four years into community projects. There would be few jobs, if any, that would come from Nestlé's business.

One hundred and seventy-five citizens show up for a presentation by Nestlé after the announcement is made. A new Water District lawyer—not the one who kept us mute—says to the curious crowd: "There's going to be plenty of opportunity for input . . . Once we get to a contract that is ready for public review, I will advise the trustees: *'Do not approve an agreement until there's been an opportunity for public input.'* So residents and customers, yes, will have an opportunity [for input]," which is another nonresponse. When the Water District trustees finally speak, their comments sound similar to, and as practiced as, a long-standing Nestlé spokesperson or employee like Mark Dubois.

Nestlé, the Water District, and the selectmen keep referring to the "data" and soon it becomes clear this is their main data point: can the aquifer maintain a sustainable draw from the water supply? The answer, at least according to Nestlé hydrologists and other experts (because nobody else can afford to hire their own), is *yes*; yes the Rumford aquifer has enough water to sustain Nestlé's pull. Climate change modeling data seems to be pinned to a bulletin board of no future concern. Estimates are given on what the Water District will make from a Nestlé contract, but nobody reveals what Nestlé stands to make in precedent. As in other Maine towns like Fryeburg and Hollis, once Nestlé ratchets in, they are as hard to boot out as a sloppy guest who drinks all your beer. Plus, who has the time to fight a megacorporation when you're making minimum wage? Other data not discussed is that Nestlé sells water back to consumers at several hundred to several thousand times the price they purchase it for, a number you can calculate by comparing the water meter bills per gallon to Nestlé's prices per gallon listed on supermarket shelves. And what about the estimated 92.6 trucks every twelve hours that could rumble through town or beat up our roads? Or the losses incurred by farmers who live near the aquifer, or the effects of a long-term drought such as the one happening now? The data they release, in fact, is Nestlé-friendly data that mainly Nestlé provides. There's other data too that isn't considered because nobody seems concerned that making plastic bottles can contribute to environmental pollution and bodily disease. Nobody in Rumford seems to care about those laborers or their communities at all. I wonder if there's any data on human emotion or response to the data they provide?

. . .

"MAKE THE SURROUNDINGS of the workmen pleasing. If this is done, they will be better satisfied to keep their positions, will take more interest in the town's success, and make better citizens," Hugh Chisholm said to the *Rumford Falls Times* in 1905.

Although Chisholm cultivated this industrial paternalism, it wasn't a bad deal for us to have his enlightened but remote management. It allowed us to feel independent even while we were being cared for by his benevolent control. His mandate to subsidize our lives with a glut of choices in stores, banks, roads, schools, churches, housing, opportunities—to be our guardian, incentivizer, benefactor, boss, town father, authority figure, persuader, and sometime inadvertent oppressor—diverted criticism away from what he earned from our labor and what we lost. And while he said his operation wasn't comparable to "working for the company store," the debt we paid was far more grand.

We didn't realize it then, but we, as part of (not separate from) the industrial complex he built, would lose our benefits and protection when Chisholm or his kin went away. In that, we were like his children but not the ones written into the will. So when the Chisholms vacated the premises by death or deed, they left a void in the legacy they so strategically built, a gap Nestlé could be all too willing to fill.

In 1994 Thomas M. Beckley conducted a sociological examination of our dependence on Maine's forest-related industries, and his work underlines the significance behind Chisholm's absent presence and how it pertained to the potential Nestlé pact. Rumford is "not on the way to anywhere," Beckley notes, and its "economic fate is and always has been decided by outside forces." This power structure creates a stubborn imbalance between nonlocals and locals, so when important decisions are made about the town's future, they are often made from the top down rather than from within. This disparity, Beckley suggests, can keep our community from self-determination and sustainable development.

Beckley also discovered few people in Rumford proclaimed themselves community leaders. Many who were named leaders by others

didn't consider themselves as such. The most common response to the question "who are the town's leaders?" was that there were *no* leaders. This type of submissiveness evolved from that unevenness where those without power were ruled and/or robbed by those at the core of it; it's a tale as old as civilization itself and plays out in mega and micro scales as infinite as a fractal. In other words, our reliance on Chisholm impaired us for such future decisions as the one required by the Nestlé ask because the latter won't deliver salvation as the former once did.

In 2016, the World Bank placed the bottled water market at $800 billion. Americans drink twenty-four million gallons of bottled water every day, and bottled water surpasses carbonated soft drinks by volume sold in the US, of which Poland Spring is the best-selling brand, and Nestlé insists Poland Spring is 100 percent from Maine. Because of their need to fulfill their advertising promises; because they need to meet the twenty-four-million-gallons-a-day consumption rate we create; because they need to keep the high market share in their grasp, Nestlé buys up water rights as fast as poor towns across the US depreciate. That seems to be the data they don't want to share or that our Water District doesn't care to know or believe—that there's a difference between need and greed. Then again, who am I to talk? Are ten pairs of clogs too much for my arthritic feet? Do I need four couches or four vehicles or is there nothing wrong with wanting more as we are all taught to do?

. . .

IN MAINE, OUR water is becoming as commodified as our forests have historically been, by outside interests who have no interest in anything but our resources. As *The Paper Plantation* suggests, when you take a natural resource and then sell it back in another package, you get a closed-loop system that fosters a colonized mentality and a colonial state where the only people getting rich are the ones in the loop.

Our Maine state motto, "Dirigo," means "I Lead," but because we allow companies like Nestlé to infiltrate our towns, we are led, not leading the way. This abdication of control to conglomerates concerned with profits and losses leaves citizens with no public voice, no transparency in how our resources are managed or shared, and, if we keep selling out to the highest bidder, quite possibly no water in our aquifers to drink.

Nestlé's statistics show that from 1965 to 1990, the consumption of tap water decreased while bottled water increased, with Nestlé getting over 30 percent of the market share. It's no surprise. Their forty-eight brands of water are visible everywhere you look: at sporting events, gyms, offices, public events, marathons, author readings, on the table at US congressional hearings for all the world to see.

Drawing millions of gallons of water a day from a local source is not what Hiram Ricker intended when he delivered barrels of Poland Spring in horse-carts to people whose wells were impure. Modern economic theory, with its template of never-ending expansion and growth, has perverted Ricker's model and arguably our entire modern world. As the World Bank notes in a study on water scarcity, our business-as-usual attitude toward water—as an inexhaustible resource—will lead us down a "parched path." But it won't be a quick decline. If water isn't managed better by governments and the people they serve, we all will be literally dying of thirst. In Rumford and Mexico there's an additional question on nobody's docket yet: is the water Nestlé's taking from our town even safe to drink?

A COMPREHENSIVE PLAN

LJ (Linda-Jean) Briggs looks out her new office window onto Congress Street and interlaces her soft hands across a stuffed seven-inch three-ring binder as if she's praying. The Board of Selectmen, the elected governing body of the town, hired LJ as town manager in February 2017, the first woman to hold the office in Rumford's history. She's not a selectman, but she and the selectmen have the same basic goals: to determine what the town needs. They work in concert but not equally; while the part-time selectmen generate policy, LJ runs the day-to-day operations of the town and implements the policies the selectmen make.

I am here to ask LJ some simple things: as an outsider to Maine, does she see things like the people she represents, and what can she do to resuscitate the town?

Born and raised in Smithfield, Rhode Island, LJ never thought she would have to deal with so much of the "you're not from here" mentality residents gruffly convey. She's willing to ingratiate herself to them rather than engage with insults or throw them back; she shows up at most town events, is incredibly optimistic about everything, and got her first deer last fall, posting pictures of the dead buck on Facebook for everyone to see. Yet some residents refuse to give her a break. A handful of people berate her online and have conjured a hall of mirrors on Facebook, creating multiple pages and identities so they can advocate their conspiracy theories regarding her motives without anyone knowing exactly who they are.

"There's so much anger pushed on somebody who just happened not to be born in Maine," she says.

"It's not much easier for me," I say, thinking about my experience in the WMWA and Poland Spring.

LJ experienced some success and some snafus in bringing businesses to economically depressed communities like ours. As town manager of Dexter, Maine, in 2013, she resigned from her position before her contract expired, with a signed and sealed agreement that both parties would not "communicate anything defamatory or disparaging about each other to any third party or entity." However, many residents had supported her, stating she "united" town departments under strong leadership and increased employee productivity. Dexter's town council chairman said to the local news that LJ and the council "often butted heads."

As town manager of Waldoboro, Maine, from 2014 to 2017, she helped shepherd into the community a Family Dollar store, a grocery store expansion, a Chevrolet dealership, and Liberty Tree Arms, a firearms dealer. Yet citizens presented a petition to the selectmen requesting to remove her, citing she has no people skills and was not town manager material. LJ, again, left on her own accord.

LJ is a gregarious, confident, broad-shouldered woman with a nose for fixing things and for community service; she, her two kids, and husband all volunteer. She's got a whiff of assertiveness some folks dislike. "I would say I have a strong personality," she says.

Her strong personality serves her well in advancing her ideas, but in a town of "local boys" who would like to maintain the status quo, a bold personality activates strong opposition even if LJ's door is always open and her ideas are pretty good.

"All my life I've said, if my personality were in a male body, it would not be an issue," she says with a sip of water. "Aggressive is good in a man. If it's in a woman, you're called a bitch." I don't disagree. Dictionary definition femininity was never my strongest suit.

LJ wants to make her mark upon this town and her approach—change from the ground up—defies the town's previous focus on beautification, through which it installed logos, signs, and benches, and produced a two-part, 172-page Comprehensive Plan written in 1998 (updated in 2013). But it appears to be less a plan than a summary of the town's history. A current selectman I speak with says of the document: "It's written with a lot of 'pet' ideas but no real action plan to get them done. I read it once and pretty much never thought about it again." It is helpful to me, and probably to LJ, as an archaeological guidepost to lives once lived, which may help determine what the forthcoming path shall be.

LJ, if nothing else, is a person of action, so she came up with her own blueprint for change. She believes Rumford suffers from an identity crisis, one she intends to fix, largely by implementing the plans in that binder she holds—the $4 million Downtown Revitalization Project—and it starts with fixing the broken sidewalks on Congress Street, and hopefully incorporates sewer and stormwater system upgrades, new water mains, LED streetlights, fiber optic broadband, and natural gas lines throughout downtown.

Congress Street, a two-lane, one-way main thoroughfare, is the commercial district with limited commercial. "Overtown," as we call it, currently accommodates a handful of stressed stores and a struggling diner that competes for customers with Dunkin' Donuts. Secondhand stores drift like plastic bags lofting in the wind. Few cars and even fewer people roam the once buzzy street except for at the post office and town hall, where new hurky granite steps lead up to LJ's recently renovated office. A once luminous gift store I prized for its small porcelain animal figurines is now encumbered with stockpiles of woebegone trinkets, secondhand furniture, two vintage inoperable Volkswagen Beetles, and dusty bottles of wine, all buoyed by an old, stained carpet paralyzed by time.

"I am here to do a job and I've got to do what I've got to do," LJ says, flipping through her binder. Her largely invisible upgrades drive LJ's confidence in the resuscitation of the downtown and the community's economic future. "Entrepreneurs and customers are staying away because of these issues. I believe if we build it, they will come," she says, paraphrasing the line from *Field of Dreams,* a film largely about second chances. LJ considers this law of attraction a manifest from which she will re-market the town, polish its identity, renovate it from the sewer up. Her certainty is contagious; down the street at the newly opened Good Karma Cafe, its owners serve organic fast food and tricolored peppercorns with the optimistic price tag of $24.95.

"There's so much potential in this town," LJ says, and she's not wrong. She looks out her window and gestures across the street toward the Strathglass Building—a four-story brick edifice with Ionic columns at the entablature built in 1906. Inside, mezzanine arches soar above an equally grand lobby that originally featured Moorish-style faux marble pillars and a stenciled ceiling. The department store—a refined establishment with a "ladies resting room" lush with thick carpets and glossy wood banisters, moldings, and floors—had once flourished on the ground floor. "The Aztec Room," a mock-Parisian cafe, operated in the basement, with trompe l'oeil murals, a pastiche of new and old, Yankee and Continental, a splendor that was anything but faux to those good people of Rumford and Mexico. The building was later converted to the Hotel Harris, and its elegant rooftop urns were replaced by an unadorned, flat-roofed fourth floor; still, its allure hasn't been vanquished.

Down Congress Street, a beaux arts building with showy vaulted ceilings and columns of Carrara marble once housed the Rumford Falls Power Company. It was also erected in 1906 and designed by the man who conceived the Copley Plaza hotel in Boston and the glamorous Waldorf Astoria in Manhattan. According to its National Register of Historic Places application, "This flamboyant structure expresses the enthusiasm and optimism of this then burgeoning community." The Oddfellows block, an art deco, curved brick structure with a roof parapet, built sometime in the 1930s, is across the street from the Cates building, also curved, a bookend to its opposite and to the town's history of architectural grace. A grant from the Carnegie Corporation funded the John Calvin Stevens–designed Romanesque revival library built in 1903 just on the other side of the island across the bridge. The Chisholm family donated monies for its shelves and books.

In the center of Congress Street, Chisholm built, as a testament to his vision for the relationship between the mill and the town, the Mechanic's Institute. Since its inception it's been an adult-education, after-hours recreation spot and social and civic forum for residents, reborn in recent years with the cheerful and hardworking administration of its director, Gary Dolloff.

"People here are thirsty for economic development," LJ says, "but everything's on simmer right now."

She cites, as proof of Rumford's bubbling future, Nestlé's relationship with the Water District; the forthcoming $5 million Best Western Plus hotel construction down by the river; Black Mountain's recently updated lodge and trails; the possibility of someone building a water-bottling factory; and a tissue machine the mill hopes to install.

"And it's ripe for a national food chain to move in. I mean, when I travel, I'd rather go someplace to eat like Applebee's instead of an unknown restaurant," LJ says.

LJ would like to hire a full-time code enforcement officer to oversee the rental inspection ordinance she also hopes to pass. "Many buildings are owned by slumlords," she says.

When I was born, US manufacturing jobs were already starting to decline, and working-class towns isolated from urban centers, like ours, started emptying out. Rumford's population was 9,363 in the 1970s, and by 2017 only 6,000 residents lived in Rumford and Mexico combined. I never noticed the exodus. It was slow, like toxic drift. With the decrease in mill employees came an increase in empty residences, which led to a glut in housing and, subsequently, these "slumlords" offering apartments for low rents.

. . .

AFTER A YEAR of citizen complaint, nothing dissuades the Water District from making a deal with Nestlé. The Water District agrees to a fifteen-year renewable contract according to Nestlé's preliminary plans.

In January 2018 Governor LePage will appoint Mark Dubois to serve on the Maine Board of Environmental Protection, the body that oversees laws that govern how water is drawn from the earth by Nestlé in seven Maine towns. That conflict of interest has precedent; Mark's boss at Nestlé, Tom Brennan, the senior natural resources manager for Nestlé Waters North America, already serves on the Maine Drinking Water Commission and has since 2002. And up until 2019, Mark Vannoy, who also worked for Nestlé, will have done double duty at the Maine Public Utilities Commission that oversees Maine water rates.

"Have we fallen into a mesmerized state that makes us accept as inevitable that which is inferior or detrimental, as though having lost the will or the vision to demand that which is good?" Rachel Carson wrote in *Silent Spring*. While allowing companies like Nestlé to help us with our short-term goals, putting life-or-death resources in private hands will certainly be our demise. Have we lost the will, as Carson asks, to demand from our leaders more than that? It depends if they make the same mistakes or admit to ones they made in the past.

SEEING RED

I turn fifty that summer of 2017 and wonder about new things like how I will die and who will be there when I do. Other reckonings configure into middle age, such as I have more years behind me than ahead and all those books I want to read will probably never get cracked. I wish I had a binder as big as the one LJ had to organize my own projects and goals. Turning fifty fosters endless computations—how much money do I need to retire? When can I pay off my mortgage? How much does long-term health care cost? I count plastic bottles of Poland Spring water I see in stores, on the street, at events, in people's homes. And more recently, when will menopause start? When will it end? I calculate:

An average woman in the US begins menstruating when she's twelve and ends somewhere around age fifty to fifty-five. I started my period when I was fifteen so I've had the luxury of thirty-five years or 420 menstrual cycles. My period, on average, lasted five days, so I've bled for 2,100 days of my life, which equals 5.75 years. If I changed my pad or tampon every four hours, as the government suggests, I would have used maybe 10,500 pads or tampons over the course of my menstruating life thus far. All the products I used were bleached white, which I know now creates dioxin that's released to the environment and contained in the products themselves. Also, these sanitary products (sanitary?!) were made using a nonorganic cotton, rayon, or synthetic fiber to increase absorbency, most of which carry pesticides.

I probably used more tampons or pads than average because when I was young my periods were above average in blood. In fact, when I was fifteen, I bled so much I needed blood transfusions. My family doctor chalked it up to a "hormone imbalance," put me on the pill, and sent me home. I tried to obtain my medical records from Rumford's hospital to see what he had noted, but they had long been destroyed. "Hormone imbalance" was a phrase so many of us women/girls/females have heard. The remedy? Besides putting us on the pill, doctors told us it was normal to bleed in abnormal ways. I know now dioxin can antagonize estrogens, cause reproduction problems, and interfere with or mimic hormones . . . was that what had happened to me?

Did you know tampons are classified as a medical device, therefore manufacturers are not required to disclose the ingredients therein? The Food and Drug Administration "recommends" tampon manufacturers monitor dioxin levels in their products, but those results are not made public. In junior high health class I was told vaginas are absorbent, permeable, and have a direct line to your reproductive organs (for obvious reasons) so all of us women/girls/females were primed for whatever those tampons contained.

While the dioxin levels for tampons are below our monthly tolerance levels, the safe intakes are set by the Joint Expert Committee on Food Additives (JECFA). While JECFA does not specifically evaluate menstrual products (they look at the safety of food additives), they claim there's no evidence bleaching them using a Totally Chlorine-Free (TCF) process is not safer than products using an Elemental Chlorine-Free process (ECF). This logic (that no evidence is evidence enough to call something safe) tells me nothing, from experts who are not experts on tampons. I am beginning to wonder if *any* experts are as reliable or trustworthy as they are supposed to be.

I do other tallies of bleached paper products: How many diapers did I use as a baby? How many notebooks have I written in? How many books have I read? How many books are published each year? The list seems endless: signs in stores, stickers on fruit, labels, junk mail, postage stamps. How many times did I blow my nose on a white tissue?

The absorption of dioxin from tampons was a concern as early as 1987 and as recent as 2015 but seems to be an area of dithering interest, and I think I know why. The National Dioxin Study, launched in 1983 by the EPA, after $400 million and over a decade of work—proposed that dioxin was a probable human carcinogen and one of the most dangerous toxics known to humankind. This was bad news for the industries that created dioxin, inadvertently or not.

Lobbyists representing beef producers, food-processing plants, farmers, Monsanto, BASF, Dow Chemical, and the paper lobby—the American Forest & Paper Association (AF&PA)—urged the EPA to revise and rethink the damning dioxin appraisal. The AF&PA, specifically, claimed bad science, limited or insufficient evidence, speculation, deficiencies in the development model, lack of clarity, and "little or no added value to the estimation of risk," which all spoke to the "flaws" they declared the EPA study contained. After contentious debates and continued pressure by industry, by the early 1990s, the EPA put the cancer risk dioxin assessment on hold, emasculating all the science and time injected into the work. The study is still incomplete, unapproved, its final draft over twenty years overdue.

I email epidemiologist and former Maine resident Richard Clapp and ask him if the negligible daily doses I receive from trace dioxin in the

J. E. Martin, M.D.
Health Officer
Town of Rumford

A lot of hard work went into this effort. I don't [expect] the townspeople to appreciate it but so what, I especially do it for them anyway. Like a mountain [needs] to be climbed because it was there. I pleased [myself] and that was enough. Someday they will admit it and I know this. What else matters?

— E.N. M.D.

tampons I use are harmful. He replies: "We're not all dying from these cumulative doses, but wouldn't it be better if we didn't even get them in the first place?" I think about the calculations needed to understand what I *collectively* consumed, even in *traces* of dioxin. So many doses in so many ways, with hundreds, maybe thousands of products, calculations impossible to make. And even if dioxin in small amounts was safe, what of the other chemicals legislated as "safe" to enter our blood?

When did it start, this fever for making things so white? Especially things that needn't be, or when we have the technology to use less harmful processes like bleaching things with oxygen or peroxide? We drive production with our appetites for such things, so maybe we need to hunger for safer products that don't leave harmful residue behind. Industry continues to say it's too expensive to change their machines, and people continue to say they're too comfortable with the status quo, but what is the ultimate cost?

PIPE DREAMS

IF YOU MET Dean Gilbert in a bar years ago, which would be the most likely place to meet him years ago, you may not have taken him seriously. In those days we called him Deano and he was a boyish, Muppet-like hell-raiser who skied like his hair was on fire. Yet he would give you the shirt off his back even if it was the last shirt he owned. Now, he's married and settled down a little, but plays drums for Crime Scene, a "High Energy Rock & Roll cover band" whose tagline is "Three Men United Under and Highly Dedicated to the Express Purpose of Creating Pure Rock & Roll Mayhem." His qualifications—loyalty, kindness, energy—are probably part of the reason he's been elected to serve as the union representative for E&I (Electricians and Instrumentation) in the Rumford mill, an institution he believes in with old-world sincerity.

My mill tour last summer was a bust. In fact, it had almost made me feel I knew less. In the forty-five years my father worked there, I never asked him what his days were like despite the mill being the place that defined every landscape he and I ever walked. It was another failure of mine—to not have asked him those questions I now want to ask. These recursive movements I've been making since calling Terry Martin years ago seem to be going nowhere fast, as recursive moments are known to do. Just when I start to connect the dots about cancer and pollution and family, more dots keep appearing like not-yet-discovered dark matter, which is only observable through its gravitational pull.

So I make a date to meet Deano at the Hotel Rumford ("The Hotel"). I want to ask him what it's like to work in the mill. I also want to know if he thinks the mill has a future or will it contribute to the community's decline? Like so many towns, ours is still orbiting around the one thing still apparently making us sick . . . and also about to go extinct. What is the legacy yet to be made, and who will lead the way? Will it be someone like Deano or LJ, or will it be Nestlé, whose path parallels the mill's in so many ways?

When I arrive, Deano's already there, drinking vodka with soda water and a "splash of cran" out of a pint glass filled with cracked ice. It's the middle of January. He gives me a hug and I order a beer. He wears a hooded flannel shirt, jeans, and a pilly wool cap smashed over his thatch of silvery-black hair. He looks a little like a well-loved sofa, which is not a horrible thing. I've known and adored Deano and his family since I was a kid. Our parents were good friends. Our mothers grew up together, our fathers worked together and retired around the same time. Our families skied together at Black Mountain. I remember he used to hit every berm on the hill, performing daffys, backscratchers, or spread eagles as he blasted down the slopes. Deano still skis every day he can, tracking his on-snow days on a device called "Trace," a small, peanut-butter-cup–sized gadget attached to his skis that records number of runs, calories burned, time skied, jumps, air time, speed— proof of his vertical successes, a modern measure of a mountain-loving man. The night before we meet for drinks at The Hotel, he climbed up nearby Mount Abram ski area at dusk using a headlamp so he could count it as a ski day.

"That's day forty-nine for the year," he says. "I do one hundred days every year." I remember he used to stutter, but now he only skids briefly over a troubling patch of words, as if they are made of thin ice.

Home from college on break, my friends and I would play pool at The Hotel and drink screwdrivers until we'd stumble down the narrow, menacing exit steps, high-fiving our former high school teachers on our way out the door. The Hotel's new owners have jettisoned the pool tables; in their place, chairs and tables and families eating supper. The smell of Lestoil bleeds out of the restroom that's notched in the back corner. The Hotel thrums with people and the constant, soundless flickering of seven large-screen TVs that populate the room. NASCAR and Miller Lite posters scab empty walls. The Hotel's hotel-ness is no longer the reason most people come here, although they do rent rooms—I think it's the only hotel in town—with the most expensive at $70/night.

Deano finished his 7–3 shift earlier today. I ask him what's his typical day, and he says his job as an electrician consists of many mundane tasks like changing lightbulbs, as well as operating high-end PLC (programmable logic controller) platforms: "Honeywell, Allen-Bradley, ABV, all systems that drive paper machines."

Electrical problems are unpredictable, so electricians are always on call. Since Deano's been trained to work with higher voltage equipment, those dependent on his skills must wait until he arrives to shut down whatever circuit needs to be shut down, using a "lock and tag" procedure to certify the line is safe to handle, per union rules. Because of the temperamental nature of his job, Deano doesn't have typical days. And his job is more than mundane; he keeps the mill running.

The mill hired Deano into the electric shop right out of high school in 1981. He says they haven't hired many people in his department since. At age 54, he's considered one of the "kids," and within five years he says something like 50 percent of employees expect to retire, not just from the Rumford mill but in the entire corporation.

"It's like having a really good baseball team full of high school seniors. And they are all about to graduate," he says and looks around the room waving to people he knows. The "high water mark" at E&I consisted of about 104 employees in 1989; today, less than half that number are tasked with doing the same amount of work.

Gary Warren, a machinist I met on my mill tour, approaches our table and says hi to Deano and looks at me.

Deano points at Gary. "These guys are very efficient."

"It all comes together," Gary says modestly.

"Everyone has stepped up," Deano pipes in as he jiggles his ice cubes. "Because of automation and other capital investments, guys like Gary can do things faster. But at the end of the day, it's their skill set, their experience that keeps the mill running. But we can't compete with China."

"Every time it's an uphill battle," Gary says. An Aerosmith guitar riff grinds out of a nearby speaker and I can barely hear a word.

"Our mill is pretty old by most standards," Deano continues. "We have some machines that were built in the 1950s and '60s. Our newest one was built the 1980s. We are competing against huge new machines like they have down in Chile and Brazil. They also grow eucalyptus trees, which reach maturity in eight years rather than sixty (like ours) and their environmental laws are pretty lax. It's unreal how they can make everything down there, ship it 3,000 miles and have it come in under our costs."

Gary: Way under.

Deano: Plus they employ children and others who work for lower wages where we are pretty fortunate to make an honest wage. We get compensated justly, but no one's getting rich. People work hard in that mill. Gary's the same way. My dad was the same way. I get up every day at 4:00 A.M. and I've never been sick. I've got thirty-five years in and I haven't missed a day in thirty years.

Gary: Doesn't pay to be sick. We don't get sick days.

Deano: Our guys work hard.

Gary: We've been told if you guys don't work hard, the mill is going to shut down.

Deano: Which is basically true.

Gary: They hold it over our heads. We feel the pressure all the time.

Deano: Maine has lost five mills in the last ten years. Six hundred people here, twelve hundred people there. And it's very real, so when they say something like *if you don't work hard, the mill will close*, we listen.

Gary: We still go in there and work hard.

Deano: It's pride. Rumford's been heralded as having the best papermakers in the world.

Jolene Lovejoy, from the Water District Board, approaches us.

"We're just talking about the mill," I say.

"The mill is still standing," she says with slight sarcasm.

"Deano works there," I feel the need to clarify.

"Well, he shows up and gets a check," she says, laughing.

Deano tells her about his plan to get in 100 days of skiing.

"I don't do anything one hundred days a year," Jolene says.

"You make trouble one hundred days a year," I say. Jolene smiles, preening with pride.

"Maybe 365," Deano says.

"I try," she says. At this, she softens a little, tells us about how she lived in Rumford until she was twelve, and later returned as an adult after going through a divorce with two kids.

"It was a good place to grow up," I offer.

"People's concept of those who live in working-class towns is not positive," she says. "The air pollution has nothing to do with cancer rates in Rumford and Mexico," she says in an answer to no question I ask. "Even though that's what people think. My daughter had cancer and we lived in California. Cancer is everywhere."

"Sure," I say. "Cancer is everywhere. It's true."

"If you've never seen anything else, you never would have left," she says not to me but in a more general way. "But most kids never get that opportunity. It's a choice to live here. It isn't always great, but unless you have something that lures you away . . ."

"If you move, there are a lot of variables," Deano starts.

". . . that you would never be included in," Jolene concludes. "You won't always walk down the street and see somebody you know. Other places? They don't know your parents. Being here is homey, it's security. It takes a lot to move away from here. It's harder to move away than it is to stay. There is such a comfort in being here. You know everybody. Everybody knows you."

Jolene and Gary leave and I think about what she's said. From 2007 to 2013 I moved five times and to three different countries. Nobody knew my parents or my family and that was okay. I could reinvent myself rather than take solace in familiarity and routine. Being unknown was a relief from the past. Spending holidays away from family never made me sad. It was always funerals that made me want to be home because there you know exactly how many people loved someone and how many loved them back.

Deano orders another vodka/cran, his last for the night. "It's a very clean drink," Deano says.

"Speaking of clean," I say, "why doesn't Catalyst make Totally Chlorine-Free paper? It's better for the environment."

When Catalyst, a Canadian papermaker, bought the mill in 2015 from NewPage, a flutter of optimism in Rumford started making the rounds, especially on the workroom floor. *Real papermakers had returned to Rumford at long last!* In a company-wide meeting, Catalyst's president also promised employees he would reinvest profits into the mill and rework the Cogen boiler so it wouldn't explode.

"It's actually cheaper to make TCF paper. But to sell? You have to make what people are going to buy," Deano says and pauses. His eyes water as he chews a big piece of ice. "It's a challenging market. For the first time in two decades though, there's a glimmer of hope. Has Catalyst met all their milestones? No. But the Rumford community has to give Catalyst a big thank you. They gave us life."

· · ·

LATER THAT WEEK when the mill holds its first informational session, made public by a note in the local news, about the new tissue machine they want to install, I attend. I am the only one there besides the three mill employees.

I ask, "Why don't you install a machine that doesn't depend on bleaching tissue with organochlorines? Why not use TCF technology?"

"It's too expensive," they say, and that's the bottom line.

· · ·

I HAVE COFFEE with Deano's mother, Luci, a few days later at Dick's. Her husband, Donald, has been living with nasopharyngeal cancer for twenty-three years and now never leaves the house. The disease had taken away his pride and his ability to be part of a life other than the dizzying array of care Luci provides. At the beginning of his treatment, Donald received three weeks of chemotherapy and radiation, which, according to Luci, killed the cancer. But it returned. At one point, food entered his lungs and when doctors removed it, they damaged his larynx and he lost his voice. He lay in bed for weeks, in a stationary position, unable to speak, with cancer's deceit compounding his slow and numbered days.

As our coffee cools and diners start to leave, she tells me matter-of-factly about her three miscarriages.

"How did you survive such a thing?" I ask.

"We didn't have a choice," she says.

After the miscarriages, Luci and Donald adopted Jodi, who was born with "crooked feet that were fixable," Luci says. "Nobody wanted her. People wanted perfect babies." When Jodi was sixteen, she was diagnosed with aplastic anemia and given four months to live.

"She had these dark spots all over her skin. We couldn't even touch her," Luci says. While Donald worked 11–7 shifts at the mill, Luci tried to keep Jodi alive.

I tell Luci about an aplastic anemia study done through the Maine Department of Human Services in 1993 in which they conducted an investigation of the high rate of aplastic anemia in our county. The report indicated seventy-four people had aplastic anemia between 1980 and 1988. A follow-up study was ordered to ascertain if the disease rates were significantly elevated, and if so, why. Each aplastic anemia case was parsed: some were eliminated from the study because they were referrals from other hospitals; some were eliminated because the state diagnosis didn't fit into the strict scientific criteria; some were eliminated because certain cancer treatments themselves caused aplastic anemia. In the final report, nobody could determine the exact cause. It was as if nobody ever had the disease at all.

Luci says she never heard about the study. "I received only two calls from the CDC," she says. "The first time, they said, 'We are just calling to let you know that Jodi's aplastic anemia is not related to the pollution at the mill,' so I figured, okay. The second time they called, they asked if I would speak to another parent whose child had aplastic anemia. By the time I got up the nerve to call those parents, their son had died."

Jodi survived, an act almost as rare as the disease itself. "How did you beat the odds?" I ask Luci.

"We prayed a lot."

. . .

DEANO SKIS THE last day of the season, May 6, 2017, at Sunday River when snow leaks down the mountain in slivers, fog and mud blemishing his line. Four days later his father, Donald, will die, an event no amount of praying could have stopped.

Seeing Deano, hearing of Donald's death, thinking about diseases strafing our town, made me reflect on my meeting with Ron Hemingway back in 2015. Ron was the United Steelworkers Local 900 union president, Deano's counterpart for a different faction of the mill. I figured he, if anyone, would have been able to tell me if the mill's safety procedures could have prevented my father's or Dean's father's deaths.

When I walked into Ron's office on the outskirts of town, a boom box in the room adjacent vented a static rendition of AC/DC's "Highway to Hell."

"One of our first priorities of the union is safety," Ron said as I sat down across from him. Photos of his family were the only decoration in the room.

Once a month, Ron said, he attended a Central Safety Committee meeting with mill management. Together they worked on choosing a "safety person," an hourly-wage employee who acted as an on-the-floor safety liaison and advocate. It was a three-year position in addition to the employee's regular job.

"The company wanted to make the safety person a full-time job, but the union said no. People get complacent doing the same thing for too long. When change does finally happen, it is not always good," Ron said and paused. "Unions are being dismembered, limb by limb, and the companies . . . well, safety is not their priority."

In September 1989, the mill had racked up 531 alleged federal work safety violations with around three hundred of the infractions "egregious" according to OSHA, which meant "a substantial disregard by this major corporation for the safety and health of its 1,600 employees in the Rumford Mill . . . and serious, willful, and repeat violations." In other words, OSHA maintained the mill's negligence involved knowing about conditions that could result in grave harm or even death to its workers but making no effort to correct them. Boise Cascade, the owner at the time, was fined $1.5 million, one of the largest fines in OSHA's history. In August 1996 Boise again was cited, for other workplace violations.

· · ·

SOMETIME AFTER THOSE OSHA and DEP admonishments, I remember Boise pushed a company-wide safety campaign called "TAKE TWO for safety." The T-A-K-E acronym stood for Think-Act-Know-Execute, the order in which you were supposed to approach a potentially dangerous task at hand. If you spent TWO minutes assessing a situation, the TAKE TWO order conveyed, then workplace injuries would subsequently decline.

Boise plastered the town and the mill and our bodies with flyers, bumper stickers, public service announcements, key fobs, and T-shirts decorated with TAKE TWO in white all caps in the center of a red circle, like a target we couldn't miss. We weathered those free T-shirts like we did our anxiety, the message TAKE TWO a constant reminder that our jobs contained a capacity for death. That slogan also told us *we* were responsible for our safety, that mere seconds could make or break our lives, that it was up to *us* to Think-Act-Know-Execute so we didn't get maimed.

Every once in a while, Boise would publish an update on how many accident-free hours accrued. But what of the billions of pounds of toxics flung into the environment for the past 1,030,152 hours since the mill opened? Yet we wore the TAKE TWO T-shirts like bulletproof vests, said nothing, and counted the hours we didn't die.

After a couple of hours of talking, Ron and I walked outside to the parking lot. He showed me the Worker's Memorial the union built to honor their members who, instead of going home at the end of the day, died while on the job. The tribute is made of a retired one-ton drying gear from Number 11 paper machine. The gear, over five feet in diameter, represents several workplace hazards millworkers constantly face: steam, weight, pinch points, power, and outdated technology like giant exposed gears. As offset gears rotate on the paper machines, their steely teeth create pinch points that could result in a crush injury; it would take seconds to lose a finger, an arm, a life. Periodically, the gears need to be changed and its rigging and enormous weight present other hazards. The gear also illustrates how much industry has changed because workers are at least now safeguarded from the machine's gnashing teeth. Also, when sixty pounds of steam enters the dryer drum, there's always a danger of thermal burns.

"Those were all accidental deaths?" I asked Ron about the names on the memorial.

"Yes," he said and looked over his shoulder toward the direction of the mill. "I guess they don't include the more invisible ones."

Like the TAKE TWO safety program, the union honored the catastrophic hazards but never the indirect ones, the ones slipping in and out of our bodies like a vengeful riptide masked by the sparkle of the ocean's lure.

At the memorial's inauguration on April 28, 2013, a small crowd collected and sat on metal chairs in front of the industrial shrine. State senator John Patrick of Rumford, who had been gassed in the mill years ago, said in his speech, nobody should have to die a needless death, which echoed what Scot Grassette, who initiated the memorial, said in the lead-up to the event in the local news: "You shouldn't have to die making a living. Everybody wants to go home the same way they came in." The president of the AFL-CIO also took care to comment on how asbestos-handling precautions and other safety issues had improved. Ron then read the names of the twenty-one people they were there to commemorate. After he finished, a bell tolled for each life, for each death.

Ron was diagnosed with mesothelioma shortly after he and I met in 2015. Over 130 people attended a benefit for him at the American Legion in Rumford in the middle of a ferocious snowstorm. At the event, they raised money for his family by holding a raffle, an auction, and a 50/50 drawing. People ate spaghetti and meatballs, danced to a live band, and sold T-shirts with "HEMINGWAY STRONG" in the design. The Facebook promotion for the event said: "Anyone who knows Ronnie and Yvonne Hemingway know that they have spent a lifetime giving to others! We want to give back!"

. . .

WHILE MY TALK with Deano was instructive about the present-day operations of the mill and how it was different from the past, I didn't learn much about the future of making paper as a whole, as it was way outside my area of expertise and maybe even Deano's. I call a paper mill consultant who's willing to tell me what he knows—but not willing to publish his name because he thinks papermaking is a dying industry and doesn't want to give up clients just yet.

"Papermaking in the US, that probably won't be around in twenty or so years," he grimly begins our conversation. The United States, he says, was so successful in manufacturing things like textiles, paper, and shoes because we had virtually no environmental or workplace protection, no unions, allowed child labor, and had immigrants willing to do the work for a lot less money. "In other words," he says, "industry in the US operated like a colonial enterprise. We were able to have an extraordinary amount of economic success that way. That's no longer possible."

He tells me China's not the problem as Deano suggested, at least not in the way I understood. China's *direct* effect on US papermaking is that it competes with us for the main raw material, OCC (or old corrugated cardboard), which kept OCC prices up for quite a while. When the Chinese government put restrictions on its import, that drove the US price of OCC down. The see-saw in OCC prices benefits and hurts producers who use OCC versus virgin fiber as their main raw material. China's *indirect* effect on US papermaking is that containerboard producers used to make boxes for nearly all US consumption of consumer goods, like sneakers and toys. Now that China supplies so much of our nondurable goods consumption, the boxes that protect them during shipment have to be made in China. The growth of US imports of goods of all kinds broke the traditional link between the growth of the US economy and the growth of domestic containerboard production. Today, box demand is related to how much we consume, not how much we manufacture.

He cites other factors contributing to the decline of papermaking in Maine, like high transportation and fuel costs and our mill's remote location. "It takes fifty to sixty years to grow an oak. It takes five to grow a eucalyptus in South America. Eucalyptus trees are cloned, so all the fibers are the same, which makes for much more pulp consistency and more efficient papermaking. In Maine, the wood pulp is a different mix every time. So it's cheaper to grow trees and manufacture paper in South America and ship it to the US than to make it in the US. That's how the industry will die."

His prognosis for the paper industry, perhaps all American manufacturing, mirrors what Ron, Deano's father, my father, my grandfather, my grandmother must have felt while they died, quite possibly from industry itself: "It's like an hourglass where the sand goes down, until finally there's nothing left."

THIS IS NOT A MAGIC WAND

WITH NESTLÉ LARGELY in the rearview mirror, I feel defensive about my hometown, more than I've ever felt, even while being rejected by it—by practically being called a fraud; my home base had been attacked. I take after my mother in that way, defending the underdog at all costs, even if the underdog was a town that has caused so much grief, even a place that took my father away. The Nestlé debacle and my talk with Deano also made me see there were other problems voiced by people of this town (underdogs themselves) when I had only been focusing largely on just one: pollution. This was a shift in the landscape for me, to look outside the confines of my own grind. There were issues equally as pressing that required attention—commerce, education, leadership, recreation, poverty, hunger, policies and politics, crime, drugs, and other assorted fears—if I was going to understand this place from all sides. Nestlé also showed me there were people willing to voice their complaints as well as wanting their town to mend.

Little by little as I back away from trying to directly help, I know this is the best place for me to be: in Maine but backstage. Change needs to come from them. That doesn't mean I can't have a voice too. It's just one that comes from another place by other means.

. . .

IN JANUARY 2017, right after the presidential inauguration, I go home to Mexico to get my hair cut at the House of Beauty, a small establishment with three hairdressers: Stephanie Young, "Original" Heidi (Heidi Merrill), and "Other" Heidi (Heidi Arsenault). Just about everyone in New England has a nickname, as if the formality of our given names is too uncomfortable to bear. Marie Therese becomes Terry and Madeline becomes Maddy and Dean becomes Deano. If your name wasn't convenient to trim or you had a certain flaw, you'd be christened something else like Stumpy if you were short or Squeaky if you had a high voice. The nicknames are not designed to demean; they're shortcuts to define who you are.

At the House of Beauty, haircuts cost $15 and a cut and color $35. If I tip another $15, it's still cheaper than getting my hair cut in Connecticut where I live. Including gas and tolls to get here. I used to come to this very place (with different hairdressers) when I was in high school and occasionally had my hair permed so it would feather better . . . but it never did.

My mother's appointment is before mine. She shifts to Original Heidi's Naugahyde chair while I wait my turn. A menace of hair products and tools litter the faux marble countertop. Combs float like preserved specimens in Barbicide, the sinister-looking blue fungicide/viricide/pesticide/germicide that kills everything from the HIV virus to lice. Over Original Heidi's station, on the wall, a comb fastened to a paper plate and scrawled in black marker: "This is a comb, not a magic wand." Below the sign, school photographs of her daughters, from kindergarten to school dances and all the ages in between. A handmade card scrawled with "Mom, you have the best heart" enclosed in a hand-drawn cartoon heart.

Original Heidi's ancestors came from Germany. "They spelled our name V-A-U-G-H-A-N but changed it to V-O-N to Americanize it," she says to me as she spins my mother around. The other side of her family is originally from Ohio. "Nothing cool like French Canadian," she says as she kicks back the chair with her clogs and tips my mother's head into the brown porcelain sink. My mother closes her eyes. Above, a vintage tin ceiling the color of fog.

"I never thought being French Canadian was cool," I say.

"It's more interesting than being from Ohio," she says.

Hairdressers hear everything, Heidi says as she washes then turbans my mother's hair. She mentions a customer who bragged about a Halloween party during which she'd dosed her five year-old daughter with Benadryl to prevent any interruptions to the festivities. A customer says in response, "There was an overdose this morning. A five-year-old."

"Did the child die?" Original Heidi asks matter-of-factly, chopping away, not looking up.

"I don't know," the customer says, returning to her magazine.

"The police carry Narcan but not EpiPens," another customer says, rolling her eyes. "Why are they saving the lives of druggies?"

Heidi stirs a pot of hair dye and paints it on my mother's head. While my mother's color sets and she reads a magazine, someone murmurs "Donald Trump," a topic that hangs over our conversation like a soggy loaf of bread: flaccid but not easy to ignore.

The voting lines were the longest Original Heidi thinks she ever saw in Mexico. "But people voted more on issues and not necessarily for the president," she says.

Mainers voted to raise minimum wage to $12/hour by 2020, to legalize marijuana, to employ ranked-choice voting rather than plurality voting, and to raise taxes on incomes over $200,000. Voters struck down a referendum for background checks before a gun sale. And in Mexico they voted overwhelmingly for Donald Trump. Four years before, Mexico had voted overwhelmingly for Barack Obama. It was the most dramatic reversal in the state.

One of the customers says to nobody in particular, "There were a lot of uneducated people voting." None of us respond.

After Original Heidi rinses out my mother's dye, I take the chair.

"Have you ever thought about moving somewhere else?" I ask jokingly as she rakes a comb across my hair. "Somewhere where you can charge more?"

She laughs. "We can't leave. People are too poor! Or single parents, like myself—I can't take my daughters away from their father. I'm sure there are other situations . . . People are also afraid. Last December, around Christmas, we kept seeing big helicopters flying low over the valley and even though the idea was ridiculous I thought, are we under attack? You get this pit in your stomach."

"Under attack?" I say.

She stops combing and looks at me in the mirror, her hand on her hip. "People were scared for a few weeks," she says, then drapes a towel over my face because she knows I worry about dye splashing in my eyes.

I lie there in the terry cloth darkness thinking helicopters can mean so many things. It could be the US Coast Guard whisking someone away to shelter or medical aid. Or the sound of a CEO taking off on a private whiskeyed flight. It's the DEA, military training, a forest fire, a news station. It's never an assault on a small town in Maine. For Heidi, maybe the fear of being attacked was the fear of uncertainty itself.

Our chatter turns to discussing people we both know: Derek Adams, who went for a hike just before a heavy snowstorm in December and is still missing; how so-and-so had been arrested or died from cancer; James Meader, who played a prince in the high school musical when he and Stephanie were teens.

"Did you know Ron Hemingway?" Original Heidi asks. "He has mesothelioma. I used to do Zumba with him before he got sick. His wife's brother Dennis just died of mesothelioma, too."

"I talked to him," I say.

"My grandparents also all died of cancer," Heidi says as she rinses dye from my hair. "Everyone dies of cancer around here." Others in the salon nod.

"It must have been so frustrating for your father," Original Heidi says about my father's cancer, trimming my bangs. "He was always so active."

"Yeah. It was. He was."

Back in Connecticut where nobody knew him, people would ask when they learned of his death: *How old was he when he passed?* as if he had an expiration date. *Not old enough,* I would say, my eyes like seeds. He outlived the current life expectancy for a male in America, that much is true, but the graceless question is a scrim of jagged fibers thrown into the air. I appreciate Heidi's words.

I flip through hairstyle magazines. I have my mother's hair: it's coarse, gains girth like a tumbleweed so I'm always trying out new cuts that never seem to work. I point to a picture of a woman with a short bob.

"Maybe this?" I say.

"That would look cute," Heidi says as she takes a step back and looks at my head.

She whacks a couple inches off, then proceeds to snip until my hair comes up to my chin. When she's done, I look in the mirror, the same one I looked in during high school, and I see my hair as I did then, uncooperative and too thick, with cowlicks in the wrong places. I put on a hat before I go. Mine, like the town's, is a beauty never quite attained. If only someone had a magic wand.

Three months later in April 2017, I learn Ron Hemingway's name is read aloud in front of the memorial for workers killed on the job—the union's admittance of the mill's role in his death. Ron, who heeded every warning, attended hundreds of safety meetings, made the mill safer for his union members, and Thought-Acted-Knew-Executed probably more than anyone in the mill, found there was no user manual, no amount of planning or sorcery or prayer, no risk assessment that kept his scarred lungs from hardening, constricting, then seizing up in a final intake of breath.

. . .

ALL ACROSS THE US, people were surprised by the working-class political flip. *What happened in four years?* they asked about the 2016 election results. The thing is, nothing happened in four years. But a lot happened in forty years. I wasn't surprised in the least.

In the seventies, not long after I was born, Nobel Prize winner Milton Friedman argued that a corporation's only responsibility was to its shareholders, not to any altruistic ideal, which influenced conservative political thinkers in DC who were also hell-bent on trusting the free market to balance itself out. The only thing to trickle down, however, was the understanding that we were on our own. It was every man or woman for themselves. Then Maine's economy crashed from the energy crisis and our manufacturing jobs took a drop but that was only a footnote in our long-term plight. In the eighties we faced the strikes, the dioxin scare, and a recession settled in like a winter that never ends. My father stared into the mouth of *make it fast and make it cheap*, which was the beginning of the end for the working-class.

Meanwhile, as thinkers shouted about the end of geography and the nation-state, we adjusted as one does when driving around a double-parked car. Our mothers went to work because our fathers' wages weren't enough and kids were left holding the physical and metaphorical keys. We hunkered down. Modified our dreams.

In the optimistic mood of the early nineties when I graduated from college and the Berlin Wall was being dismantled, democracy and liberalism swanned all around. In my town? Lives were collapsing faster than that damn wall coming down. Our movie theater? Gone. Clothing stores? Gone. Churches? Gone. A place to buy a bicycle, underwear, a wedding ring? Gone. Restaurants? Gone, gone, gone. Businesses thinned out like an old man's hair. Megastores moved in to our towns and rightly so. We needed their aggressively low prices and their full-time jobs to employ our mothers who had been laid off their other jobs since. In the background, the opioid crisis every town felt; at least we weren't special in that.

Corporations became people then globalization came like a shooting star but we had been left out of its orbit altogether. We were detached from this new global currency, where information was the raw material and tangible commodities like logs or paper were not. As

America began to deindustrialize the upward mobility of the working-class corkscrewed shut and opportunities limped away with the gazebos and bandstands that once furnished our towns with happy diversions. Our hope for future prosperity went into a tailspin as furious as when a Stuka got shot down. Meanwhile, pollution hovered like sorties flying low over our lonesome town.

Our undoing was a gradual assault, almost indiscernible, like ice hardening over a culvert. We tightened our belts and tried to keep our lives from collapsing from high taxes or disease. The wealth gap widened until we couldn't even see the other side. The recession of 2008 terrified America, but nobody in my town found it remarkable. We had been living with a shitty economic decline for decades. Nobody noticed because they had been looking the other way.

Those decades fed into the architecture that led to our forty-fifth president and the vote in Mexico, Maine. Robert D. Kaplan provides insight to this parade in his 1994 book *The Coming Anarchy*: "Think of a stretch limo in the potholed streets of New York City, where homeless beggars live. Inside the limo are the air-conditioned postindustrial regions . . . with their trade summitry and computer-information highways. Outside is the rest of mankind, going in a completely different direction."

Most people riding in limos didn't even bother looking out their tinted windows as they sped past our towns. We watched as we had been doing, from the other side of the paved road, a stone's throw away from the message but not the action, simultaneously within sight of wealth but without access to it. Trump, however, saw us. And even if he too was riding in a limo or using a gold leaf toilet, even if in the end he didn't provide what we needed, at least he stopped, opened his door, and said hello.

As Original Heidi said, the election wasn't about *who* people voted for, but *what* they voted for (or against). And believe it or not, Mexico voted for hope, just as it had done in 2012. People hungered for change, *any* change even if it required making a Faustian bargain of sorts. Trump tapped into years of broken promises, broken policies, and our mistrust of government that even Obama's celestial presence couldn't erase. His gaudy, gold-tinged gleam, which I had admired in a previous life, still resonated as a manifestation of success. Trump also spoke our language, or a facsimile thereof, in a rough-edged, direct, every-man-or-woman-for-themselves kind of voice we had been trained to value. That kind of talk exploited our admiration of and participation in the independent, no bullshit life we had lived.

In the lead-up to the election, it seemed Democrats had already accepted the deconstruction of the working-class and had moved on to more cerebral things. I remember their discourse about gender-neutral bathrooms, but those conversations didn't pay the rent; it's not that we were unsympathetic to such causes but we had nothing left to give. We already had enough to worry about, like the possibility of being crushed by a paper roller, getting cancer, or how to make ends meet. We also wanted to be reasonably sure that the *whop-whop-whopping* of helicopter blades was not because the town was under attack. Losing your mill job is like losing your identity (as the strikes of the 1980s had shown). Those are identity politics in a working-class town.

In the acute aftermath of the election, the only thing I *was* surprised about was my friends' surprise at the result. Many blamed the working-class—in part—for America's presidential faux pas. All across social media and at cocktail parties I attended, Trump voters were called racists, bigots, rednecks, conspiracy theorists, religious nuts, or just too ignorant to know what's good for them. One friend said Trump voters "aided and abetted" the election, as if voting itself was a punishable crime. This kind of dialogue reduced people in my town to labels, to clichés, to a reductive configuration instead of humans voicing their feelings of injustices sharply felt.

This censure, by those who previously championed the working-class felt like a moral injunction; it was as if another flip had occurred; people disparaged the working-class for doing exactly what they pressed us to do: vote. They just didn't like the result. They thought we were wrong, said *they* knew better, said our ignorance was a determining factor, dehumanizing a people who had already been dehumanized enough for the past forty years. And if I know one thing about the people in my town or Maine as a whole, it's that we don't like being told why we do what we do, especially by those who have no understanding of our lives. Ours, not unlike Trump's, was a struggle for recognition, to have a voice in our future even if that meant compromising the present.

. . .

HERE ARE A couple of things *nobody* voiced in the election cycle; first, manufacturing paper is a dirty process. It uses and produces toxic, dangerous chemicals that we all knew about to some degree. For decades, we buried contaminants beneath our soil, released them into our air and water. People in Mexico and Rumford got sick, appeared to die in curious clusters. Most said nothing. Questioned nothing. Cashed our paychecks at the end of every week and accepted the fact our illnesses were a fact, told ourselves it was acceptable to accept the inevitable. Everyone in town, including my own family, remained mute for over a century. Where was the pageant of empathy then? Where were our goddamn voices then? These economic strikes against us were reinforced by the actual union strikes, and on the final pitch—the environmental strikes against us were almost too much to bear—everyone just watched the ball go by like my father told me never to do. The 2016 election was our last at-bat.

Second, a large contingent of people in Mexico have descended from French-speaking Canadians, people subjected to the same kind of prejudice and intolerance Trump started to embrace. I was surprised Mexico voters could not see that connecting line, a straight line from fear to their heart of hearts. Then again, silence deadened our anxieties about the flecks that floated into our milk or landed on our fields. Silence kept our feet adhered to the ever-shifting ground of a week-to-week life and stifled our fears, fears that were better left unsaid. Without silence, without the stories we told ourselves, we would have helicoptered away ourselves into curdled skies. We had been trained by the mill to fear gears that churned near our heads, to fear losing our jobs, to fear the day when the death bell tolled for us. And we learned to fear the unknown, but the unknown was all we ever knew. Even the safety guy at the mill couldn't usher safety to us or himself. Who in the world could? So it was easy to miss that historical link, the one dot we didn't connect.

There's no singular catastrophe that brought this town to its knees and no single solution to bring it back. Trump is the symptom not the disease, like a boil on your ass, which denotes an imbalance in diet or in skin pH. In fact *everything* is lopsided in the US right now: our incomes; our politics; our access to power, recognition, and global affairs; even our bodies' cells. And those of us just on the other side of the foul line, outside the seats of power and progress, suffer the worst.

TESTIMONY

In Mexico, voting for Trump was a backlash to all the prosperity out of reach, a backlash to the world going global while Rumford and Mexico just ran in place, a backlash to the working-class not having a loud enough voice. I start snooping around town in bars and salons and schools: to listen more closely to what these voices have to say. I had been so involved with drumming up the past, with trying to figure out why Doc Martin's pleas went unheard, that I wasn't paying attention to folks who had been ignored, people right in front of my face.

After our haircuts, I meet up with an old friend and ask about his work in the mill some years ago. "I worked in chemical unloadin' for a while," he says, speaking with that familiar Maine accent and manner I've known all my life.

In my first year in Beloit College, friends would ask me to say certain words where I dropped my *r*'s, like in "rivah," then they'd laugh at my accent, so I laughed too, and my accent vanished as quick as the teasing it provoked. Their reaction and my dialect, if that's what you call it, made me feel dumb, like I had an unsophisticated way of talking that betrayed an unsophisticated background.

While they wore L.L. Bean sweaters I couldn't afford, I washed dishes for work-study coin. I never let on at college I didn't know about Greenwich Village (Where is it? Why wasn't it pronounced "green witch?") or that grilled cheese sandwiches were not called, as I thought until then, *gorilla* cheese. Their accents and behaviors and clothes, they were all a new language I simply had to learn. So I adopted and adapted, sampling identities like I did the cereal bar in the campus cafe. But assimilation didn't always turn out so well. One summer when I came home wearing the style of shredded jeans that were popular among my new well-to-do friends, the dad of my best friend in high school saw me and said, "You wouldn't wear those if you had to," and I never put them on again.

When I hear the Maine accent mimicked in movies by actors whose mouths don't quite wrap around the *r*-less speech of the non-rhotic kind, their studied fake accents are the target of my own laughter now, not for sounding like Mainers, but because they don't. I listen to my friend's testimony, for that's what it is:

Mercury. And that's all in the ground down there. They didn't tell nobody nothin'. They buried it down there. You know what? The cancer rate in that mill is un-be-liev-a-ble! Can you imagine how much mercury is in the water down there? It's there for-evah. I don't care how high in spring the rivah is. That don't wash away. Mercury's too heavy. That's in the watah. Do I know anybody else who wuhked in chemical unloading? Ha ha ha. They're all dead. Please don't put my name on this. When you live in this town it's amazin'. See, I get my pension through the mill. There's a little clique down there. You ain't gonna believe it. This town is smaaaaallll. My sister still works there. I'm afraid they'll go after her and she'll lose her job. They even pushed doctors out. One time, the mill doctor told me I had pneumonia and it wouldn't get any better so my wife called another doctor. He did X-rays and a culture. He says, "Where do you work," I says, "the mill," he says, "you got chemical burns." They tried to cover it. So my health records in the mill say one thing and my real health records say another. Yeah, so he sent me to Lewiston to see a specialist and I had to have surgery. Then I had to get a lawyah because the mill still said it's pneumonia. Then they started sayin' it's from cigarette smokin'. Even the doctor who did my surgery signed a paper that said it's not pneumonia, it's not cigarettes. Chemical burns. That doctor that told me I had burns? The mill pushed him right out. He left town.

You're around chemicals, asbestos, you name it, it's in there. They hid so much from people it's scary. The chlorine leaks. We've all been gassed. My friend got trapped in an elevator durin' a chlorine leak. It almost killed him. There was quite a few of 'em trapped. My friend said, ya know, you're up five hundred, six hundred feet in the air and there's thoughts of even jumpin'. Ya know you're goin'.

To make paper you need chlorine, black liquor, green liquor, and sometimes the mixture when they're making it escapes. I worked in the chip loft in the Kraft room. There was gas alahms everywhere. There was so much gas they disconnected the alahms. They could give a shit about me. They just didn't want to hear the alahms. I'd go home and you couldn't get that shit out of your clothes, your hair. The stink. But I would never take a salaried job there. Because they own ya.

Working-class people and Acadians (he is both) in my town, we were never known for our ability to speak up, but we always spoke out as if we were learning the world with our mouths open. This was a kind of public performance; unless we were saying it out loud, it wasn't happening, we weren't sorting it out, as if to say, *We are all in this room together so let's not pretend otherwise.* Our urge to talk belies all the times we couldn't or didn't because of all those prohibitions on language itself. Words hold weight when spoken. This is a language unto itself.

I can't calculate how many hours I loitered with friends or family doing nothing but taking turns saying our piece—in kitchens or anywhere we shared a social moment: the bank, the grocery store, the picket line, the VFW, a basketball game. My mother's running commentary—like a leaf blower, like a bee—as she goes about her daily tasks. My father's teasing zingers when he saw an old friend walking toward him on the street. Doc Martin's speeches at town meetings. Terry's stories I try to prove. Dot Bernard's genealogy files that began other conversations too numerous to list. My whole town, with one voice layered over another in a symphony of complaint and community. These voices contain every voice that has ever been maligned, ignored, vaporized, marginalized, their testimonies like a prayer, a recitation, an invocation, all uttered as if to say, *Here I am, here is a space I can exist.* Those spaces

have always been limited for people like us, like the nook in the *aboi-teaux* that squeezed salty water out of our ancestral land. But we can reclaim language like we did the land, within the gaps of history we find ourselves dominated by. For if we articulate our thoughts in these spaces where we are recognized, then we exist. Isn't that what identity or having a voice is all about?

VARIABLES

I flip through my mother's high school yearbook, *The Pep,* she keeps in a side table drawer by her sofa. In 1960, the year she graduated, most girls wore short white socks with knee-length skirts and arranged their hair into wavy pin curls with micro bangs. Boys wore buttoned-up shirts and ties. Their neat flat tops—apogees of the current moment—drew a horizontal line across the page linking one boy to the next. Under my mother's headshot, the phrase "NEVER AN IDLE MOMENT."

Only fifty-eight kids made up my mother's graduating class, yet there existed the enthusiasm and a sense of heightened engagement with the community larger towns enjoyed. Her school hosted social clubs of all kinds, and advertisers in the yearbook end pages show a place anyone would want to live—Lamey-Wellehan shoes and stockings, the Lowe Brothers paints and varnishes, Cal's barber shop, Ferland's dairy, Fournier's foods, Hamann's wallpapers, Vito Umbro the tailor, Gleason's hardware, Lee's butcherette, Bouffard's furniture, Bisson and Hebert auto shop, Puiia's hardware and lumber, Kersey's jewelry, Georgette's hat shop, Larry Stanley's menswear, Meader & Son ambulance service—because they were all run by people who everyone knew.

After high school, kids got a job at the pharmacy, the mill, the grocery store, or became a housewife, a teacher, a milkman, the guy who delivers oil, or worked as a secretary as my mother did until she had kids. She returned to the labor force during the strikes and retired in 2009 from the school district, where she still works part-time. As a special education aide, she cares for those kids as if they are her own. One day she'll make spaghetti and meatballs and the next she'll be listening to their furious wails, calming them with *It'll be ok. No need to yell,* then receiving their cheery hugs. The school offered her a full-time position because they also have the highest percentage of special education students in the state. My mother balked. She values her time as much as the money she gets from the work, and balances the two like she still balances her paper checkbook: to the penny. I look out the plate-glass window, and there goes my mother at age seventy-five still leaving for work.

I'm heading to school as well, to meet Lisa Russell, my childhood friend, for lunch, then observe her math classes. Lisa was street smart, cool-headed, practical, yet also user-friendly—like a well-designed Danish chair. I had Facebooked her, somewhat, out of the blue and we started talking right where we left off at age eighteen. I asked her what it was like to teach high school in the same community where we grew up and she invited me to come and see for myself. My day in her class doesn't require any special permission since my mother is so well liked and connected to the school. I just say *I'm Maddy's daughter* and that statement opens doors I cannot alone.

• • •

"I'M HERE TO visit Lisa Russell's classroom," I say to the intercom and get buzzed in. When I check in to the main office, the secretary gives me a visitor pass and asks if I'm Maddy's daughter. "One of three," I say.

Above the whiteboard in Lisa's classroom: RESPECT, BELIEVE, PERSEVERE, STRIVE, ENCOURAGE, EMBRACE in cheery, multicolored letters. Polygon tables dot the room. I give Lisa a hug.

Lisa's daughter Marie, age twenty-five, teaches French and is installed in the classroom next to Lisa's and has joined us. "Nice to finally meet you," she says, vaguely avoiding my outstretched hand.

Mother and daughter often eat their twenty-minute lunch together. The fare usually consists of foods like yogurt, hummus, pita chips, raw broccoli, and fruit. Maybe a granola bar. We talk about Marie's recent engagement and the practice of women who change their last name when they marry. Marie plans to change hers.

"Feminism is about choice," she says a little defensively, as if she's had this conversation a thousand times. "And that's my choice." I can see Marie wrestles with this choice and her choice to live in Rumford, which she declares she has a "love/hate relationship" with. She sometimes dreads the possibility of living here the rest of her life. "It's a bit like living in a bubble, but it's also comfortable and easy to stay," she says, mirroring what Jolene Lovejoy expressed at The Hotel.

Lisa owned and operated a travel agency in Rumford until September 11, 2001, forced her to close. "Nobody was traveling anymore," she says. With no other promising job opportunities, she started working at the school as an education technician while taking classes at the University of Augusta. In 2003, a high school math teacher died from a heart attack and the school asked Lisa to fill his position. She's worked there ever since.

While I headed out the door after high school, Lisa, like Marie, stayed. She stayed despite and because of all the variables pulling her away. For small-town kids, it was the biggest decision we faced. Leave and you cut yourself off from everything familiar, everything you love. Stay, you may isolate yourself from other comforts and opportunities you don't yet know.

Lisa is happy Marie stayed but would be fine if she decided to leave and fine if she kept her surname. Lisa, however, does want grandchildren.

"Tell my mother you can lead a fulfilling life without children!" Marie pleads.

"I reserve my opinion," I say.

"She has her softball team!" Marie says.

"They are like my daughters," Lisa admits. I've seen Lisa's players cluster around her, as if any amount of her attention, her high expectations, her constancy, will somehow rub off on them. It usually does.

Brenda, the special education teacher, joins us. After she introduces herself, sits down, asks me, "Who'd you marry?"

"Nobody you'd know."

"Kerri doesn't live here anymore," Lisa says.

"My husband's from Massachusetts," I say.

Brenda bites into a celery stick and nods her head.

Such misdemeanors, like not living in Maine anymore or marrying someone from Massachusetts (from "away"), can lower your percentage of likability, your credibility, your authenticity. Flatlanders, I used to jokingly call them, which was anyone not born in Maine or those who moved away and are gone too long. *Tick tock* says the clock the minute you depart. If you lived on Maine's southern coast you may be considered a flatlander because of your proximity to Massachusetts, whose residents we also called "Massholes," a specific breed of know-it-alls on our ski slopes even though they never quite deciphered the ski codes or perhaps human etiquette; they'd barge down the hill in neon outerwear and spill all their beer before it reached their mouths. You'd be wrong if you think after a certain number of years of living in Maine you'll be "from Maine" because it doesn't work that way either.

Maine has always been a place of almost undetectable change, because we didn't like change. *If it ain't broke don't fix it,* we always joked, but we were rabid in our defense of this concept; i.e., don't change unless you absolutely must, which relates to moving away, the biggest change you could make. Yet change happened anyway all around us while we stood still. And the flatlanders, they blustered around our towns, skied our mountains, tailgated our cars, and even if they boosted our economy for a season or two, we couldn't wait to see the red flash of their taillights skidding down the snowy roads.

When my father first met my husband-to-be, he told him a joke: *Why can't you get a blowjob in Massachusetts on the weekends?* [pause] *Because all the cocksuckers are up here!* My father eventually loved my husband as much as, if not more than, he loved me, but his initial words were a territorial warning like Brenda's big crunch of celery that staccatos our lunch conversation.

"How do you know each other?" Brenda asks Lisa, not looking at me.

"We grew up together," I say. "We got into a fistfight in fifth grade."

"Fighting was how we settled our differences back then," Lisa says.

"Speaking of fights," Marie says, "have you seen the documentary *The Rivals*? It's about how you love and hate where you grew up. That's what it's like for me here."

The bell rings and Marie leaves before I can ask what she means.

Lisa suggests I talk with Jeanne Lapointe, the food and nutrition director for the school district, if I want to understand what it would be like if I had stayed or what it's like to be a kid or a parent facing the future my town will face.

In a mass of ponytails and leggings, girls in Lisa's honors algebra class shuffle in and muster together. Lisa and I table the discussion at hand. Boys wade in, their boots swooshing on the low piled rug, and satellite themselves to the girls.

Backpacks zip and unzip. Papers rustle. Half the kids look half asleep. Lisa starts recapping inverse functions in Morse code, hammering her felt-tip pen on the white board. "So, flip the X and the Y, so Y becomes X and X becomes Y. Then replot the points." She looks at their flat, quiet faces. One girl twirls her long hair and a boy jiggles his right leg. Lisa turns back to the board. "When I square root this side, it's plus or minus, right? Now what?"

A thin, quiet girl sits across from a boy who slumps in his chair, his chin barely level with the edge of the table. He looks at her when she's not looking and she looks at him as soon as he looks away. Outside, bare birch trees shiver in the winter midday. The sky is bright and blue and deceitful. It is ten degrees. The fluorescent classroom lights strangle the sunshine and the carpet muffles the repetitive sounds teenagers make when they tap their feet or their pencils.

One boy stands up and declares, "I hate F of X so much!"

"But X can be anything," Lisa calmly reminds him.

The students scribble on their worksheets, talking to each other in discreet voices. After a few minutes, one student stands up and waves his paper.

"I got it correct! I should get something! A gold star!"

Lisa keeps writing on the whiteboard in her reasonable black slacks, her white button-up shirt. She turns and her eyes scissor the room, ignoring the boy's plea to recognize him for doing what he is supposed to do.

"Do you remember how to find a vertex on a quadratic?" she asks. "You made a table of value, right? How did you guys do your graphs?" Silence. A whiff of impatience from Lisa. "You have to be able to read the language of math."

Math *is* another language, of logic and organization and of solving problems, concepts Lisa knows well as the third-youngest of fourteen children. Lisa grew up in my neighborhood near the Chessie family, who harbored thirteen kids of their own, both homes a circus of meals, chores, and boys who were sometimes treated like kings. Eating dinner at Lisa's was like approaching a traffic rotary: if you didn't move fast enough, you would lose your entrance. But there was always a hot meal served up by Lisa's mother; those baked bean and mayo sandwiches were delicious.

"Find the length of the tether when you are walking in terms of the height of the balloon," Lisa says as she draws a stick figure holding a balloon. The students laugh.

I find myself floating in and out of attention, as if I am back at my own high school math class where fractions and formulas congregated in the tiny unresponsive space in my brain until I hear Lisa say the word "slope" and think of skiing.

"You guys need more work on bearings," I hear Lisa say and I rivet my eyes ahead.

There's something hopeful about math, in the anythingness of X, in that problems can be solved by transposing the question, or that we can work on bearings until we find a solution, something I have been trying to find since before my father's death . . . his dying an X factor I hadn't foreseen, a blank he left unsolved. At times I still don't know its function—his death—except when it propels me to ask questions about his life, my town, and myself I hadn't thought to ask.

. . .

WHILE SOME PEOPLE have the freedom to move in and out of whatever space they choose—in large part due to money, class, education—most of the world is relegated to landscapes fixed in more territorial constraints. Lisa, Marie, Heidi, Deano, my mother, they stayed and figured out how to make a life in a place that did what it could to prevent them from doing just that. Over the past few decades, we had experienced an exponential exodus, a state of dehiscence where kids left for more lucrative metropolitan landscapes and never returned, taking their capacity for prosperity with them. At some point, more of us left than stayed, which contributed to the persistent decline of rural towns and to the uneven economic growth across the nation. In Maine, 20 percent of residents are over sixty-five. It's the oldest state in the states. The Rumford hospital, that served our elders and our disease, became the second-biggest business in town. This redistribution of money and talent shuttered those businesses named after fathers and grandfathers and we didn't really have a plan B for the *mise en abyme*.

And where we live matters: not only for our health as I already could see, but because our backgrounds predict our economic destinies, too. It's not like it was in the good old days where college, hard work, hard knocks, and loyalty ratcheted us up and out of the stratum we were born into. Now, those in the middle with the middle skill sets were seeing the steepest earning declines. Globalization, with its open cultural and economic borders, couldn't remove those kinds of barriers no matter how hard it tried.

What does it mean to come from such a place (like so much of America), a place that causes as much harm as it does good? Or maybe people like Lisa see only the good in this town, a good I sometimes struggle to see in my bubble of distance and a less anxious life. Because they stayed, it meant they never had to return as I did. Leaving is a transgression, especially if you return with things you've acquired while away like husbands from Massachusetts or ideas about what the town needs or does not, or if you threaten the status quo. *It's not you, it's me,* you have to tell your hometown as if you are breaking up. But can we ever truly move on and away from the place we are from?

My parents invested in me as they would in a less risky stock, but then I left; is that what they wanted me to do? Urging me out the back door was also an underinvestment in the future of our community and helped quicken the hollowing out of the working-class and the town they loved. By leaving, I had put an end to the repetition of what small towns used to encourage: stay and open a store using your surname or pick up where your parents left off. I *was* the American Dream in ambition and scope while at the same time I was killing that dream with every step farther from home.

"You can't go back home to your family," Thomas Wolfe famously wrote, ". . . back home to your childhood . . . back home to the father you have lost and have been looking for . . . back home to the old forms and systems of things which once seemed everlasting but which are changing all the time." But we can and probably should go back home to confront what made us leave, what made us fall in and out of love with the places that create us, or to see what we left behind. Because each time I go home, I face a referendum on the success or failure of my relationship with it, like a dialogue between two people in a deep and complicated relationship.

NO SUCH THING AS A FREE LUNCH

Across America, June signifies the end of school. When I was that age, we got jobs, got into trouble, lounged carelessly around town until classes resumed in the fall, or were left to ourselves, finding distractions in our backyards or swimming in the cold dark river. Today, in Mexico and Rumford, and in many communities across the US, June signifies hunger.

The poverty level in Maine is increasing at more than twice the rate of neighboring states and eight times the rate of the rest of the nation. One out of five kids in Maine don't have enough to eat. For Rumford and Mexico, four out of five kids suffer from food insecurity.

. . .

OVER THE INTERCOM at the end of the morning announcements, as I walk into Jeanne LaPointe's office the day after visiting Lisa, Mountain Valley High School's principal says, "Make it a great day! The choice is yours!"

Jeanne is the food and nutrition director in the school. She's tasked with feeding the four out of five hungry kids throughout the school year as well as all summer. The summer program, sponsored by the USDA, is in its sixth year, with local organizations like Full Plates and the Oxford Federal Credit Union chipping in. For the school year, the bulk of the funding comes from the Community Eligibility Provision, a meal service "option" for schools in low-income areas that allows the nation's poorest schools and districts to serve breakfast and lunch at no cost to all enrolled students without making parents face the burden or humiliation of submitting applications. Figuring the eligibility of a school involves its own special math problem, taking in state poverty guidelines, family size and income, and other social programs available in the area.

Jeanne generally eats three meals a day, she says, unlike most kids she feeds, whose only source of food is often school meals. "That includes breakfast and weekends," Jeanne says as she glances at her phone. "On Fridays, kids make as many as eight trips to the self-serve salad bar because that is the only food they will eat until Monday."

Today Jeanne's a little distracted. Randy Brown, her brother, is fifty-seven and has been moved to a hospice facility because his death is imminent. She keeps checking her phone, her eyes soured red as I ask her about her job and the kids she feeds. Her dirty blond hair is a little askew, pulled back by a headband to keep it off her face.

"Let's go have lunch!" she says cheerfully and we walk down to the cafeteria. It's barely eleven o'clock. Her smile is as big as the sun.

The cafeteria is like every cafeteria in America. Football players at one table, cheerleaders at another. Freaks, geeks, loners, nerds, kiss-asses, smarty pants, the beautiful, the homely, the poor, the popu-lar, all arranging themselves strategically around the room as if in a staged play. The clatter of trays and silverware heightens the smell of the steam rising from the various bins of food: the oily slug of pizza, withering vegetables, and today's main offering, box-made stuffing littered with a generous amount of chicken hiding in a spongy mass that smells like damp oregano. "It goes a long way," Jeanne says about the chicken.

Even though kids are hungry, Jeanne and her team of lunch ladies still have to puzzle out each week what kids will actually eat. "They don't drink white milk," Jeanne says as lunch ladies scoop food onto our trays. "So we provide chocolate milk. These kids need calories and they need calcium. Chocolate milk provides both."

The chocolate milk plan didn't go over so well with the school board, but Jeanne's team will try pretty much anything to get food in kids' mouths. They launched a smoothie "program" where they smuggle healthy, low-sugar nutrients into drinks. Kids like pizza, so they hide vegetables in the sauce. The school has even hosted themed lunches, like on Cinco de Mayo, when they served Mexican food and festooned the cafeteria with colorful crepe paper while the music teacher played mariachi music.

It's even trickier in the summer. Kids are embarrassed, shy, some-times too proud, and they don't want to be seen lined up for free food while other kids are doing more enjoyable things. Jeanne works in con-cert with the school's summer programs with the idea that if meals accompany activities, people are less likely to feel ashamed eating free food. Signs advertise the meals: "FRIENDS, FUN, & FREE FOOD" with a big cartoon sunshine in the backdrop of smiling cartoon kids.

We find a spot to eat in the center of the room and I look around. The mingling of food and teenage sweat—sour, sweet, heavy, reassuring, emphatic—seeds the air. Dim lights and low ceilings buffer the room's noise to a soft murmur in a potluck of sounds and smells. A shriek from a girl who jumps out of her chair, then a wave of giggles from the floor.

"Eighty-five percent of our kids are eligible for free lunch," Jeanne says. "And if that many kids qualify, according to a complicated matrix, everyone gets free lunch."

"You can tell by the way they dress," says another educator at our table.

"They?" I ask, a little alarmed.

"The kids who qualify for free lunch," she says.

I look over at a group of boys throwing pens at each other. To me, they look like all teenage kids: a little sloppy, misunderstood, too big or too small for their clothes. Pimply and raw. But there's a code, she's implying, in the off-brand sneakers or in the slightly unfresh T-shirts worn on repeat that someone points out. These codes create an imaginary line between who's on the inside and who's on the outside track. The more fortunate kids, they glide confidently across the linoleum floor as if the very air around them is oiled.

People tend to comment on differences (no-name clothes, poverty) rather than sameness (boys, teenagers, all receiving free lunch, all friends), which mirrored something I had been seeing everywhere—in classrooms, boardrooms, living rooms: even though we are generally alike in our desire to be fed, clothed, housed, loved, we zero in on differences—in political parties and at dinner parties—perpetuating a cycle of divisiveness that does nobody any good.

I poke around the edges of the beige wad on my plate. Jeanne digs into her meal. "Comfort food," she says as she sees me eyeballing her stuffing. "It's familiar to the kids and it helps us use our commodity items."

It's been years since I've eaten institutional food. When I was in high school, we were served fresh bread and homemade meals every day for the insignificant price of fifty cents and I paid it absentmindedly. Arrogant jerks called kids who received free or reduced lunch derisively and uncreatively the "free lunch kids." And we let them.

Jeanne uses words like "commodity" for chicken, "offerings" for lunch, "barriers" instead of poverty, "nutrients" for food, and "programs" for menus, more codes I'm beginning to unravel, ones that keep us at arm's length from actual things. If we institutionalize the words that describe the food we serve to the hungry or the poor, it's easier to swallow when we can't provide full plates.

I take a bite. The chicken and stuffing taste pretty good so I eat it all. Still, I chase it down with a big gulp of water and watch the salad bar empty out.

Jeanne's passion for nutrition arises not just out of her dietetic studies at the University of Maine in Farmington, or out of having kids of her own, or feeding her husband while he trains for Ironman competitions. She also understands how the human body can define you—and how you can define it, too.

In the summer of 2012, Jeanne's bras didn't fit her well. As a fifty-something-year-old woman, however, she knew the shifting mechanics of the female form. Around Thanksgiving, while putting on deodorant, she looked in the mirror and saw an odd dimple in her breast. A month later she was diagnosed with breast cancer. By then, it had infiltrated her lymph nodes. She had a lumpectomy, six rounds of chemo, thirty-seven rounds of radiation. She was prescribed aromatase inhibitors, which she still takes and which contribute to her recently diagnosed osteoporosis. She's also developed atrial fibrillation and sees a cardiologist in addition to an oncologist.

"Cancer is the gift that keeps on giving," Jeanne says as she laughs. In fact Jeanne smiles all the time, even when she tells me that one out of five women over the age of fifty get breast cancer nationally. Jeanne doesn't emotionally connect with the cancer survivor narrative. "I just survive," she says.

After lunch, Jeanne and I walk back to her office and in the wide unencumbered carpeted hallway, five students are fanned out on the floor piecing together quilts for an art class project; four of them, according to statistics, are food deprived.

"We don't know what will happen out of Washington," Jeanne whispers after we pass the kids, "but I can tell you there's a conservative arm—the Heritage Foundation—and our new Department of Education secretary [Betsy DeVos], who believe parents, not bureaucrats, should decide what their children eat."

"I'm surprised there are detractors to feeding hungry kids," I say. "Food is a basic necessity like water or air or love, three essentials kids shouldn't have to earn."

But the Heritage Foundation insists that funding food programs is the type of federal overreach it abhors. "Everything the bottom 95 percent can benefit from they oppose," Jeanne says in disgust. "Many people don't even have the ability to walk out and find a job, never mind drive your nonexistent vehicle to that nonexistent job. We live in rural Maine where there's no infrastructure, no buses, no trains. I'm so fortunate, but many people are not. There's already so many strikes against them out here. Then they have to hope like hell they get a job that pays something! Or what if you had to move last weekend or are hungry? What if you don't even have a stove? What if you are sick or have a disease like cancer? These are just some of the stresses many of our families face. Everyone gets hungry but when you're food insecure, you live in a whole different way." My great-grandfather Pierre cooked enough to fortify logging platoons, as did my grandmother and mother. I adopted their approach, always preparing too much for the numbers I'm feeding, and to express my love through food. So hearing kids don't have enough food pokes at my heart and my deepest concerns.

. . .

AT HOME IN Connecticut I think of what Jeanne had said before I left: "Hunger is a stress we can't measure." I wonder if that's true. Children who suffer from food insecurity can develop serious health problems in their adult lives. And children who suffer from lack of food are almost all afflicted by poverty. While I inherited my family's propensity for cooking too much, parents who can't feed their kids, I fear, will pass down an endless hunger loop. I still catch myself saying *I am starving* in between my organic potato chips and $4.99 kombuchas. It's shameful to make light of such a thing when so many times *any* out of five children are far hungrier than I. Do people *against* feeding children understand there really is no such thing as a free lunch? These kids pay mightily every day.

Jeanne calls a week or so after my visit to tell me her brother died later in the day I was there, four days before a spaghetti supper benefit to help with his medical expenses at $8.00 per person.

. . .

I HEAR FROM Jeanne from time to time, especially about the forthcoming election in November 2018, the results of which could crimp the funding of free food for students. Maine congressman Bruce Poliquin, who is running for reelection in Rumford and Mexico's district, suggests anyone applying for food stamps should be required to work twenty hours a week "to become independent of welfare so they're not trapped in poverty." His mandate, lifted straight from the Heritage Foundation's arguments, is counterintuitive to reality and his constituents' needs.

As part of his campaign, he hosts a meet and greet at the mill and posts about the event on his Facebook page afterward: "Folks at the Rumford Mill work hard and just want a fair shake. This is why our trade deals must be fair and why I've fought so hard against bad actors like China. . . . If Mainers are on a level playing field, we can win." The "bad actors"? A Chinese company had just bought the mill; they own the place.

In the fall, Poliquin attends a Rumford nighttime football game, grinning and glad-handing everyone—including Jeanne—by the ticket booth in his new red flannel shirt, pressed jeans, and perfectly white, Maine-made New Balance sneakers. After the game starts, he circles the track that encompasses the field a few times while his assistants corral and funnel people into more handshakes. Before the game is over, he heads up the steep, grassy embankment to use the bathroom, which is a medium-sized effort for anyone not in reasonable shape, then he wanders off, not to be seen again that night.

Poliquin's wandering off—the football field or outside his awareness—is common among politicians running for office. They show up at your events or where you work, buy your local goods, and wear clothes that signify they understand you—but where are they when your kids are looking for their next meal or for a way up and out of poverty? Where are they when burning tires are eclipsing the sun? Where are they when neighbors and family wither away to straw, to concave doppelgängers, to coffins? Like a neglectful parent, politicians like Poliquin are always there when they want something and never there when you need them, persistently legislating what's on your plate or in your air even if they don't give a shit what you eat or breathe as long as it's what they serve up. And those loops they make around football fields are just like the poverty cycle they avoid. Then they give out double-wide grins and fair-weathered handshakes and slink out the back door.

Ciphers of poverty are all around: what kids eat for lunch, the kind of winter jacket someone wears (if they have one), the hunger or disease paralyzing someone's ability to work twenty hours a week. Poverty is not only calculated in dollar amounts, as I was learning on the ground. The opioid crisis is bludgeoning my hometown. Our special-education population is the highest in the state. Rumford also has the highest rate of crime. And on top of it all, our environment is like a garbage can. As a news headline on NBC said in 2016, "WHERE YOU LIVE DETERMINES WHAT KILLS YOU"—and in Rumford and Mexico we have been living in a cathedral of trauma.

GOING DOWNHILL

SPENDING TIME WITH Jeanne in the lunchroom and with Lisa in math class made me realize I wasn't moored to one spot. I could eat at my leisure with no consequence felt. I could drink chocolate milk for pleasure, not survival. I could leave when the stink of the town got too bad.

From the outside looking in, it seems Rumford and Mexico can't win, even if they won all those football games in the past. But from the inside looking out, our towns, they had hills and they had snow and our fathers and mothers made sure we had access to both. If the mill was the spine of the community, Black Mountain was the guts.

In between overtime and/or double shifts in the 1960s, my father and other millworkers carved up rocky slopes and felled trees on the eastern slope of Black Mountain, then jammed iron ski lift poles into unsympathetic soil to install a T-bar to scrape us up the hill. The ski area they built was modest but challenging, like everything else in our town.

As was fashionable in those days, the club erected three ski jumps. Sometimes my father would thunder down the largest, I think it was a 45-meter one, on a regular pair of skis and still land with grace despite the trembling g-forces under his feet.

It was a town-wide effort, Black Mountain. Even the mill provided workers on its dime. The Chisholm Ski Club, of which my father was a member until the day he died, raised money and sold stocks; the fifty shares he bought entitled our family to lifetime passes, which made skiing affordable, egalitarian, a lifetime sport I still enjoy.

Lisa had asked me if I would help chaperone "Ski-Free Day," a collaboration between the high school and Black Mountain that gives kids an opportunity to try skiing for the low cost of $10, which includes equipment and a day pass. Student participation is not mandatory but most kids join in while others stay inside and play video games or Monopoly. Others go tubing on the far side of the mountain or just fiddle around with their phones, gossip, flirt, or collapse their heads on their crossed arms and slumber fitfully across the long wood tables in the lodge.

Some kids stay home because they don't have winter clothing. "I feel so bad I didn't think of it," Lisa says. "I should have known better." She starts calculating how many jackets or pairs of mittens she will need for next year.

Jim Aylward, a high school English teacher and former football coach, walks over and interjects. "There's so much poverty in Rumford and Mexico," he says, looking around. "It's not like it used to be."

Another teacher interjects: "I know a first grader who showed up one day with only one shoe."

"One shoe?" I say.

"Yeah," the teacher says. I think of those parents who may not even have a stove or are hungry themselves. "They were probably on drugs," the teacher says, ending my trance.

Three hundred and seventy eight people in Maine in 2016 die of opioid overdoses, I find out, in a huge increase (40 percent) from the year before. Maine's per-capita rate of drug overdose deaths was the thirteenth-highest in the nation in 2015 and in the top ten in 2017. The Maine Department of Health and Human Services received $4.8 million to treat those affected by opioids. But within a year, they spend less than $60,000. And if drug users don't die, our towns have no treatment to offer them in their follow-up care, according to the assistant deputy chief of the Med-Care Ambulance Service in Mexico. I'm not sure if that one shoe is because just the parents didn't care; it's as if nobody cared.

. . .

BLACK MOUNTAIN, LIKE the town itself, ebbed in times of economic and population downturns and bad weather. In the 1980s we were forced to relinquish our lifetime passes when the mountain went through financial trouble and a change of ownership (it couldn't afford to carry us for free anymore), but it remained our first true love.

When I was little, almost every weekend my father piloted our station wagon along the frost-heaved roads winding through the outskirts of town, past the smokestacks, past the Swift River where he learned to swim, past the Catholic cemetery where his father lay buried, and past the Black Mountain sign my grandfather Ernie painted, to where I would lug my steely equipment uphill through the icy parking lot, collapse on the snow, and thwack down the metal buckles on my leather boots, pinching my fingers. I was small, the runt in a pack of kids who were already small, and tried to keep up with them and my father, who was one of the best skiers on the hill. As I followed them, my boots and gloves went through an endless cycle of becoming soaked with sweat then freezing, then thawing from sweat again. We would ski until the T-bar stopped clinking and growling, lolling to rest like an iron dinosaur, and the last light of dusk would slam shut over the smudged hills. We'd return the following week just as the T-bar purred awake. Once in a while, we skied under the stars and beneath a few lighted trails, where interstitial shadows made it feel like we were going faster than we were.

A home movie: I am four. My father crouches over me on skis and I stand in front of him on skis too, between his legs, facing forward, gaining speed as we race down the mountain. He warns me to watch what's in front of me, but to also look far enough downhill to see what lies ahead. I think I'm skiing on my own volition. Unbeknownst to me at the time, I couldn't have stood for two seconds without his arms there to carry me.

Even in summer, our lives centered on Black Mountain, where we took swim lessons and attended day camp. But the hill without snow always seemed blasphemous, naked and muggy, the long ribbons of white changed to lumpy mounds of straw-colored slopes that hissed with cicadas.

. . .

AFTER I GEAR up, I head outside to take a few runs. A slashing wintry mix of ice and snow nicks my face.

A boy in a cotton jacket with a hooded sweatshirt underneath, unzipped to midchest, asks if he can ride the lift with me. Ice crystals crust his lashes. When the lift scoops us up, he hits his hip on the chair and loses his balance for a second. He pulls the bar down quickly.

"I am afraid of heights," he says. "But I want to prove autistic people can do anything regular kids can do." He wants to be a Marine, he says, more specifically a field medic, wants to save people's lives. "But I don't like being yelled at. That makes me anxious," he says, laughing. "So likely not the Marines."

The wind gusts, and our chair leans a little to the left. He closes his eyes. His nose piercing looks cold in its silvery case. He says, with the authority of a doctor or at least someone who has spoken with many doctors: "I am diagnosed with anxiety disorder, bipolar disorder, and autism. But I am going to do something big, something the world will remember." Something in his tone makes me feel a little anxious myself.

We watch below the lift as a small pack of elite skiers—kids who race on the downhill team—bomb straight down expert terrain on mixed conditions: ice, steeps, granular, slushy snow, dirt patches, as if there are no obstacles in their way, as if they never knew how to fall. Their racing suits shine like oil slicks. The boy next to me gives a deep-throated yell and stands up in the chair. I grip the seat.

"I see my friend up there on the lift," he says pointing a few chairs ahead.

When we get to the top, we lift the safety bar and ski off. His friend is there at the top, typing something on her smartphone, doesn't respond when the boy asks her what trail they should ski down.

He turns and asks me, "Will you ski with me?" His friend continues typing away then skis off without saying a word. It's as if he is not there at all. I follow him until he gets lost in the crowd mulling at the bottom of the hill outside the lodge.

My next run, I ride up the lift with another boy, an exchange student. "I love it here," he says. "I'm having the best experience." He says that he won't advance in his school back home even after attending Mountain Valley High School for a year because his country's schools are too strict. "The grades are too easy here," he goes on. "The work is too easy." It's not about school credit, he says, it's a cultural and social experience, a year to socialize and make friends.

He takes off down the hill, and I ski a few runs by myself, remembering the crests and curves of each trail and finding turns anew. On the beginner slope, I see a girl struggling to uncross the tips of her downhill-facing skis and I stop next to her. It's the thin quiet girl from Lisa's math class.

"Do you need help?" I ask.

"I'm okay," she says, her eyes tenacious, her jacket flapping open as she flails around.

I take another run but check on her on the way down. She's moved about five feet. She still doesn't need help, she insists. The weather changes with each chairlift ride. Gusty, granular snow hits my helmet like buckshot. Then it's sunny. Then sleeting again. Then a cold, white sky. The third time down, I check on her again and see a boy helping her try to get up. About two hours later I see her at the bottom of the hill in the lift line. I watch as she takes the chairlift right back up to the top. Is it weird I feel proud of her, this girl I don't even know, who could take such punishment and face the same obstacles that caused the beating all over again?

At the end of the day as the sun drifts downward, ski patrollers clear the trails. The head patroller lets me ride the chairlift down as dusk colonizes the hills. In the middle of the ride, the lift stops, and I am hammocked by a small wind, a few stars, eight degrees, and the violet sky. No sound but for the cruel wind grazing the edges of my helmet. I love winter, its ability to equalize everything with a skin of clean smooth white snow and the way that snow filters out the noise of civilization and its discontents. Soon the sky turns to gray tones, tamping down the bustle of day.

The chair creaks in a slap of wind. It feels good to be here, in this simplicity of being in my own skin. Then the lift starts up with a sudden lurch and carries me downhill. At the bottom, I ski off the lift. I can barely feel my fingers.

HALF-LIFE

I was always fascinated by what other people didn't want, not what I didn't have. As a kid, my mother always shepherded me to yard sales and junk stores, weaning me on a love of castoffs and remnants of throwaway things.

My parents furnished their house this way, with resurrected bits and bobs they ferried home from weekend yard sale hauls. My father would refinish the beat-up dressers and cabinets and chairs in the dark timelessness of our barn, sanding each turned leg as if he were carving it himself, and my mother would accessorize the refurbished furniture with doilies and lamps. It was my job to massage lemon oil into the creases of the various woods my father made anew. Veneer never stood up to my father's handiwork or to the test of time. If they found a table with chipped white paint they wouldn't consider it "shabby chic," they would just consider it shabby and my father would rehabilitate it to its better form. That whole "one person's trash is another's treasure" never rang true; to me calling it trash conceals the capacity of the item discarded by hasty hands. Then, as now, I resurrect things from dumps. I have a soft spot for anything tossed aside.

Could my parents have afforded new furniture? Maybe. Their habits weren't borne out of necessity or trying to affect a certain style, even though my mother had a weakness for Victorian oak; it was the idea of betterment. The hardwood of every chair that caught my mother's eye, every table that survived paint stripper or my father's hand, signified desire.

My mother favored Corelle dinnerware, of all things, a cross between china and paper plates, as they were the only dishes she couldn't break. She preserved the "good dishes" (ushered out for Christmas), the platinum-edged place settings she received for her first marriage, in the curved-glass oak china cabinet I also kept dust-free.

. . .

AFTER SKI FREE day, the weather turns and my mother and I are holed up together in the house. It's still eight degrees but now with a horizontal wind and a fresh snow glazing the sidewalks and roads. I ask her if she wants to drive to Overtown to look at the stores.

"You can't buy anything over there!" she says in frustration.

We head to Marden's instead, a store that replaced the yard sales that had all but frittered away. We shop there every time I am home, me looking for cheap necessities like underwear or sheets, her looking for clothes or something to do. Today, we cruise the store at a slow pace, avoiding the confines of the weather.

Marden's Surplus & Salvage moved into Rumford in the 1990s: "I should have bought it when I saw it at Marden's!" croaked the radio advertising jingle that besieged you like a burr with its insistent, cheery commercialism. We took the demand seriously and filled our shopping baskets with Marden's orphaned goods. The store was founded by Mickey Marden on the principle "buy great stuff and sell it cheap." Marden, a treasure hunter who pilfered off salvage, fire sales, and bankruptcy courts, was a hucksterish Robin Hood who took from the poor and sold it to the poorer. "Don't buy anything you have to feed," he quipped.

The building used to house Zayre department store, a New Englandish phenom discount chain not unlike Marden's but more consistent in its inventory and less obvious about its status as a lower-price venture. Zayre became Ames until Marden's overtook the low-slung, flat-roofed building. It's a touchstone really, from when I left town in 1985 to when I returned to New England in 2013, with everything in between behind the onion skin of time.

We stop to talk with a former student my mother knows. He hugs her. When she asks how he is, he says he and his wife plan to get divorced. He says he's moved on, lost a little weight, but his chubby face is crushed with defeat, curdles red every time he speaks. My mother responds with that wilting, sympathetic face nobody ever wants to see. Every time he starts to walk away, he comes back and says something else to my mother, looking both for that sympathetic face and despising what cultivated it.

"I'm doing good, really I am," he says unconvincingly. My mother gives him a hug.

She always attracted kids who needed her, and she was attracted to them, especially when she was the high school principal's secretary. She became to any stray kid a de facto counselor, helping addicts through drug and alcohol rehab or counseling them herself. She wasn't such an emotional philanthropist to me but helped me win college grants by writing long pleading letters to financial aid staffers.

In Marden's forty-four-thousand-square-foot space, you never know what you will find, which is part of its charm: cheap spices, gardening gloves, triangular-shaped pizza storage containers, shrink-wrapped socks, remaindered books, off-season clothing, vinyl and laminate flooring, notions, hardware, big puffy couches, many things tossed on shelves or bins or crouched low on the tan, lusterless floors under mean fluorescent lights. I feel sorry for the small ceramic angels in the home goods section and their big doe eyes.

As I look across the store for my mother, neon sale signs violate every sightline. I pick up a $4.99 apron that says "NO BITCHIN' IN MY KITCHEN," which I actually find pretty funny, and another: "WHAT'S A NICE GIRL LIKE ME DOING IN A PLACE LIKE THIS?" My mother and I drive home under glowering skies.

FOR THE WIN

The grass is always greener to most of us. Roger White? He just makes it green. I hadn't seen Roger (my seventh-grade boyfriend, one of the nicest guys I knew) since high school until he appeared one summer morning in 2016 while I was home to check up on the work he'd done to my parents' disgruntled lawn.

Sometime in the 1950s, when the house was being erected, builders buried loose fill and construction debris in the backyard. The lawn heaved with ankle-breaking divots and creases whose shapes and locations suspiciously changed in the middle of the night as if the landscape were melting. My mother called Roger and he and his landscaping crew shored up the turf, fought back the menacing poison ivy dithering on the edge of the property, and replaced some overgrown shrubs with indigenous perennials.

"You broke up with me on Valentine's Day," he had said when I saw him that day.

"I did?! I'm sorry," I offered. I pretended to not remember but I did.

While I had been flinging myself from place to place, walking down avenues I hardly knew, Roger stayed and made his mark in yards all over town. The terrain of past and present was forever entangled in the work Roger regularly did; it lived in the soil under his nails, in the earth he sculpted, in the people he sought to help, in remaining behind. We had different calibrations, he and I: mine was distance and his was proximity. I imagined that his repeated transactions of seasonal yard work emphasized how much things change or how little, as he watched each summer peter out to fall until winter moved in and ravaged the lawns he so carefully toned, until spring once again came round. Through it all, he kept his eye on each year, each snowstorm, each drought, each football game.

• • •

BEFORE THE SUPER Bowl in February 2017, Roger counted down the hours to kickoff, and during the game, he counted up, as his blood pressure rose to unprecedented numbers. In the end, the Patriots won in the greatest comeback of all time, at least according to nearly every sportscaster alive, and Roger's blood pressure returned to normal. While many viewers abandoned their television sets by the end of the third quarter with the Patriots losing 28–9, Roger never gave up.

After Roger watched the parade in Boston celebrating the Patriots' win, he purchased a replica of the Vince Lombardi Trophy and decided to hold his own celebratory parade in Rumford and feature the trophy alongside his five Super Bowl replica rings, one for each Patriots championship win. He said jokingly if he didn't spend so much money on Patriots memorabilia, he'd probably be able to afford a new stove.

In the lead-up to his parade, Roger asked the Patriots organization for permission to borrow the real Lombardi Trophy, but his modest request was in direct competition with mayors from Bangor, Brewer, and Portland who also wanted to display the trophy in a convention center. The Patriots lent the trophy to the mayors and furnished a cheerleader and an iteration of Pat the Patriot (the team mascot) to Roger.

Roger contacted the local news stations but they didn't seem interested in covering his parade. He figured they were too busy investigating a recent storm and the apartment-block-sized snowbank scraped up by Rumford's plows.

I drive home specifically for Roger's parade.

In the early afternoon, Patriots fans line the streets on the 1.5-mile mile route from the high school all the way to Rumford's town hall to watch. I stand with my mother, a high school friend, a woman who wears Patriots logo earrings, and a few others from my mother's neighborhood where the parade passes by. Gray skies muffle the commotion and escort the cold deep into the layers of wool I'm wearing.

Spectators stand on top of crusty snowbanks the same color as the sky as high school kids in Patriots jerseys toss candy into our outstretched cold hands. Other people wave giant banners custom-made for the parade. Light chatter and laughter bursts and subsides up and down the street. We stomp our feet and blow breath into our fists as the sun darts behind a cloud. Darlene Cormier, an old friend of mine, sneaks a small package into my mother's hands. It's the last of her homemade poutine. "Don't tell anyone," Darlene whispers. My mother squirrels the package into her coat.

About twenty floats, made of flatbeds and trucks and cars, inch toward us in celebratory shouts, with police cars and fire engines tailing the cheerful cavalcade. The Patriots cheerleader shakes her foil pom-poms while the jug-headed mascot dances alongside her, both terrifying and happy, like a clown waiting in the woods. The Mountain Valley

Falcons' mascot sashays along the pavement in a white mangy costume. "PATS NATION" signs and balloons billow alongside many wearing Tom Brady masks. Baby carriages decorated in red, white, and blue. A squall of truckers blow their horns. Roger hoists and shakes his faux Lombardi Trophy out the window of his truck, its silvery success gloating along the frozen terrain of the road.

Roger wasn't a football player himself, that much I recall. He was a skinny kid making his way the best he could in a close-knit, working-class family of nine. His "one wish in life," he admitted on Facebook, was to be able to retire with enough money so he could help as many other people as possible.

His plan to help others began to manifest long before retirement was in view. He started a campaign called "Take out the Trash," a crusade against drug dealers he considered worse than the refuse buried in my parents' backyard. He also sold T-shirts to earn money for the longtime fire chief in Mexico, who was diagnosed with terminal cancer. The fire chief died before the shirts were made, but instead of making the T-shirts or reimbursing donors, Roger simply gave the $2,692 to the fire chief's widow. Roger also helped raise money for my mothers' neighbor whose child was impaired by cystic fibrosis and had been waiting for new lungs. In response, Roger challenged his 370-pound friend to lose weight and for every pound he did, Roger would donate $5.00 to the child's cause. Other citizens got wind of the pact, and soon the amount ballooned to $626.12 per pound.

As the last police car brings up the rear of the Patriots parade, with a few quick siren bursts, my mother and I and the poutine head back to her house. While hope flickers in the white lattice fence holding back a squadron of daylilies wanting to make their spring debut; in the "STOP NESTLÉ" signs poking out of the dirty snowbanks; in the triumph of each building's past, the shine of optimism is tempered by a gray wash that settles over the town, particularly in late winter, as if the sun has stolen everything from the sky.

After the parade, everyone meets up at Black Mountain's bar. I'm happy to be here in the scrum of the after-party and warmth of old friends. I talk to LJ and Lisa and congratulate Roger on his efforts.

"I'm only a poor boy from Rumford," he says modestly over the din.

I turn and talk for a moment to Bonnie Aleck, who I haven't seen for decades. She works as an accountant in town, mainly for millworkers.

"They do well, but they live simply," Bonnie says, then asks what I do, where I work.

"There's nothing here for me," I say, tipping back my plastic beer cup and swallowing hard. "I don't even have a job where I live. But you . . . you can be an accountant anywhere. Why stay here?"

"I went to a funeral today," she says, "and ninety percent of the people there, I love. Love keeps me here."

THE END OF THE LINE

FROM ARTHUR AND Sheila Meader's back deck you can hear the 176-foot drop of the Androscoggin's falls plowing over rocks, but we meet in Arthur's "arrangement office," where normally a different rush of water occurs: people are breaking into tears.

Arthur runs a funeral home—Meader & Son—the same one his father and grandfather owned, first as a partnership and then as a wholly owned operation. Sheila maintained a beauty shop in Mexico for years and, though she retired from that business some time ago, still cares for the hair of the deceased at Meader & Son.

Their house and the business are basically one and the same, changed, appended to, refurbished over the years; the upstairs apartment Arthur's parents lived in became a casket room; a neighbor's property became a parking lot; and the Meaders purchased a large house next door that became their residence, which they later connected through a small overpass to the funeral home. It's a property where the past never recedes and the personal is always mixed with business; much of Arthur's "bread and butter" is from the mill.

"My dad told me years ago, the one who truly feeds you is the man who works in that mill." Arthur leans forward in his office chair, his voice deep, confident. "Those are the ones you want to keep happy." The early afternoon sun dusts his face.

He says his one rule is to lead by example. And he is a man of rules, either making them or complying with them. Arthur's father had rules too. When Arthur started working at the funeral home full-time as a young man, his father laid down the law: "If you want to go to a party, that's fine. It doesn't give you the next day off. If you don't show up at work, you and I are going to have a conversation. The second time, I'm going to give you a warning. The third time, I'm going to ask you, where are you working now?" Arthur always showed up.

Arthur shows up for families, too. We engaged Meader & Son when my father died. In his office, we discussed what my father would have wanted, what we wanted, what other people may want, and were shepherded gently through those final tasks: photos to display, writing the obituary, settling financial matters, where to go at the church. They gave us multiple-choice questions, which made it easier in our grief: which kind of urn to use, which flowers wouldn't make me gag. Meader & Son's website, which I consulted at the time, also advises on funeral and cemetery etiquette, like what to wear, what not to say, what you'll need, how to memorialize someone you love. During my father's wake, funeral, and burial, we were shown where to stand, where to sit, where to shake everyone's hand as they lined up. Rules and procedure got us through.

In 1982, on Meader & Son's sixty-fifth anniversary, the local paper profiled the funeral home and Arthur. Proud at his longevity, Arthur said at the time he hoped his then three-and-a-half year-old son, Jayme (James), would take up the profession after him. When James was in high school, however, Arthur wanted him to do bigger and better things. Arthur hired David Blouin, who is like a son, when he was thirteen. He'll take over the business when the time comes. The name is still Meader & Son, but there's no longer a son involved.

I look at the article Arthur has copied for me. "James always had a goal and if he reached that goal, he'd set another one, and another one, and another one," Arthur says.

While four generations of Meader men made goals, showed up, did what they said they would do, James's goals didn't include managing the funeral home or living in Rumford, Maine. Yet James still returns to Rumford every chance he can, to ski, to see his friends and family, and to remain close to that small, intimate community atmosphere.

As Arthur and I talk, the unleafed trees outside magnify the sound of birds hiding in them. You can almost hear spring releasing its frost like a cracked rib, the sound of soil shifting in its skin. Spring is when the funeral business tends to pick up, Arthur says, when Meader & Son "serves" more families. I like Arthur's choice of words, because death is not the kind of business you want to propagate and it's a more accurate description of Arthur's allegiance to the community: to serve.

Arthur and Sheila—as well as Heidi, Deano, Roger, Terry, Lisa, Jeanne, Gary Doloff, my mother—they were the true leaders of this community, though I'm not sure they'd admit as much, but what good leaders ever do? Duty-bound, uncorrupt, and beholden to their "constituents," serving this community, to them, was never just about doing things right, but also about doing the right thing. They worked hard and saw what hard work could build: a town, businesses, families, children's confidence.

$\bullet \quad \bullet \quad \bullet$

ARTHUR AND I have been talking for hours, and by now the sun has tilted west. "How about a glass of scotch?" he asks with a quick lift of his eyebrows. We leave his office and walk up the back stairs, through the casket showroom, through a private office on top of the garage, bang a left, and we are in the overpass. From there we walk through a fire door built into a two-foot-thick wall in the basement of the house, which then empties into a big sunroom. From there, we walk up to a landing, and into the kitchen.

"Now I'm thirsty," I say after the hike. He offers me a glass of his favorite, a fifteen-year-old Glenlivet matured in French oak casks.

"I want to show you something," he says.

On the wall of a downstairs guest bedroom, a photo of him skiing at Black Mountain in 1963, heading through a slalom gate. Next to it, a photo of James, also skiing, also heading through a slalom gate. A generation apart, skiing in tandem to his father, crouched over in the same stance, the same distance from the gate, taking the same tight line, the two of them racing time.

James and I—like Arthur, like my dad—always kept one eye on immediate obstacles and one eye downhill in order to determine the best line to ski. But what James and I didn't know, as we carved through those gates in our earlier years, was that we were the last in our line. We broke the rules of our family's way of life, rules they encouraged us to break; we chose different paths.

. . .

AFTER I LEAVE Arthur and Sheila's house, I walk over to the Tourist Information Booth parking lot to see the falls. Water stampedes over the crisp edge of the dam. Trees along the Androscoggin are still naked in their transformation. A motorcycle growls by.

A huge Paul Bunyan statue looms over the river where Bunyan-sized logs once floated downstream toward the mill. In blue pants, a matching blue watch cap, and a short-sleeve red polo shirt exposing his brawny arms, Bunyan proffers an equally enormous ax that could clear-cut even the Amazon. That statue has been around as long as I remember, although it used to tower above the Village Shoppe across the street where I bought charcoals and sketch pads for my juvenile renderings of horses. I never paid much attention to Bunyan despite his size. He blended into the background, as improbable as that seems.

Small towns from Maine to Minnesota claim Bunyan as their own, yet everyone agrees the boy giant was the hero to all woodsmen. Legend maintains when Bunyan's cradle rocked, the motion caused huge waves that sank ships. He also whittled a pipe from a hickory tree and could outrun buckshot. Our Bunyan, I learned, was crafted from the mold of the Muffler Man, a giant fiberglass statue who held mufflers in his outstretched hands as an advertisement on US byways in the 1970s. Other Muffler Men held hot dogs, fried chicken, and one in Illinois was found holding a rocket. The model was a blank slate for whatever fairy tale we chose. No matter the myth, there our Bunyan stands as a guardian for those ambling through the waning mill town of my youth, his shadow sometimes as brooding as the hurtling river beyond.

He was overhauled between 2000 and 2002, including a paint job, a new ax, and steel supports secured to a huge block of concrete. To add the new supports, workers had to remove Bunyan's head and shimmy down his neck. Inside his torso, after they assembled his improved skeleton, workers wriggled up and out of the neck, one at a time—like the snakes on Medusa's head come to life in a lumberjack disguise—then reattached his head. In honor of the statue's resurrection, Rumford held a festival featuring a lumberjack breakfast, zip line rides over the waterfalls, a facial hair contest, a flannel shirt dinner dance, and an ax-throwing competition.

We commemorate resource development and industry with memorials like Bunyan or the marble bust of Chisholm, but we don't memorialize the environmental consequences of their work. We keep those legacies hidden in the earth, invisible to the naked eye. What if we began to enshrine those kinds of legacies, the ones that don't want to be found? "HERE IN THIS SPOT LIES A TOXIC CATASTROPHE" would be a sign of something we are not yet ready to admit. I'd love to see in the Information Booth some real information—a pamphlet outlining the path of mercury, dioxin, and other toxics that are part of our heritage, too. Or maybe an interactive feature like they created for the Old Man of the Mountain so future generations can see what the world was like before we choked it with garbage that contains the half-life of a zillion years. I wonder what kind of festival we'd have for such dangerous shrines as those, or if we'd bother to maintain their perpetual care as lovingly as we shored up Bunyan's spine.

Down at the river's edge, I see Edmund Muskie's smaller, more serious memorial of squat, dark gray granite. Bookish and six feet four inches tall, he was a giant in real life although painfully shy (admittedly so) and smart: so smart that, as a student, he was asked more than once to substitute for his teachers when they fell ill. He pushed to overcome his shyness, a flaw he wore like a hair shirt, yet it vanished when he stood in front of a chalkboard or in front of the debate team, which he joined despite his reticence. When I was young my grand-mother Bridget dated Muskie, but I can't imagine the couple: he, with his stooped quietness and a card-carrying Boy Scout, and my grand-mother, an explosive miniature force, like BB gunshot, scattered but sharp, all at the same time.

Muskie always saw both sides to every argument, the kind of guy who went hunting as a kid but would never shoot anything. Chris Matthews, in the *Sarasota Herald Tribune* in 1966, said of Muskie, he "did not enter politics to have his sentences appear in the newspaper. . . . He sought election to make the country better." So Muskie adopted a tailor's mien and went to work. Against a resistant president and House of Represen-tatives and industry inaction, he helped enact the Clean Air Act and the Clean Water Act by trying to answer a question he often asked himself: how do you create an environment people can enjoy while pro-tecting it?

In Rumford, however, Muskie was no match for the silhouette cast by Bunyan. Both giants memorialized and their acts equally signifi-cant, however, one deforested the woodlands and the other tried (in a way) to reclaim them, the rocky pools on the edge of the Androscoggin spanning the gap between them.

My father used to make fun of Bunyan and the ludicrous blue hoof-prints made by Babe, Bunyan's sidekick blue ox, that started at the Information Booth and colored the sidewalks of Overtown, the same sidewalks LJ plans to tear up to replace. The Rumford selectmen had voted in 2009 to use $6,500 from their economic development fund to create Babe, figuring he would encourage tourists to follow his me-andering line around town. What they forgot to consider was there's not much left in town to see but Bunyan himself and those garish blue hoofprints that end abruptly at Rite Aid.

When we leave home, as James and I did, we leave behind our past but when we return, we encounter a version of home built of legends true and false. For me, those legends are so big—Chisholm, Muskie, Thoreau, Longfellow, Bunyan, Black Mountain, Anne of Green Ga-bles, my family, and trees, endless trees—that it is hard to see beyond their shadows. So when I drive back over the Piscataqua River Bridge with Mexico and Rumford in my rearview mirror, I may not see "true love," as E. B. White did, but I can see where my lifelines are drawn.

. . .

WHEN I GET back to Connecticut, I examine my father's death certificate, which I had gotten from Arthur. It indicates his immediate cause of death was esophageal cancer "due to (or as a consequence of)" lung carcinoma; "due to (or as a consequence of)" prostate cancer; "due to (or as a consequence of)" coronary artery disease, with "other significant conditions contributing to the death but not resulting in the underlying cause given in the above consequences: COPD, respiratory failure with PE, failure to thrive, aspiration."

Those two words "underlying cause" precipitating his death seem a mockery of the phrase. "Under" means less than or below, the condition beneath his actual death, and "lying" is something the death certificate may do—lie—because his esophageal cancer was supposedly gone, as the doctor indicated just months before he died. And "cause"—his condition before his death was obvious, he was sick. But why? Was it because the sacs in his lungs took all they could take? What about before he was sick, playing golf on Farrington Mountain near the landfill, or working in the mill? Where those conditions of his sickness—playing golf? No mention of asbestosis at all in this record of death or the smoking he did back in 1986. If they were listing all underlying causes, "veteran" should probably be there, as he probably was exposed to asbestos then, too; many veterans were, including my husband. There's nothing in the recent medical records to show my father's triple bypass decades ago contributed to his death. Why was his heart weak in the first place? Was it stressed from working amid chloroform, benzene, mercury, dioxin, and butadiene? I read somewhere that asbestosis can contribute to cardiac issues because the heart and lungs work together. Was that lying under his prognosis? His prostate removal in 2008 was successful, and, in the year before he died, the word "prostate" was never discussed as a risk factor for lung cancer so why was it on his death certificate now? Wasn't prostate cancer one of the things the NOCC committee found was high in our town? Doc Martin died of prostate cancer. There was no mention of my grandfather's metastatic stomach cancer or that he worked in the bleach room before there were many rules. Did toxics like dioxin bioaccumulate in my grandfather's blood, and in doing so, crawl up the food chain to my father and probably to me? I mean, if we are talking about underlying conditions as a consequence of things, we should try to be thorough. Do these record keepers even consider the words they are writing down?

At least the doctors had the decency not to say: "at least" he lived a long life. Because that would be rude.

My father's obituary says he died peacefully with his family by his side, but that's not true either. I was there. There was nothing peaceful about it. Everyone's emotions were splintered and raw. He died a terrible death, which cancer often accommodates, his chest working overtime like he often did in the mill. And as my mother stated in her letter to the nursing board, he "died in excruciating pain." The nurse tending him inserted a catheter improperly. He got an infection from the mistake, and died of sepsis four days later; wasn't the fucked-up catheter insertion an underlying cause?

My mother was his best caregiver and spent every minute of every day trying to get him to live. His "failure to thrive," mentioned on the death certificate, I daresay, may have been because the last nurse was careless and the nursing board even more so. My mother had wanted to sue them for medical malpractice, but she didn't have definitive proof; no autopsy was ever done. The nursing board determined there was no violation of the law and voted to dismiss my mother's complaint a year after my father died in their care, and they considered the matter closed. But if no autopsy was done, how did they determine these causes of his death?

I want to review his medical files, but my mother's pain of unburying everything would be too great. She tried to remedy what she could and has moved on. Besides, what could I do? If I learned anything in my research, it was that records are wrong all the time. I'll never know the answers, or possibly even the right questions to ask about how he or anyone in my town died, especially if the documents were written by people who have their own story to tell. One more question: why wasn't my father's name on his union's memorial alongside Ron Hemingway? They both died of indirect causes from the mill, the net effect of their work. Speaking of cause and effect, that's what I've been looking for all these years: in my ancestors' migrations, in cancer rates, in wealth disparity, in the disappearance of the working-class, and in the past itself and all the concomitant truths it holds. I'd found no shortage of effects but determining causes was like catching smoke in the wind, as Terry's group tried to do. My father's death certificate is testimony to these things. All I can do is continue to connect the dots, drawing one line to another until some kind of shape emerges.

It's almost impossible to draw a straight line from our mill to cancer. Someone leaves Mexico. They get cancer. Some people never leave. They get cancer. Or vice versa. Some people smoke, like my grandmother Hortense, who inhaled cigarettes furiously every day. She didn't get cancer. You work in a paper mill like my father, grandfather, and great-grandfather, you get cancer. Some people do not. At least not yet. There are long delays between environmental exposures and cancer, too long to calculate, and each cancer comes with individual risk factors, symptoms, causes. If you think your town contains a cancer cluster, consider the criteria: clusters require a greater-than-expected number of cancers in a narrowly defined group, i.e., the people must have the same type of cancer, in a limited geographic area, over a limited period of time, and all these factors have factors, including the limitations of science itself. In addition, if several family members get cancer, it doesn't count toward the cluster evidence you need. Ordinary cancers don't count either. And it doesn't appear the CDC analyzes how individual bodies respond to specific environmental factors. And even if a cancer cluster is found in your neighborhood, they may not be able to determine the exact cause or do anything about it. One in three people develop cancer over their lifetime, so maybe the question is, *when* will we get cancer?

• • •

WE LEAN ON science for proof but it rarely provides it. Science thrives on skepticism, interpretation, hypotheses, predictions, assumptions, uncertainty. Scientists are trained to be inconclusive and cautious. If you go to the doctor and ask, *am I going to die tomorrow?* she'll say she's not 100 percent sure you won't. When science fails to answer or explain, we sometimes turn to law, a recourse my mother considered in her grief. But the proof is no less elusive. Tort laws and regulation provide some protection for people with cancer but, as William Boyd writes in his paper "Controlling Toxic Harms," laws are "inadequate" because of their demand for scientific precision and evidence of harm, especially when trying to prove community exposure, where risk factors can be as diverse as the people who live there. The law also includes the EPA, which has been accused of colluding with industry at the expense of humans and the planet it's tasked to protect. How can we trust the law?

The European Union's method for regulating chemicals is *better safe than sorry* or "the Precautionary Principle," whereby industry must provide rigorous proof people or ecosystems won't be affected by industrial substances. "No data, no market" is their approach. In the US the regulatory approach is largely innocent until proven guilty. This places the burden of proof on us to prove toxics cause harm. In addition, testing of chemicals is standardized to a degree, but it depends on the country where they will be used and the will and power of the agency regulating them. Nobody is coordinating such a thing. So if the law fails us, what else can we do? I'm not sure I know.

The standards for permissible amounts of toxics allowable for humans to intake usually only deal with one substance at a time, and don't consider the burdens of one chemical or carcinogen or toxic in coordination with another, or the cumulative effects of all of them or some of them together. Tampons, diapers, beef, breast milk, cheese, air: what's the total intake? Nobody knows.

And if they did? Imagine for a moment the United States eliminated all the toxic chemicals it has created. Who's to say China, Germany, Japan, Finland, Canada, Brazil would do the same? The permutations mirror what it's like when we look at galaxies in outer space. As for the two thousand new chemicals introduced into the US every year and the eighty thousand chemicals still untested, how can any agency—let alone an underfunded, understaffed, and often industry-friendly government agency—possibly keep up?

While cancer is not provincial, neither are pollutants; they do not stay where we put them. They move and seep into silt, get ingested by cows and babies, soar through smokestacks across the world, or crawl downriver into the ocean and into lobster flesh.

Rachel Carson called chemicals "sinister" in her 1962 landmark work *Silent Spring*. Our post–Agent Orange, post–atomic bomb, post-DDT, R&D industrial defoliated landscape proved her claim. Then, people started fearing chemicals of any kind, even ones exonerated by science. It didn't help that industry fought back against regulation with corruption and lies, deploying an alphabet soup of sinister acronyms like CERCLA, which sound like chemicals themselves.

Yet because you can't draw a straight line doesn't mean there's no line. While we largely accept the risks of our own bad behaviors—smoking, drinking, lying in the sun with iodine on our skin—we are trapped in a much bigger environment, one in which we don't know what all the risks are. Our body burden—the total amount of toxic chemicals present in a person's body—is exactly that: the burden an individual must bear because our regulatory organizations, science, and laws can't or won't. It is also our burden to decode the vernacular of toxicologists and environmentalists and academics and journalists who feed us the news; don't we already have burdens enough? In the meantime, toxics accumulate in our bodies like Hummel figurines accrue, their presence a placeholder for something that may or may not multiply out of control.

· · ·

IT'S NOT FAIR, I thought, when the doctor delivered my father's prognosis of cancer, for which she gave no definitive cause. But asbestosis, which my father definitely had, can develop into lung cancer in ten, thirty, or fifty years, and if you ever smoked like he did, the likelihood increases with every puff you take. Yet connecting asbestos exposure to lung cancer is difficult to do. Many cancers are "idiopathic," a Greek word meaning "of local origin," i.e., not seemingly caused by something outside the body: idio (one's own) and pathos (suffering). An idiopathic diagnosis, like in my father's death certificate, blames the body itself for its own undoing.

Perhaps it was our fault in the end. We've been creating the very thing that could be destroying us in the landscape of the American Dream. But blame, like a river's flow, is a fugitive act, because its target shape-shifts as the current of time presses forward, as fugitive as finding ancestors who died long ago.

For years, asbestos manufacturers knew about the dangers of the fiber and did nothing except block the government from regulating it. Today scientists are certain: asbestos causes harm. It's a known human carcinogen, and like dioxin, there's no safe level of exposure. You'd think that's the end of the line for asbestos—a carcinogen banned in most developed countries except a few (including the US), a substance that ruined a generation of lives. Yet on June 1, 2018, the EPA announced a "significant new use rule" to allow US companies to manufacture, import, and process new asbestos-containing products, despite the enormous number of studies done on the health risks resulting from its use.

At a 1964 conference on asbestosis sponsored by the New York Academy of Sciences, scientists presented data showing that asbestos was found in people "who lived in the same house with workers who came home with asbestos dust on their clothes." It turns out asbestos can cling not only to someone's clothes, but to their lunch basket, shoes, hair, car, bedding, skin, sofa, and subsequently end up in their family's lungs, too. My father always showered after work at the mill but it didn't matter. My mother, who laundered so many clothes, didn't know the shit didn't wash off.

There are lines we follow (family lines), lines we shouldn't cross (picket lines), and lines we hardly dare to bridge (silences among ourselves). There are also lines that lead us down an odd path (Babe, the blue ox) or lines that bisect the haves and the have-nots (sacrifice zones, football teams). Then there are lines we follow because it's the fastest way downhill (skiing). The only straight line I've found in this whole damn mess is the clothesline where my mother hung her wash.

BURIED IN PAPER

TO UNDERSTAND THE past and the future it foretells—in family, in disease rates, in our governmental and societal rules—for ten years I gathered information from historical societies, academic journals, the EPA, experts, legal briefs, sociological studies, poets, environmental historians, lobbyists, courts, lawyers, news articles, chemists, death certificates, and took thousands of photographs. I sent out surveys, talked to high school classmates, teachers, millworkers, students, lunch ladies, my mother, my father, their friends. I traveled to Canada, France, and fifteen or so other countries along the way and made endless trips to Maine. I read about organochlorines, Acadian history, labor unions, logging, economics, chestnut trees, Agent Orange, and long boring essays about how boilers work. I tried to understand cancer studies written in a forgettable language like: "Workers exposed to volatile organochlorines experienced a deficit of all-cause [SMR = 0.91; 95% confidence interval (CI), 0.89–0.93] and all-cancer (SMR = 0.93; 95% CI, 0.89–0.97) mortality, with no evidence of increased risks for any cancer of a priori interest." There's no end to what I don't know, can't know, can't translate, won't ever have the time or capacity to understand because I'm not an expert of any kind except for following rabbit holes that tunnel far below what the naked eye can see.

As I stockpiled this mass of things I thought I needed in order to connect the dots, I simultaneously had been compiling a list of all the documents I didn't have, would need, couldn't seem to find, were withheld from me, didn't have access to, all the information I'd seen spelled out in the negative by the countless stories accumulating in town. I added to and deleted from this list as each year went by.

Sometime in 2014, I met with a Pulitzer Prize–winning journalist who told me the point of my investigation was to find the absolute truth, and to get at the truth I'd have to sacrifice the unvetted, unverifiable stories from people I'd meet. *Nobody wants to read about characters,* he said. But there are a few problems with his stance: One, that facts alone can produce rational decision-making or arrive at some greater good place because they can't. Science, the ultimate venue of facts, is also the greatest source of uncertainty. Two, nonempirical belief systems are strong adversaries to facts. Take tuberculosis, which everyone originally thought was caused by personality flaws. Or consider anti-vaxxers' sentiment on preventative medicine. Or people who believe in different gods. Beliefs, while not provable, shouldn't be dismissed as ignorance or sociopathy, because they are "an integral part of the process of coping with and adapting to invisible threats" and help reduce the stress of ambiguity, as Henry Vyner states in his book *Invisible Trauma.* Three, authorities are not always authorities on the evidence they wish to convey. The EPA, tire-derived-fuel experts, archivists, lobbyists— they all embody subjective truths. Four, so much of the information I sought was inaccessible due to cost or access, like academic journals, ancestry.com, or laws like the ones that protect our president's tax records. Most humans are simply not privy to the political and financial worlds whose verdicts affect us. Five, human error is a fact itself. Yet here I was, gathering facts as if in a maelstrom. Obviously, that journalist's words had an effect on me.

Under the Maine Freedom of Access Act, I write a letter and address it to the Maine DEP, figuring they would have the missing facts I sought so I can resolve the puzzle of whatever it still is I'm looking for. In the letter I ask the "custodian of records" for all "documents," "internal communications," "records," "written communication," and/or "electronically stored information" in thirty-six numbered points that identify everything from environmental permits to Doc Martin and whatever lay in between. I even define "documents" in a separate 223-word paragraph. I cover the bases, as my father would appreciate, to an alarming degree. I had success with these kinds of official requests before, in my job as a litigation paralegal from 2001 to 2005 and, more recently, investigating Nestlé and Poland Spring. I know the lingo to use, just how specific to be, where to file such requests, and what will make the recipient nuts. When I finally feel I can include all I can include on my Freedom of Information Act request, on January 8, 2018, I email my appeal. Within a week, I get a phone call in return.

"Many of the older files are buried," the DEP Compliance and Procedure specialist says.

"Can we unbury them?" I ask.

He says the DEP staff will pull seven to ten boxes and then I can go from there, and they'll help me once I go through all that. A few emails back and forth and he accommodates most of my needs. One set of files is too large—license transfers of the mill—so he downloads them to a flash drive for ten dollars payable upon receipt. Everything else I can look at for free. I schedule a meeting for March 2018.

· · ·

I DRIVE TO Maine the week before my appointment and attend Easter service with my mother. It's one of my favorite Catholic holidays, for the incense and for the magical tale it tells. When Jesus's disciples visit his tomb to grieve, bringing the spices they prepared, Jesus himself was nowhere to be found, just a stained piece of linen lay where his body once did. An angel appeared and informed them: *he has risen.*

The otherworldly and inexplicable aspect of rising from the dead is the part I love; how a corpse can transform into something else, how a man's death can start a religion, and how advocates of the Shroud of Turin believe an image of Christ appeared in the negative on a fabric remnant. It's a bit of sorcery, this cosmic resurrection, and it's easy to see how the Romans thought the Jesus act was part of a cult. Jesus's

Easter performance perhaps wasn't much different than seeing Bigfoot or UFOs, which are all supernatural, near-divine events given credence by testimonials of credible witnesses like the disciples also did on Easter day. Take Jesus and the Bible out of the mix, the story would make a good Stephen King novel.

As my mother I and kneel at church, I can't help but compare King's book sales to the Bible's: the former around 350 million and the latter around 5 billion, allegedly the best-selling book of all time. I wonder how much paper those Bibles use, and was any of it Totally Chlorine Free?

Yet somehow the service commemorating all of this is sweet and solemn, the mass made more intimate by the candles everyone holds in their hands. The priest pendulums the thurible of ancient incense through the nave, a prayer for the faithful heading to heaven. The song, the incantations, the whispered *Amen*s speak of resurrection, communion, cooperation, amends. The priest with his underlit face delivers the liturgy and we respond in a monotone: *This is the day the Lord has made; let us rejoice and be glad,* with rustling missals we retrieve from the pockets on the back of the pews. When the lights go on, I see the church is not even half full. A few children are baptized. Everyone claps.

The next morning, as my mother leaves for work at the school, I pack up my car: my new scanner purchased just for this day, a digital camera, my laptop, my phone as a backup camera, my iPad as backup to my backup camera, a voice recorder, pens, pencils, Post-its, and notebooks—all the tools I think I'll need to record the truth. Under a light drizzle, I drive to Augusta to the DEP.

The closer I get, the more my focus sharpens, like when I was a paralegal helping attorneys build a legal case. I never got stressed by difficult work or the unknown because I was brought up to not watch the ball go by on the third strike, to take the quickest line downhill, to work my fingers to shreds if that's what needed to be done. And never, under any circumstances, throw like a girl.

I park and look at a congregation of turn-of-the-century brick buildings. I can't tell where to go. I look for a sign, try a few doors that are locked, walk behind the buildings and along paved paths to a garden in disrepair. I look at my watch. I'm already ten minutes late and it's starting to pour. Finally, I see someone else walk through an unlocked door and follow them in.

A woman behind bulletproof glass directs me to the file room. I proceed through a warren of narrow halls with walls the color of mold. Down the first set of stairs, I take a left and pass through a small canteen and look around. The short-order cook points to a side door without saying a word. I ring a buzzer and a file room clerk opens it and says hello.

Here and there, stacks of boxes billeted in makeshift corrals wait until clerks can place them in more permanent quarters. The bent of white winter light smuggles through small windows just above the foundation. The smell of copy machine ozone commingles with the waxy cheese pizza from the canteen just on the other side of the locked door. When someone enters the file room, a dense whirr of industrial refrigerators, then a vacuumed *whomp* as the door slams closed, delivering a fresh wind of pizza.

I sit down to ten boxes and a desk of my own. "Let us know if you have any questions," one of the staff offers. If they only knew.

• • •

THE DEP IS housed on the grounds of the former Augusta Mental Health Institute (AMHI), where for over 160 years Maine stashed away its mentally ill, the "insane," "lunatics," and, later, substance abusers, addicts, and troublesome teens. Like many mental health institutions of yore, here patients were treated with shameless disregard, bullied, even served cruelty by hand: caged, handcuffed, or given electroshock or insulin shock therapy without consent. Threats of suicide were also routinely and recently (allegedly) ignored. Patients were fed sedatives, laxatives, Succus Alternans (a blood purifier), tincture of Passiflora Incarnate (passionflower, a sleep aid), and given injections of Trypasamide (used chiefly for African sleeping sickness), Bismuth Sodium Tartrate and Marpharsen (for venereal disease), Serpasil (high blood pressure), Thorazine, Lithium—a whole estate of pharmaceuticals. The hypnotic agent chloral hydrate used with bromides of potassium and ammonia was used as an antimasturbatory solution. Other treatments included radiant heat, ultraviolet, hydrotherapy, diathermy, sine wave (for women), galvanism, faradism, electric needle, and eventually psychiatric counseling and therapy.

"If you dared think for yourself, you found yourself in trouble," one former patient said about her experience. "We walked like zombies up and down the corridor with the Thorazine shuffle."

I remember when I was a kid, adults and friends alike would threaten us with the image of being detained there if we were acting a little offbeat: *You're going to be sent to Augusta,* they'd say. I imagined AMHI to be a place like the hotel in Stanley Kubrick's film *The Shining* or like the sadistic psychiatric hospital in *One Few Over the Cuckoo's Nest,* both movies I had seen. They were refractions of AMHI in my mind's eye; AMHI was a place I never wanted to go.

"There are tunnels under the buildings," the DEP file clerk says, handing me another box. "It's creepy. In one place, you can see the outline of sweat of a person's body where they used to chain them against the wall."

The former Kennebec Arsenal, the largest ammunition depot along the east coast during the Civil War, also stood on these grounds. When the federal government closed the arsenal in 1901, the property was conveyed to the state and the surviving granite buildings were absorbed into AMHI's grip. Much of the wood structures got torn down. Stone tunnels under the buildings had shuttled munitions during the war, and after AMHI moved in, they sheltered patients and staff who commuted between buildings during bothersome weather. Parts of the arsenal were sold to a private developer with historic-preservation restrictions, but the developer deferred its next evolution and left the interior walls peeling like roasted skin.

With changes in the treatment for mental illness came change in the buildings that housed the patients. Society demanded more healing environments with such things as courtyards and private rooms and natural light. AMHI vacated the premises in 2004. The DEP moved in a short time later, and I'm pretty sure not much has changed in the overall architectural design. The three uses for the site—as arsenal, psychiatric hospital, and DEP headquarters—shared parking lots, history, and a capacity to harbor pain, suffering, and societal ills.

. . .

When DEP administrators evacuate their congested inboxes, those papers are interred in the rooms of the basement where I now sit. Imagine the aggregate of such complicated and drawn-out work as the ongoing efforts to keep water and air clean tossed haphazardly into the nearest container with observable relief: *One file goes here, a file there, maybe I will just stick this here.* Month after month, year after year not having the time or an assistant to sort it all out. *The past is past* they must say to themselves once a matter is laid to rest as they move on to the kingdom of other matters accumulating on their desks.

I ask the file room clerks what the organizing principle is, and they laugh. "We are not responsible for organizing anything," one of them says. "We just file what they give us."

And that's what it feels like as I comb through the boxes in front of me. Many are disorganized, redundant, some faxes indecipherable, like a pressed flower a century old. I'm sure the filing system made sense at the time, but thirty years later it's unclear. And perhaps the person with expertise on the subject has died or retired or both. Email didn't exist early on, so any oral conversations that occurred have been lost to the annals of time and air.

A 112-page operations manual for "Farrington Mountain Landfill, 2005" is in three different boxes, one has what seems to be a full appendix, one has *some* of an appendix, one doesn't have any appendix at all. Is the appendix really complete? One file from 1997 abuts a file from 1983 and they don't seem related. Were they accidentally stapled together when someone's inbox had overflowed?

I remember something the paper consultant had told me, how when a paper mill is sold, the buyer is responsible not just for the property taxes owed, but for toxics they inherit even if they are buried ten feet deep. However, if the mill goes bankrupt, there's no one to fund accompanying environmental mitigation or cleanups, so the state is left with the mess. And if the state doesn't have the money, the site is left in limbo to be dealt with at a future date. If the state sells the property to someone else, environmental obligations may or may not go along with the sale and the whole circuitry of responsibility starts all over again. In the end, communities like ours may be the ones who pay. The flash drive I obtained from the DEP contains those license transfers for the mill's most recent sales. I put in the thumb drive and at least one page looks like this:

```
≤∫
ˇÆ∏ˌê$
ˇÆ∏ˌê$
ˇÆ∏ˌê$
ˇÆ∏ˌê$
fl˘ÛÏÏ«¿∫≥≥éáÅzzUNHAAˇÆ∏ˌê$
ˇÆ∏ˌê$
ˇÆ∏ˌê$
fl ˇÆ∏ˌê$
ˇÆ∏ˌê$
ˇÆ∏ˌê$
ˇÆ∏ˌê$
˘ÛÏÏ«ˇÆ∏ˌê$
```

· · ·

THE MAIN AMHI structure was built in 1840 across from the Maine State House as a reminder to legislators not to overlook the disenfranchised people of the state. Yet nearly a quarter of AMHI's residents—11,647 people—died on its premises over 165 years, and almost all records of where their bodies were buried are as lost as their tragic souls. Mental health institutions all over the country were guilty of warehousing humans and then burying them in unmarked plots. And why not? They had been treated even more cruelly when they were alive.

All told, across the US, over 300,000 former psychiatric patients were carelessly interred without a paper trail left behind. We've a long history of stockpiling the unwanted in such institutions or landscapes of no relevance or concern: prisons, homeless camps, Section 8 housing, small industrial towns. Even with years of research and efforts by advocacy groups and concerned individuals, most of those missing AMHI graves were never found.

As I watch the soft ruffle of papers slide through my scanner, I can't stop thinking about those forgotten people. They were like unchristened babies in lonely cemetery spots. Time clocks by at the speed of an IV drip. I snack at my desk, saving the potato chips for later when I'm not embarrassed by their crunch.

In one box, pinched between two maps, I find documents about the mill's first landfill, "Olsky." Joseph Olsky's property contained a natural crater between the low hills of Mexico, a perfect dimple in the earth. It rested on the side of Farrington Mountain, three-quarters of a mile from John DeSalle's Motor Inn and adjacent to the Oakdale Country Club where my father played his daily game.

Around 1967, the year I was born, Mexico's selectmen negotiated a contract that designated Olsky's property as a landfill for the mill's wastes. Terry remembers the meeting when one selectman, pleased with the thought of the good he was doing for the town, said, *Rumford gets all the tax breaks from having the paper mill. Mexico gives a lot of workers to that paper mill and we don't get any of the tax benefits from it, so let's have a landfill!* A round of mild applause stippled the room.

Terry and Jenny from the Toxic Women activist group snuck up to Olsky one day in the early 2000s. They were told fish floated in a putrid stream and wildlife sported strange tumors near the capped debris and so they wanted to see for themselves. A few kids my brother knows said when they field-dressed deer they shot near Olsky, the animals' insides were so destroyed, they discarded or buried the carcass and meat. Jenny's adventurous mood served the deed on the eve of the caper, but she forgot to tell Terry that she badly needed hip replacement surgery.

An acquaintance led Terry and Jenny up the back way in his truck, stopped at the end of a dirt road, gave them fresh donuts, coffee, and directions, and sent them on their way. After they skirted the golf course, they found Olsky. Nearby, pools of black "stuff" glistened in shallow impressions in the land. Then Jenny slipped on a wooded slope and couldn't quite get up. Her hip had given out. Terry considered pressing on to find the source of the oozing black gunk but decided against abandoning poor Jenny alone in the woods. Every time they saw each other until the day cancer brought Jenny down for good, they regretted not sampling the goo emerging from those woods. Here, in the DEP file, amid other Olsky material, I find a picture of a pool of the black stuff they must have seen, marked "Photos 1/10/83. Boise Cascade Sludge Landfill 26-0686."

Before I came here, I had requested and received a document from the EPA showing the disposition of the Olsky landfill indicating Terry and Jenny were on the right track. At Olsky the EPA had found elevated levels of mercury, chromium, lead, and many volatile organic compounds (VOCs) and semi-VOCs in the soil and additional chemicals in the groundwater all exceeding state standards. So here is one trail I can follow today and this is what I find:

Ethyl Corporation (the mill) purchased the Olsky property in 1967 and used it as a landfill for mill waste from 1970 to '73. Olsky consists of four unlined lime mud basins, one site just called "dump" and another called "Elect. Chem 1970-71." From 1910 to 1979, the Sorensen Electrochemical Plant (abbreviated above as "Elect. Chem") at our

mill produced chlorine and caustic soda by the electrolysis of sodium chloride in a mercury cell process for use in the bleaching of paper. The process resulted in asbestos waste and mercury releases to soil and water under and near the facility. The electrochemical plant was razed in 1979 in order to build a recovery boiler and a cogeneration plant. During its demolition, half the building's remains were left on site and covered with six inches of soil. Mercury and polychlorinated biphenyl (PCB) debris was stockpiled in the North Mill Yard. About four thousand to nine thousand cubic yards of the same debris was trucked to the Olsky landfill and some of the mercury-contaminated soil was used as backfill on site. As was the practice (law?) at the time, no landfill liner impeded migration of the toxics in the waste.

The mill never sought the DEP's permission for removing the demolition debris because they, the mill, classified it as "mill yard waste," not hazardous waste. Approximately 1,347 tons of the mercury-contaminated "mill yard waste" was taken to Consolidated Waste Services (CWS), a landfill in Norridgewock and the largest commercial landfill in Maine.

By the mid-1980s, when I graduated from high school, Olsky was full. The mill put a lid on it and planted grass over the cap, as if it were never there at all. In 1990, John DeSalle, who owned a motor inn on the banks of the Androscoggin just downhill from Olsky, wanted to expand, so he drilled another well to accommodate the RVs he anticipated camping on his property. When he hit the water table, up bubbled pea soup. The DEP tested DeSalle's water and determined the chemicals in the well were the same chemicals found in Olsky. The mill suggested there could have been another source. *The tests proved nothing*, they argued. The DEP ultimately agreed. The mill, as a neighborly gesture, built DeSalle a new well and provided bottled water to a few nearby residents. And the pea soup stayed covered up, like so many things in our valley.

I also found out that earlier, in 1982–1983, the EPA required the mill to test the North Mill Yard's soil to see if any hazardous wastes were still present from the Sorensen Electrochemical Plant. Supposedly nothing worrisome was found. I was surprised, considering how much mercury had remained after they leveled that facility to the ground. In 1995, portions of the cogeneration plant floor built on the former mercury mess needed repair. It was jackhammered and tiny beads of mercury clung to the cement chips that flew all around. The mercury, apparently, was just below the surface and not so deep at all and at levels above the levels it was supposed to have.

Subsequently, the DEP put in place a "Declaration of Restrictive Covenant" that outlines the status of Olsky as it stands today, which is "operation and maintenance," meaning there's nothing additional to be done. The covenant also indicates that in 1999 and 2000, the "Owner" (the mill) performed their own assessment and found only low concentrations of VOCs in the shallow earth and slightly elevated levels of mercury in other spots. The covenant also indicates the former "Electro-Chem Disposal Area" and "1970 Lime Mud Basin Area" were "eliminated" by "waste removal," meaning (I think but am not sure) that the debris was sent to the Norridgewock landfill. The covenant also establishes "institutional controls" placed upon the owner, which means the mill is required to control erosion, grow native vegetation in the open space, and allow for passive recreational pursuits (snowmobiling or ATVs) but not to do anything that might disturb the napping toxics embedded in the ground.

I drive back to my mother's at the end of the day, we eat dinner, watch CNN, and go to bed by eight.

. . .

IN THE MORNING, I look online for AMHI information before driving back to Augusta for another round. I find an article about an art therapist who began working with AMHI's patients in later years to help "translate . . . feelings into visual metaphor." In her enthusiasm, the art therapist encouraged patients to paint over ugly photographs that adorned the hospital's walls in a more creative form. Then she rehung the obscured images where they were first found. Colorful murals and poetry also appeared on the tunnel walls, the bright blues casting off the gray of the stone. A few poems still caress the underground paths, like this one written by an anonymous convalescent: "Among

These books, a great amount of Knowledge There must be, / But what good is Knowledge where others carry the keys . . ."

Some of AMHI's adolescent patients weren't comfortable with painting large landscapes and asked if they could just trace themselves on the walls. Their outlines cataloged a more diminished and transient mood than the big cheery murals others had left behind. The tunnels are now pretty much off limits, mainly because of their dangerous neglect, but it's a place nobody likes to go anyway to face specters and imprints of human pain.

Back at the DEP, the more I learn, the more there is to learn, and sometimes I end up further from my main question; is the pollution from our mill connected to the diseases in our town? Did the pollution harm my family, my friends, and will it harm me? Much of what I seek seems missing or misplaced or maybe never added to the file at all, and some I'm sure is buried deeper than the mercury on that bulldozed land. Even so, do all these documents about pollutants to land, air, and water tell the whole story, half a story, or even a sixteenth? Are they even worth the paper they're printed on?

. . .

THIS THING I started over twenty years ago began with my grandfather's obituary and ends with my father's, but is it really the end? Months after I leave the DEP, papers still rain in on my desk every day and I try to make sense of them the best I can. I find no smoking gun, no magic bullet, no conspiracy, no Shroud of Turin to condemn or acquit the mill, my family, or the state or federal government. The truth, it seems, is not about hard evidence in your hand. It's about examining and poking at long-held beliefs in the portals of history then pushing back on them, like my ancestors pushed back the Acadian tides with the palms of their hands.

Just a few towns away from where I live, Danbury, Connecticut was once known as the "Hat Capital of the World." The hatters, as the hatmakers were called, used boiling hot mercuric nitrate to shape and convert animal pelts into their desired form. The mercury-tinged vapors and sweat from the solution drizzled down on the hatters' heads in poorly ventilated rooms. Over time, hatters got the "Danbury Shakes," or mercury poisoning. The symptoms ranged from tremors and jerky movements to irritability, lack of coordination, poor memory, insomnia, and psychological traits such as pathological shyness, mental confusion, and emotional disturbances. Mercury poisoning in the modern era can occur through ingesting fish or the burning of coal, or even overexposure to caustic soda and industrial debris. Those mad hatters, as they were known because of their tattered mental state, like so many working-class laborers, were poisoned by their own careers.

The Annual Report of the Bureau of Statistics of Labor and Industries of New Jersey wrote of the hatters: "The surprise is that men can be induced to work at all in such death producing enclosures. It is hard to believe that men of ordinary intelligence could be so indifferent to the ordinary laws of health. . . . It does not seem to have occurred to them that all the efforts to keep up wages . . . [are] largely offset by the impairment of their health."

How men can be "induced" to working in less than great conditions is like the Hatter asking Alice in Wonderland, "Why is a raven like a writing desk?" Sometimes there's no clear answer to the riddle at all.

THE TRUTH LIES SOMEWHERE

IN MID-NOVEMBER 2019, over a year and a half after my Maine DEP visit and three days before this book is due to start production, Mike Matthews texts me about some documents he and his wife, Angela, found while cleaning their house: "What we r sending you, vindicates everything you have ever written or said about Cancer Valley. We are against pollution, innocent people being exploited like a 'Renewable Resource' and the corruption and coverup of these issues by the State and Federal Government." Naturally, I'm intrigued.

I had not forgotten about Mike, whom I met on July 4, 2017, but back then, I wasn't sure where he fit in. I hadn't known him growing up and he orbited around other people and things. I knew he worked in the mill, and during my research I found out he was a stakeholder on the NOCC investigation team where he positioned himself as someone who cared about the mill and the people it employed, while also caring about the pollution he helped make. I asked around about Mike and one person smiled and said "he's a little odd" and left it at that. Another person said he "talked A LOT." But as I got to know him I found he had a lot of interesting things to say. And not many people had listened.

. . .

"Did you see my chestnut tree?" Mike asked, pointing to a tree in his driveway as I got out of my car.

An American chestnut grew next to the driveway, a tree he and Angela planted fifteen years ago. It was tall and perfectly formed, like a first grader's hand-drawn tree. Long catkins feathered the dark green of its toothy leaves. By fall, nuts will plonk to the ground.

I knew a little about chestnuts, being the believer in underdogs that I am. The American chestnut was an American story: a tenacious, fast-growing tree, adaptable, hardworking, and mythical. At one time chestnuts were so prominent a squirrel could travel from Georgia to Maine across their canopy. Its rot-resistant wood helped expand the American West with telephone poles and railroad ties. Pioneers and craftsmen used chestnut to build furniture, houses, coffins, pianos, musical instruments. Its lightweight wood was easy to work, the bark was used for tanning, and its nuts, a nutritional food for animals and humans alike. The tree was determined to be a keystone species, meaning it provided habitat and sustenance for nearly everything in its circumference; it was an ecosystem unto itself and essential to, and part of, daily life in America. Chestnuts were useful, common, dependable—until they disappeared. They were the working-class of trees.

A fungus was accidentally imported to the US around 1900 and it quickly spread to the chestnut, entering wounds on its bark until cankers developed, eventually girdling the trunk and shutting off nutrients and water from its roots. The fungus spread until killing the entire tree outright. In just fifty years, the product of thousands of years of evolution was decimated: from four million to fewer than one hundred trees remained.

I followed Mike into his house through the garage, so as to not disturb the birds mobbing the feeders near the front door: two species of nuthatches, purple finches, chickadees, cardinals, doves, a nesting pair of flycatchers, and either an Eastern Phoebe or "two similar possibilities: an Eastern Pewee or the Least Flycatcher," Mike said. Four to five pairs of rose-breasted grosbeaks who flew up from Venezuela or Panama also summered there. Goldfinches flashed their feathers as I scraped the door across the threshold, closing it behind me. "Birds have been on the decrease for the last thirty years or so," Mike said over his shoulder as we walked into the kitchen. "Very few people care. It's *Silent Spring* all over again."

Angela was preparing lunch. I said hello.

Mike and I shifted into the living room, a cool, dark den adorned with shelves of old-fashioned hurricane lamps, a huge TV, and soft, antimacassared chairs and sofas, which cushioned the clatter and flash of the midday news. Pictures and other decor colonized every square inch of the walls. I submerged into a nearby chair. Zieg, their Doberman, nosed my knee.

Mike and Angela lived on the outskirts of Rumford in a house built in 1940, put together originally, Mike said, by Mickey Mouse. Their son Erik was learning carpentry by renovating the kitchen; so far, he outfitted the walls with antique vertical chestnut boards, replaced the old double-hung windows, and inserted two metal doors. His work buttressed the walls . . . walls that tilt. Erik also did odd jobs around town too, unable to get work in the mill, Mike believed, because of Mike's "big mouth."

"Those of us who feel strongly compelled to speak up when we see a problem are demonized," he said, explaining what he means by his big mouth. "I was never against 'our mutual way of life,' as Jolene Lovejoy once said to me. I wanted to meaningfully address our public health problems in the River Valley. But politicians impede net gains for everyone. We are far more than just a disposable, renewable resource."

He made a lot of sense to me.

• • •

MIKE WAS A kid when he first came through town on the way to Byron, where his father owned property. As they drove by the Androscoggin, Mike never forgot the image: "cakes of gunk" drifting on the water like dirty, mean ice floes. His father, after working years at a tissue factory in Lewiston, eventually moved to Byron full-time. Mike moved with him, graduated from Mexico High School in 1968, and worked in the mill the summer of 1969 before going to college. When Mike walked into the mill that summer he was teased. *Hippie. The new guy with the attitude problem. A radical.*

"People rely heavily upon image," he said. I looked at him: his chin-length, thin, curly hair spilled over his silver wire-framed glasses he kept pushing up on his nose, his face soft.

He wasn't a radical, even in appearances. I got the feeling he always wanted to do the right thing, keep a balance between speaking up and doing his job without making too many waves. He was the kind of guy who followed protocol to an alarming degree, and he wasn't a hippie but for his longish hair. He was just the new guy in town with a last name and a father nobody knew. He was also the only guy questioning the mill's practices.

Mike started working full-time in the mill in 1976. He noticed, among other things, "dangerous processes" and "a collective denial" in the millworkers he knew. He would ask coworkers about cancers they had or observed and would write down their answers in the notecards he carried around in his shirt pocket. They humored him because he was smart, young, and a little naive. In the lunchroom, he'd show them the statistics he was compiling. *Wow,* they'd say, *look at all those people who died of cancer!*

"Then we'd go back to our jobs," Mike said, "back into denial again. I knew then I was onto something. The truth is hidden."

Mike talked like this: *The truth will set you free. Knowledge is power. The end justifies the means. The truth is hidden.* But his clichés felt earnest, like he invented them. He said he's "no good at politics" but it didn't prevent him from questioning authority, which itself was a political act. Mike didn't see his inquisitiveness that way. He simply believed he saw what nobody else saw.

"In politics the perception is the reality," he said. "The *perception* in the mill was that everything was fine. It wasn't. Your dad was exploited."

"Did you know my father?" I asked.

"I'd see him around from time to time. He was one of the good guys," Mike said, petting Zieg. "I die a bit inside knowing how your dad and many others suffered various horrible diseases. I know he had asbestosis, where you have significant loss of lung function but not the actual cancer. Was your father a smoker?"

I nodded.

"See, they hold that against you."

"He hadn't smoked in a long time, though," I said.

"It's a smokescreen they use. No pun intended," Mike said. "You're the victim but it's still your fault. *Shine the spotlight over here,* they'll say. It's a tactic. But you're playing with fire if you shine the spotlight on them."

Despite his constant suspicions about smokescreens, Mike liked his job and played a key role in getting his union to help pay for masks, goggles, and steel-toed boots and convinced the mill to test and label all asbestos products. His careful consideration of other people's health, he believed, earned him a troublesome reputation, that of someone who secretly wanted to shut the mill down.

"Do you?" I asked.

"As if I have some sort of economic suicidal death wish for myself?" he said, his words broken, malignant. "Or the whole area?!" Then he softened. "I just want to follow the law in worker health and safety."

Angela walked in the room. "You know she's saved two of our children's lives," Mike said, gesturing toward her: one choked on a sour ball while running and the other had a seizure. They have also lost two children: one to suicide and one to a freak river accident. "I'm in awe of her," Mike said.

"Lunch is ready," Angela said, deflecting the compliment and the conversation.

We sat down to platters of thick Omaha Steaks, hot dogs, and marinated chicken with a big bowl of potato salad garnished with bacon.

"Protein," Angela said, laughing. I helped myself to all of it.

Afternoon breezes of hot dry grass slipped through the kitchen as we watched catbirds feed and made small conversation in between mouthfuls of food.

"Love it or hate it, if this mill shuts down a lot of people are going to be hurt. Call me pessimistic, but I don't see the 'innovative creative minds' here being able to pursue Plan B, which truly is right there," Mike said, pointing out the window. "Our recreation, our water, our mountains. We have such great groundwater upstream from this valley, and we have such old laws that there's nothing to prevent someone like Poland Spring from taking it. That right there is the ultimate potential of this state—to lower taxes and a path to prosperity: water. It's becoming more and more valuable, more valuable than gold—water and the environment. We don't even give it a thought."

Mike and I had more in common than I thought. I asked if he knew how involved I had become with Nestle's invasion of our town, and how I had felt ejected from my own group.

"I know what rejection feels like," Mike said, and told me about his "soul dog," Kaiser. Kaiser went missing one day. Four days later he showed up with over four hundred porcupine quills in his body. Mike was pissed, scolded him, punished him by not making eye contact with the dog.

"Then Kaiser stopped eating," he said, his voice cracking. "I come from a broken family. Both my parents were functional alcoholics. You can't bond very deeply with an addict. They are too into themselves. Kaiser, he didn't want to live anymore because he thought I had broken my bond with him." Mike sobbed into his potato salad.

Angela sat down, reached out, and touched the top of his hand. I set down my fork and stared at the enormous pile of meat.

Angela looked at me, at the steak. "It won't go to waste. The kids will come over later for leftovers. I always cook enough for them."

Mike, his eyes still wet, said, "Since he died, nothing has been the same. I didn't tell him how much I loved him right before he died. One never gets a second chance."

As we talked of their love of animals, Angela and Mike said they were getting ready to go on a six-week vacation in August to the Washington State National Forest to do wilderness research.

"Wilderness research?" I asked. Nobody said anything in response. "What kind of research?" Silence. I felt like I said something wrong.

Mike mumbled through a bite of steak. Took a sip of water. Angela cleared our plates, walked over to the sink. Mike said something that sounded like "did he?"

"What did you say?" I asked. "Did you say 'did he'?" I turned to Angela.

"Actually, he said Biggie," Angela said.

"Where's that?" I asked.

"Bigfoot. But we call him Biggie," Mike responded, looking me squarely in the eyes.

I considered myself a person who didn't rule anything out, open to all possibilities.

"I've always been fascinated with Bigfoot," I said, which was totally true. But not to the degree I would try to find such a thing. Mike looked visibly relieved. "How do you know where to look?"

"Thank you," he said. "Usually when I mention Bigfoot people think I'm crazy. I look for protein clusters."

I look back at the pile of steak. "If one can believe in God, why not Bigfoot?" I said, stabbing my fork into the mass. "Likely, there's more possibility of Bigfoot. Religious people would argue that God's work is all around. But I daresay God's work would include Bigfoot if such a thing exists."

"Oh it exists," Mike said.

Both Bigfoot and God, I think, require oceans of faith, yet only one requires evidence to prove it exists: Bigfoot.

"Why can't the *lack* of evidence allow the possibility Bigfoot exists?" I asked. Mike then felt comfortable to tell me about a few of his expeditions to find Bigfoot. After a while, it occurred to me to ask: "*Why* do you look for Bigfoot?"

"It's about confronting your fears, about pushing the envelope, discovering something that most people can hardly talk about—the unknown. It's also about doing something that I wanted to do over half my life. I was an anthropology major with only sixteen hours from getting a bachelor's of science degree and so I'm leveraging my natural inclinations, alone in woods, off the grid. It's also nonconfrontational and I go to places where I would normally never go. The longer you study it the more compelling it becomes. There are many things in this world we don't understand."

• • •

I LOOK AT the eighty pounds of materials he sent to me on this November day, wishing they would go away. The files are organized, dated, he's included handwritten notes on some, and a few loose documents are bundled together with maroon yarn tied in a bow. I'd be stupid not to dip in.

One whole box is filled with binders containing the Maine Chronic and Sentinel Disease Surveillance Project from around 1980 to 1990, with tabs and tabs of data on asthma, leukemia, liver cancer, non-Hodgkin's lymphoma, aplastic anemia, all diseases I encountered in my research for the past ten years, all diseases showing up in my town, some in large percentages. Some material is from Mike's NOCC committee research, including meeting agendas, draft reports, and grassroots organizing tools. A whole binder delegated to studies related to paper mills and pollution. I put it aside. A few of his handwritten notes, in toned-down tones from how he speaks and without the clichés: "Public officials are rarely impressed by the facts," he wrote about the health survey NOCC planned to conduct. Many newspaper articles refer in some way to dioxin. Some of this stuff I've seen before. Some of it I have not.

Many records reference the high point in Maine's dioxin debate: when Maine's then governor, now senator Angus King voiced his opinion about dioxin at a 1995 conference on pollution prevention in the paper industry. The EPA's damning draft assessment on dioxin had just been published; dioxin was on everyone's mind.

King said in his speech to forty state environmental officials and forty paper industry officials who attended the conference: "You could make my life a lot easier if you could figure out a way to get rid of the dioxin." I know what he meant.

After the speech, allegedly, dioxin was not discussed at the conference. Not in the agenda or the breakout sessions or keynotes. It was relegated to a silence of another sort. A writer for *The Maine Sportsman* opined on the omission of dioxin discussions: "This is akin to holding a conference about the dangers of cigarette smoking where the attendees spend all day talking about the bad smell the smoke leaves on your clothes."

. . .

ALTHOUGH I HAD skimmed the EPA's draft assessment on dioxin years ago, trying to sum it up was like trying to sum up the Bible, and trying to understand it was like trying to understand God their/him/herself. It's hard to compute. I search through the notes on my computer to see what I wrote about that report and find an email exchange with Stephen Lester, the science director at the Center for Health, Environment & Justice, an organization led by Lois Gibbs, an activist who brought public attention to the Love Canal crisis. I had written to Stephen in 2017, asking if he could school me on the EPA's dioxin assessments, which was his area of expertise. He said to call; however, I dropped the ball.

I email Stephen again today, to see if he can clarify a few things, like why nobody's talking about dioxin when it seems a critical health issue, at least to me.

He says there were two studies the EPA released on dioxin—one was the *cancer* risk assessment released in draft in 2003; the other was the *non-cancer* risk assessment released in final form in 2012. I hadn't understood the difference until now. This was a change in the agency's strategy, Stephen said, to exclude the cancer risks from the final EPA dioxin study. That 2012 report only discussed non-cancer risks such as reproductive and immune problems associated with dioxin exposure. The 2003 draft determined that dioxin was carcinogenic and that the cancer risk was very high. Exposure to any amount of dioxin increased the risks of getting cancer.

"At the time of the 2012 report, the agency told us and the public in general that it was continuing to work on the *cancer* risk portion of assessment, that they were not done," Stephen writes. "But since that time, I've been told repeatedly by staff at EPA (often off the record) that the *cancer* risk portion is on the shelf with no plans by the agency to go back to it."

"Why?" I ask, innocently enough. "Why won't the EPA go back to finish the job and publish the final report?"

"When the EPA ran the [dioxin] risk numbers for cancer, those numbers came out so high it would have significant ramifications . . . a debilitating economic impact for the entire U.S. economy."

"What?" I hear myself asking him, not quite registering what he's saying.

"Put it this way, if the EPA used *cancer risk* rate data to determine how much dioxin would be allowed in food, you wouldn't be able to buy a McDonald's hamburger."

"McDonald's specifically?" I ask.

"No," he says, and says that the threshold for dioxin is so low, based on the 2003 *cancer risk* assessment, that almost all meat, fish, and animal by-products like butter and milk would have dioxin levels that exceed government standards for how much would be allowed in food. Even one simple hamburger could do a person harm. McDonald's is just a handy reference. He reiterates that the EPA doesn't currently list dioxin as a carcinogen.

"Will the EPA ever publish this data?" I ask. "Will they ever make these claims?"

"What they did was brilliant," he says. "They published the study on *non-cancer* risks in 2012 then walked away. Dioxin is no longer a problem in the public eye because the EPA stopped thinking about it and stopped analyzing it."

"So everyone thinks the study is done?" I say.

"It seems that way. No one worries about dioxin anymore."

But for Stephen, me, Terry, Mike Matthews, and others—it is never the end. Even if paper mills stopped releasing dioxin, it would not be the end of the problems it carries. Dioxin drifts downstream and in the wind that carries it up and out to sea, where it will someday be ingested by animals then by us and given to our babies in our own mother's milk. What a legacy we have made. In fact, when we are all dead and gone, when the planet has taken its last breath, I'm betting dioxin will be the only thing that remains. "Now this is not the end. It is not even the beginning of the end. But it is, perhaps, the end of the beginning," Winston Churchill said at the turning point of the war. It's how I feel about dioxin's endless harm and the discoveries I continue to make.

Mike would say this unpublished EPA assessment is a "smoking gun," a phrase I've heard him use before, but what if there's no smoke arising from that gun, or smoke nobody can see, and the only smoke is the smokescreen that's suspended over our town? Trying to find the center of this dioxin narrative is like unwrapping a set of infinitely smaller nesting Russian dolls or opening a Pandora's box where you can't tamp down the unforeseen but continuously appearing problems that manifest from their release. Both metaphors work. It's an endless negotiation trying to find what doesn't want to be found, as Mike experienced in his Bigfoot quests. Bigfoot, the truth, the missing members of my family tree, the effects of dioxin on our bodies, all exist in a liminal space, which is not a space in which we want to live most days.

Mike and I chase something that's near impossible to prove, and that ambiguity can traumatize us, as sociologists who studied the effects of Love Canal found. "Perception is the reality," another key phrase of Mike's, applies here as well. Whoever controls the story, controls the discourse (or the perception), and if you control the discourse, you establish the reality people accept. If the reality served is uncertainty, where do we go from there?

After I hang up the phone with Stephen I look at Mike's life's work hunkering at my feet, and I think about his chestnut tree, an important and overlooked accomplishment; to grow something for twenty-five years that, according to the USDA, has become functionally extinct. But the blight may have finally found Mike's tree he tells me; its leaves are distorted and full of holes and there are no insects to be found.

There still exists a small window of hope for the American chestnut's resurrection, however. The killing fungus cannot live in the soil surrounding the tree, and in that uncontaminated earth, the chestnut's root system begins to re-sprout. Saplings will prosper for a while, or years as Mike's has done, but when their bark cracks or is injured, the blight exploits the open wounds and kills the trees before they become mature and the cycle of death and life starts all over again. One strategy to recover the chestnut is to inject the trees with a virus to suppress the blight, indicating the solution is buried within the problem, that is, a fungus will be parasitized by a virus. Robert Frost, in his poem "Evil Tendencies Cancel," enumerated this idea that life and death were two sides of the same coin and that the trophic levels of nature could end the chestnut's demise.

CODA

THIS RECURSIVE MOTION of looking at the past and the present at the same time is as rocking as the watery tide. With each passing year, water conceals the more egregious crimes, diluting them until they become derivatives of themselves, their half-lives cut in half as our lives may be, too. Maybe the water is where that paper machine nameplate ended up—the one my father scraped from a paper machine—sunk to the bottom of some river, where it lost its shine, as time, space, and abuse took its toll.

We are so mesmerized by things that glitter, magpies that we are: Big Incidents, Urgent Incidents that make good TV like measles outbreaks, airplane crashes, white girls gone missing, people mowed down by lunatics with guns. Most of us never experience such tailspinning highs and lows. Our lives are assembled of less acute moments like homemade parades, distant trips with our dads, or low-priority, low-level contamination concerns like those found in Township E. Updates to those less glamorous crimes are stalled in agencies across the world, working their way slowly to the top of the inbox, just as slowly as toxics work their way up our food chain from groundwater, to sheep, to parmesan cheese, to our DNA. There must be hundreds, maybe thousands of sites like Township E. We only hear of a few, if any at all.

The news is that it's not news, because such people and landscapes drift in the peripheries where it's hard to see or where we don't bother to look, in isolated places of no tenable or fiscal concern. Such quiet tragedies only flicker in the headlines, which makes their consequences hard to pin down and difficult to voice. And voice is the very thing absented, invisible like the people themselves. This silence presages the slow corruption of all bodies—of water, of systems, of the human form.

The ambiguous boundaries of this corruption prophesy a future we don't want our children to see. If they even have a future at all. The environmental legacy we leave to them may be bigger than the United States debt. And we won't even know where those legacies will be found, for the memorials people build always honor and legitimize the perpetrators of those crimes, never the crimes themselves.

Maine's "Vacationland" narrative has become as polished as the steely urn that holds my father's ashes, as wrongheaded as our resolute silence, and as one-dimensional as ersatz postcards furnished at Tourist Information Booths across the state. It's been reinforced, too, by a landslide of books, artwork, tourists, clam shacks, and transplanted residents who bought property upwind or away from the mouths of dirty rivers.

Those who can't move become receptacles for our trash. We have always remanded garbage to the margins, to silent locations of despair, or tossed it into streams and watched it float away like a toy boat we can't trace. *Out of sight, out of mind* allows us to rest easier because we want to believe there is no lead in our tap water, no dioxin in our kids' blood, no legal, well-designed, well-operated, and well-maintained combustion device throwing shit up into our backyards. After all, there's always someone else carrying the burden for us. It's an illusion, this "poison-redistribution," because what we expel from our backyards eventually returns—but in more diabolical forms. Mass cannot be destroyed, only dispersed or rearranged.

The journal my father had started to keep ends up in my hands after Mike's boxes arrive. It consists of only four pages, but everything in them is about the river. The last two paragraphs read:

I remember one day in particular, I was waiting to dive but wouldn't because I was all alone. After about 15 minutes a man, a tourist I think, showed up. So I dove off. When I got out of the water he said to me, that was a beautiful dive. I thanked him. The reason I waited was because if something happened to me on the dive or I needed help, there would be someone there to assist.

The river, I found out later in life, was a vast sewer for all the people that lived on or near the river. I guess it didn't do me any harm.

John McPhee once wrote, "Rivers are the ultimate metaphors of existence" and my father knew this, too. But ours is an existence shaped by natural forces *and* human intervention, capitalism and its consequences, economic crimes without punishment, war without peace. In this existence we vowed to keep each other for richer, for poorer, in sickness and in health, but mostly we just keep the richer afloat, which has littered our landscapes with abandoned towns, mauled forests, toxics napping in the ground, poisoned fish that can't swim upstream, and ravaged human beings who thought such neglect didn't do them any harm. It's a neo-feudalistic future, the foreground to the background of burdens almost too much for our bodies, my body, to bear. We are all complicit to different degrees, even in those things we omit, like the silence we fail to break—the things we can't bear to say. This existence is only a glimpse of what's to come. What would the world be like if we all changed our demands?

The river also gave my town life, carved out from Chisholm's magic mind. The Androscoggin gave us money, jobs, softball games, tiaras and desires, fish before the tides turned. It provided water when there was none, acted as a receptacle for what we didn't want to keep around. It will power our mill until the day comes when trees, paper, or humans are all dead.

As the Androscoggin gains speed and intent, twining through everything like strands of DNA, it gathers up everything we fed to its belly in grotesque detail—dioxin, sawdust, mercury, our broken cars and lives, the memories my father wrote down, his battered dreams. There's no dramatic climax before it leaves the winding alley of its design. Paths with tidy resolutions never really occur. Finally, slowly, cumulatively, almost indecipherably, but inexorably with an exhausted flush, the river debouches and slips softly into the arms of the Atlantic Ocean.

ACKNOWLEDGMENTS

Thank you to:

Linn Rottem and Andreas Wiese at Litteraturhuset in Oslo, Norway, for giving me a beautiful space and time and cheese and bread and salmon and the key to Oslo; Bread Loaf Environmental Writers Conference, for a week in Robert Frost's room; 100W Corsicana, Texas gave me two months and two weeks of freedom to write and I was supported by incredible people who scaffolded the whole operation; Nancy Rebal, your enthusiasm and joy inspires me; David Searcy, my words are more tender and strange because of you; and Kyle Hobratschk, your generosity, friendship, and laughter saw me through.

Early readers, who kindly led the way: Melanie Gideon, Charlie Haas, Jesse James, BK Moran, Ryan Chard Smith, Mary Ann Walsh, and Matthew Zapruder.

Later readers, who kept my feet on the ground: Lisa Huber and Victoria Sahadevan Fossland. My MFA thesis group, you kept me on task: Sharon Cole, Arly Evensen, Tatiana Serafin, and of course, Samuel Evensen; my two secret weapons, Heather Wichman Marx and Georgette Miller, your comments located the good, the bad, and the ugly. And James Meader, you grew up under the same skies as me and we skied the same lines.

Even later readers who gave me time they probably did not have:

Kate Christensen, Ben Fountain, John Freeman, Jonathan Lethem, Robert Macfarlane, Emily Raboteau, Richard Russo, David Searcy, and Dani Shapiro.

People who offered their expertise on matters large and small: Rebecca Altman, Michael Blumenthal, Mary Booth, Richard Clapp, Bathsheba Demuth, Barry Mower, Barbara Bartlett, Dennis Fulbright, Thomas Beckley, Robert Forrant, Greg Howard, Steve Lester, Dave Schauf, Nickie Sekara, Nancy Smith, and all the folks at the Maine Department of Environmental Protection.

Supporters, advocates, friends, neighbors, teachers, mentors, and cheerleaders: Nicole Aragi, Joan Baxter, Josh Bodwell, Jane Brox, Jess Bruder, Carolyn and Kevin Bruen, Belinda Burkhardt, Alexander Chee, Joel Cyr, Marcia DeSanctis, Joyce Desroches, Colin Dickerman, Rebecca Fitting, Jon Franzen, Erik Madigan Heck, Jack Huber, Kendra Huber, Brady Huggett, Zia Jaffrey, Denise James, Barbara Jones, Elizabeth Kaney, Brianna Killion Heck, Megan Labrise, Mark Lamster, Suzannah Lessard, Alane Mason, John McPhee, Letitia Montgomery-Rogers, Honor Moore, Leigh Newman, Patricia Pelehach, Becky Saletan, Elisabeth Scharlatt, Jill Schoolman, Holly Stark, Gay and Nan Talese, Pamela Talese, Ken Theriault, Joey Tillinger, Sophie Treppendahl, David Vermette, Joan Vermette, Matt Weiland, and Michelle Weinberg.

Past and Present Rumford and Mexico Residents: Heidi Arsenault, Roland Arsenault, Jim Aylward, Georgette Beauschene, James Bernard, Nancy Bourgea, Chris and Heidi Brennick, Druscilla Breton, LJ Briggs, Greg Buccina, Mo (Chessie) Brodeur, Walt Buotte, Barbara Caron, Gena Cloutier, Darlene Cormier-Martin, Sheila Delameter, Matt Desroches, Gary Dolloff, Bruce Farrin, Dean Gilbert, Luci Gilbert, Matt Gilbert, Scot Grassette, Nghia Ha, Janet Hall, Jan and Lou Irish, Blue Keim, Billie Koris, Marie Lane, Jeanne Lapointe (and the lunch ladies of RSU 10), Melissa Litalien, Frank Martin, Louie Marin, Rebecca Martin, Mike and Angela Matthews, Arthur and Shelia Meader, Heidi Merrill, Anne Morin, Jane Peterson, Lee Petrie, Pat Pineau, Barb Radmore, Scott Reed, Lisa Russell, Beverly Soucy, Jeff Sterling, Gary Warren, and Roger White.

Applause goes to: At St. Martin's Press—Dori Weintraub, publicist, you are the calm in every storm I make; Alan Bradshaw, your editing and proofing expertise made me a better writer; proofreader Rima Weinberg; and grand assistance from Danielle Prielipp and Alex Brown; and a million thanks to Jonathan Bush for your thoughtful book cover design. Beyond St. Martin's, transcribers Alison Richter and Elizabeth Rushe; Nat Reade, for your early footwork; and Alexander H. Schmidt, Esq., Rachel Doughty, Esq., Elisa Rivlin, Esq., you kept me from my worst self.

Everyone who died while I wrote this book: my father, Tom Arsenault, Wilma Belanger, Dot Bernard, Doris Gaudin, Don Gilbert, Ron Hemingway, Edmund Morris, Jenny Orr, Dan St. Cyr, and Cathy Taylor. I'm sure there are others.

Editors **Sumanth Prabhaker** for finding the plot then working through it word by word and offering to do it for chocolate; and **Anna deVries**, for your patience, enthusiasm, and knowledge in bringing this across the finish line with grace and levity.

My most discerning critics—my siblings, Kelly Arsenault Fitz-Randolph, Amy Cox, Tom Arsenault, Joel Arsenault, you always kept me in line; my father, Tom Arsenault, who taught me to keep my eye on the ball; and my mother, Maddy Arsenault, for keeping my story straight even if we disagree on whose version is best, for putting up with arbitrary visits, and for opening doors I never even knew existed.

Terry Martin, your story led me to my own.

Sarah Burnes, you are a fierce, smart, buoyant agent and champion of humans and like me, hater of social injustice.

John Freeman—mentor, editor, friend—I would have been lost without your generosity, kindness, and humor. You helped me connect the dots in so many ways. Let's hope this book is worth the paper it's printed on.

Finally, my criminally supportive husband, **Andrew Wood**, you read and listened to all versions of every page and worked hard so I could have the time, money, and space to do the same.

NOTES

PREAMBLE

1   *slow caress of lava and despair*: This is an ode to William Empson's 1937 villanelle "Missing Dates."

2   *to catch salmon lofting*: "A River's Journey: The Story of the Androscoggin," Exhibit on display at the Bethel Historical Society from June 2, 2007, through September 9, 2011, https://www.bethelhistorical.org/legacy-site/A _River%27s_Journey.html.

CHAPTER 1

7   *cretons on their toast*: Cretons are a French Canadian pâté made with ground pork, onions, and spices. We always bought the brand Mailhot's, which is still made in Lewiston, ME.

15   *In an 1894 letter*: Letter from Hugh J. Chisholm to Charles A. Mixer, September 12, 1894, in the files of the Rumford Falls Power Company and Rumford Historical Society and reprinted in the *Rumford Falls Times*, September 14, 1901.

15   *to usher in slum violence*: While *The Oxford Story* provides insight to Chisholm's reasoning for Strathglass Park, I corresponded with Robert Forrant, Ph.D., Distinguished University Professor of History, University of Massachusetts, Lowell, and he said for Lowell and Lawrence, Chisholm's claim about housing problems in those areas depends on the time period.

In the nineteenth century, especially before the Civil War, most millworkers lived in company-owned boardinghouses and while conditions were spare, there was not the overcrowding and conditions we'd think of when we consider urban worker housing from the 1870s forward. Workers who arrived from difficult lives overseas often saw their first housing in Lowell and Lawrence as a step up. But across the 1880s to the 1920s in both cities, the housing was substandard and overcrowded. Lack of plumbing caused frequent typhoid outbreaks in the summer. There was a lack of clean water. But, there is no evidence he's seen that crime was rampant. In most mill cities where the owners controlled housing, they used that control to hold workers' wages down and make it really difficult for workers to form unions. The threat was always there to evict any workers who even hinted at unionization. Most New England mill owners would brag about their housing to make it seem like they cared, but wages and dangerous working conditions often suggested otherwise. John J. Leane, *The Oxford Story: A History of the Oxford Paper Company 1847–1958* (Rumford, ME: Oxford Paper Company, 1958).

18 **harmful levels of vanadium pentoxide**: Janene Pieters, "Carcinogenic Debris Falls on Curacao, Puts Refinery in Spotlight," *NL Times*, June 9, 2015, https://nltimes.nl/2015/06/09/carcinogenic-debris-falls-curacao-puts-refinery-spotlight.

18 **disadvantaged people in Oakland's port**: When I lived in Oakland, new California Air Resources Board (CARB) regulations were being implemented during my husband's time as chief, Prevention Department, US Coast Guard Sector San Francisco. His department was the leading federal authority for shipping in the Bay Area.

After years of study, CARB determined ships transiting San Francisco Bay and conducting cargo operations at the Port of Oakland (among many other California ports) contributed significantly to poor air quality, which affected the health of nearby residents, who were, more often than not, lower income. To save money, ships use a low-quality fuel oil for their propulsion and power generators. The new regulations required ships to switch over to a cleaner fuel within twenty-four miles of the California coast. While this fuel was higher quality (cleaner), it affected the performance of ship engines, which resulted in increased hazardous conditions, such as fuel leaks into the machinery spaces of the ship and even loss of power (e.g., the engine shutting down—not a good condition while the ship is maneuvering in congested San Francisco Bay). Prior to and during the implementation period, my husband's office worked closely with CARB to minimize the negative consequences and collateral hazards created by these regulations.

The following articles refer to some of the pollution issues outlined: Pingkuan Di et al., "Diesel Particulate Matter Health Risk Assessment for the West Oakland Community: Preliminary Summary of Results," California Environmental Protection Agency, Air Resources Board, March 19, 2008, https://ww3.arb.ca.gov/ch/communities/ra/westoakland/documents/draft summary031908.pdf; Juliette De Guyenro, "Port of Oakland, Officials Work to Resolve Air Quality in West Oakland," *Oakland North*, March 12, 2019.

18 *plastics and petrochemical companies*: Much has been written about the dangers of living in parts of Louisiana near petrochemical plants. See: Mara Kardas-Nelson, "The Petro-Chemical Industry Is Killing Another Black Community in Cancer Alley," *The Nation*, August 26, 2019; Mark Schleifstein, "New EPA Rules Aim to Reduce Toxic Emissions. But Many 'Cancer Alley' Chemical Plants Won't Have to Change," *ProPublica*, November 14, 2019; Erin L. Pulster, "Assessment of Public Health Risks Associated with Petrochemical Emissions Surrounding an Oil Refinery" (2015). University of South Florida. *Graduate Theses and Dissertations*, https://scholarcommons.usf.edu/etd/5761.

18 *industrial projects in the Niger Delta*: A gloomy article on how globalization, capitalism, and climate change is reshaping the planet and the people who live on it. Raffi Khatchadourian, "The Long View: Edward Burtynsky's Quest to Photograph a Changing Planet," *The New Yorker*, December 11, 2016. Patrick Radden Keefe, "Reversal of Fortune: A Crusading Lawyer Helped Ecuadorans Secure a Huge Environmental Judgment Against Chevron. But Did He Go Too Far?," *The New Yorker*, January 1, 2012.

18 *edges of Israeli settlements*: J. A. Allen, "Water in the Middle East and in Israel and Palestine: Some Local and Global Issues," in E. Feitelson and M. Haddad, eds., *Identification of Joint Management Structures for Shared Aquifers* (Washington, DC: World Bank, 1998). Also, I have witnessed this myself as a journalist in the West Bank.

18 *infernos of another kind*: Robert D. Bullard, "Environment and Morality: Confronting Environmental Racism in the United States," United Nations Research Institute for Social Development, Identities, Conflict and Cohesion Programme Paper No. 8, October 2004, http://www.unrisd.org/unrisd/website/document.nsf/(httpPublications)/543B2B250E64745280256B6D005788F7?OpenDocument.

19 *It contained seven fireplaces*: Doc Martin journal entry, April 8, 1989.

CHAPTER 2

25 *The package contained*: For ten years I tried to find the American College of Surgeons report. I found a mention of it in the news article by Wendy

Hazard listed below, which indicates that the study includes records from 1976 to 1980. Later I found what appeared to be a cover page from the report which indicates the survey covered the years 1972 to 1986 and includes over 700 hospitals and over 1.5 million cancer cases. I never did find the entire study. Cover page: *Summary & Survival Report for: Maine*, Prepared by the American College of Surgeons, n.d. Wendy Hazard, "In 'Cancer Valley' Doctor Battles Boise Cascade Polluters," *Maine Progressive*, June 1992.

25 ***dioxin—a toxic by-product***: Dioxin, or polychlorinated dibenzodioxin (PCDD), is the generic term for a group of seventy-five related chemical compounds. These are produced unintentionally due to incomplete combustion, such as from waste incinerators, and also through some chemical processes, like the process of bleaching paper with chlorine. Dioxins contaminated the herbicide blend Agent Orange, due to poor quality control in the chemical manufacturing process, and are largely responsible for the toxicity of that famous substance.

Dioxins (and other dioxin-like compounds, including polychlorinated furans) are classified as persistent organic pollutants (POPs), because they are persistent in the environment, they bioaccumulate in the body and in the food chain, and they are toxic. Dioxins and furans were on the original "dirty dozen" list of POPs identified by the international Stockholm Convention as requiring immediate action.

As noted, dioxins are unintentional by-products. The same processes also usually produce furans (PCDFs), which are very similar. PCBs (polychlorinated biphenyls) are different and were intentionally manufactured for a long time, but they share the same basic structure. A general discussion of dioxins as (for example) combustion by-products often includes all the PCDD (polychlorinated dibenzodioxin) congeners and the PCDF congeners as well. PCBs are a little different, but many congeners have similar toxic action, so all three groups are usually lumped together as dioxin-like compounds. Information provided by Gregory J. Howard, environmental health scientist and chemicals policy consultant based in Dhaka, Bangladesh.

25 ***paper mills, including ours***: United States Environmental Protection Agency, "National Dioxin Study: Report to Congress," Office of Solid Waste and Emergency Response, August 1987.

25 ***"not very severe at all"***: Stephen Groves, DEP, director of Bureau of Water Quality Control, was the person who downplayed the dioxins found. "Dioxin Trace Found in Androscoggin Fish," *Bangor Daily News*, May 20, 1985.

25 ***used in the herbicide/defoliant***: Agent Orange killed millions of acres of forest and farmlands in order to improve US military defense. What happened, however, was that Agent Orange also started killing people. A large

epidemiological study began in 1979 to assess and understand the health effects of Agent Orange on US veterans. As of 2011, about $140 million had been spent on the study, which found that there *was* enough evidence to link Agent Orange with diseases such as non-Hodgkin's lymphoma, a disease that also cropped up in our town in larger numbers than normal. In fact, the study showed that those who served in Vietnam in sprayed areas had a 110 percent higher rate of non-Hodgkin's lymphoma and a 58 percent higher rate of lung cancer, than those who served in unsprayed areas of Vietnam.

The Red Cross says as many as three million Vietnamese were affected by dioxin, including their children and their grandchildren and so on, both directly and indirectly.

The US Veterans' Association has accepted the military's responsibility for using Agent Orange. Its website lists all cancers it believes are caused by contact with Agent Orange and how veterans can seek help. https://www .va.gov/disability/eligibility/hazardous-materials-exposure/agent-orange/.

Other resources include: Ronald A. Hites, "Dioxin: An Overview and History," *Environmental Science & Technology* 45 (2011): 16–20; Institute of Medicine (US) Committee to Review the Health Effects in Vietnam Veterans of Exposure to Herbicides, *Veterans and Agent Orange: Health Effects of Herbicides Used in Vietnam* (Washington, DC: National Academies Press, 1994), Chapter 2, "History of the Controversy over the Use of Herbicides," https://www.ncbi.nlm.nih.gov/books/NBK236351/; Fred A. Wilcox, *Waiting for an Army to Die: The Tragedy of Agent Orange* (New York: Vintage, 1983).

25   ***savaged the town of Love Canal***: In the book *Dying from Dioxin*, Lois Gibbs, who was affected by the Love Canal disaster, wrote that she wanted "to provide every reader with enough information to help stop dioxin exposure." The book is a great history of dioxin and a very readable resource on dioxin and organizing strategies for activist groups; in addition, it pinpoints the dioxin controversy at a specific place and time. Lois Marie Gibbs and Citizens Clearinghouse for Hazardous Waste, *Dying from Dioxin: A Citizen's Guide to Reclaiming Our Health and Rebuilding Democracy* (London: Black Rose Books, 1997).

25–26   ***rendering the town uninhabitable***: Times Beach residents evacuated in 1982. Their homes were eventually bought by the EPA using Superfund monies under the leadership of Anne Gorsuch Burford.

26   ***declare dioxin a probable human carcinogen***: The EPA's declaration in 1985 that dioxin was a probable human carcinogen began a protracted process in which the intended result was to issue a comprehensive risk study analysis (for cancer and non-cancer risks) for dioxin.

26   *"paper companies own the town"*: Letter from Edward Martin, Ph.D., to Governor Angus King, October 20, 1995.

28   *twenty-mile radius of Rumford*: What Dan St. Cyr said about twelve of the twenty-eight children in the children's ward at Dana-Farber being from the Rumford-Mexico area was confirmed by epidemiologist Richard Clapp, via a phone conversation with me in 2016.

28   *metastasized to his colon*: Doc Martin's journal entry, December 18, 1990.

29   *to augment the water supply*: "Cancer Valley," *Chronicle*, WCVB TV, Boston, December 18, 1991.

29   *"doubtful it played many places in Maine"*: Email from *Chronicle* to Kerri Arsenault, "Query About Past Program," February 17, 2015.

29   *violating environmental regulations*: Letter from Edward Martin, Ph.D., to Douglas Daniels, Regional Manager, Boise Cascade, cc: DEP and Selectmen of Rumford and Mexico, April 7, 1988.

35   *a tiny forest pantry*: The winter stockpiles consisted of 110 truckloads that dumped 6,000 tons of sludge—without the town's knowledge—near our watershed. Luther also informed Senator Mitchell that IP planned for 1,000 such sites. Ida Luther, Letter from Ida Luther to Senator George Mitchell, February 23, 1989.

35   *5,000 cubic yards of sludge*: Also, about 15 to 30 inches of topsoil was "mistakenly" removed to prepare the land for the sludge load. The DEP maintained the soil would have acted as a filter to hold the leachate. Instead, they dug a trench around the pile. Neither the trench nor the soil would have been enough to contain the mass. And it didn't. It ran over the riverbank. The DEP, which issued IP the license to spread the sludge, insisted the sludge was safe, that there wasn't enough runoff to cause problems. We now know that is not true, as evidenced by toxic persistent chemicals showing up in groundwater and animals on Maine farms where the sludge was also spread. When I visited the DEP, I saw a lot of sludge permits for other nearby towns. I wonder if those residents know/knew. Rich Plante, "Residents Voice Concerns about IP Sludge," *Lewiston Daily Sun*, January 4, 1989; Donna Buttarazzi, "Maine Dairy Farm Plagued by Chemical Contaminants May Be the 'Tip of the Iceberg,'" *Bangor Daily News*, March 23, 2019; Kevin Miller, "Public Health Experts Aim to Stop Spreading Sludge: Fred Stone Says He Can't Sell Milk from His Herd Because of Exposure to PFAS, Chemicals Linked to Cancer That Were Found in the Sludge He Spread on His Fields for Decades," *Portland Press Herald*, March 19, 2019.

35   *risks weren't exactly defined*: Rich Plante, "Residents Voice Concerns About IP Sludge," *Lewiston Daily Sun*, January 4, 1989.

35   *the mill's "sludge recycling program"*: From Russell E. Keenan, Ph.D., Risk Assessment Division, Envirologic Data. Report to Mr. William Ginn, January 3, 1989.

38   *accusations leveled by the films*: Letter from Jeff Nevins to Chris Stirling at *Chronicle*, February 28, 1991.

38   *Andy Drysdale, a Boise spokesperson*: From Andy Drysdale, Boise Cascade spokesperson, "Replay of 'Cancer Valley,'" email memo to "U4PGL" (presumably a distribution list), December 20, 1991. Handwritten note on printed copy of same memo by Ben Groce, a senior VP for Boise Cascade.

38   *toxics would increase too*: Carbon monoxide would increase from 30.2 tons a year to 525.6 tons; nitrous oxide, from 448 tons a year to 1,182 tons; sulfur dioxide, from 391 tons a year to 683 tons; volatile organic compounds would increase by 40 percent; particulate matter would increase by 19 percent; and particulate matter that may be inhaled would increase by 10 percent. This information came from a letter from Doc Martin to DEP Commissioner Dean Marriot, September 2, 1992. I am unsure of his source for those numbers, but because they are specific, I presume they are relatively accurate.

38   *About two hundred alarmed residents*: Tux Turkel, "Rumford Pollution Debate Pits Property Against Health," *Maine Sunday Telegram*, October 11, 1992.

38   *public hearing about the emissions*: In 1994, Maine DEP enacted "Rules Concerning the Processing of Applications and Other Administrative Matters," which required industry to notify all abutters by certified mail, place a public notice in the newspaper, and hold a public hearing whenever a company wanted to revoke, modify, or suspend any operation license. This change in DEP decorum was propelled, in part, by the dioxin scare.

39   *"smell of death and suffering"*: Letter from Doc Martin to Maine DEP Commissioner Dean Marriot, September 2, 1992.

39   *1981–83: Ann Gorsuch*: The Gorsuch controversy centered on the EPA's Superfund, a $1.6 billion program established by Congress to help cleanups of hazardous waste. Of the 14,000 possible Superfund sites, only five cleanups were completed under Gorsuch's supervision. An article in the February 21, 1983, issue of *Newsweek* referred to the domino effect of the dispute as having "eerie overtones of Watergate, or 'Sewergate.'" Gorsuch was cited for contempt of Congress because she refused to turn over subpoenaed documents about the enforcement of Superfund. She eventually resigned and died of cancer herself. Philip Shabecoff, "House Charges Head of E.P.A. with Contempt," *New York Times*, December 17, 1982; Joanna Brenner. "Neil Gorsuch's Late Mother Almost Annihilated the EPA. Is History Repeating Itself?" *Newsweek*, February 1, 2017, https://www.newsweek.com

/anne-gorsuch-new-bill-abolish-epa-551382; Philip Shabecoff, "Threat Posed by Dioxin Subject of Growing Fear," *New York Times*, February 12, 1983.

39   **1985: Dioxin found in fish**: "Dioxin Trace Found in Androscoggin Fish," *Bangor Daily News*, May 20, 1985.

40   **1986: Activist Carol Van Strum**: One month after Van Strum and Merrell released their report "No Margin of Safety," the EPA released their two-year National Dioxin Study, confirming Van Strum's and Merrell's contention that dioxin from the bleaching of paper was a big problem. Carol Van Strum and Paul Merrell, "No Margin of Safety: A Preliminary Report on Dioxin Pollution and the Need for Emergency Action in the Pulp and Paper Industry," Greenpeace USA, 1987; Carol Van Strum, "Statement before the Subcommittee on Water Resources, Committee on Public Works," US House of Representatives, July 13, 1988, cited in *Dioxin Pollution in the Pigeon River, North Carolina and Tennessee: Hearing Before the Subcommittee on Water Resources of the Committee of Public Works and Transportation, House of Representatives, One Hundredth Congress, Second Session, July 13, 1988*, Washington, DC: US Government Printing Office, 1989; Craig Collins, *Toxic Loopholes: Failures and Future Prospects for Environmental Law* (New York: Cambridge University Press, 2010); Peter von Stackelberg, "White Wash: The Dioxin Cover-Up," *Greenpeace* 14, no. 2 (April 1989): 7–11; *Carol Van Strum, Plaintiff-appellant, v. United States Environmental Protection Agency, Defendant-appellee*, 892 F.2d 1048 (9th Cir. 1990), US Court of Appeals for the Ninth Circuit, 892 F.2d 1048 (9th Cir. 1990), argued and submitted June 28, 1989, decided January 4, 1990.

40   **1987: Dioxin residue found in paper products**: Phillip Shabecoff, "Traces of Dioxin Found in Range of Paper Goods," *New York Times*, September 24, 1987, https://www.nytimes.com/1987/09/24/us/traces-of-dioxin-found-in-range-of-paper-goods.html.

40   **1987–88: Van Strum verifies**: After the *New York Times* broke the story on dioxin contamination in paper goods, the paper lobby (the American Paper Institute, or API) mounted a public relations plan to subvert consumer concerns about dioxin and to suppress the negative findings. Part of the PR plan (led by the firm of Burson-Marsteller) included: (1) keeping all allegations of health risks out of the public arena—or minimizing them; (2) avoiding confrontations with government agencies, which might trigger concerns about health risks or raise visibility of issue generally; (3) maintaining customer confidence in product integrity; and (4) achieving an appropriate regulatory climate. The API claimed there was nothing to prove these trace levels were a risk to human health and that their main goal was to get the EPA to rethink their dioxin assessments. An anonymous source leaked to Van Strum

(after reading her "No Margin of Safety" report) a letter from the EPA to the API showing basically that they agreed to help this PR effort by supressing, modifying, or delaying any results of the congressionally mandated National Dioxin Study that indicated the seriousness of dioxin's harm. The EPA basically did, and subsequently stated that they may have overstated dioxin's risk to the public. See: "The Poison Papers Documenting the Hidden History of Chemical and Pesticide Hazards in the United States," most of which were collected by Carol Van Strum and digitized by Peter von Stackelberg. All 200,000 pages available at PoisonPapers.org. This article gives a concise and thorough narrative of dioxin's history in the paper industry, in the EPA, and how it relates to the legal concept of "harm": William Boyd, "Controlling Toxic Harms: The Struggle over Dioxin Contamination in the Pulp and Paper Industry," *Stanford Environmental Law Journal* 21, no. 345 (2002): 2012, https://papers.ssrn.com/abstract=2079802. See also, M. Weisskopf, "Paper Industry Campaign Defused Reaction to Dioxin Contamination," *Washington Post*, October 25, 1987; *Dioxin Pollution in the Pigeon River North Carolina and Tennessee*, Hearing before the Subcommittee on Water Resources, One Hundredth Congress, Second Session, July 13, 1988, Washington, DC: US Government Printing Office.

40 ***1987: Maine's state toxicologist***: Robert A. Frakes, who worked as the Maine DEP's state toxicologist, became the state's top dioxin expert. From 1986 to 1990, he issued advisories for Maine residents to lower their consumption of fish from certain state rivers. He also recommended limits on dioxin discharges from mills. Frakes narrowed the scope of his warnings based on industry pressure, and raised the dioxin intake limits. The paper mills had hired consultants in collaboration with the DEP to review Frakes's findings. Frakes objected and, in the end, quit his job due to "nobody listening" to him. Dieter Bradbury, "Dioxin Fighter Prevails over Mills in Long Run," *Maine Sunday Telegram*, April 11, 1993; "State's Top Dioxin Expert Quits in Frustration," *Lewiston Sun Journal*, 1994 (no day listed).

40 ***colon, endocrine, and thyroid cancer***: As for the air emissions, elevated levels of chloroform, benzene, and 1,3-butadiene, all hazardous and all exceeding state guidelines, had swished through our air.

41 ***money and energy flatlined***: In the report there was a nod to possible environmental exposures: "Lastly, some cancers may be caused, in part, by occupational exposures. . . . These exposures might be reduced through changes in the workplace including pollution control, pollution prevention and remediation." Northern Oxford County Coalition, "A Report on Cancer Incidence in the Rumford, Maine Area from the Technical Subcommittee to the Northern Oxford County Coalition," April 5, 1996.

41   ***confines of this town***: Sarah McKearnan and Patrick Field, "The Northern Oxford County Coalition: Four Maine Towns Tackle a Public Health Mystery," in Lawrence Susskind, Sarah McKearnan, and Jennifer Thomas-Larmer, eds., *The Consensus Building Handbook: A Comprehensive Guide to Reaching Agreement* (Thousand Oaks, CA: SAGE Publications, 1999). http://dx.doi .org/10.4135/9781452231389.n21; Victoria E. Cluck, "The Northern Oxford County Coalition: An Analysis of Representation and Communications" (master's thesis, Massachusetts Institute of Technology, June 1997), https://pdfs .semanticscholar.org/ec29/a70fb89f6f433f1975302a7eda0a9d3bb70e.pdf? _ga=2.254518472.1303715941.1580152224-1754606651.1580152224.

41   ***they made us feel small***: Joan C. Williams, "What So Many People Don't Get About the US Working Class," *Harvard Business Review*, November 10, 2016.

41   ***or felt what we felt***: Maria Eriksson Baaz, *The Paternalism of Partnership: A Postcolonial Reading of Identity in Development Aid* (London: Zed Books, 2005).

42   ***In the winter of 2004***: Journalist Nat Reade had been researching writing a book about Rumford himself. On March 9, 2017, he gave me all his notes and research and permission to use them.

42   ***book of the same name***: Steve Lerner, *Sacrifice Zones: The Front Lines of Toxic Chemical Exposure in the United States* (Cambridge, MA: MIT Press, 2010).

42   ***"this is for environmental crimes"***: Denny Larson launched the Bucket Brigade concept in 1995 in California in response to the Costa County case against UNOCAL oil refinery, and the idea spread as far as South Africa, Louisiana, England, and the Philippines. There's a Q&A with Denny about his work at "Free Speech in Citizen Science: Q&A with Denny Larson," *Medium*, May 16, 2017, https://medium.com/@crowdandcloud/free-speech -in-citizen-science-q-a-with-denny-larson-f9142a6957cb. Denny Larson died in March 2019. Thousands mourned the loss.

43   ***Many of the toxics (around 93 percent)***: William Boyd, "Controlling Toxic Harms: The Struggle over Dioxin Contamination in the Pulp and Paper Industry," *Stanford Environmental Law Journal* 21, no. 345 (2002), https:// papers.ssrn.com/abstract=2079802.

43   ***706,236 pounds of toxics***: Jean English, "2003 MOFGA Teach-In: Cancer and the Environment," *Maine Organic Farmer & Gardener*, December 2003–February 2004, https://www.mofga.org/Publications/The-Maine-Organic -Farmer-Gardener/Winter-2003-2004/Cancer-and-the-Environment.

44   ***the tests were inconclusive***: The Toxic Waste Women group received a small grant from the New England Grassroots Environmental Fund in 2001. The

organization funded community organizations engaged in environmental stewardship and social change projects.

45 *"just like [Doc Martin] said"*: John Patrick, Maine Legislative Record—House, One Hundred and Twentieth Legislature, First Regular Session, 69th Legislative Day, June 19, 2001.

45 *things we can't see*: Henry M. Vyner, *Invisible Trauma: The Psychosocial Effects of Invisible Environmental Contaminants* (Lexington, KY: Lexington Books, 1988).

46 *invisible, stealthy threats*: Thom Davies, "Toxic Space and Time: Slow Violence, Necropolitics, and Petrochemical Pollution," *Annals of the American Association of Geographers*, June 14, 2018, 1–17; Rob Nixon, *Slow Violence and the Environmentalism of the Poor* (Cambridge, MA: Harvard University Press, 2013); Rachel Carson, *Silent Spring* (Boston: Houghton Mifflin, 1962).

CHAPTER 3

51 *"The entrance into our political"*: John J. Leane, *A History of Rumford, Maine, 1774–1972* (Rumford, ME: Rumford Publishing, 1972). (A second edition, credited to John J. Leane and Elliot E. Burns, and updated to the year 2000, was published in 2005.)

51 *then you needed to go*: "The Coolidge Era and the Consumer Economy, 1921–1929," Coolidge-Consumerism Collection, Library of Congress, http://lcweb2.loc.gov:8081/ammem/amrlhtml/dtimmig.html; Kenneth T. Palmer et al., *Maine Politics and Government* (Lincoln: University of Nebraska Press, 2009).

51 *the KKK's message and acts*: For further reading about the KKK in Maine, see Raney Bench, "Maine's Gone Mad: The Rising of the Klan," Mount Desert Island Historical Society, n.d., https://mdihistory.org/wp-content/uploads/Maines-Gone-Mad-The-Rising-of-the-Klan_ocr.pdf.

51 *disguised racism with national unity*: Sociologist Jan Nederveen Pieterse wrote that "endorsing the myth of national culture and cultural unity, it glosses over the dark side of nationalism." Pieterse, *Globalization and Culture: Global Mélange* (Lanham, MD: Rowman & Littlefield, 2009).

51 *1881 Report of Labor Statistics from Massachusetts*: *Twelfth Annual Report of the Bureau of Statistics of Labor*, January 1881 (Boston: Rand, Avery, 1881), 469, http://archives.lib.state.ma.us/handle/2452/757017.

52 *twelve to thirteen million bags*: The approximate number of bags made comes from Continental Paper Bag Company commemorative brochure, 1900–1905, 38. Available from Rumford Historical Society, Rumford, ME. Also see Peter A. McKenna, "Hugh J. Chisholm's Magic Town, 1882–1912" (master's thesis, University of Maine, n.d.).

53   ***blanket of dried peas***: "Elles Sont Venues, Elles Ont Servi" was an exhibit on the Grey Nuns at the Franco-American Center in Lewiston, ME, 2012. Text for the exhibit is available here: http://www.francocenter.org/education -heritage/heritage-museum/elles-sont-venues-elles-ont-servi-the-grey-nuns -exhibit/. As part of the exhibit, a thirty-minute documentary was commissioned. Mary Rice-DeFosse, *The Grey Nuns: They Came, They Served*. Edited and produced by Colin Kelley, 2012. Video, 26:51, https://vimeo.com /56111325.

55   ***read a few studies***: Frances J. Milliken et al., "Linking Workplace Practices to Community Engagement: The Case for Encouraging Employee Voice," *Academy of Management Perspectives* 29, no. 4 (2015): 405–421; Frances J. Milliken, E. W. Morrison, and P. F. Hewling, "An Exploratory Study of Employee Silence: Issues That Employees Don't Communicate Upward and Why," *Journal of Management Studies* 40 (2003): 1453–1476; Brandon B. Johnson and Vincent T. Covello, *The Social and Cultural Construction of Risk: Essays on Risk Selection and Perception* (D. Reidel, 1987).

55   ***rather than speak out***: Margaret Heffernan, "The Shameful Cost of Saying Nothing," *Financial News,* August 19, 2013; Margaret Heffernan, *Willful Blindness: Why We Ignore the Obvious at Our Peril* (New York: Simon & Schuster, 2011).

55   ***becomes a powerful norm***: Leslie Perlow and Nelson Repenning, "The Dynamics of Silencing Conflict," *Research in Organizational Behavior* 29 (2009): 195–223.

57   ***polled residents about disease***: Terry was inspired by Michael Brown, who went door-to-door in Love Canal, New York, and found an astronomical number of birth defects, miscarriages, and other health anomalies in nearly every home near Hooker, the chemical company partly responsible for the toxic mess in Love Canal. Michael H. Brown, "Love Canal and the Poisoning of America," *The Atlantic*, December 1, 1979, https://www.theatlantic .com/magazine/archive/1979/12/love-canal-and-the-poisoning-of-america /376297/.

CHAPTER 5

72   ***coarse windows from greased paper***: William B. Lapham, *History of Rumford, Oxford County, Maine. Its First Settlement in 1779 to the Present Time* (Augusta, ME: Press of the Maine Farmer, 1890).

72   ***Mexico's commercial pursuits***: George J. Varney, *The Gazetteer of Maine* (Boston: B.B. Russell, 1886).

73   *"and of course healthy"*: Reverend Daniel Gould, *The History of Rumford, 1826,* eds. Randy L. Bennett and Peter A. McKenna (Augusta, ME: Pennycook Press, 1975).

73   **eight hundred years old**: Richard G. Wood, *A History of Lumbering in Maine: 1820–1861* (Orono: University of Maine Press, 1971), 20.

73   **depleted agrarian towns**: John J. Leane, *The Oxford Story: A History of the Oxford Paper Company 1847–1958* (Rumford, ME: Oxford Paper Company, 1958).

74   **A History of Rumford**: John J. Leane, *A History of Rumford, Maine, 1774–1972* (Rumford, ME: Rumford Publishing, 1972).

74   **Chisholm . . . as a "genius"**: *Rumford Falls Evening Herald,* April 14, 1903.

74   **with "dazzling accomplishments"**: *Biographical Review Cumberland County, Maine* (Boston: Biographical Review Publishing, 1896), 310.

74   **always there "in spirit"**: "Hon. Hugh Chisholm," *Lewiston Evening Journal,* September 22, 1905.

74   **"minimum of basic data"**: Hugh Joseph Chisholm, *A Man and the Paper Industry, Hugh J. Chisholm (1847–1912)* (New York: Newcomen Society in North America, 1952).

75   **"a gentle and lovable scholar"**: Leane, *The Oxford Story.*

75   **"fluctuations of the stock market"**: Peter A. McKenna, "Hugh J. Chisholm's Magic Town, 1882–1912" (master's thesis, University of Maine, n.d.).

75   **L.A. Times in 1908**: James B. Morrow, "A Modern Aladdin. Hugh J. Chisholm, Head of the 'Paper Trust,' Builder of Cities. His Plans for a Great Industrial School for Workingmen's Children," *Los Angeles Times,* September 8, 1908.

75   **Chicago, Illinois, to Portland, Maine**: Chisholm, *A Man and the Paper Industry.*

75   **patent leather visors**: Morrow, "A Modern Aladdin."

76   **In 1872, Chisholm**: When Chisholm filed for US citizenship the day after Lincoln's assassination, he said, "A Staunch republican and a great union and anti-slavery boy, I believed the North would be successful." See Morrow, "A Modern Aladdin."

77   **Chisholm began to gather data**: McKenna, "Hugh J. Chisholm's Magic Town, 1882–1912."

77   **raw goods, power, and transportation**: In the early 1800s, Maine rivers fell under the jurisdiction of common law. If you had riparian rights to the water, you were allowed "reasonable use" of that water, as long as you didn't make a nuisance.

77   **He inserted water mains**: Randy L. Bennett, "Bowler Versus Chisholm, and the Ill-Fated Bethel-Rumford Electric Railway," *The Courier* 30, no. 2 (Summer 2006); McKenna, "Hugh J. Chisholm's Magic Town, 1882–1912."

77   ***donated land to almost every church***: McKenna, "Hugh J. Chisholm's Magic Town, 1882–1912"; *Lewiston Sun Journal*, July 8, 1912, cited in ibid.

77   ***"healthful outdoor amusement"***: McKenna, "Hugh J. Chisholm's Magic Town, 1882–1912"; *Lewiston Sun Journal*, September 18, 1912, cited in McKenna, "Hugh J. Chisholm's Magic Town."

77   ***he also furnished turkeys***: McKenna, "Hugh J. Chisholm's Magic Town, 1882–1912."

78   ***tricked by Pettengill***: Bennett, "Bowler versus Chisholm, and the Ill-Fated Bethel-Rumford Electric Railway."

78   ***The success and expansion of "Magic Town"***: McKenna, "Hugh J. Chisholm's Magic Town, 1882–1912."

80   ***raft the flotilla of trees***: Alfred Ames, *From Stump to Ship*, video recording (Orono: University of Maine, 1985), 27:56, https://www.youtube.com/watch?v=cIKCjQdxtO0; Sumner McKane, *In the Blood*, video recording, 56:51. 2010. Available by contacting filmmaker at http://sumnermckane.com.

80   ***"the great trinity"***: Joseph R. Conlin, "Old Boy, Did You Get Enough of Pie? A Social History of Food in Logging Camps," *Journal of Forest History* (October 1979): 164–185, https://foresthistory.org/wp-content/uploads/2018/03/Conlin.pdf.

81   ***homes heaved with relatives***: Sometimes French-speaking Canadians housed multiple families in precarious company-owned tenement structures. David Vermette, who writes about such Franco-American settlements in Maine, indicates these *petit Canadas* were disparaged by Clare de Fraffenried, special agent in the US Department of Labor, who called them "a reproach to civilization" that wrought fear from neighbors. In Rumford, Chisholm protected workers as much as he could from that attitude. David Vermette, *A Distinct Alien Race: The Untold Story of Franco-Americans* (Montreal: Baraka Books, 2018).

89   ***suffocating downriver in 1816***: Doug Watts, "Androscoggin: A Brief History," Maine Rivers, n.d., https://mainerivers.org/watershed-profiles/androscoggin-watershed/.

89   ***evolving river cocktail***: The first paper mill was established in the 1730s on the Presumpscot River. By 1890, there were twenty-five pulp mills in Maine, and the state was the top producer in the nation in making pulp and third in producing paper. Rachel Bouvier, "The Natural Environment as Field-Level Actor: The Environment and the Pulp and Paper Industry in Maine," *Journal of Economic Issues* 44, no. 3 (2010): 717–735, https://doi.org/10.2753/JEI0021-3624440307.

90　***Citizens demanded action***: Such problems fell under "nuisance cases," and citizens' legal recourse was to sue the offending factory to have the nuisance abated. Courts didn't always side with plaintiffs because of their antibusiness, antigrowth stance. The Sanitary Water Board's actions were the beginning of a nascent environmental movement against the paper industry. Even so, the inertia was too great and the desire to attract more industry to Maine kept interest in the movement lukewarm. The Sanitary Board was cripplingly underfunded. Wallace Scot McFarlane, "Defining a Nuisance: Pollution, Science, and Environmental Politics on Maine's Androscoggin River," *Environmental History*, no. 17 (April 2012): 307–335.

90　***by-product of the wood-pulping***: Walter A. Lawrance, "Androscoggin Pulp and Paper Industry and Pollution Abatement 1942–1977: Final Report of the Androscoggin River Technical Committee," Lewiston, ME, August 1, 1978.

90　***hovered around ten thousand***: "Rumford Comprehensive Plan Update," Town of Rumford, ME, November 5, 2013.

91　***"lost industry and ghost town"***: McFarlane, "Defining a Nuisance."

91　***Lawrance tried***: Lawrance, "Androscoggin Pulp and Paper Industry and Pollution Abatement 1942–1977: Final Report of the Androscoggin River Technical Committee."

92　***the river's natural aeration***: McFarlane, "Defining a Nuisance: Pollution"; Lawrance, "Androscoggin Pulp and Paper Industry and Pollution Abatement 1942–1977: Final Report of the Androscoggin River Technical Committee."

93　**Better Homes and Gardens, Good Housekeeping**: Address by Mr. Hugh J. Chisholm [the son], President, Oxford Paper Company, before the New York Society of Security Analysts, November 5, 1952.

93　***make paper for* National Geographic *magazine***: Leane, *A History of Rumford, Maine, 1774–1972.*

94　***mill invested over $130 million***: Leane, *The Oxford Story: A History of the Oxford Paper Company 1847–1958.*

94　***ten filthiest rivers***: Kenneth Auchincloss, "The Ravaged Environment," *Newsweek*, January 26, 1970.

94　***some of the highest dioxin***: "'Environmental Leader' Mantle Not for Maine," *Maine Sunday Telegram*, February 6, 1994.

95　***Maine's* Kennebec Journal**: "**Toxins** are poisons produced within living cells or organs of plants, animals, and bacteria. **Toxicants** are synthetic, human-made, toxic chemicals. The difference is not merely one of semantics." Max Liboiron, "Toxins or Toxicants? Why the Difference Matters," *Discard Studies*, September 11, 2017, https://discardstudies.com/2017/09 /11/toxins-or-toxicants-why-the-difference-matters/.

95   ***number one producer***: Information from article derived from Maine Toxic Release Inventory (TRI), generated by the EPA.

95   ***"lack of health insurance"***: Tom Walsh, "Age, Lifestyle Contribute to High Cancer Rate in Maine," *Bangor Daily News*, May 2, 2013, https://bangordailynews.com/2013/05/02/health/age-lifestyle-contribute-to-high-cancer-rate-in-maine/.

96   ***1989: Our mill discharges***: Environmental Protection Agency Toxic Release Inventory Report: "TRI On-Site and Off-Site Reported Disposed of or Otherwise Released (in Pounds), for All Chemicals, by Industry [Paper] for ZIP code 04276, 1989, from Toxic Release Inventory," https://enviro.epa.gov/triexplorer/tri_release.industry.

96   ***1989: Our mill is fined***: "OSHA Fines Boise Cascade $1.5 Million," *UPI*, September 13, 1989; Frank Swoboda, "$1.6 Million Fine Proposed Against Paper Mill Owner," *Washington Post*, September 14, 1989; David Andersen, "Boise Cascade Fined $98,150 for Violations at Rumford Mill," *Sun-Journal*, June 13, 1989.

96   ***1990: The National Institute for Occupational Safety and Health***: R. A. Rinsky, Health Hazard evaluation report: HETA-89-020-L2070, Boise Cascade, Rumford, Maine, 1990. https://www.cdc.gov/niosh/hhe/reports/pdfs/1989-0020-2070.pdf?id=10.26616/NIOSHHETA89020L2070.

97   ***1991: According to Maine's chronic disease***: Statistically, two to twenty-five cases of aplastic anemia per million people are usually found. Rumford's population around that time hovered in the low thousands. Aplastic anemia had been monitored because of its etiology: often, environmental pollution. I'm not sure what the aplastic anemia rates were in the 1980s, but currently only around 600 to 900 people are diagnosed with aplastic anemia each year in the United States, according to the Aplastic Anemia and MDS International Foundation, https://www.aamds.org. Maine Chronic and Sentinel Disease Surveillance Project Final Report, Maine Health Care Finance Commission, Maine Department of Human Services, October 1991. A follow-up study was inconclusive. Kenneth P. Burke and Linda J. Huff, "A Study of Aplastic Anemia in the Rumford Community Health Planning Area Final Report," Appropriation #013-10A-2586-032, Department of Human Services, Maine, March 1993.

97   ***1991: Five millworkers are diagnosed***: William C. Hidlay, "Paper Mill Chemicals Form Pall of Controversy over 'Cancer Valley': Several Cases of a Rare Lymphoma in Maine Town Raise Concerns. But Not Everyone Blames Exposure to the Pulp Process," *Los Angeles Times*, September 8, 1991.

97   ***1988–2002: Our mill releases over 25 million***: Environmental Protection Agency Toxic Release Inventory reports: "TRI On-Site and Off-Site," 1989 to 2005.

97   ***2005: Maine's death rate***: Data provided by the Maine Cancer Registry and analyzed by the Maine Cancer Consortium shows that Maine has a relatively larger cancer burden when compared to the rest of the nation. Tom Walsh, "Age, Lifestyle Contribute to High Cancer Rate in Maine," *Bangor Daily News*, May 2, 2013.

97   ***2008: Our mill is among the top***: "Toxic List Includes Mills," *Maine Sunday Telegram*, February 23, 2008.

97   ***2010: Toxic environmental exposures***: Mary E. Davis, "Economic Assessment of Children's Health and the Environment in Maine," *Maine Policy Review* 19, no. 1 (2010): 36–44, https://digitalcommons.library.umaine.edu/mpr/vol19 /iss1/6.

97   ***2011: Rumford releases***: Environmental Protection Agency, "EPA Analysis Shows Increases in 2011 Toxic Chemical Releases in Maine," press release, January 16, 2013.

97   ***2012: Cancer is the leading cause***: Maine Center for Disease Control and Prevention, Maine State Health Assessment, "General Health and Mortality, 2012," https://www.maine.gov/dhhs/mecdc/phdata/sha/SHA_General HealthMortality.pdf; Jackie Farwell, "Cancer Kills at Higher Rate in Maine Than National Average," *Bangor Daily News*, October 1, 2012; Environmental Protection Agency, "EPA Analysis of Toxic Chemical Releases in Maine Shows Pulp and Paper Mills Account for Nine of the Top 10 Sites," press release, February 11, 2014.

97   ***2014: Cancer remains***: Maine Cancer Surveillance Report, 2014. Also, in 2014, the Rumford mill increased its toxic release to about three million pounds. Matt Hongoltz-Hetling, "Skowhegan, Jay Mills Named Among Maine's Biggest Polluters in Federal Report," CentralMaine.com, February 10, 2014.

CHAPTER 6

99   ***history and migration of Acadians***: In the seventeenth and eighteenth centuries, Canada and Acadia were two separate geographies. Acadians and Canadians have different histories and different accents. Acadians are careful to preserve the distinction between themselves and the French speakers of Quebec and elsewhere in Canada. David Vermette, *A Distinct Alien Race: The Untold Story of Franco-Americans: Industrialization, Immigration, Religious Strife* (Montreal: Baraka Books, 2018), 18–19.

100   ***my tenth great-grandfather***: The records for where most Acadians came from are fragmented and differ depending on the authority or source. Most are lost or missing. The first Acadian census was taken in 1671. Nearly all the names on this census appear in my family tree, including a Jehan

Terriau/Terriot. A transcription as well as the graphic scan of the original census appear on the website Acadian-Cajun Genealogy and History: http://www.acadian-cajun.com/1671cens.htm. J. Henri Blanchard, *The Acadians of Prince Edward Island: 1720–1964* (Charlottetown, PEI: Self-published, 1964); Bona Arsenault, *Histoire des Acadiens (Mise à jour de Pascal Alain). Nouvelle édition revue et augmentée* (Paris: Fides, 2004).

100 **an aversion to war**: Geneviève Massignon, "Les Parles Francais d'Acadie: Enquete Linguistique (The French dialects of Acadia: A linguistic inquiry)" (PhD thesis, University of Paris, 1962).

100 **fleshy mass**: Arsenault, *Histoire des Acadiens*; John Mack Faragher, *A Great and Noble Scheme: The Tragic Story of the Expulsion of the French Acadians from Their American Homeland* (New York: W. W. Norton, 2005); Douglas Baldwin, *Land of the Red Soil: A Popular History of Prince Edward Island* (Charlottetown, PEI: Ragweed, 1998).

100 **perceived little threat**: Faragher, *A Great and Noble Scheme*.

100 **100 billion tons of seawater**: Christopher Hodson, *The Acadian Diaspora: An Eighteenth-Century History* (New York: Oxford University Press, 2012).

100 **U-shaped wood sluices**: Sarah Robinson, Danika van Proosdij, and Hank Kolstee, "Change in Dykeland Practices in Agricultural Salt Marshes in Cobequid Bay, Bay of Fundy," in J. A. Percy et al., eds., *The Changing Bay of Fundy: Beyond 400 Years*, Proceedings of the 6th Bay of Fundy Workshop, September 29–October 2, 2004, http://www.bofep.org/PDFfiles/BoFEP6thProceedings.pdf.

101 **since around 1024**: Hugh Clout, ed., *Themes in the Historical Geography of France* (London: Academic Press, 1977).

101 **"so in the hameaux"**: Faragher, *A Great and Noble Scheme*.

101 **distinct culture and identity**: A. J. B. Johnston, "Défricheurs d'eau: An Introduction to Acadian Land Reclamation in a Comparative Context," *Material Culture Review* 66 (Fall 2007), https://journals.lib.unb.ca/index.php/MCR/article/view/18101.

101 **ten to twenty children**: Blanchard, *The Acadians of Prince Edward Island: 1720–1964*.

101 **protein-rich diet**: John Frederic Herbin, *The History of Grand-Pre*, 4th ed. (St. John, NB: Barnes, 1911).

101 **orchards and shared gardens**: N. E. S. Griffiths, *From Migrant to Acadian: A North American Border People, 1604–1755* (Quebec: McGill-Queen's University Press, 2005).

101 **Disease, pests, weather**: Ibid.

101 ***pushing back the forests***: Allan Greer, *Peasant, Lord, and Merchant: Rural Society in Three Quebec Parishes, 1740–1840 (Studies in Atlantic Canada History)* (Toronto: University of Toronto Press, 1985).

101 ***stemming the salty seas***: Griffiths, *From Migrant to Acadian.*

102 ***pillaged by jealous New Englanders***: Herbin, *The History of Grand-Pre.*

102 ***desired their fertile meadows***: Mason Wade, "The Acadian Background," in *Smokestacks and Steeples: A Collection of Essays on the Franco-American Experience in New England,* ed. Claire Quintal (Worcester, MA: Assumption College, Institut français, 1996).

102 ***persist to this day in their descendants' DNA***: The following source contain information on the aspects of Acadian identity: James P. Allen, "Franco-Americans in Maine: A Geographical Perspective," *Acadiensis* 4, no. 1 (Autumn 1974): 32–36; Carl A. Brasseaux, *The Founding of New Acadia: The Beginnings of Acadian Life in Louisiana, 1765–1803* (Baton Rouge: Louisiana State University Press, 1997); Clive Doucet, *Notes from Exile: On Being Acadian* (Toronto: McClelland & Stewart, 1999); Claire Quintal, ed., *Smokestacks and Steeples: A Collection of Essays on the Franco-American Experience in New England* (Worcester, MA: Assumption College, Institut français, 1996).

102 **goals and primed to revolt**: Griffiths, *From Migrant to Acadian.*

103 ***"Let us bear the cross"***: Colonel John Winslow, *Report and Collections of the Nova Scotia Historical Society for the Year 1878: Journal of Colonel John Winslow of the Provincial Troops While Engaged in Removing the Acadian French Inhabitants from Grand Pre and the Neighbouring Settlements in the Autumn of the Year 1755* (Halifax, NS: Morning Herald, 1879). Transcribed excerpts are also available from http://www.acadian-home.org/John-Winslow.html.

104 ***some ships sank***: For those interested in what ship went where, a website on Acadian history and genealogy managed by Denis St. Cyr (a rock star in lay Acadian genealogy and history) offers a boatload of well-documented information: https://www.acadian.org/ships.html.

104 ***wrested what land and homes***: Griffiths, *From Migrant to Acadian*; Michael Rosano, "Mapping the Acadian Deportations," *Canadian Geographic*, July 28, 2016.

104 ***winter didn't come early***: Quintal, *Smokestacks and Steeples.*

105 ***one-sided narrative***: Faragher, *A Great and Noble Scheme*; Jane Slemon, "Liminal Space of the 'Aboiteaux': Pilgrimage in Maillet's 'Pélagie,'" *Mosaic: An Interdisciplinary Critical Journal* 36, no. 4 (2003): 17–32, http://www.jstor.org/stable/44029993.

105 ***mouths of empty cellars***: Herbin, *The History of Grand-Pre.*

105 ***the Acadian removal***: F. A. Landry, "The Historical Origin of the Poem Evangeline," La Société Historique Acadienne, 23rd notebook, 1969.

105 ***persecuting the French***: Faragher, *A Great and Noble Scheme*.

105 ***Longfellow's sentimental tone***: Katie Macleod, "The Unsaid of the Grand Derangement: An Analysis of Outsider and Regional Interpretations of Acadian History," *Graduate History Review* 5, no. 1 (2016).

106 ***as a creation myth***: Naomi Griffith, "Longfellow's Evangeline: The Birth and Acceptance of a Legend," Acadian.org, https://www.acadian.org/history /longfellows-evangeline-birth-acceptance-legend/.

106 ***Some scholars and politicians consider***: Caroline-Isabelle Caron, "On the Acadian Diaspora: A Proposal for a Renewed Debate," *Transnational Subjects: History, Society, Culture* 1, no. 1 (2011): 29–51.

108 ***original dike-building work***: Hugh Clout, ed., *Themes in the Historical Geography of France* (London: Academic Press, 1977).

109 ***the lowlands of France***: Slemon, "Liminal Space of the 'Aboiteaux': Pilgrimage in Maillet's 'Pélagie.'"

109 ***latent and negative effects***: Virginia Hughes, "Epigenetics: The Sins of the Father," *Nature* 507, no. 7490 (March 6, 2014): 22; Bastiaan T. Heijmans et al., "Persistent Epigenetic Differences Associated with Prenatal Exposure to Famine in Humans," *Proceedings of the National Academy of Sciences* 105, no. 44 (November 4, 2008): 17046–17049, https://doi.org/10.1073/pnas .0806560105; Carl Zimmer, "The Famine Ended 70 Years Ago, but Dutch Genes Still Bear Scars," *New York Times*, February 6, 2018; Elmar W. Tobi et al., "DNA Methylation as a Mediator of the Association Between Prenatal Adversity and Risk Factors for Metabolic Disease in Adulthood," *Science Advances* 4, no. 1 (January 1, 2018).

109 ***suggests DNA plays a part***: A. Abdellaoui et al., "Genetic Correlates of Social Stratification in Great Britain," *Nature Human Behaviour* 3 (2019): 1332–1342.

109 ***finger-sized cutting***: "Trees with Acadian Roots Planted on Local School Grounds," *Truro News*, June 5, 2014, http://www.trurodaily.com/news/local /trees-with-acadian-roots-planted-on-local-school-grounds-144845/.

CHAPTER 7

112 ***declared it a "brownfield"***: According to the EPA, a "brownfield" is "a property, the expansion, redevelopment, or reuse of which may be complicated by the presence or potential presence of a hazardous substance, pollutant, or contaminants." From EPA, https://www.epa.gov/brownfields/overview -brownfields-program.

113 **alongside Doc Martin**: Cancer registries act as repositories—required by law now—for medical facilities to collect data on cancer diagnoses and treatments. The registries share information interstate, so if a Rumford resident seeks treatment in Boston, say, details are reported back to Maine's registry.

113 **like fish, clams**: "Tests Find Dioxin in Clams Near Mills," *Bangor Daily News*, December 31, 1993.

113 **butter, eggs, and cheese**: According to Richard Clapp and others, 90 percent of the dioxin that enters our bodies comes from foods that contain animal fat. Also see: "Dioxins and Their Effects on Human Health," World Health Organization, October 4, 2016, https://www.who.int/news-room /fact-sheets/detail/dioxins-and-their-effects-on-human-health.

113 **the human body**: Victor Turoski, ed., *Chlorine and Chlorine Compounds in the Paper Industry* (Chelsea, MA: Sleeping Bear Press, 1998); Joe Thornton, *Pandora's Poison: Chlorine, Health, and a New Environmental Strategy* (Cambridge, MA: MIT Press, 2001).

113 **products like tampons**: Michael J. DeVito and Arnold Schecter, "Exposure Assessment to Dioxins from the Use of Tampons and Diapers," *Environmental Health Perspectives* 110 (2002): 23–28, https://doi.org/10.1289/ehp .0211023.

113 **filters, tissues, baby food**: Phillip Shabecoff, "Traces of Dioxin Found in Range of Paper Goods," *New York Times*, September 24, 1987, https://www .nytimes.com/1987/09/24/us/traces-of-dioxin-found-in-range-of-paper -goods.html.

113 **in human placenta**: Go Suzuki, Masuo Nakano, and Shiro Nakano, "Distribution of PCDDs/PCDFs and Co-PCBs in Human Maternal Blood, Cord Blood, Placenta, Milk, and Adipose Tissue: Dioxins Showing High Toxic Equivalency Factor Accumulate in the Placenta," *Bioscience, Biotechnology, and Biochemistry* 69, no. 10 (2005): 1836–1847, https://doi.org/10.1271/bbb .69.1836.

113 **In 1994, researchers also discovered**: Peter Jackson, "Dioxin Advisory Issued for Lobster Tomalley," *Lewiston Sun Journal*, February 3, 1994; Ned Porter, "State Issues Advisory for Lobster Eaters," *Bangor Daily News*, February 3, 1994.

114 **In 2009, the Maine Center**: Maine Division of Environmental and Community Health: Maine Center for Disease Control & Prevention, "Saltwater Fish & Lobster Tomalley Safe Eating Guidelines," revised June 3, 2009, https://www.maine.gov/dhhs/mecdc/environmental-health/eohp/fish /saltwater.htm.

114 **equipment and access to a lab**: In March 2015, I contacted Reagen LLC in New Jersey, which sells dioxin test kits. One to five kits would cost $3,000 each. If I ordered more than twenty kits, they would be only $2,300 each. Update: As of November 24, 2019, dioxin tests cost $4,695 each.

121 **art critic John Berger**: John Berger, *Ways of Seeing* (New York: Penguin Books, 1990).

CHAPTER 8

130 **longing for an ancestral home**: Maria Gravari-Barbas and Nelson Graburn, eds., *Tourism Imaginaries at the Disciplinary Crossroads: Place, Practice, Media* (New York: Routledge, 2016).

131 **kicked to the street**: Rob Shiels, "Lifelong Sorrow: Settler Affect, State and Trauma at Anne of Green Gables," *Settler Colonial Studies* 8, no. 4 (2017): 518–536.

132 **US entered the war**: Daile Kaplan, *The Story Behind Ansel Adams's "Moonrise, Hernandez, New Mexico,"* Swann Auction Galleries, New York, February 18, 2016, YouTube video, 4:50, https://www.youtube.com/watch?v=-3cLJBPEDCM.

139 **"Familiarity is the thing"**: E. B. White, "Home-Coming," in *The Points of My Compass* (New York: Harper & Row, 1962).

143 **serious groundwater problems**: Environmental Protection Agency, "Burning Tires for Fuel and Tire Pyrolysis: Air Implications," Office of Air Quality, Research Triangle Park, NC, December 1991, https://nepis.epa.gov/Exe/tiff2png.cgi/9100LGXA.PNG?-r+75+-g+7+D%3A%5CZYFILES%5CINDEX%20DATA%5C91THRU94%5CTIFF%5C00002284%5C9100LGXA.TIF.

143 **when chlorine combusts**: Mary Booth, "Trees, Trash, and Toxics: How Biomass Energy Has Become the New Coal," Partnership for Policy Integrity, April 2, 2014, https://www.pfpi.net/trees-trash-and-toxics-how-biomass-energy-has-become-the-new-coal.

143 **remedying the stockpiles**: Michael Blumenthal, "Colorado Is King of the Mountain—of Tires," *Denver Post*, April 17, 2014.

144 **without an engineering degree**: When tires are used for fuel, they are normally de-wired, but even so, 5 to 10 percent metal is left, which can release zinc when burned. Zinc is not regulated by the Maine TDF regulations. All the ash from the boiler is deposited at Farrington Mountain landfill in Mexico. Memo from Susan Parrella to Gail Geraghty, May 8, 2000.

144 **"very efficient" boilers**: In an email dated July 30, 2014, Scott Reed, the environmental manager at the mill, wrote: "These solid fuel boilers are circulating

fluidized bed (CFB) design that are recognized as a very efficient design for burning solid fuel. The boilers inject high pressure air into the furnace to burn the fuel in suspension resulting in more complete combustion and better heat transfer. The ash particles from combustion are collected and removed in cyclones and an electrostatic precipitator which results in very high removal efficiency. The CFB operates at relatively low combustion temperatures which results in lower emissions of Nitrous Oxides (NOx) and Volatile Organic Compounds (VOC) emissions. The boilers also inject limestone into the furnace which reacts with the sulfur in the fuel to reduce emissions of Sulfur Dioxide (SO2)."

144 *the mill also incinerates*: Letter from Scott Reed, Environmental Manager, Rumford Paper Company to River Valley Healthy Communities Coalition, "Looking for Info," March 16, 2000.

146 *"Best Available Control Technology"*: Maine Department of Environmental Protection, "A Summary of EPA and Maine DEP BAQ Instructions for Conducting a BACT Analysis," December 2, 2015, https://www.maine.gov /dep/air/publications/docs/BACTGuidanceA-L-0082.pdf.

147 *constant and optimum conditions*: Email from Bryce Sproul to me copy Marc (subject "Tire Burning"), June 27, 2011, and follow-up telephone conversation.

147 *look up more rules*: "Facilities are required to stack test according to applicable requirements for the emissions unit in question. These applicable requirements may come from federal New Source Performance Standards (NSPS), found at 40 CFR Part 60, or from federal National Emissions Standards for Hazardous Air Pollutants (NESHAP), found at 40 CFR Part 63. There may also be applicable requirements from state rules and/or written into a specific facility's air emission license as the way to demonstrate compliance with a license limit. In addition, both federal and state regulatory agencies have the authority to require stack testing upon request from the regulatory agency." Email from Jane Gilbert, P.E., Air Licensing Unit Manager, Maine Department of Environmental Protection, Bureau of Air Quality, November 15, 2019.

148 *one of the dirtiest rivers*: Booth, "Trees, Trash, and Toxics."

148 *low-level source of dioxin*: J. Reisman, "Air Emissions from Scrap Tire Combustion," Environmental Protection Agency, Washington, DC, EPA /600/R-97/115 (NTIS PB98-111701), 1997.

148 *TDF could pollute as badly as the worst*: Booth, "Trees, Trash, and Toxics."

149 *open to debate*: In 2017, 30 million tires were burned as fuel in pulp and paper mills, which is 29 percent of all TDF. Cement kilns burn 46 percent and electric utility boilers burn 25 percent. Colorado still has the most stockpiled tires. US Tire Manufacturers Association, "2017 US Scrap Tire

Management Summary," July 18, 2018, https://www.ustires.org/system/files /USTMA_scraptire_summ_2017_072018.pdf.

151 **in absentia** *visitors*: Robert Frost, "In a Disused Graveyard," available at https://www.poetryfoundation.org/poems/148651/in-a-disused-graveyard.

INTERLUDE

155 *even a corpse*: Darcie Moore, "Body Recovered from Merrymeeting Bay Identified as Missing Wisconsin Man," *Portland Press Herald*, May 17, 2019.

155 *aperture of the sea*: Resource Services, "Merrymeeting Bay, an Environmental Review," Prepared for Friends of Merrymeeting Bay with funding from the Davis Conservation Foundation, January 5, 1998, http://cybrary.fomb .org/ahayden/mmbenvre.html.

156 *"the epicenter of Hell on earth"*: John McPhee, *Encounters with the Archdruid: Narratives About a Conservationist and Three of His Natural Enemies* (New York: Farrar, Straus and Giroux, 1971).

CHAPTER 9

160 *shut down operations*: "Rumford in Mourning for Hugh J. Chisholm," *Paper Trade Journal, 41st Year*, May 2, 1912, 26.

160 *employed four servants*: The servants were James W. McFarland, 43; Agnes Clancy, 42; Lily M. Sharp, 42; and Franny Nauden, 32. Taken from 1910 Census: Year: *1910*; Census Place: *Manhattan Ward 19, New York, New York*; Roll: *T624_1043*; Page: *9A*; Enumeration District: *1163*; FHL microfilm: *1375056*.

160 *leather-bound literature*: Purchase College states Chisholm's home was in Port Chester; however, in his will, the farm and property are noted as being in Rye and Harrison, New York. Subsequent research shows that the residence in Port Chester was eventually used as Highpoint Hospital, a forty-three-bed psychiatric facility founded by Dr. Alexander Gralnick. Also, in Hugh J. Chisholm's will, he states $2 million be set aside to establish a scientific university in Maine. I'm not sure what happened regarding that directive. Purchase College, State University of New York, "Purchase History: 20th Century History (1900–1964)," https://www.purchase.edu/purchase -history/20th-century-history-1900-1964/; Museum of the City of New York, "Photographs of the Interior of Hugh J. Chisholm's Home in Purchase, New York," https://collections.mcny.org/C.aspx?VP3=SearchResult&VBID =24UAYWIB1L38&SMLS=1&RW=1046&RH=1013.

161 **lived more extravagantly**: James B. Morrow, "A Modern Aladdin. Hugh J. Chisholm, Head of the 'Paper Trust,' Builder of Cities. His Plans for a Great Industrial School for Workingmen's Children," *Los Angeles Times*, September 8, 1908.

161 **He sold the ARAS**: "Navy Buys Large Yacht: Aras. ARAS, Owned by H.J. Chisholm, to Be Taken Over Today," *New York Times*, April 30, 1941.

161 **gave it up for good**: The *Williamsburg* (as the ARAS was called as a private vessel) was "a bedraggled, listing vessel" with "grass, weeds and even small trees" sprouting "from the sodden pulp of her once-gleaming teak decks." Ken Ringle, "Keeping a Piece of History Afloat," *Washington Post*, July 27, 1990, https://www.washingtonpost.com/archive/lifestyle/1990/07/27/keeping-a -piece-of-history-afloat/b2355e3e-c3f7-40d9-bf05-1d73b95933d4/.

Some photos of the *ARAS* can be viewed here: Cruise Line History, "The USS *Williamsburg*, President Harry Truman's Presidential Yacht Scrapped," https://www.cruiselinehistory.com/the-uss-williamsburg-president-harry -trumans-presidential-yacht-scrapped/; and here: Portland Terminal, "Look How Harry Truman's Presidential Yacht Ended Up Before It Sank into the Mud," https://www.portandterminal.com/look-how-harry-trumans -presidential-yacht-ended-up-before-it-sank-into-the-mud/.

161 **fend off overdevelopment**: Purchase College, "Purchase History: 20th Century History (1900–1964)."

162 **properties are billeted**: Brooklyn Museum, "Atlante, One of Four, from Hugh J. Chisholm Mansion, 813 Fifth Avenue, NYC. On View: Steinberg Family Sculpture Garden, 1st Floor," https://www.brooklynmuseum.org /opencollection/objects/87514.

162 **triumph of the fiscal kind**: "High-rise offices are outfitted as self-contained world citadels, a crusty core set within a jittery field held behind stealthy and/or slippery perimeters. The slippery perimeters are further reinforced by the tendency of world citadels to cluster together as a means of facilitating face-to-face contact between business interests." Steven Flusty, "Building Paranoia: The Proliferation of Interdictory Space and the Erosion of Spatial Justice" (West Hollywood, CA: Los Angeles Forum for Architecture and Urban Design, 1994), http://architectureofwar.artun.ee/wp-content /uploads/Steven_Flusty_-_Building_Paranoia1.pdf.

164 **sighed to the ground**: Robert D. McFadden, "Developer Scraps Bonwit Sculptures," *New York Times*, June 6, 1980. For vintage photographs of Bonwit Teller's architecture, see Driving for Deco, "Vanished New York City Art Deco: Stewart and Company/Bonwit Teller," 2014–2020, https://www .drivingfordeco.com/stewart-and-company/.

165   *imprisoned for fraud*: Department of Justice, U.S. Attorney's Office, District of Minnesota, "Colin Chisholm Sentenced to 48 Months in Prison for Stealing More Than $2 Million from Investors in Television Network Startup," press release, August 17, 2017, https://www.justice.gov/usao-mn/pr/colin-chisholm-sentenced-48-months-prison-stealing-more-2-million-investors-television.

CHAPTER 10

169   *The millworkers underestimated*: The article contains detailed information on the arc of the strike, testimony from local residents, and description of the hostile atmosphere in town. Timothy J. Minchin, "Broken Spirits: Permanent Replacements and the Rumford Strike of 1986," *New England Quarterly* 74, no. 1 (2001): 5–31, doi: 10.2307/3185458; Julius G. Getman and F. Ray Marshall, "Industrial Relations in Transition: The Paper Industry Example," *Yale Law Journal* 102, no. 8 (1993): 1803–1895, https://digitalcommons.law.yale.edu/ylj/vol102/iss8/1.

169   *"an unambiguous signal"*: Harold Meyerson, "Class Warrior," *Washington Post*, June 9, 2004, https://www.washingtonpost.com/archive/opinions/2004/06/09/class-warrior/5fcf246d-f571-43d8-b236-064bbac8e407/.

170   *2:1 in favor of returning*: UPI, "Boise Cascade Strike Ends," September 15, 1986, https://www.upi.com/Archives/1986/09/15/Boise-Cascade-strike-ends/6536527140800/.

171   *and about 850 returned*: "Maine Town Divided by Bitter Strike," *New York Times*, December 28, 1986.

172   *called the art one-sided*: Scott Thistle, "Mills Says Labor Mural That LePage Removed from Labor Department Will Stay Put," *Portland Press Herald*, January 8, 2019.

172   *right to "government speech"*: "Judge Rules Removal of Labor Mural Was Justified," *Portland Press Herald*, March 23, 2012.

176   *Maine has lost 13,000*: Phoenix McLaughlin, "Where the Paper Industry Went," *Bangor Daily News*, December 14, 2015.

183   *demise of what they provide*: Fred Pearce, "Why Green Pledges Will Not Create the Natural Forests We Need," *Yale Environment 360*, April 16, 2019.

183   *careful restoration of their lines*: Michèle Valerie Cloonan, "The Paradox of Preservation," *Library Trends* 56, no. 1 (2007): 133–147.

183   *glacial ice and ancient geology*: Woodrow B. Thompson, "Glacial and Postglacial Geology of Grafton Notch State Park," Maine Geologic Facts and Localities, Maine Geological Survey, Department of Agriculture, Conservation & Forestry, November 2001, https://digitalmaine.com/cgi/viewcontent.cgi

?referer=https://www.google.com/&httpsredir=1&article=1346&context
=mgs_publications.

184 *nature and self-reliance*: Loch Adamson, "Roxanne Quimby for Governor!,"
Fast Company, December 1, 2003, https://www.fastcompany.com/47877
/roxanne-quimby-governor.

185 *in diners and onto bumpers*: Frederick Reimers, "Lucas St. Clair Turns
Recreation into Political Capital," *Outside Magazine*, June 2, 2018.

185 *"our way of life alone"*: Adamson, "Roxanne Quimby for Governor!"

185 *largest exported goods*: Maine Economic Growth Council, "Measures of
Growth: Performance Measures and Benchmarks to Achieve a Vibrant and
Sustainable Economy for Maine 2017," 23rd Report of the Maine Economic
Growth Council, April 2017.

185 *halfway ruined themselves*: "Map: Maine Paper Mills Operating or Closed
Down," *Portland Press Herald*, July 19, 2017. For a snapshot of forest-related
products, see also Maine Forest Products Council, "Maine's Forest Economy," 2016, https://maineforest.org/wp-content/uploads/2016/09/Maines
-Forest-Economy-10-12-2016.pdf.

185 *"They're tone-deaf"*: Quoted in Michael Charles Tobias, "Maine vs. Thoreau: The Roxanne Quimby Question?," *Forbes*, October 3, 2011.

186 *Maine's national parks will bring in*: In 2017, 3.5 million park visitors
spent an estimated $285 million in gateway regions while visiting Na-
tional Park Service lands in Maine. This spending supported a total of 4,410
jobs, $127 million in labor income, $224 million in value added, and
$395 million in economic output in the Maine economy. Catherine Culli-
nane Thomas, Lynne Koontz, and Egan Cornachione, "2017 National Park
Visitor Spending Effects: Economic Contributions to Local Communities, States, and the Nation," Natural Resource Report NPS/NRSS/EQD/
NRR—2018/1616, April 2018, https://www.nps.gov/nature/customcf
/NPS_Data_Visualization/docs/NPS_2017_Visitor_Spending_Effects.pdf.

186 *Quimby argued she wasn't*: Phyllis Austin, "Roxanne Quimby Purchases
High Priority 24,000 Acre Township East of Baxter Park," *Maine Environmental News*, November 24, 2003, http://www.meepi.org/files03/pa112403
.htm.

186 *seven major paper companies*: William C. Osborn, *The Paper Plantation:
Ralph Nader's Study Group Report on the Pulp and Paper Industry in Maine*
(New York: Grossman Publishers, 1974).

189 *"species of moderate concern"*: James A. Kushlan et al., *Waterbird Conservation for the Americas: The North American Waterbird Conservation Plan*,
Version 1 (Washington, DC: Waterbird Conservation for the Americas,

2002), https://www.fws.gov/migratorybirds/pdf/management/northameric
awaterbirdconservationplan.pdf.

189 **unhatched eggs and livers**: "Loon Preservation Committee Takes a Close
Look Inside Loon Nests," *Union Leader*, August 30, 2017.

189 **the demise of species we poison**: BirdLife International, *State of the
World's Birds: Taking the Pulse of the Planet* (Cambridge: BirdLife Interna-
tional, 2018), https://www.birdlife.org/sites/default/files/attachments/BL
_ReportENG_V11_spreads.pdf.

189 **the CDC will release data**: D. A. Siegel et al., "Geographic Variation in
Pediatric Cancer Incidence—United States, 2003–2014," *Morbidity and
Mortality Weekly Report* 67 (2018): 707–713.

190 **Marine biologist Susan Shaw**: Peter McGuire. "Decades of Chemical Pollution Suspected in Maine's Seal Die-Off," *Portland Press Herald* (August 19,
2018).

191 **"smooth, but still varied landscape"**: Henry David Thoreau, *The Maine
Woods* (New York: HarperCollins, 1987) (1864).

CHAPTER 11

193 **coffee in June 2016**: Bruce Farrin, "Nestlé Waters Eyeing Rumford's Primary Water Source," *Lewiston Sun Journal* (blog), June 15, 2016, http://www
.sunjournal.com/Nestlé-waters-eyeing-rumfords-primary-water-source/.

200 **"Cures Dyspepsia"**: Hiram Ricker & Sons, *Poland Spring Centennial: A Souvenir* (Poland, ME: Author, 1895), 81. A facsimile of first circular issued on
Poland Water: https://babel.hathitrust.org/cgi/pt?id=loc.ark:/13960/t1jh3r36
p&view=1up&seq=85.

200 **to the leisure class**: Maine History Online, Maine Memory Network, "Poland Spring: Summering in Fashion," n/d, slideshow, 25 slides, https://
www.mainememory.net/sitebuilder/site/304/slideshow/309/display?format
=list&prev_object_id=570&prev_object=page&slide_num=1.

201 **impure or contaminated**: "How the States Got Their Shapes," *Maine's Healing Springs,* video, The History Channel, n.d., 2:16, https://www.history
.com/shows/how-the-states-got-their-shapes/videos/maines-healing-springs.

201 **Franco-American millworkers**: Maine History Online, "Poland Spring:
Summering in Fashion."

201 **a class action lawsuit filed against them**: The original class action suit was
filed on August 15, 2017, and was dismissed without prejudice. Plaintiffs
filed an amended complaint in two parts: in July 2018 and March 2019.
Then plaintiffs supplemented their amended complaint to add Rumford's

well sites to the suit. *Mark J. Patane, et al., Plaintiffs, v. Nestle Waters North America, Inc., Defendant,* US District Court, District of Connecticut, No. 3:17-cv-01381 (JAM), March 28, 2019.

204 **drinking from plastic bottles**: Sherri A. Mason, Victoria G. Welch, and Joseph Neratko, "Synthetic Polymer Contamination in Bottled Water," *Frontiers in Chemistry* 6 (2018): 407.

209 **Hugh Chisholm said**: "Hon. Hugh Chisholm," *Rumford Falls Times,* September 16, 1905, https://news.google.com/newspapers?nid=1913&dat=1905 0922&id=o8ogAAAAIBAJ&sjid=4moFAAAAIBAJ&pg=3462,3891384 &hl=en.

209 **would lose our benefits**: Donald Reid, "Industrial Paternalism: Discourse and Practice in Nineteenth-Century French Mining and Metallurgy," *Comparative Studies in Society and History* 27, no. 4 (1985): 579–607, https://doi .org/10.1017/S0010417500011671.

209 **In 1994 Thomas M. Beckley**: Thomas M. Beckley, "Pulp, Paper, and Power: Social and Political Consequences of Forest-Dependence in a New England Mill Town" (Ph.D. diss., University of Wisconsin-Madison, 1994).

211 **forty-eight brands**: As of September 29, 2019, from Nestlé, "Get to Know Us," https://www.nestle-waters.com/get-to-know-us/through-our-waters/all -brands.

211 **study on water scarcity**: Richard Damania et al., *Uncharted Waters: The New Economics of Water Scarcity and Variability* (Washington, DC: World Bank, 2017), doi:10.1596/978-1-4648-1179-1.

212 **hired LJ as town manager**: LJ started working as town manager on February 1, 2017. Her initial contract ran only through June 2018. In March 2018 the town selectmen unanimously approved LJ's contract beginning July 1, 2018, and ending June 30, 2021, so there would be no interruption in her service or her job.

213 **signed and sealed agreement**: Mike Lange, "Former Dexter Town Manager's Separation Agreement Includes Six Months Salary," *Bangor Daily News,* November 27, 2013.

213 **she "united" town departments**: Alex Barber, "Dexter Residents Voice Support for Town Manager During Meeting," *Bangor Daily News,* April 25, 2012.

213 **Yet citizens presented**: Beth A. Birmingham. "Updated: Citizens Petition to Remove Waldoboro Town Manager," *Village Soup Knox,* February 11, 2015, knox.villagesoup.com/p/updated-citizens-petition-to-remove-waldoboro -town-manager/1303535.

213 **172-page Comprehensive Plan**: Rumford Comprehensive Plan Committee and Androscoggin Valley Council of Governments, "Rumford

Comprehensive Plan: Section I, Inventory & Analysis," November 1998, https://rumfordme.org/wp-content/uploads/2015/12/rumford-comp-plan-ia-sm.pdf.

214   **and it starts with fixing the broken sidewalks**: LJ wrote in an email to me on November 16, 2019: "In addition to the 990,000 grant for the original scope, we applied and received $400,000 grant from northern borders commission for the broadband and [his] portion of the project."

214–15   **toward the Strathglass Building**: From photos viewed at Rumford Historical Society, Rumford, ME.

218   **manufacturers monitor dioxin levels**: Rep. Carolyn Maloney (NY) has introduced legislation nine times since 1997 to require manufacturers to be more transparent regarding the composition of tampons and their testing. Since tampons are considered to be and are regulated by the FDA as medical devices, manufacturers are not required to disclose what's in them. Maloney's latest attempt to demand transparency was in 2017. Rep. Carolyn B. Maloney, H.R. 2379, Robin Danielson Feminine Hygiene Product Safety Act of 2017, introduced May 4, 2017; Michael J. DeVito and Arnold Schecter, "Exposure Assessment to Dioxins from the Use of Tampons and Diapers," *Environmental Health Perspectives* 110, no. 1 (January 2002): 23–28, doi: 10.1289/ehp.0211023; Nadia Kounang, "What's in Your Pad or Tampon?," CNN Health, November 13, 2015. If you want to read about the sanitary device market, it will cost you $900. Euromonitor International, "Sanitary Protection in the US," March 2019, https://www.euromonitor.com/sanitary-protection-in-the-us/report.

218   **the dioxin levels of tampons**: In 2009 the FDA funded a test to see how much dioxin was absorbed by women from their use of tampons. Another study was done in 2013 by Naturally Savvy, which also examined pesticide residue in tampons and found traces of malaoxon, malathion, dichlofluanid, mercarbam, procymidone, methidathion, fensulfothion, pyrethrum, and piperonyl butoxide. Another study found glysophate in tampons. I learned the above information from: Rose George, *Nine Pints: A Journey Through the Money, Medicine, and Mysteries of Blood* (New York: Metropolitan Books, 2018); Titania Kumeh, "What's Really in That Tampon," *Mother Jones*, October 20, 2010; Roni Caryn Rabin, "Period Activists Want Tampon Makers to Disclose Ingredients," *New York Times*, May 24, 2017.

219   **a concern as early as 1987**: Philip Shabecoff, "Traces of Dioxin Found in Range of Paper Goods," *New York Times*, September 24, 1987; Ashley Fetters, "The Tampon: A History," *The Atlantic*, June 1, 2015.

219 ***they declared the EPA study contained***: American Forest and Paper Association, Environment and Health Department, "Dioxin: Science Advisory Board Critical of EPA's Dioxin Reassessment," Newsletter May–June 1995.

CHAPTER 12

224 ***"Our mill is pretty old"***: Ben Casselman, "Americans Don't Miss Manufacturing—They Miss Unions," *FiveThirtyEight*, May 13, 2016.

226 ***so it wouldn't explode***: As one had done at the Lincoln, Maine, paper mill. See Darren Fishell, "Documents Show Financial Devastation from Lincoln Mill Boiler Explosion," *Bangor Daily News*, October 21, 2015.

227 ***seventy-four people had aplastic anemia***: Kenneth P. Burke and Linda J. Huff, "A Study of Aplastic Anemia in the Rumford Community Health Planning Area Final Report," Department of Human Services, Maine, March 1993.

228 ***"egregious" according to OSHA***: "OSHA Fines Boise Cascade $1.5 Million," UPI, September 13, 1989.

229 ***Boise again was cited***: "Violations of Safety and Health Regulations by Federal Contractors," Report to Congressional Requesters, Washington, DC: Occupational Safety and Health, Health, Education, and Human Services Division, August 1996, https://www.gao.gov/assets/230/223113.pdf.

229 ***called "TAKE TWO for safety"***: The TAKE TWO program was developed by DuPont, the storied chemical manufacturer, as a way to "stimulate thinking and conversation about safety in the workplace and at home." See DuPont Sustainable Solutions, "Take Two . . . for Safety," at https://www.dsslearning.com/take-two-for-safety/DUP001/.

230 ***tolled for each life***: Terry Karkos, "River Valley's First Worker's Memorial Held," *Lewiston Sun Journal*, April 30, 2013.

237 ***Milton Friedman argued***: Milton Friedman, *Capitalism and Freedom* (Chicago: University of Chicago Press, 1962); and Milton Friedman, "The Social Responsibility of Business Is to Increase Its Profits," *New York Times Magazine*, September 13, 1970.

237 ***Then Maine's economy crashed***: Charles S. Colgan, "The Maine Economy: Yesterday, Today, and Tomorrow," Charting Maine's Future: An Action Plan for Promoting Sustainable Prosperity and Quality Places, Brookings Institution, October 2006.

237 ***logs or paper were not***: Yong-Sook Lee and Brenda S. A. Yeoh, "Introduction: Globalisation and the Politics of Forgetting," *Urban Studies* 41, no. 12

(November 2004): 2295–2301; Jan Nederveen Pieterse, *Globalization and Culture: Global Melange* (London: Rowman & Littlefield, 2003).

238 ***"completely different direction"***: Robert D. Kaplan, *The Coming Anarchy: Shattering the Dreams of the Post Cold War* (New York: Penguin, 2001).

238 ***within sight of wealth but without access***: Two important books on globalization's effects on those who are outside its sphere: Pieterse, *Globalization and Culture*; and Zygmunt Bauman, *Globalization: The Human Consequences* (New York: Columbia University Press, 1998).

240 ***Trump started to embrace***: I think it's important not to conflate those who voted for Trump in 2016 and those who support him in 2019. In this section I am specifically talking about the election of 2016.

250 ***more territorial constraints***: Bauman, *Globalization: The Human Consequences*.

250 ***for prosperity with them***: Patrick J. Carr and Maria J. Kefalas, *Hollowing Out the Middle: The Rural Brain Drain and What It Means for America* (Boston: Beacon Press, 2009).

250 ***where we live matters***: Isabel Sawhill and Eleanor Krause, "Seven Reasons to Worry About the American Middle Class," Brookings Institution, June 5, 2018.

256 ***federal overreach it abhors***: Rachel Sheffield and Daren Bakst, "Child Nutrition Reauthorization: Time for Serious Reform, Not Tinkering," Issue Brief, Heritage Foundation, May 26, 2016; Rachel Sheffield and Daren Bakst, "Getting the Facts Straight on School Meals and Child Nutrition Reauthorization," Welfare, Heritage Foundation, November 3, 2016.

256 ***all afflicted by poverty***: "The Impact of Poverty, Food Insecurity, and Poor Nutrition on Health and Well-Being," Food Research & Action Center, December 2017.

257 ***"not trapped in poverty"***: Bruce Poliquin, "Rep. Bruce Poliquin: Work Requirements for Welfare Are Common Sense," *Kennebec Journal and Morning Sentinel*, September 8, 2018.

258 ***news headline on NBC***: Maggie Fox, "Where You Live Determines What Kills You," Health News, NBC News, December 13, 2016.

CHAPTER 13

260 ***in a huge increase***: Megan Gray, "Maine Overdose Deaths Soared Nearly 40 Percent Last Year, to Record 378," *Portland Press Herald*, February 2, 2017; Joe Lawlor, "After a Year, LePage Program to Treat Opioid Addicts Falling Far Short of Target," *Portland Press Herald*, February 15, 2018; "Maine Opioid

Summary," Opioid Summaries by State, National Institute for Drug Abuse, March 2019 (revised).

260 *Med-Care Ambulance Service*: Marianne Hutchinson, "King Gets Firsthand View of Opioid Crisis in Rumford Area," *Lewiston Sun Journal*, June 29, 2019.

268 *was in direct competition*: Nick Sambides Jr., "Patriots' Super Bowl Trophy Coming to Bangor," *Bangor Daily News*, March 29, 2017.

CHAPTER 14

274 *holding a rocket*: Matt Hickman, "Meet America's Mightiest Muffler Men," *Mother Nature Network*, July 26, 2015.

279 *One in three people*: See https://www.cancer.org for most updated numbers. One in three was current for 2017.

280 *protection with people with cancer*: William Boyd, "Controlling Toxic Harms: The Struggle over Dioxin Contamination in the Pulp and Paper Industry," *Stanford Environmental Law Journal* 21, no. 345 (2002); University of Colorado Law Legal Studies Research Paper No. 12–08. Available at SSRN: https://ssrn.com/abstract=2079802.

280 *"the Precautionary Principle"*: "The Precautionary Principle: Decision-Making Under Uncertainty," Science for Environmental Policy, Future Brief 18. Produced for the European Commission DG Environment by the Science Communication Unit, UWE, Bristol, September 2017, http://ec .europa.eu/science-environment-policy.

280 *permutations mirror what it's like*: "Combination Effects of Chemicals," Science for Environment Policy. European Commission. Issue 21, June 2010, https://ec.europa.eu/environment/integration/research/newsalert/pdf /21si_en.pdf.

281 *cancer is not provincial*: Joe Thornton, *Pandora's Poison: Chlorine, Health, and a New Environmental Strategy* (Cambridge, MA: MIT Press, 2001).

281 *people started fearing chemicals*: D. Ropeik, "On the Roots of, and Solutions to, the Persistent Battle Between 'Chemonoia' and Rationalist Denialism of the Subjective Nature of Human Cognition," *Human & Experimental Toxicology* 34, no. 12 (December 2015): 1272–1278.

282 *EPA announced a "significant"*: Matt Mauney, "EPA Releases New Rules for TSCA Asbestos Review," Mesothelioma Center, Legislation & Litigation (blog), June 5, 2018, https://www.asbestos.com/news/2018/06/05/epa -asbestos-review-snur-scott-pruitt/; Aileen Kwun, "Under Trump's EPA, Asbestos Might Be Making a Comeback," *Fast Company*, July 31, 2018; Lisa

Friedman, "E.P.A. Staff Objected to Agency's New Rules on Asbestos Use, Internal Emails Show," *New York Times*, August 10, 2018.

282 ***enormous amount of studies***: Emily Goswami, Valerie Craven, Fionna Mowat, et al., "Domestic Asbestos Exposure: A Review of Epidemiologic and Exposure Data," *International Journal of Environmental Research and Public Health* 10, no. 11 (October 31, 2013): 5629–5670.

282 ***"asbestos dust on their clothes"***: Paul Brodeur, *Expendable Americans* (New York: Viking, 1974).

CHAPTER 15

284 ***"cancer of a priori interest"***: David McLean et al., "Cancer Mortality in Workers Exposed to Organochlorine Compounds in the Pulp and Paper Industry: An International Collaborative Study," *Environmental Health Perspectives* 114, no. 7 (2006): 1007–1012, www.jstor.org/stable/3651769.

285 ***some greater good place***: D. Ropeik, "On the Roots of, and Solutions to, the Persistent Battle Between 'Chemonoia' and Rationalist Denialism of the Subjective Nature of Human Cognition," *Human & Experimental Toxicology* 34, no. 12 (December 2015): 1272–1278.

285 ***"adapting to invisible threats"***: Henry M. Vyner, *Invisible Trauma: The Psychosocial Effects of Invisible Environmental Contaminants* (Lexington, MA: D.C. Heath, 1988).

285 ***whose verdicts affect us***: No book better shows this abuse of power than Éric Vuillard's *The Order of the Day* (New York: Other Press, 2018). With a filmmaker's eye and using fiction, Vuillard zooms in on Hitler's slog to annex Austria, and asks us to find another means to access reality—our imagination.

288 ***shameless disregard, bullied***: Anonymous 65-Year-Old Man, Maine Department of Health and Human Services, "Oral Histories of People at AMHI," interview by Diana Scully, September 9, 2003, https://www.maine .gov/dhhs/riverview/history/oral-history/anonymous2.html.

288 ***whole estate of pharmaceuticals***: "Augusta Mental Health Institute Timeline: 1840–2004," Maine Department of Health and Human Services, November 24, 2019, https://www.maine.gov/dhhs/riverview/history/timeline .html.

289 ***"the Thorazine shuffle"***: Karen Evans, Maine Department of Health and Human Services, "Oral Histories of People at AMHI," September 14, 2003, https://www.maine.gov/dhhs/riverview/history/oral-history/evans.html.

291 ***carelessly interred without a paper trail***: Kelley Bouchard, "Maine's Forgotten Dead," *Kennebec Journal*, May 26, 2012.

292 ***were never found***: In the 1990s a nationwide movement called "The Cemetery Project" began locating these forgotten graves. When Karen Evans, an AMHI patient in the 1960s, learned of the project, it triggered memories of patients she knew who had, in her words, "seemingly disappeared overnight." With the help of advocacy groups, Evans wrote a letter to the Maine Department of Health and Human Services to inquire after those patients. They responded: "Most people who died when they were patients at the hospital were, indeed, returned to their towns of origin for burial . . . and a few were buried in the cemetery across [the] street. . . . There is no other AMHI burial ground."

294 ***exploitation of vulnerable populations***: Rachel Culley, "Norridgewock's Dump: A David and Goliath Story: The Creation and Growth of the Largest Commercial Landfill in Maine" (final research paper, University of Michigan, 2012).

295 ***nothing additional to be done***: Olsky is also no longer listed in the CERCLIS database (which is where you find information about Superfund sites), and as far as the EPA is concerned, as they told me, the case and the site have been archived as of October 31, 2000.

295 ***"feelings into visual metaphor"***: Natasha Mayers, Maine Department of Health and Human Services, "Oral Histories of People at AMHI," interview by Ed Oechslie, October 7, 2003, https://www.maine.gov/dhhs/riverview/history/oral-history/mayers.html.

296 ***Much of what I seek seems***: Documents I do find:

- 1/14/1988: Letter to the mill's environmental engineer from the DEP's Bureau of Land Quality Control outlining how to handle approximately 40 cubic yards of mercury-contaminated soil and groundwater at the mill subject to the conditions they lay out.
- 2/9/1988: The mill's environmental engineer responds to the DEP in a letter that "the volume of 'mercury containing' soil removed to Farrington Mountain [the mill landfill] amounted to 300 [cubic] yards" was "isolated and covered in a remote section of the landfill."
- 5/3/1988: The Bureau of Oil and Hazardous Materials Control sends an internal memo regarding a May meeting with Peterson. In summary, the mill's environmental engineer takes exception to the DEP's "Order" of 1/14/1988 and states that the mill "would like to dispose of the contaminated soil on the characteristic of E.P. Toxicity instead of as a listed hazardous waste. This would enable Boise to dispose of most of the soil at an in-state commercial landfill."
- 6/17/1988: The DEP commissioner sends an internal memo to the Acting Director of Land Bureau about the mill's mercury-contaminated soil

that "there is, however, some confusion as to whether or not the mercury-contaminated soil is hazardous waste. With approval from the DEP, the contaminated soil is stockpiled under cover at the Farrington Mountain Landfill site until a determination is made regarding the soil's status."

297 *"Hat Capital of the World"*: At its peak, around 1880, Danbury hatmakers churned out nearly five million hats a year. "The Mad Hatters of Danbury, Conn," New England Historical Society, https://www.newenglandhistoricalsociety .com/mad-hatters-danbury-conn/; "The Danbury Hatters," ConnecticutHistory .org, August 2, 2014, https://connecticuthistory.org/the-danbury-hatters/.

297 *Annual Report of the Bureau*: "Twelfth Annual Report of the Bureau of Statistics of Labor and Industries of New Jersey. For the Year Ending October 31, 1889" (Camden, NJ: F. F. Patterson, 1890).

CHAPTER 16

299 *daily life in America*: Susan Frienkel, *American Chestnut: The Life and Death and Rebirth of a Perfect Tree* (Los Angeles: University of California Press, 2007).

306 *"bad smell the smoke leaves"*: Douglas Watts, "Paper Mills' Dioxin Discharges Annoy Governor," *Maine Sportsman*, January 1996.

308 *sociologists who studied the effects of Love Canal found*: Martha R. Fowlkes and Patricia Y. Miller, "Love Canal: The Social Construction of Disaster," Federal Emergency Management Agency, October 1982.

309 *the trophic levels of nature*: Dennis Fulbright, Ph.D., professor emeritus, Michigan State University, letter to Kerri Arsenault, "Inquiry About Chestnut Trees," July 15, 2017.

CODA

312 *throwing shit up*: "Air Emissions from Scrap Tire Combustion," Washington, DC: US Environmental Protection Agency, October 1997.

312 *"poison redistribution"*: Rob Nixon, *Slow Violence and the Environmentalism of the Poor* (Cambridge, MA: Harvard University Press, 2013).

313 *John McPhee once wrote*: John McPhee, "Encounters with the Archdruid," *The New Yorker*, April 3, 1971.

Erik Madigan Heck

KERRI ARSENAULT is the book review editor at *Orion Magazine* and contributing editor at *Literary Hub*. Her writing has appeared in *Freeman's, The Boston Globe, Down East* magazine, *The Paris Review, The New York Review of Books, Air Mail,* and *The Washington Post,* among other publications. *Mill Town* is her first book.